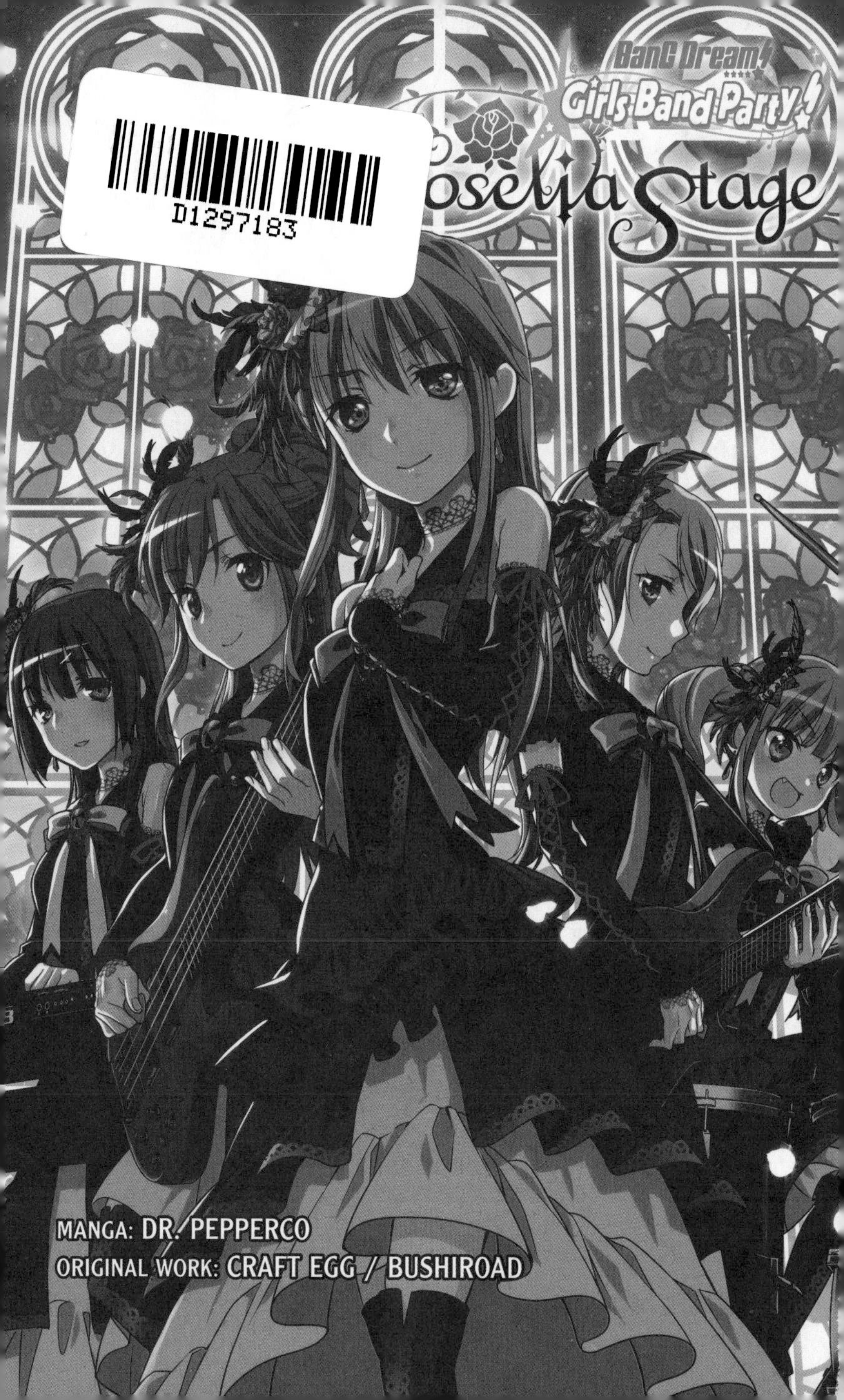
BanG Dream!
Girls Band Party!
oselia Stage
MANGA: DR. PEPPERCO
ORIGINAL WORK: CRAFT EGG / BUSHIROAD

Contents

Chapter 6

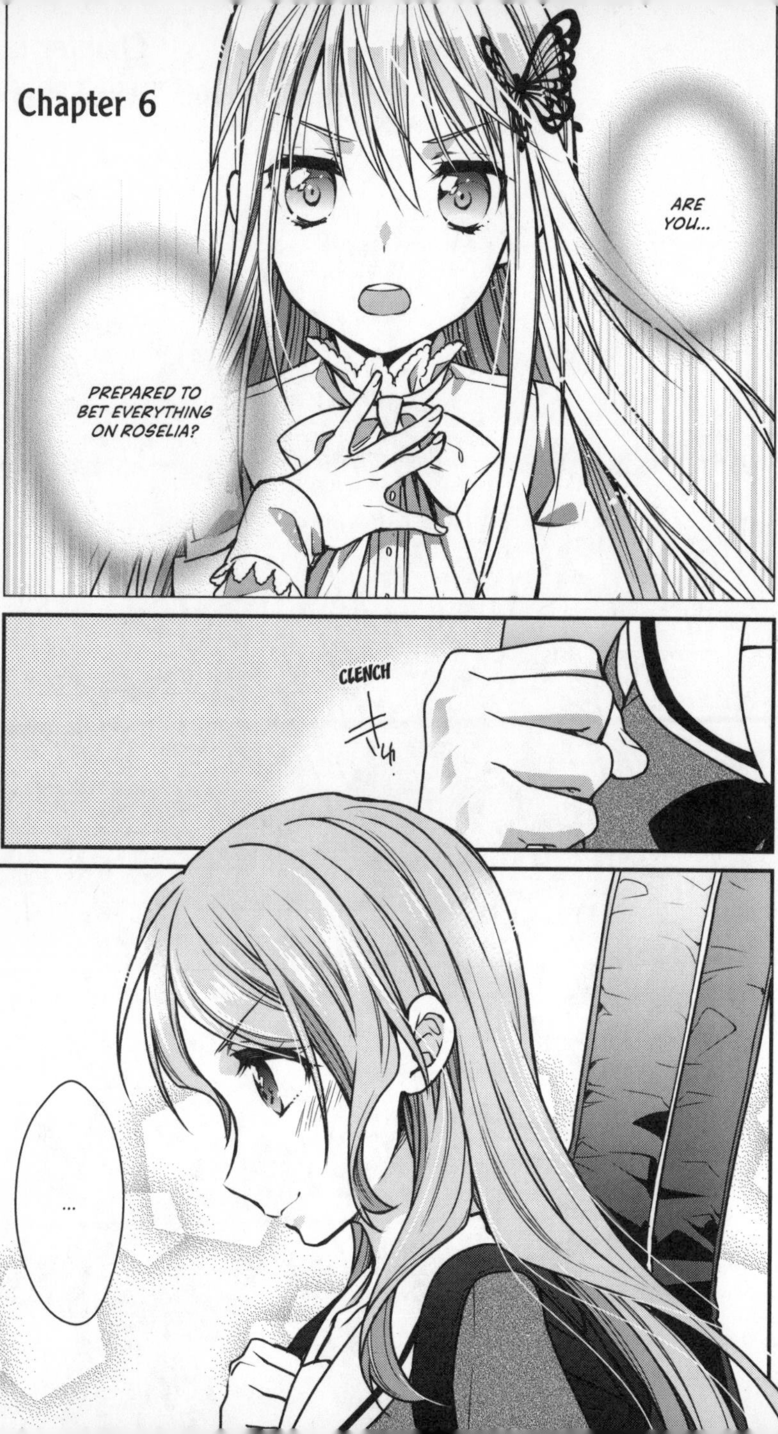
ARE YOU...
PREPARED TO BET EVERYTHING ON ROSELIA?
CLENCH
...

Chapter 6
The Younger Twin Sister

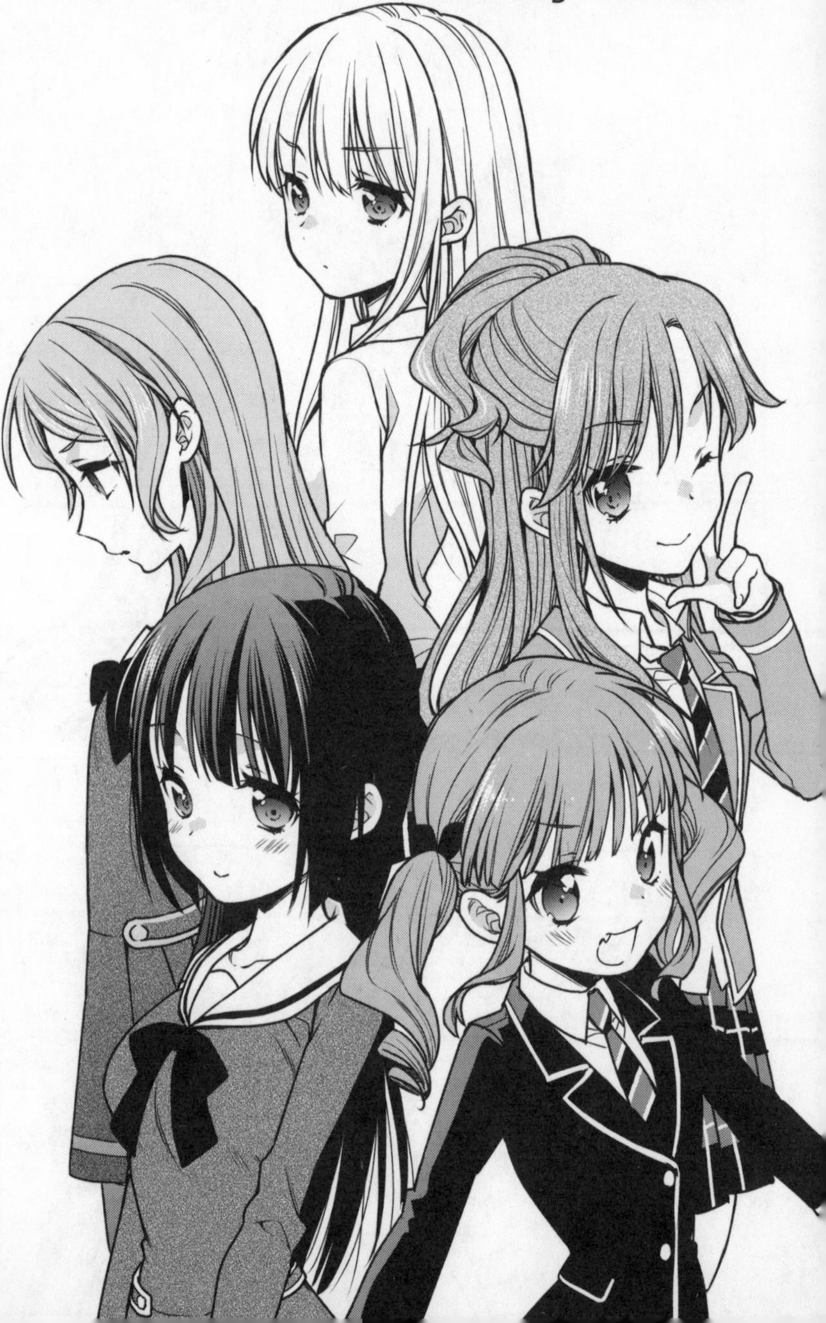

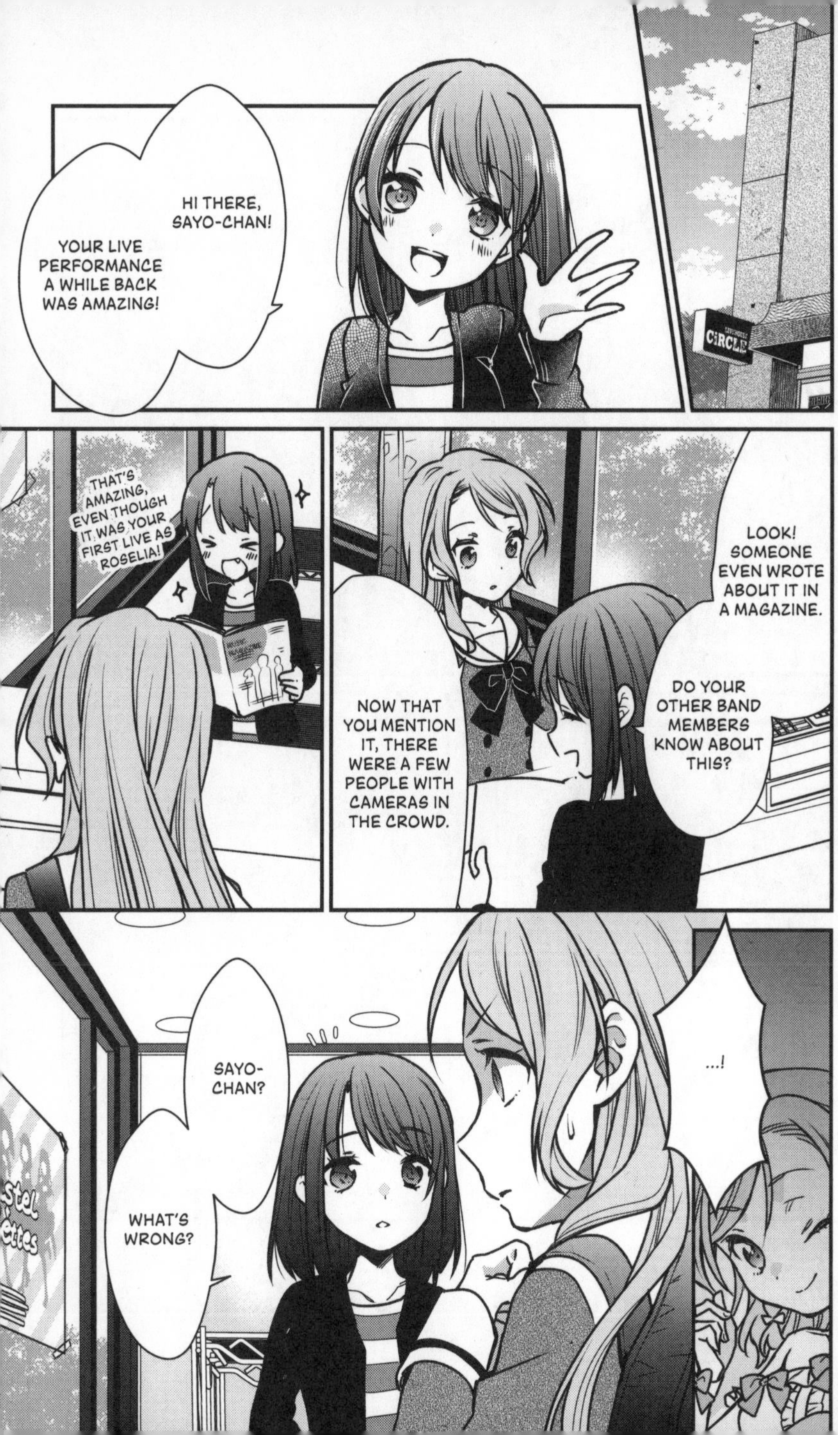
HI THERE, SAYO-CHAN!
YOUR LIVE PERFORMANCE A WHILE BACK WAS AMAZING!
CiRCLE
LOOK! SOMEONE EVEN WROTE ABOUT IT IN A MAGAZINE.
DO YOUR OTHER BAND MEMBERS KNOW ABOUT THIS?
NOW THAT YOU MENTION IT, THERE WERE A FEW PEOPLE WITH CAMERAS IN THE CROWD.
THAT'S AMAZING, EVEN THOUGH IT WAS YOUR FIRST LIVE AS ROSELIA!
...!
SAYO-CHAN?
WHAT'S WRONG?

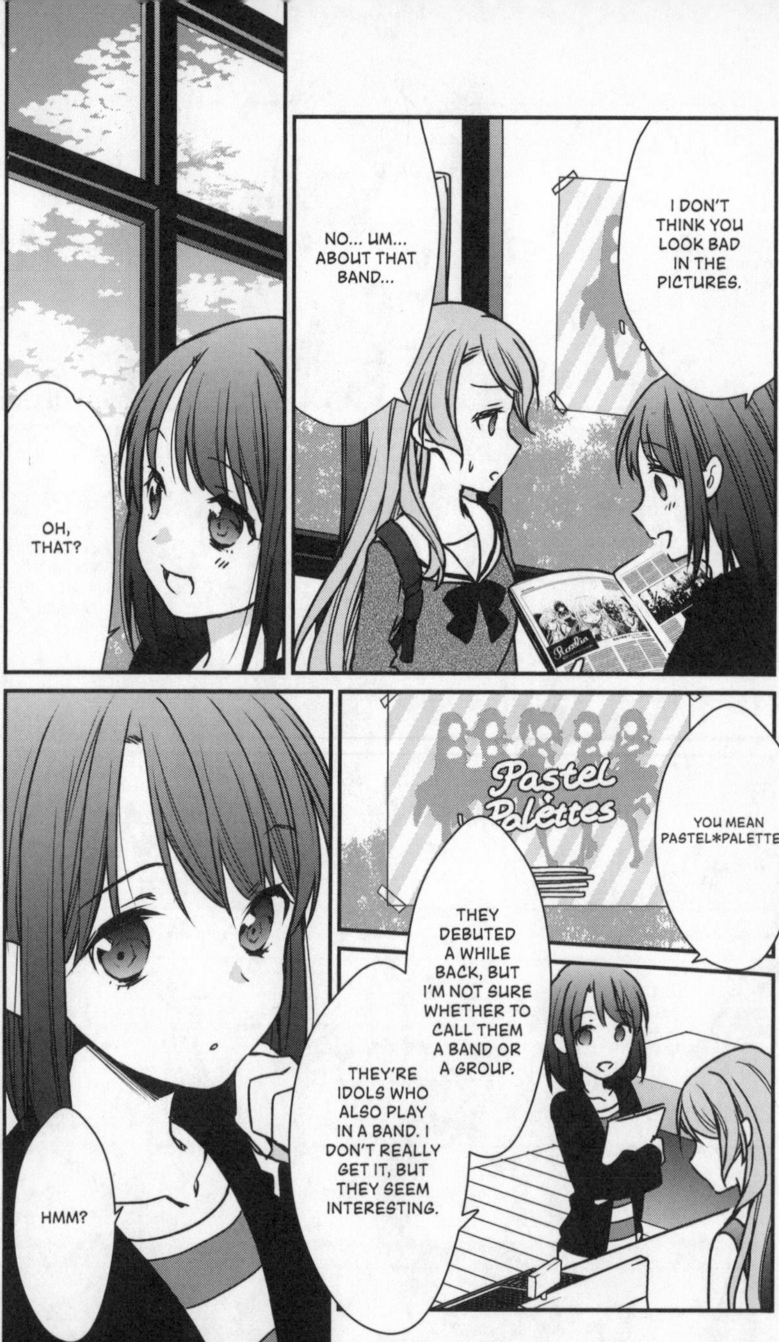
I DON'T THINK YOU LOOK BAD IN THE PICTURES.
NO... UM... ABOUT THAT BAND...
OH, THAT?
Pastel Palettes
YOU MEAN PASTEL*PALETTES?
THEY DEBUTED A WHILE BACK, BUT I'M NOT SURE WHETHER TO CALL THEM A BAND OR A GROUP.
THEY'RE IDOLS WHO ALSO PLAY IN A BAND. I DON'T REALLY GET IT, BUT THEY SEEM INTERESTING.
HMM?

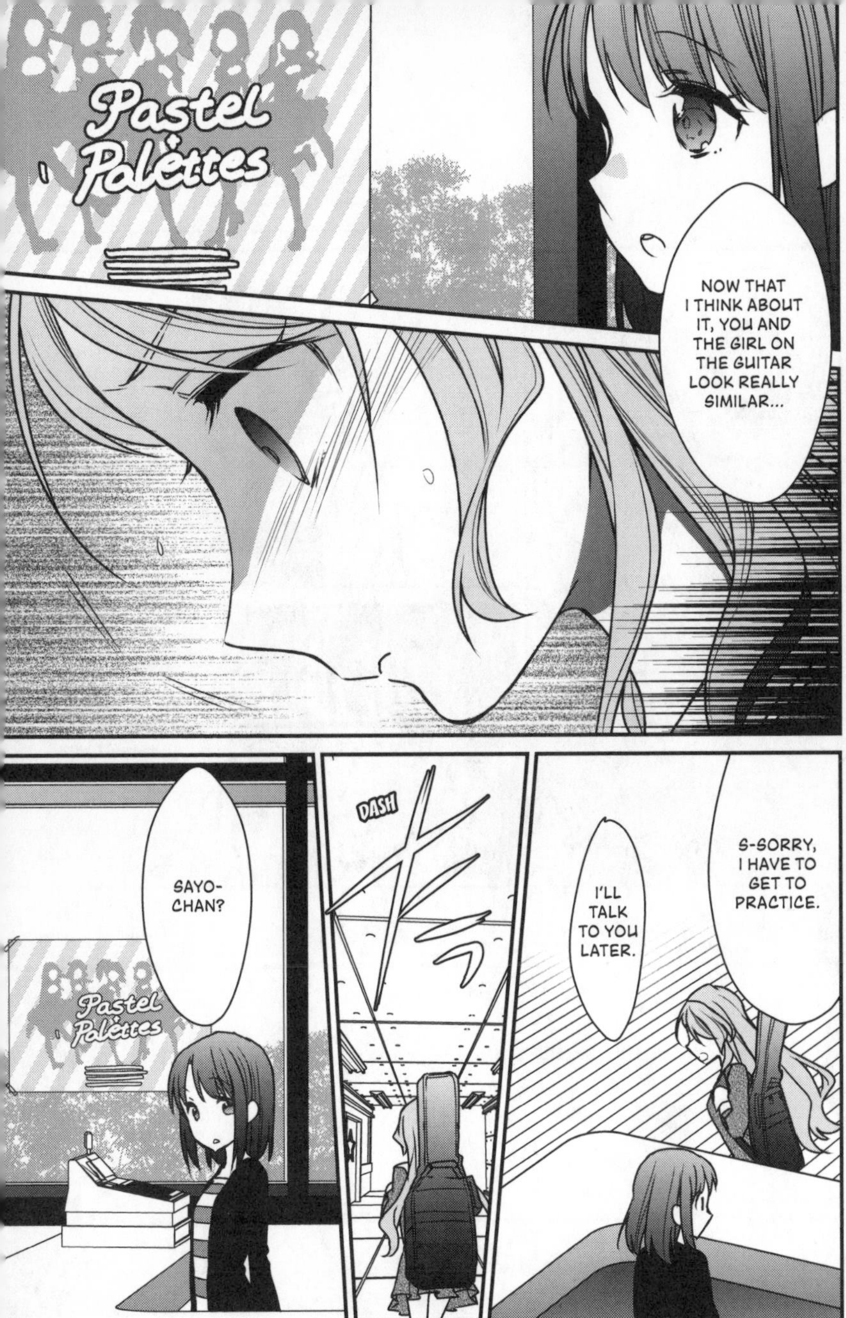
NOW THAT I THINK ABOUT IT, YOU AND THE GIRL ON THE GUITAR LOOK REALLY SIMILAR...
Pastel Palettes
S-SORRY, I HAVE TO GET TO PRACTICE.
I'LL TALK TO YOU LATER.
DASH
Pastel Palettes
SAYO-CHAN?

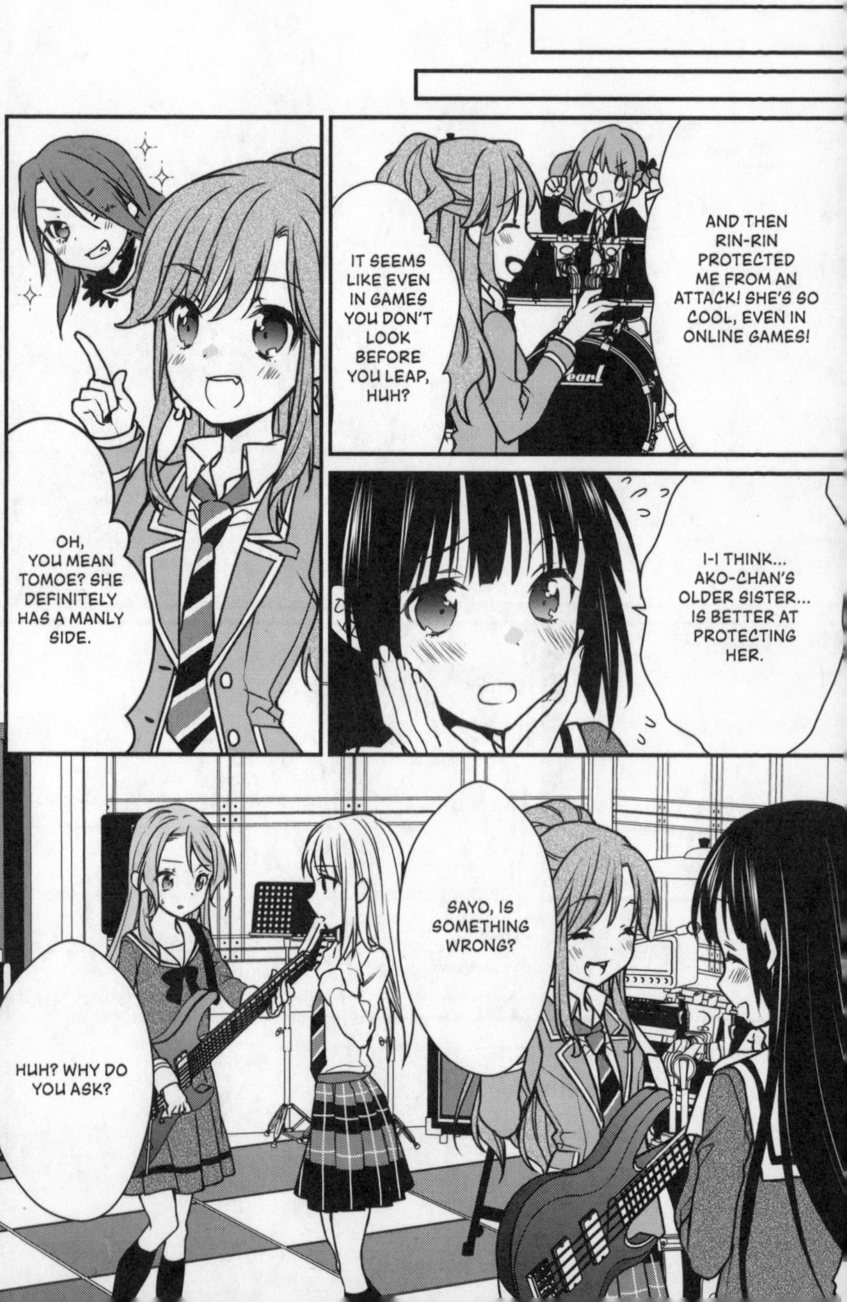
AND THEN RIN-RIN PROTECTED ME FROM AN ATTACK! SHE'S SO COOL, EVEN IN ONLINE GAMES!
IT SEEMS LIKE EVEN IN GAMES YOU DON'T LOOK BEFORE YOU LEAP, HUH?
I-I THINK... AKO-CHAN'S OLDER SISTER... IS BETTER AT PROTECTING HER.
OH, YOU MEAN TOMOE? SHE DEFINITELY HAS A MANLY SIDE.
SAYO, IS SOMETHING WRONG?
HUH? WHY DO YOU ASK?

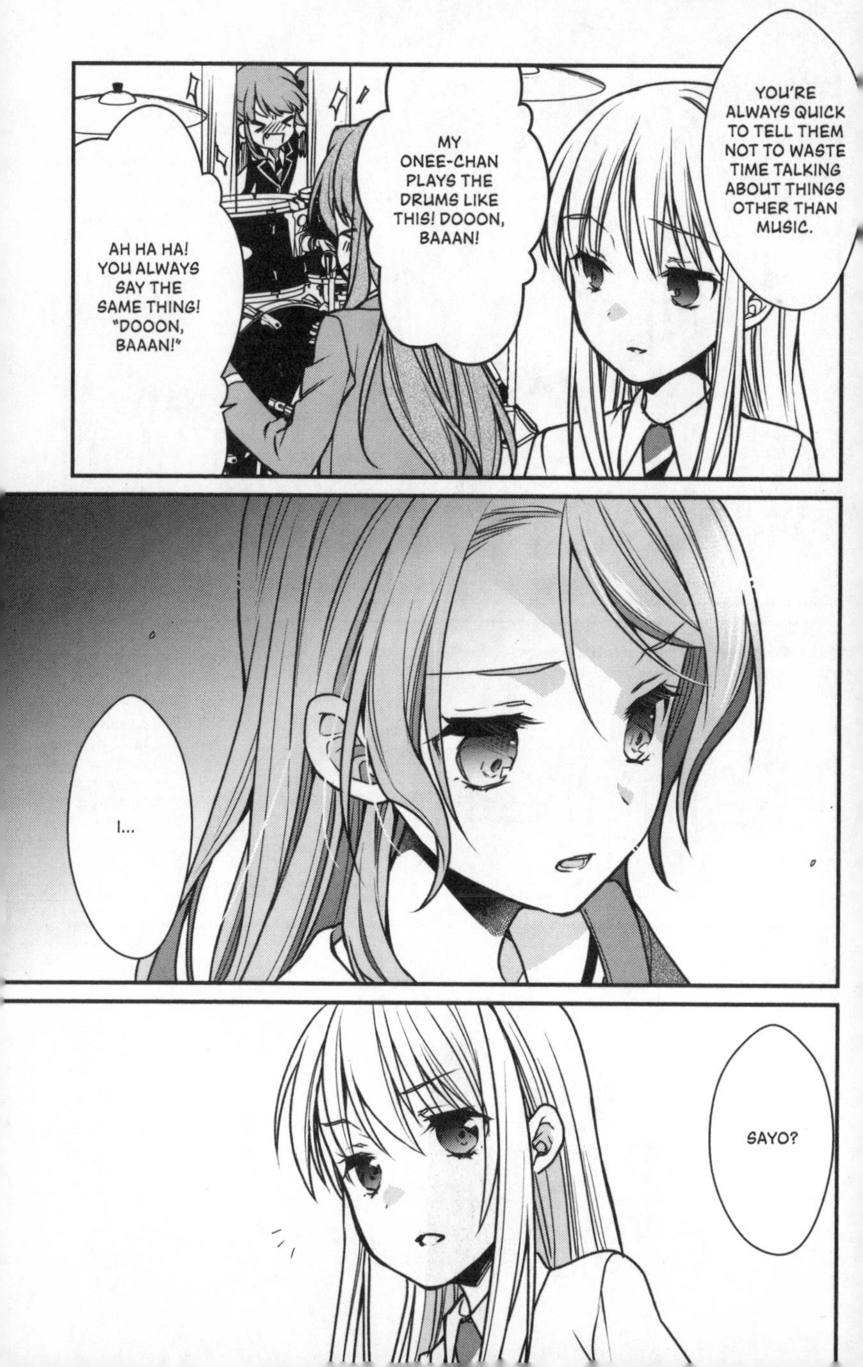
YOU'RE ALWAYS QUICK TO TELL THEM NOT TO WASTE TIME TALKING ABOUT THINGS OTHER THAN MUSIC.
MY ONEE-CHAN PLAYS THE DRUMS LIKE THIS! DOOON, BAAAN!
AH HA HA! YOU ALWAYS SAY THE SAME THING! "DOOON, BAAAN!"
I...
SAYO?

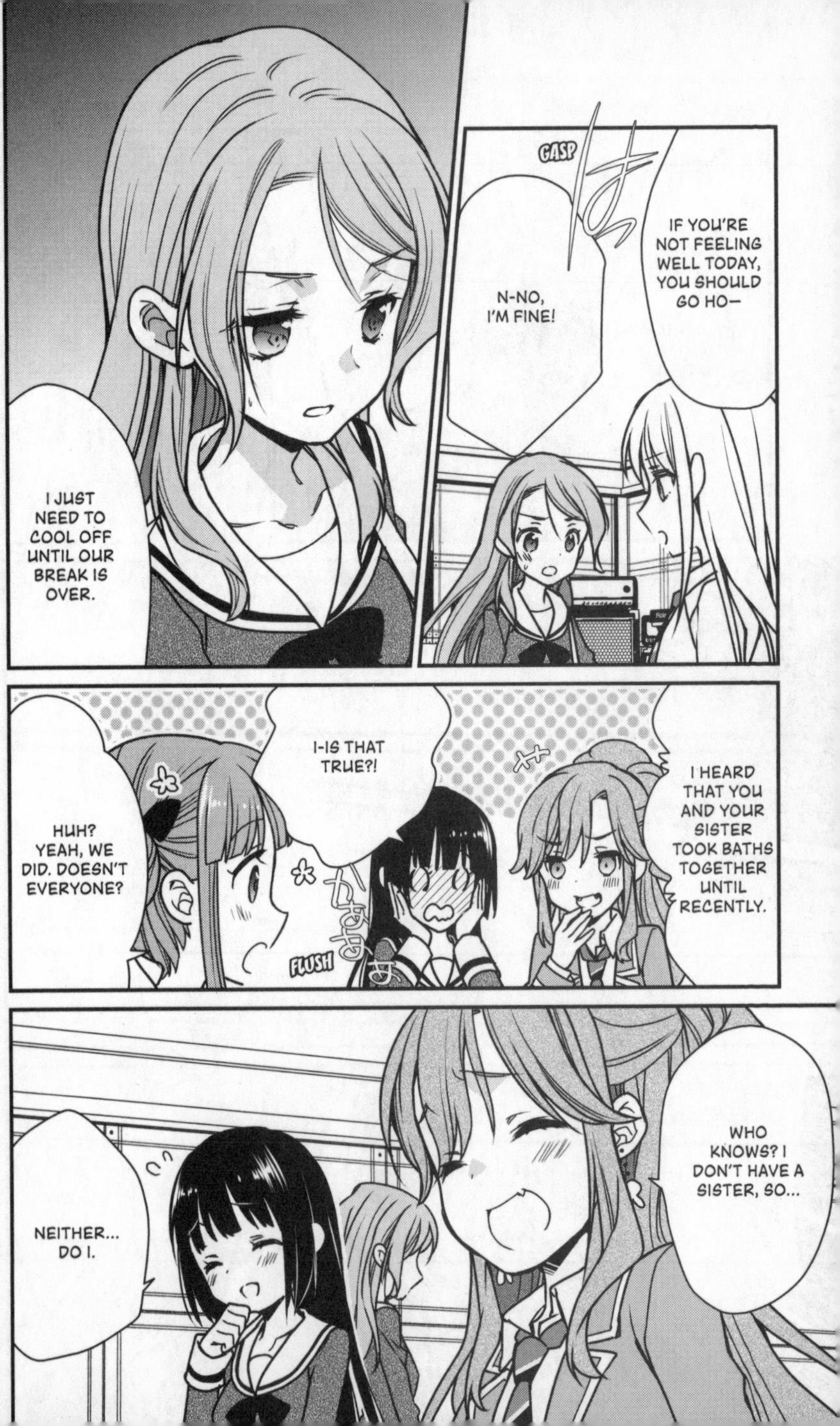
GASP
は
IF YOU'RE NOT FEELING WELL TODAY, YOU SHOULD GO HO—
N-NO, I'M FINE!
I JUST NEED TO COOL OFF UNTIL OUR BREAK IS OVER.
I HEARD THAT YOU AND YOUR SISTER TOOK BATHS TOGETHER UNTIL RECENTLY.
I-IS THAT TRUE?!
FLUSH
HUH? YEAH, WE DID. DOESN'T EVERYONE?
WHO KNOWS? I DON'T HAVE A SISTER, SO...
NEITHER... DO I.

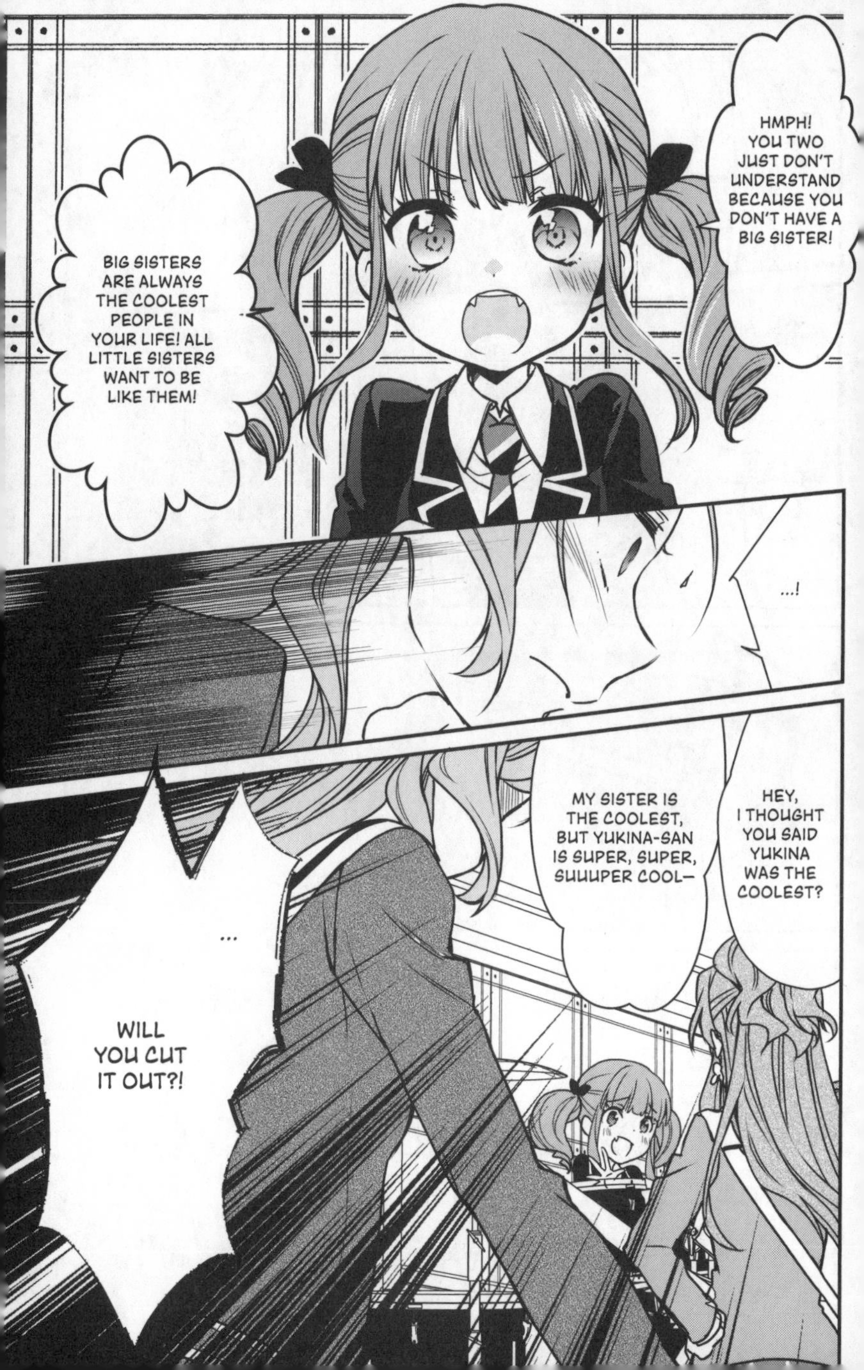
HMPH! YOU TWO JUST DON'T UNDERSTAND BECAUSE YOU DON'T HAVE A BIG SISTER!
BIG SISTERS ARE ALWAYS THE COOLEST PEOPLE IN YOUR LIFE! ALL LITTLE SISTERS WANT TO BE LIKE THEM!
...!
HEY, I THOUGHT YOU SAID YUKINA WAS THE COOLEST?
MY SISTER IS THE COOLEST, BUT YUKINA-SAN IS SUPER, SUPER, SUUUPER COOL—
...
WILL YOU CUT IT OUT?!

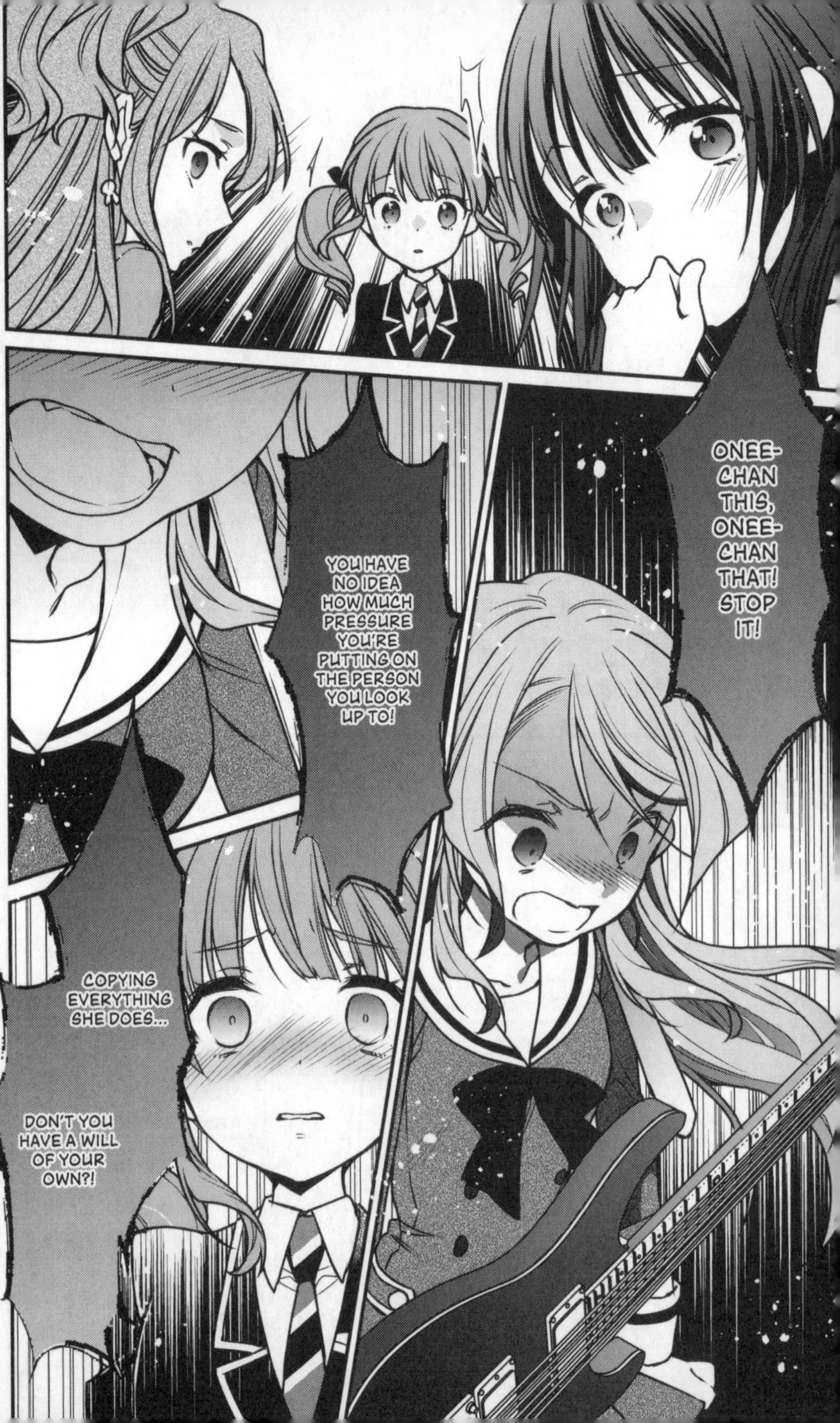
ONEE-CHAN THIS, ONEE-CHAN THAT! STOP IT!
YOU HAVE NO IDEA HOW MUCH PRESSURE YOU'RE PUTTING ON THE PERSON YOU LOOK UP TO!
COPYING EVERYTHING SHE DOES...
DON'T YOU HAVE A WILL OF YOUR OWN?!

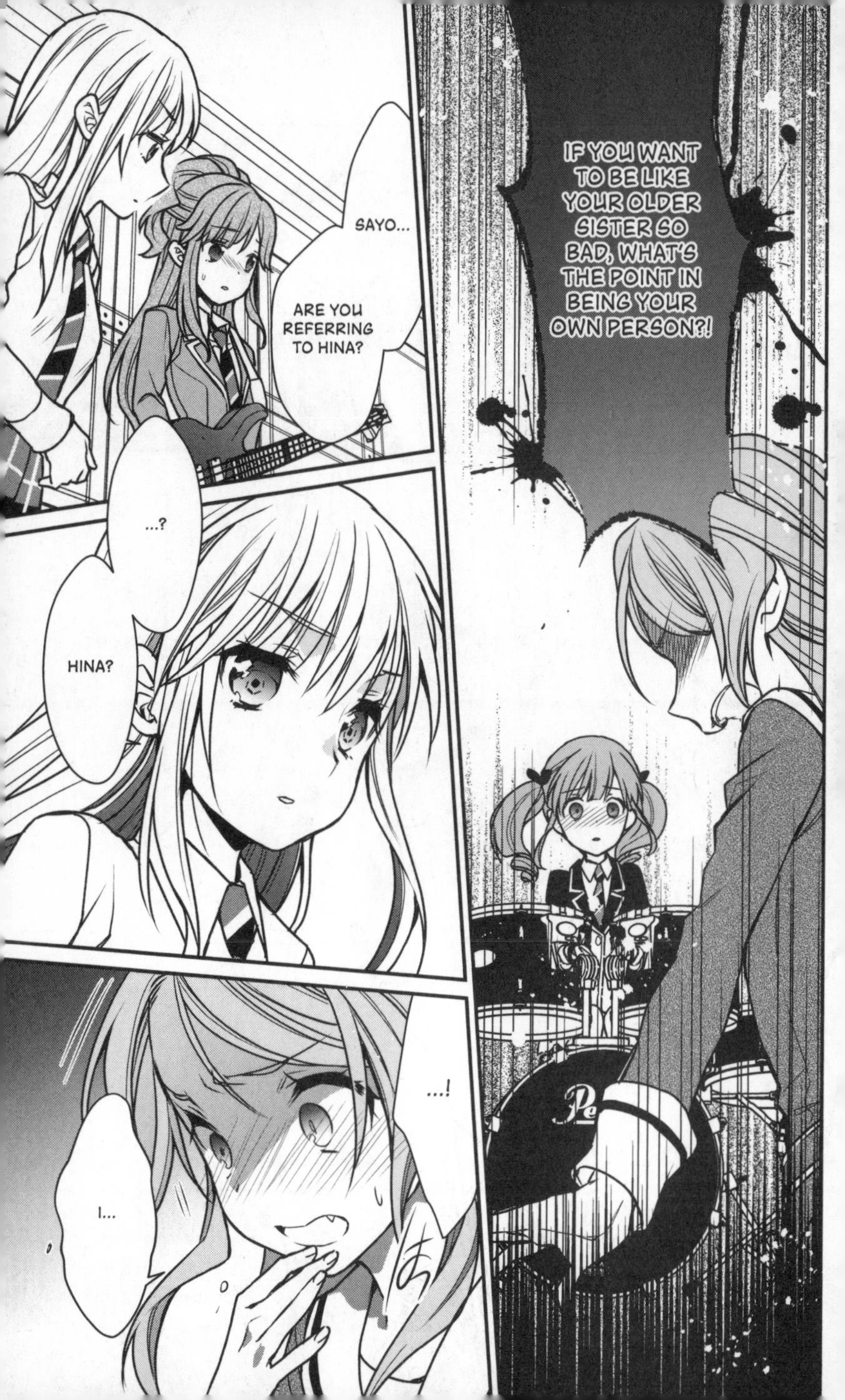
IF YOU WANT TO BE LIKE YOUR OLDER SISTER SO BAD, WHAT'S THE POINT IN BEING YOUR OWN PERSON?!
SAYO...
ARE YOU REFERRING TO HINA?
...?
HINA?
...!
I...

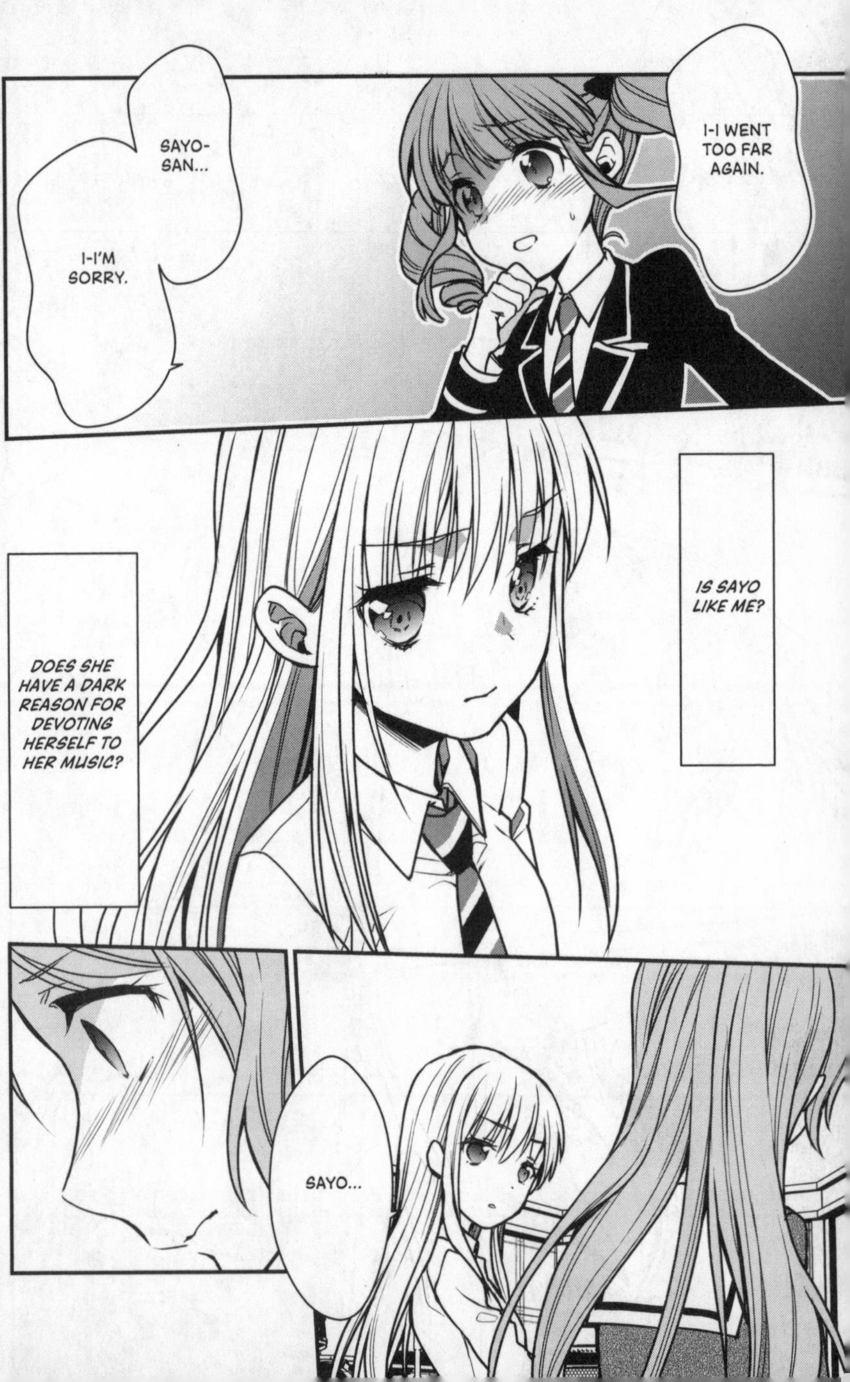
I-I WENT TOO FAR AGAIN.
SAYO-SAN...
I-I'M SORRY.
IS SAYO LIKE ME?
DOES SHE HAVE A DARK REASON FOR DEVOTING HERSELF TO HER MUSIC?
SAYO...

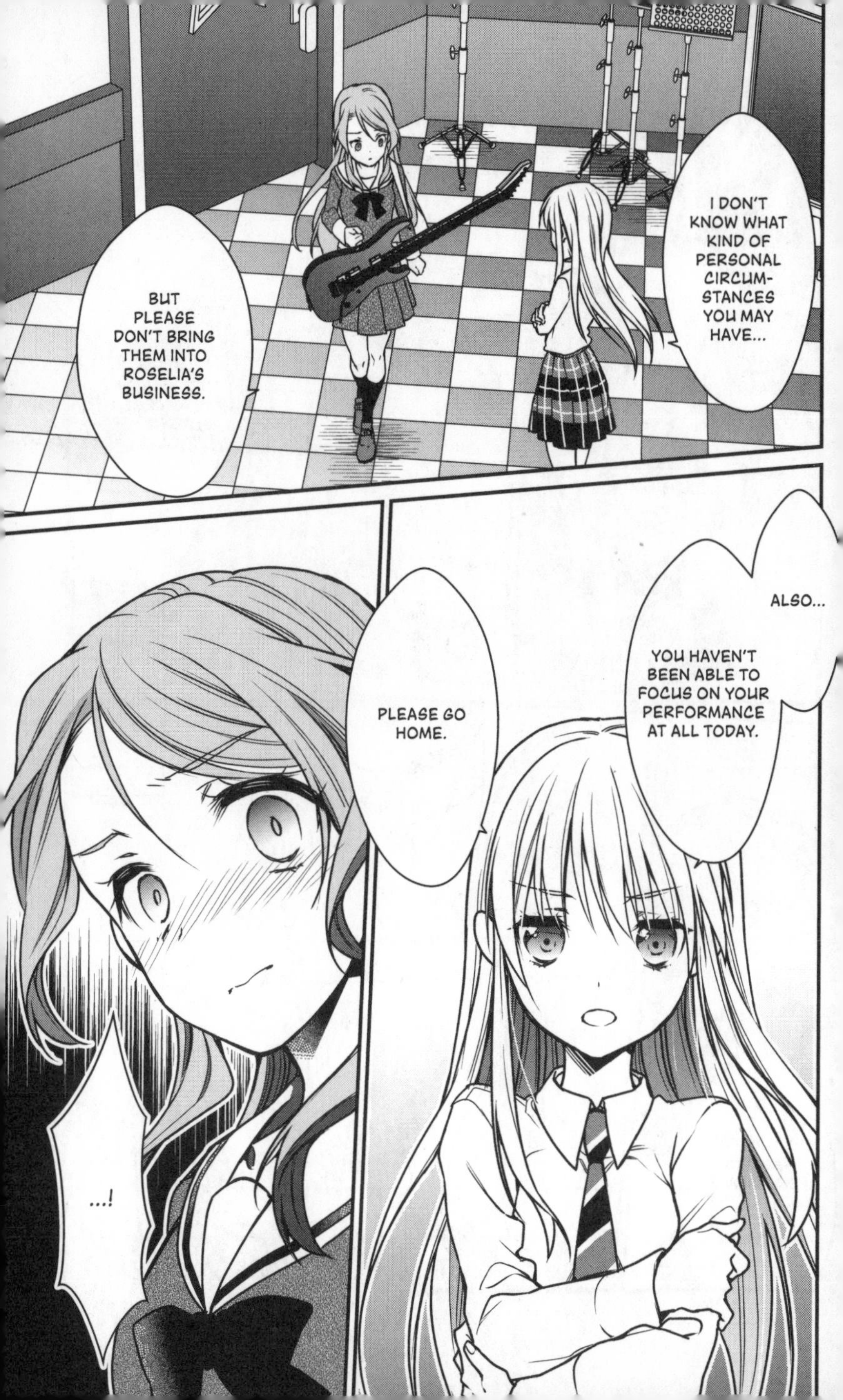
I DON'T KNOW WHAT KIND OF PERSONAL CIRCUM-STANCES YOU MAY HAVE...
BUT PLEASE DON'T BRING THEM INTO ROSELIA'S BUSINESS.
ALSO...
YOU HAVEN'T BEEN ABLE TO FOCUS ON YOUR PERFORMANCE AT ALL TODAY.
PLEASE GO HOME.
...!

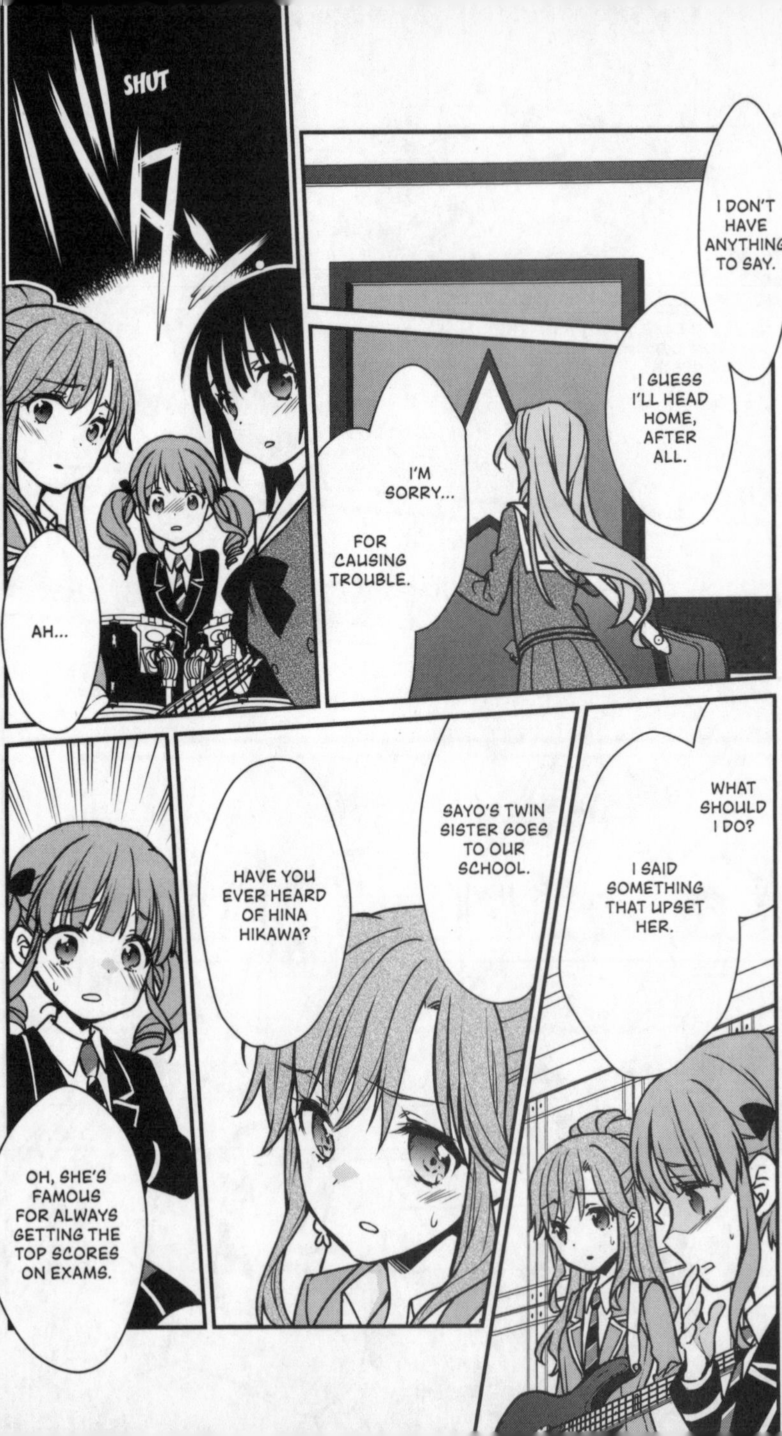
I DON'T HAVE ANYTHING TO SAY.
I GUESS I'LL HEAD HOME, AFTER ALL.
I'M SORRY... FOR CAUSING TROUBLE.
SHUT
AH...
WHAT SHOULD I DO? I SAID SOMETHING THAT UPSET HER.
SAYO'S TWIN SISTER GOES TO OUR SCHOOL.
HAVE YOU EVER HEARD OF HINA HIKAWA?
OH, SHE'S FAMOUS FOR ALWAYS GETTING THE TOP SCORES ON EXAMS.

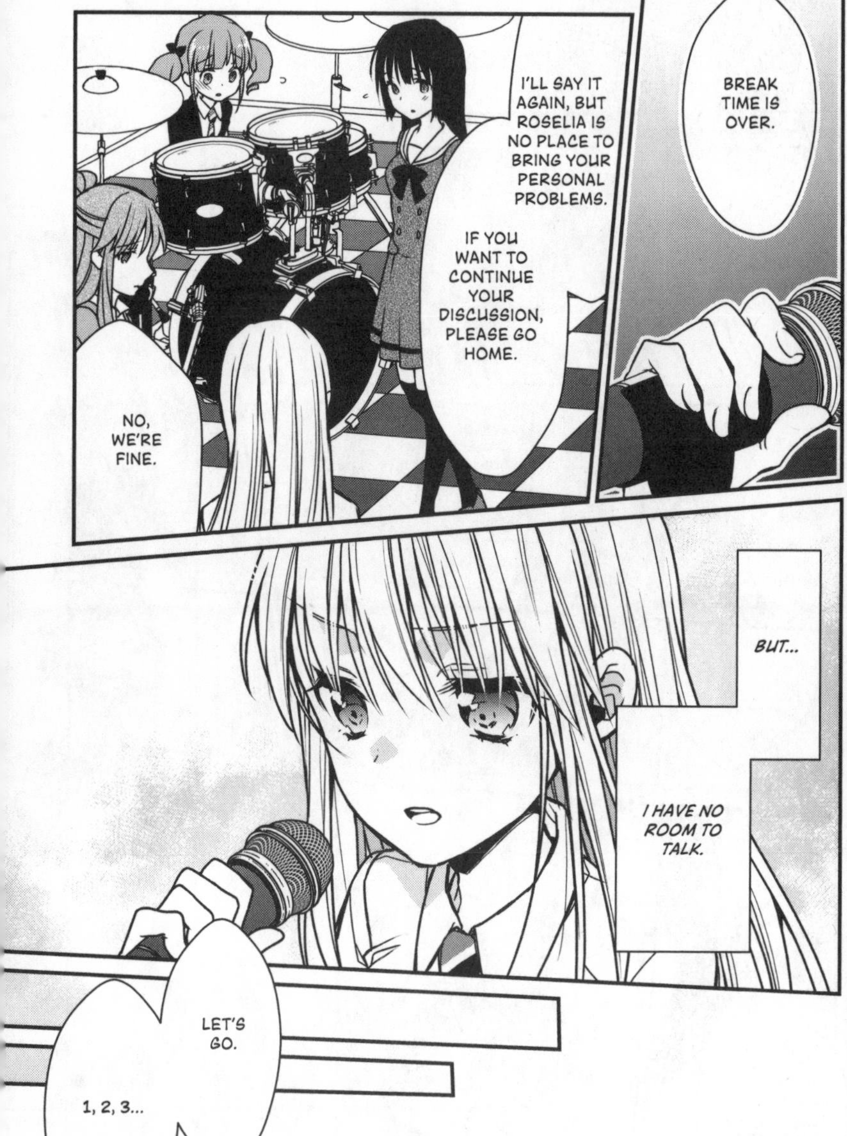
BREAK TIME IS OVER.
I'LL SAY IT AGAIN, BUT ROSELIA IS NO PLACE TO BRING YOUR PERSONAL PROBLEMS.
IF YOU WANT TO CONTINUE YOUR DISCUSSION, PLEASE GO HOME.
NO, WE'RE FINE.
BUT...
I HAVE NO ROOM TO TALK.
LET'S GO.
1, 2, 3...

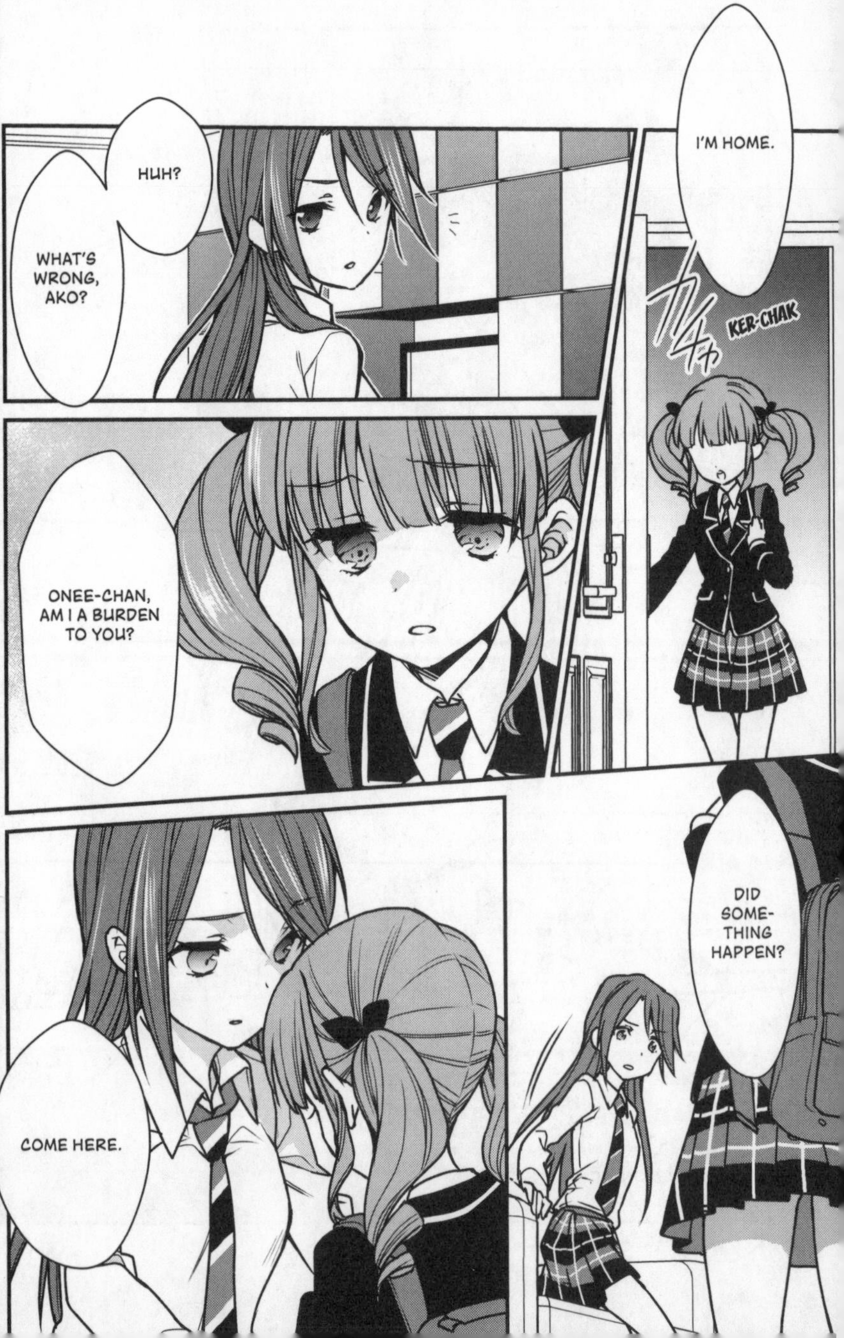
I'M HOME.
KER-CHAK
HUH?
WHAT'S WRONG, AKO?
ONEE-CHAN, AM I A BURDEN TO YOU?
DID SOME-THING HAPPEN?
COME HERE.

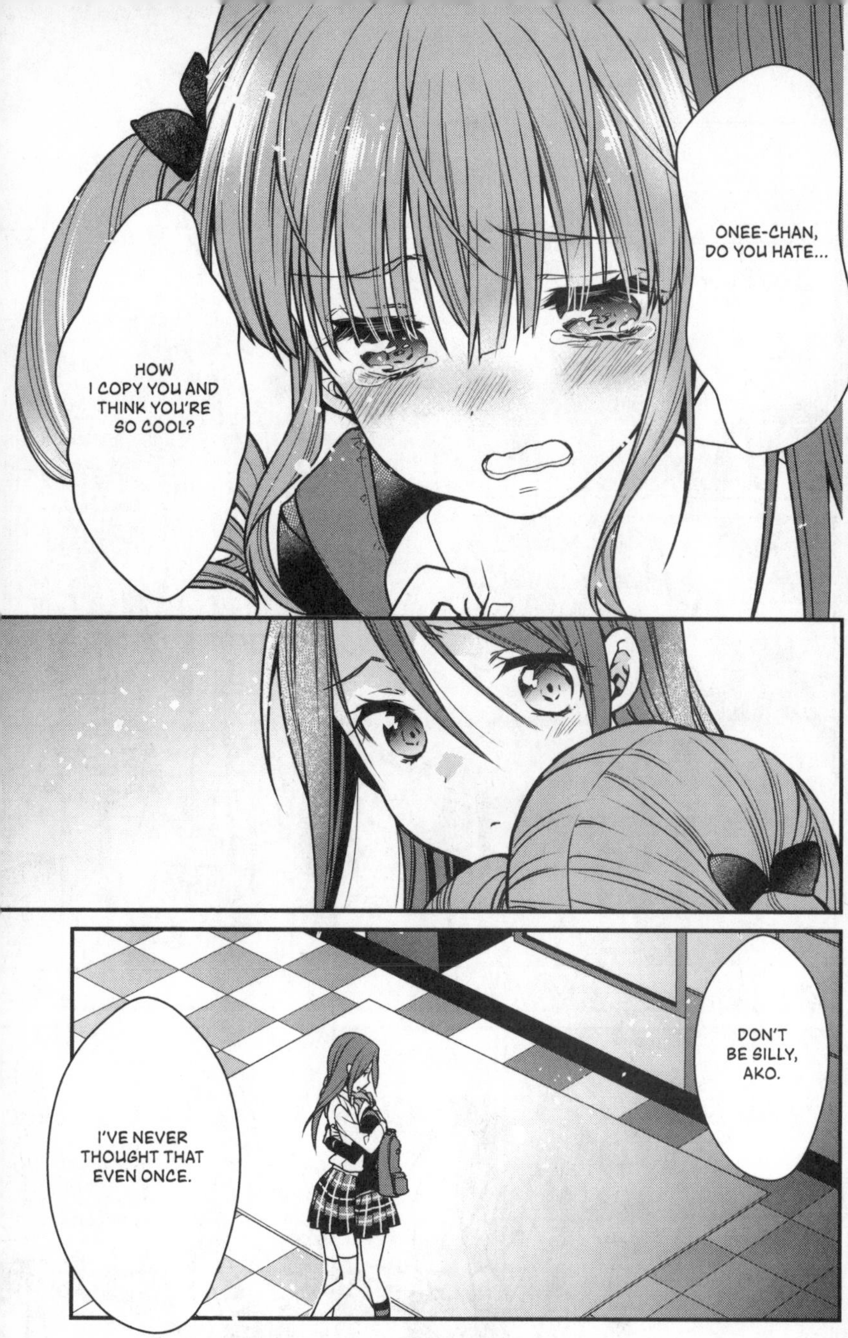
ONEE-CHAN, DO YOU HATE...
HOW I COPY YOU AND THINK YOU'RE SO COOL?
DON'T BE SILLY, AKO.
I'VE NEVER THOUGHT THAT EVEN ONCE.

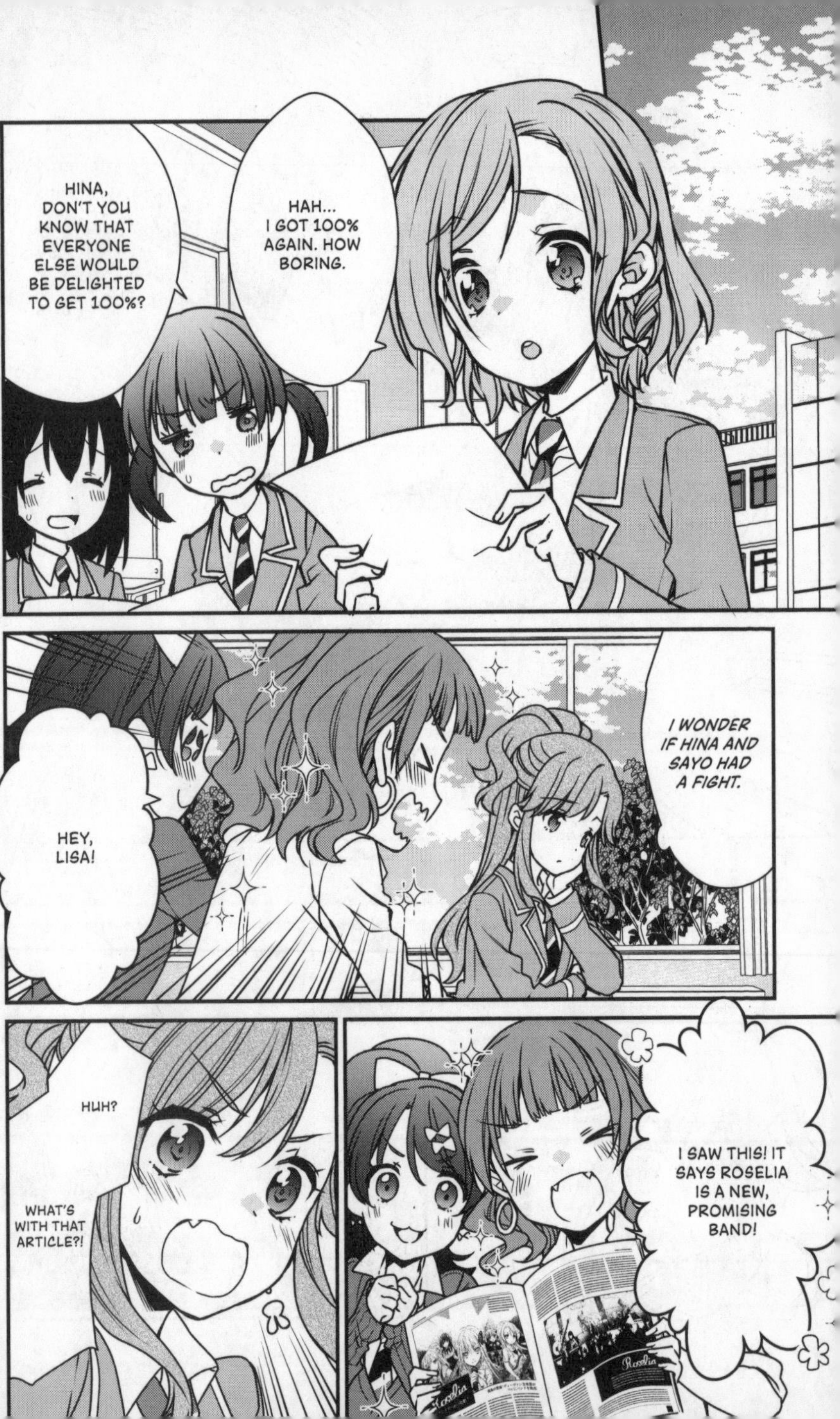
HAH... I GOT 100% AGAIN. HOW BORING.
HINA, DON'T YOU KNOW THAT EVERYONE ELSE WOULD BE DELIGHTED TO GET 100%?
I WONDER IF HINA AND SAYO HAD A FIGHT.
HEY, LISA!
I SAW THIS! IT SAYS ROSELIA IS A NEW, PROMISING BAND!
HUH?
WHAT'S WITH THAT ARTICLE?!

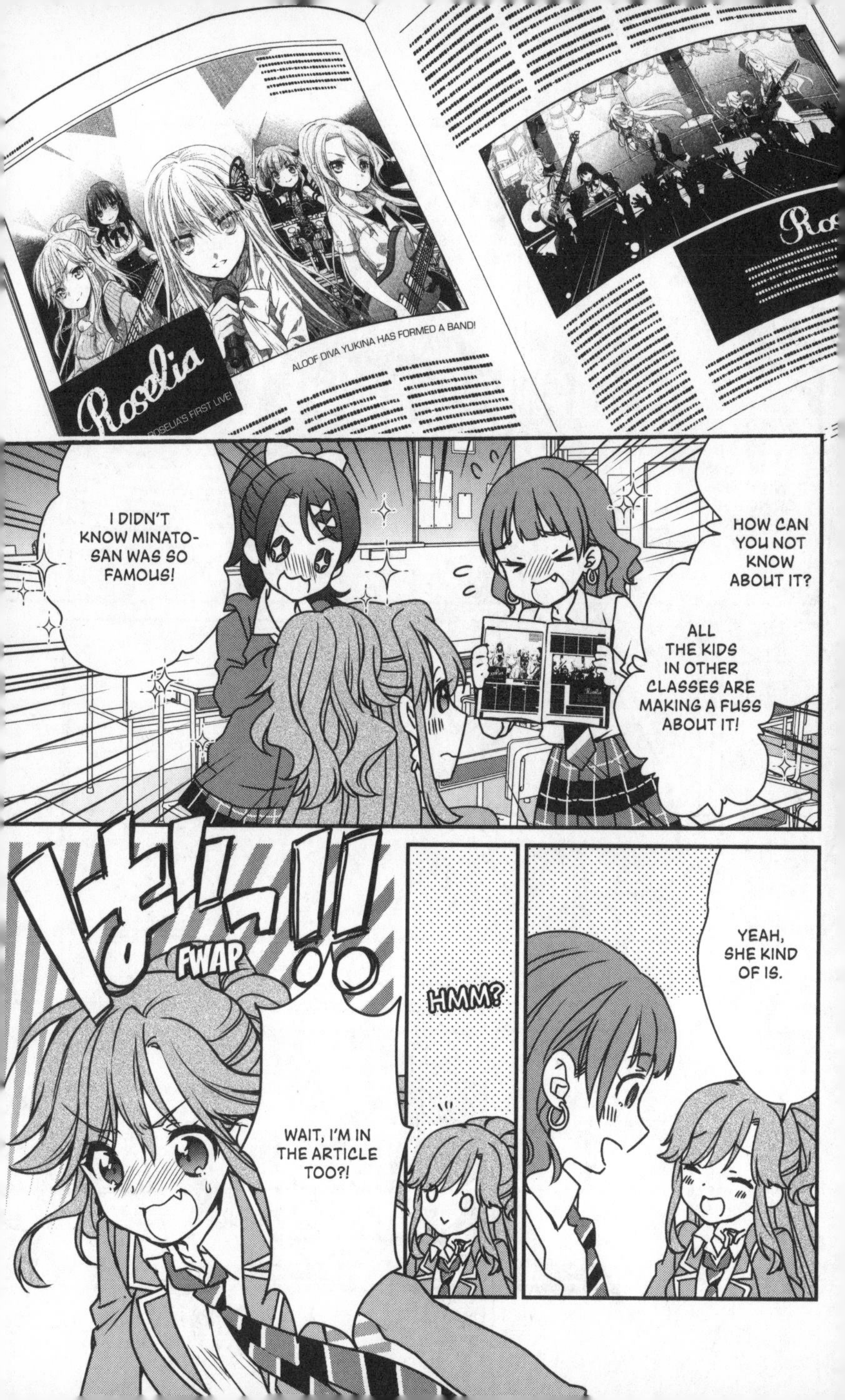
ALOOF DIVA YUKINA HAS FORMED A BAND!
Roselia
ROSELIA'S FIRST LIVE!
HOW CAN YOU NOT KNOW ABOUT IT?
ALL THE KIDS IN OTHER CLASSES ARE MAKING A FUSS ABOUT IT!
I DIDN'T KNOW MINATO-SAN WAS SO FAMOUS!
YEAH, SHE KIND OF IS.
HMM?
FWAP
WAIT, I'M IN THE ARTICLE TOO?!

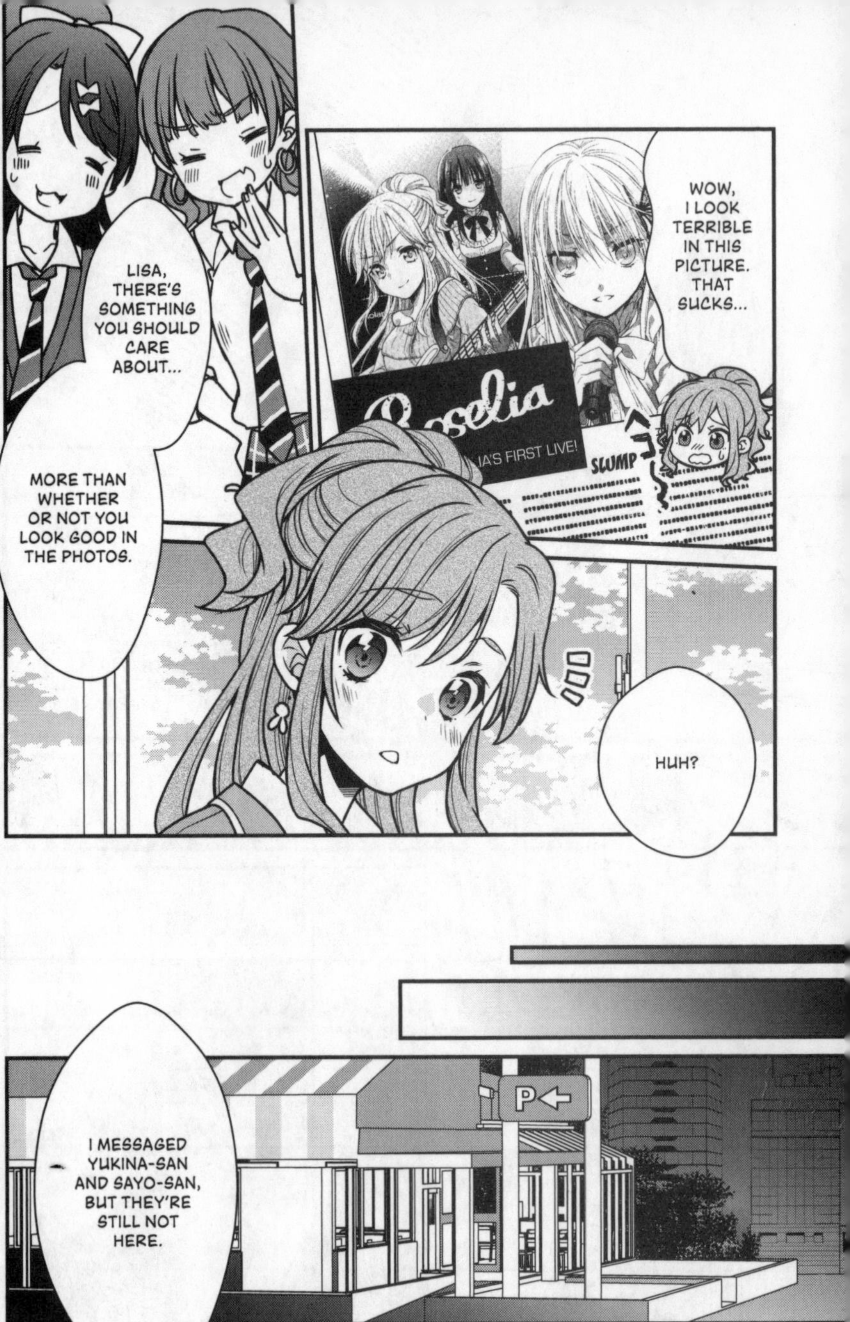
WOW, I LOOK TERRIBLE IN THIS PICTURE. THAT SUCKS...
SLUMP
LISA, THERE'S SOMETHING YOU SHOULD CARE ABOUT...
MORE THAN WHETHER OR NOT YOU LOOK GOOD IN THE PHOTOS.
HUH?
I MESSAGED YUKINA-SAN AND SAYO-SAN, BUT THEY'RE STILL NOT HERE.
P

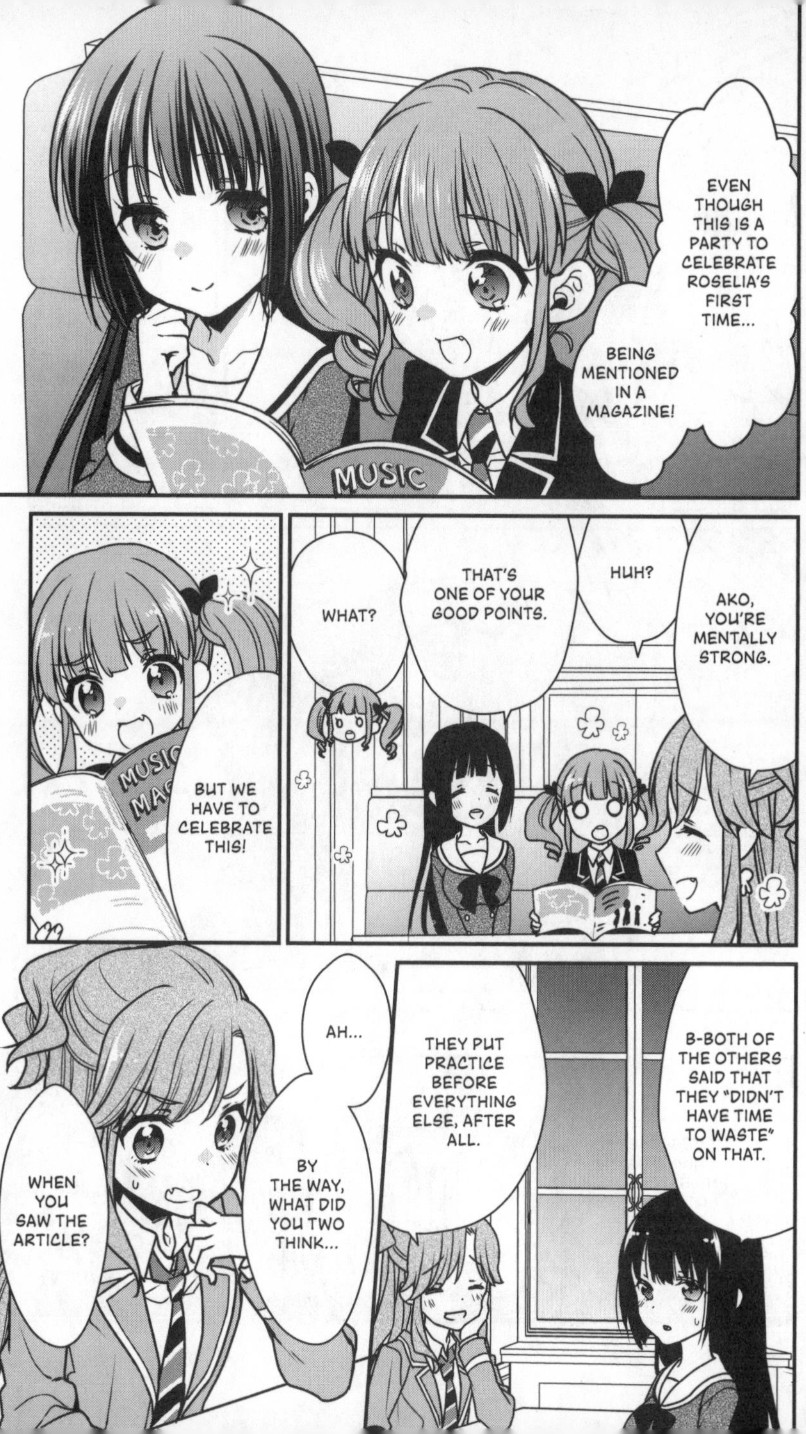
EVEN THOUGH THIS IS A PARTY TO CELEBRATE ROSELIA'S FIRST TIME...
BEING MENTIONED IN A MAGAZINE!
MUSIC
AKO, YOU'RE MENTALLY STRONG.
HUH?
THAT'S ONE OF YOUR GOOD POINTS.
WHAT?
BUT WE HAVE TO CELEBRATE THIS!
B-BOTH OF THE OTHERS SAID THAT THEY "DIDN'T HAVE TIME TO WASTE" ON THAT.
THEY PUT PRACTICE BEFORE EVERYTHING ELSE, AFTER ALL.
AH...
BY THE WAY, WHAT DID YOU TWO THINK...
WHEN YOU SAW THE ARTICLE?

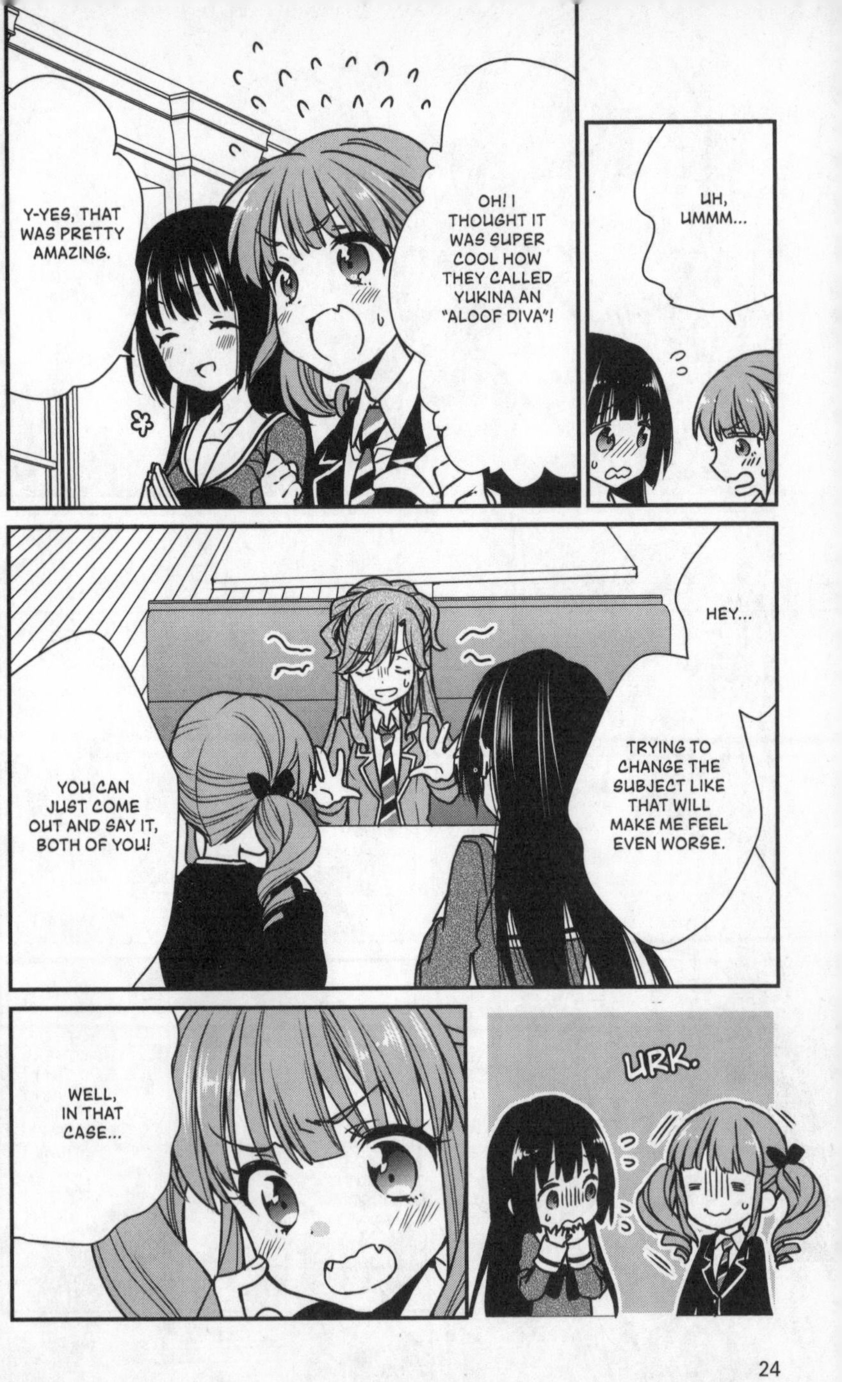
UH, UMMM...
OH! I THOUGHT IT WAS SUPER COOL HOW THEY CALLED YUKINA AN "ALOOF DIVA"!
Y-YES, THAT WAS PRETTY AMAZING.
HEY...
TRYING TO CHANGE THE SUBJECT LIKE THAT WILL MAKE ME FEEL EVEN WORSE.
YOU CAN JUST COME OUT AND SAY IT, BOTH OF YOU!
URK.
WELL, IN THAT CASE...

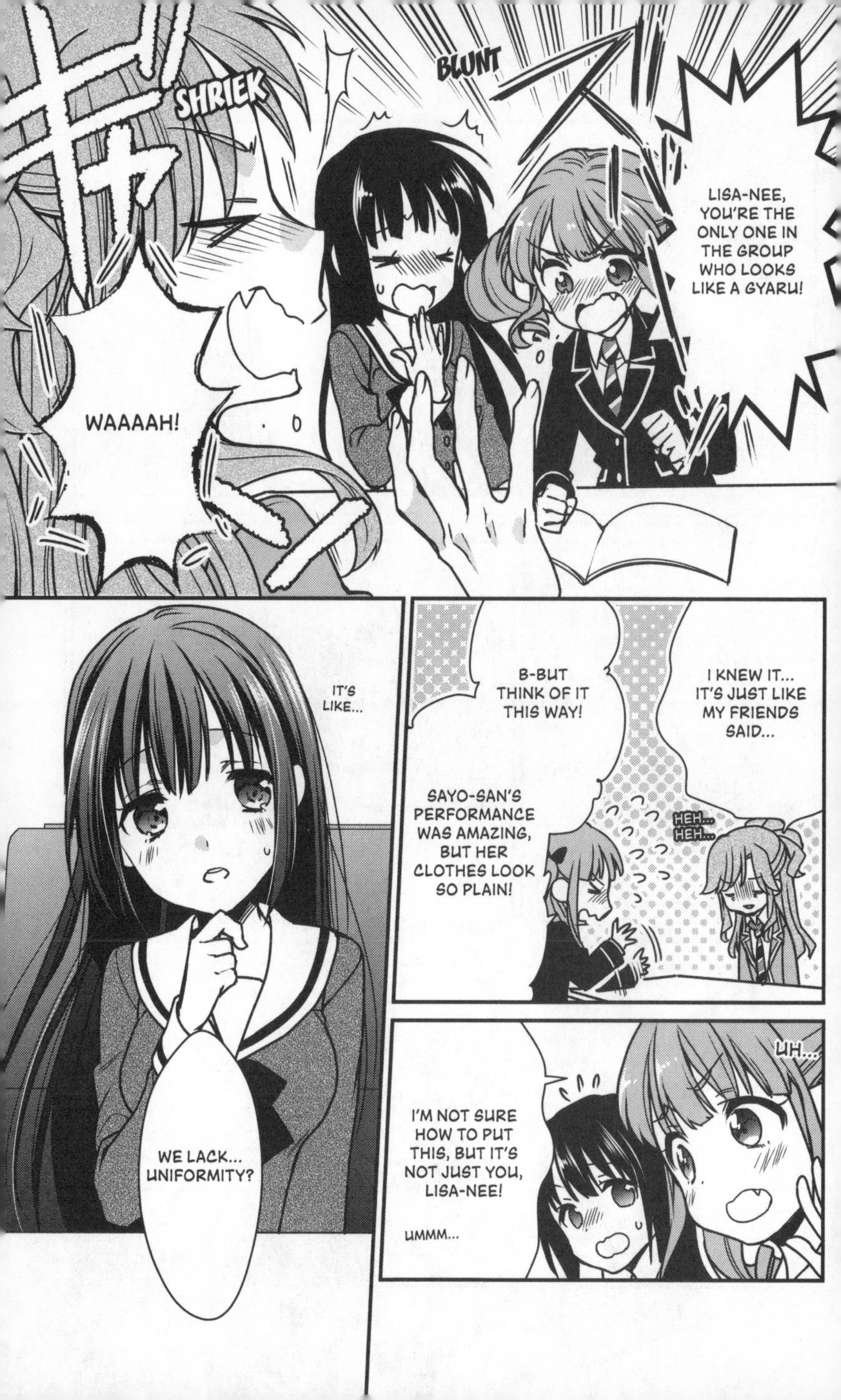
LISA-NEE, YOU'RE THE ONLY ONE IN THE GROUP WHO LOOKS LIKE A GYARU!
BLUNT
SHRIEK
WAAAAH!
I KNEW IT... IT'S JUST LIKE MY FRIENDS SAID...
HEH... HEH...
B-BUT THINK OF IT THIS WAY!
SAYO-SAN'S PERFORMANCE WAS AMAZING, BUT HER CLOTHES LOOK SO PLAIN!
UH...
I'M NOT SURE HOW TO PUT THIS, BUT IT'S NOT JUST YOU, LISA-NEE!
UMMM...
IT'S LIKE...
WE LACK... UNIFORMITY?

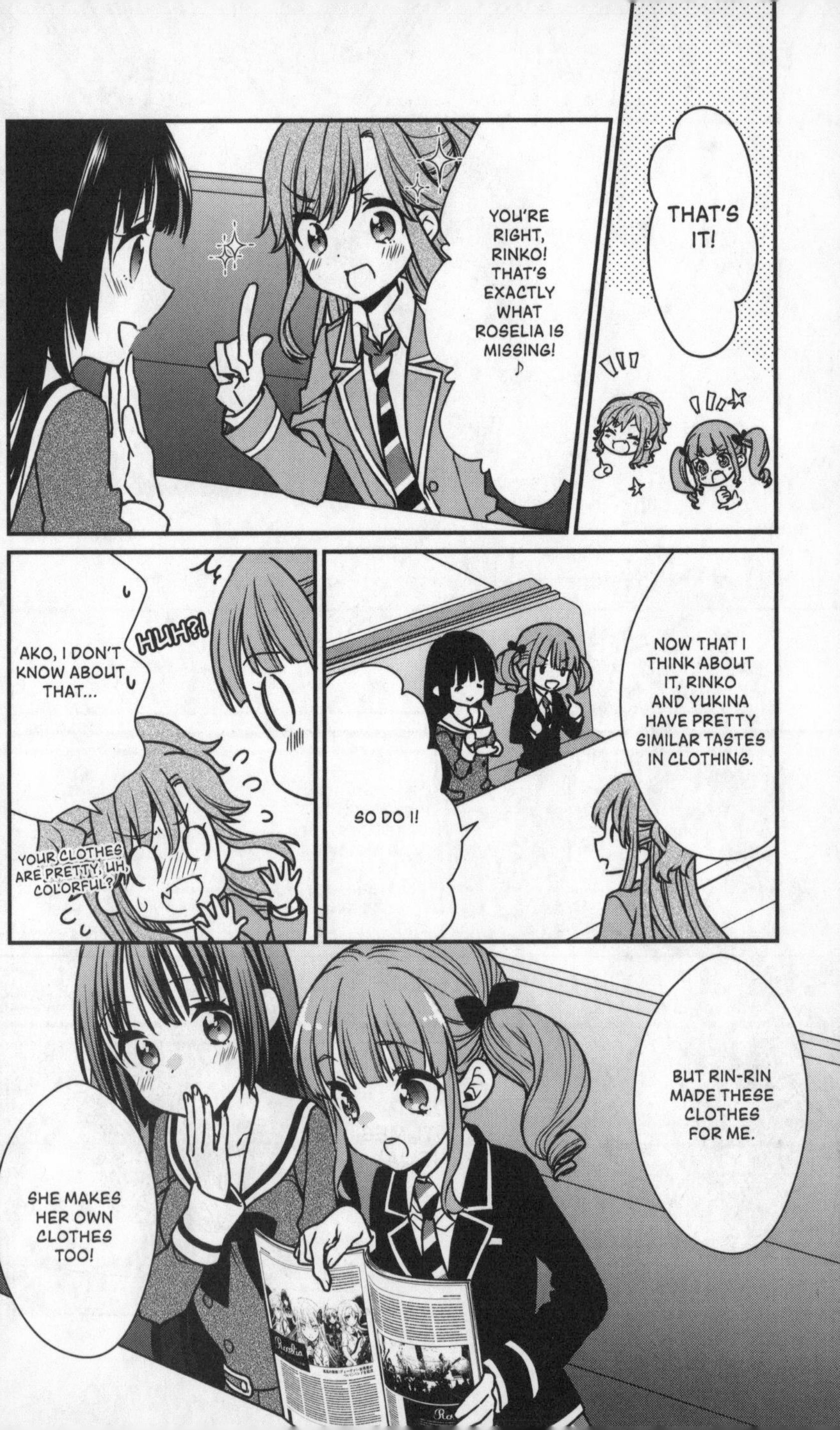
THAT'S IT!
YOU'RE RIGHT, RINKO! THAT'S EXACTLY WHAT ROSELIA IS MISSING! ♪
NOW THAT I THINK ABOUT IT, RINKO AND YUKINA HAVE PRETTY SIMILAR TASTES IN CLOTHING.
SO DO I!
HUH?!
AKO, I DON'T KNOW ABOUT THAT...
YOUR CLOTHES ARE PRETTY, UH, COLORFUL?
BUT RIN-RIN MADE THESE CLOTHES FOR ME.
SHE MAKES HER OWN CLOTHES TOO!

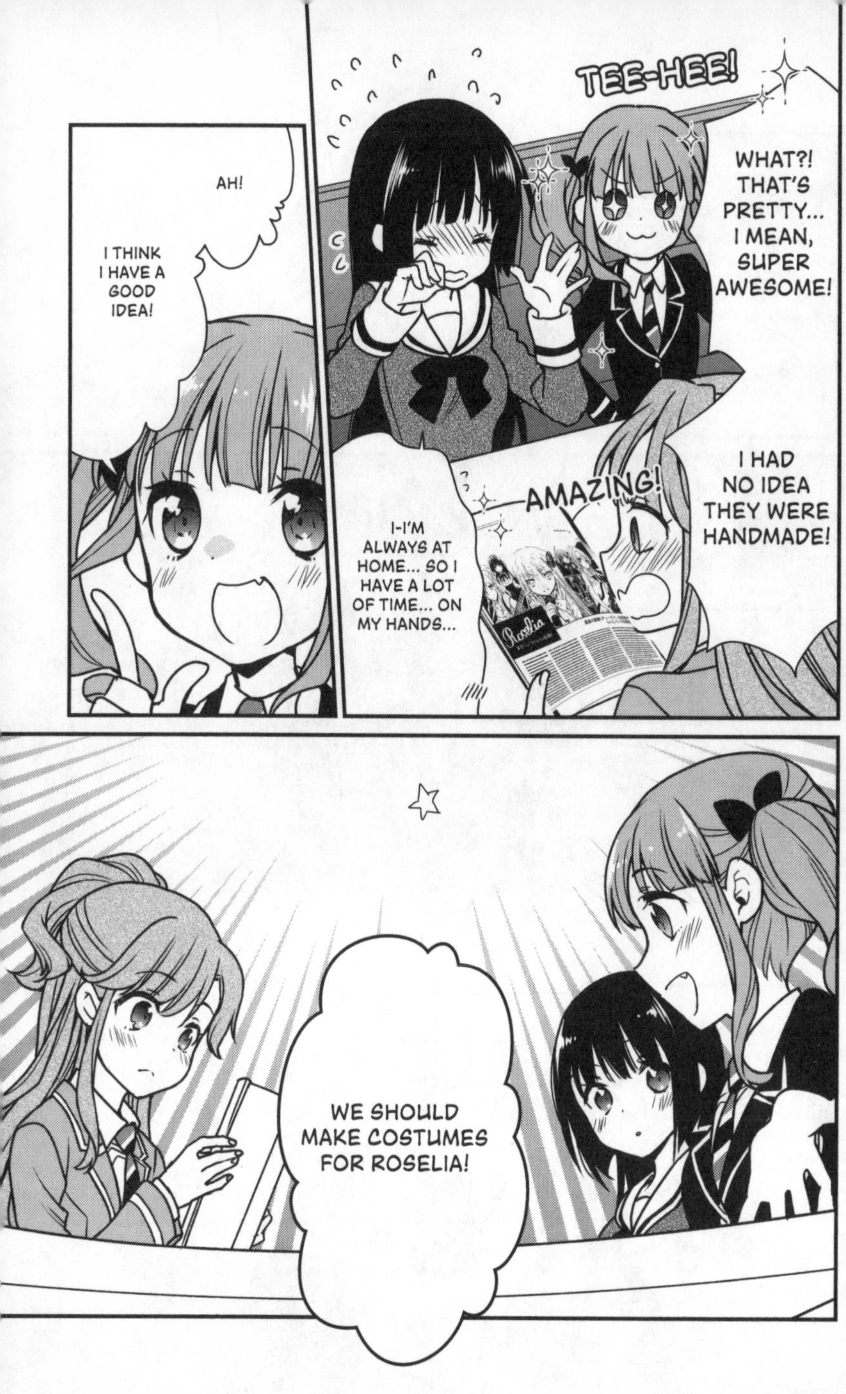
TEE-HEE!
WHAT?! THAT'S PRETTY... I MEAN, SUPER AWESOME!
I HAD NO IDEA THEY WERE HANDMADE!
AMAZING!
I-I'M ALWAYS AT HOME... SO I HAVE A LOT OF TIME... ON MY HANDS...
Roselia
AH!
I THINK I HAVE A GOOD IDEA!
WE SHOULD MAKE COSTUMES FOR ROSELIA!

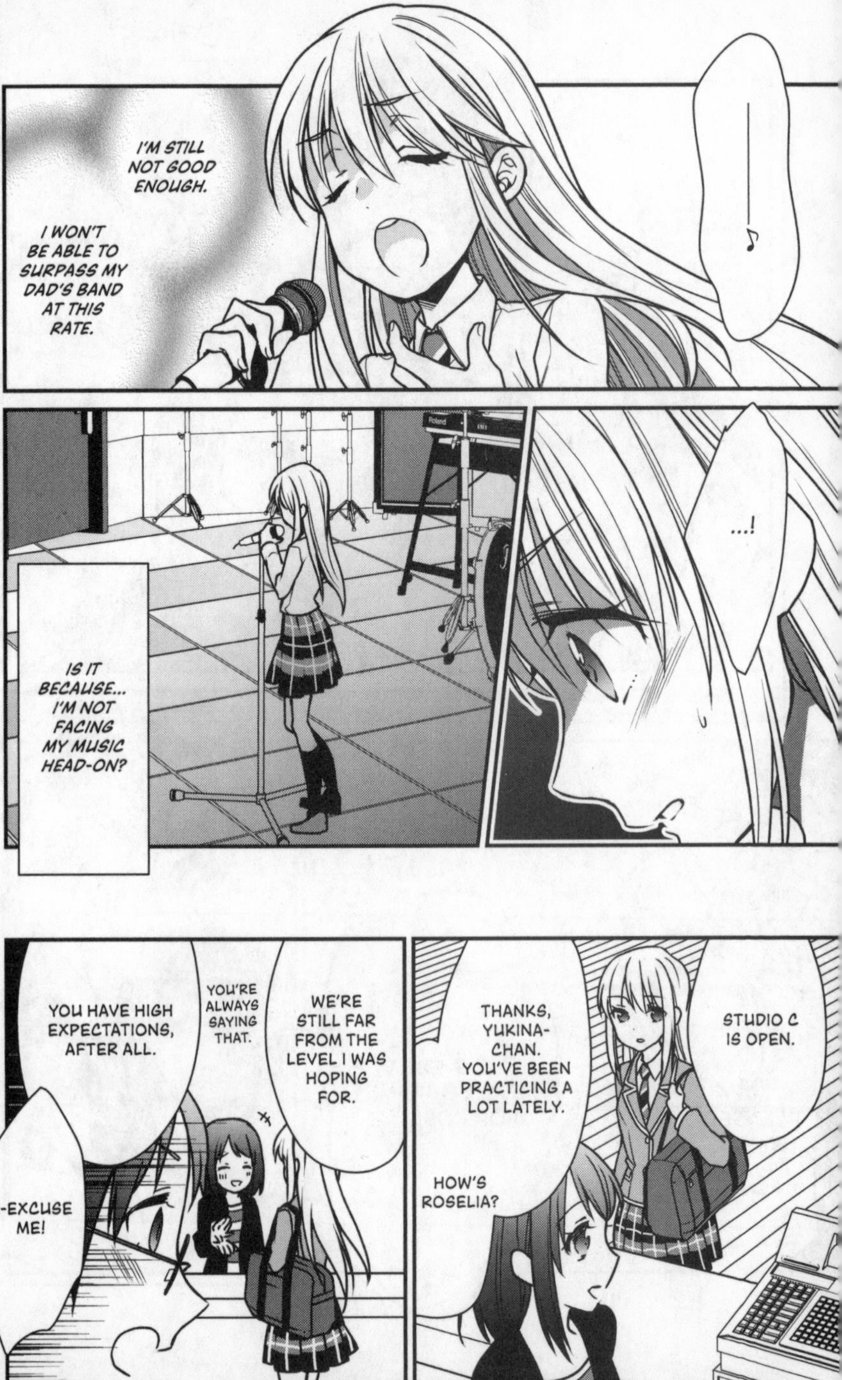
I'M STILL NOT GOOD ENOUGH.
I WON'T BE ABLE TO SURPASS MY DAD'S BAND AT THIS RATE.
...!
IS IT BECAUSE... I'M NOT FACING MY MUSIC HEAD-ON?
STUDIO C IS OPEN.
THANKS, YUKINA-CHAN. YOU'VE BEEN PRACTICING A LOT LATELY.
HOW'S ROSELIA?
WE'RE STILL FAR FROM THE LEVEL I WAS HOPING FOR.
YOU'RE ALWAYS SAYING THAT.
YOU HAVE HIGH EXPECTATIONS, AFTER ALL.
E-EXCUSE ME!

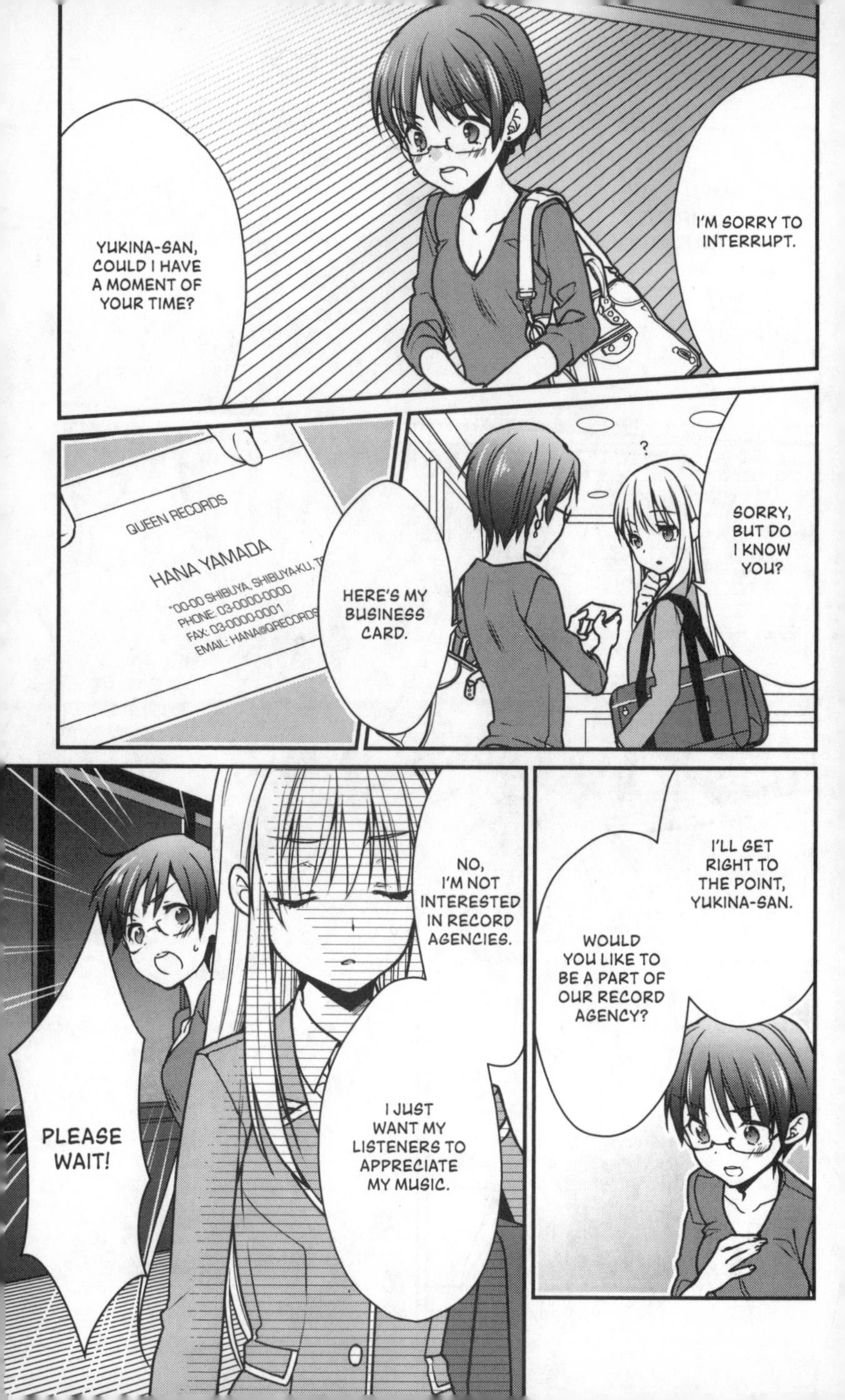
I'M SORRY TO INTERRUPT.
YUKINA-SAN, COULD I HAVE A MOMENT OF YOUR TIME?
?
SORRY, BUT DO I KNOW YOU?
HERE'S MY BUSINESS CARD.
QUEEN RECORDS
HANA YAMADA
00-00 SHIBUYA, SHIBUYA-KU, T
PHONE: 03-0000-0000
FAX: 03-0000-0001
EMAIL: HANA@QRECORDS
I'LL GET RIGHT TO THE POINT, YUKINA-SAN.
WOULD YOU LIKE TO BE A PART OF OUR RECORD AGENCY?
NO, I'M NOT INTERESTED IN RECORD AGENCIES.
I JUST WANT MY LISTENERS TO APPRECIATE MY MUSIC.
PLEASE WAIT!

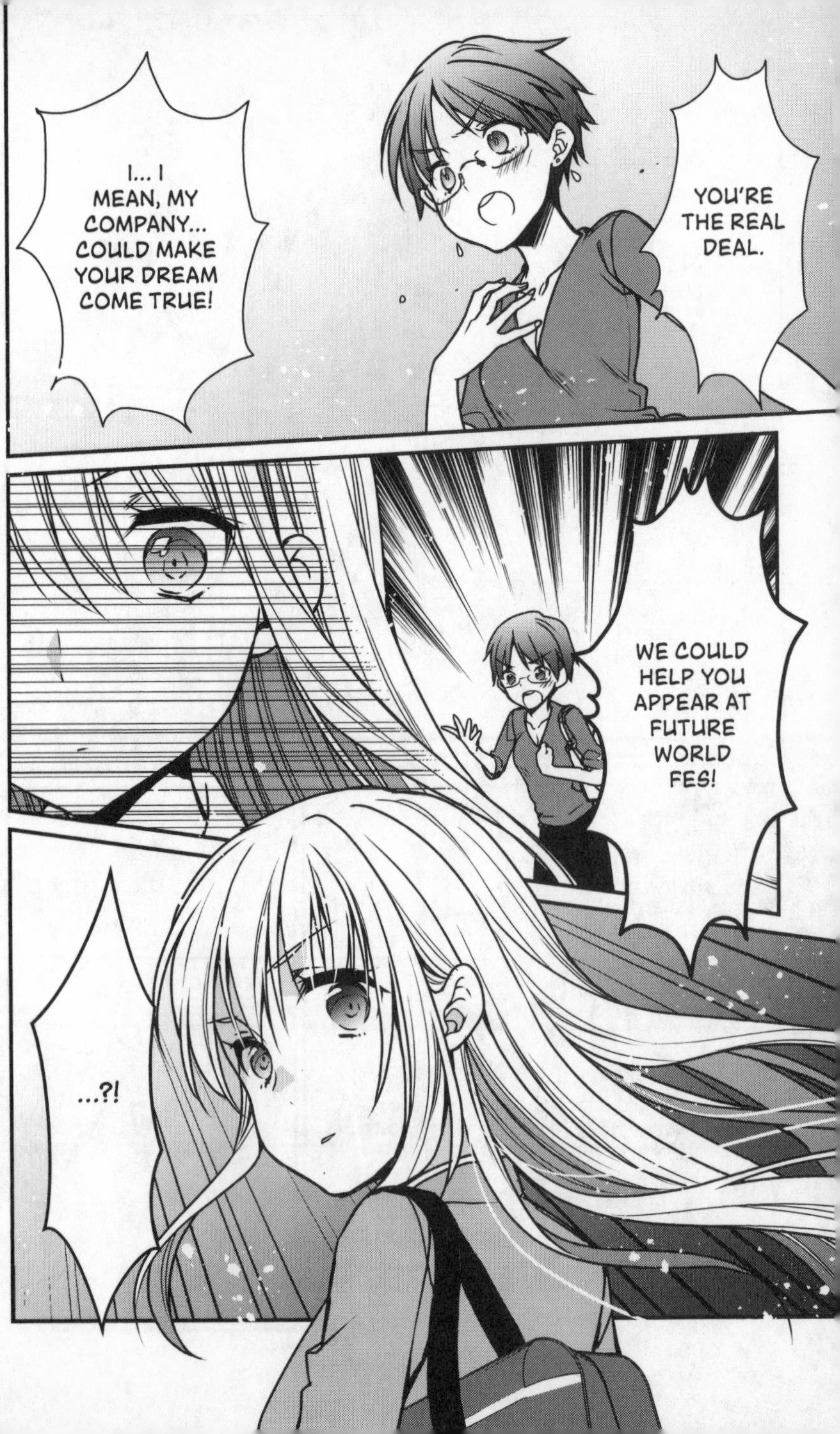
YOU'RE THE REAL DEAL.
I... I MEAN, MY COMPANY... COULD MAKE YOUR DREAM COME TRUE!
WE COULD HELP YOU APPEAR AT FUTURE WORLD FES!
...?!

Chapter 7
A Sudden Invitation

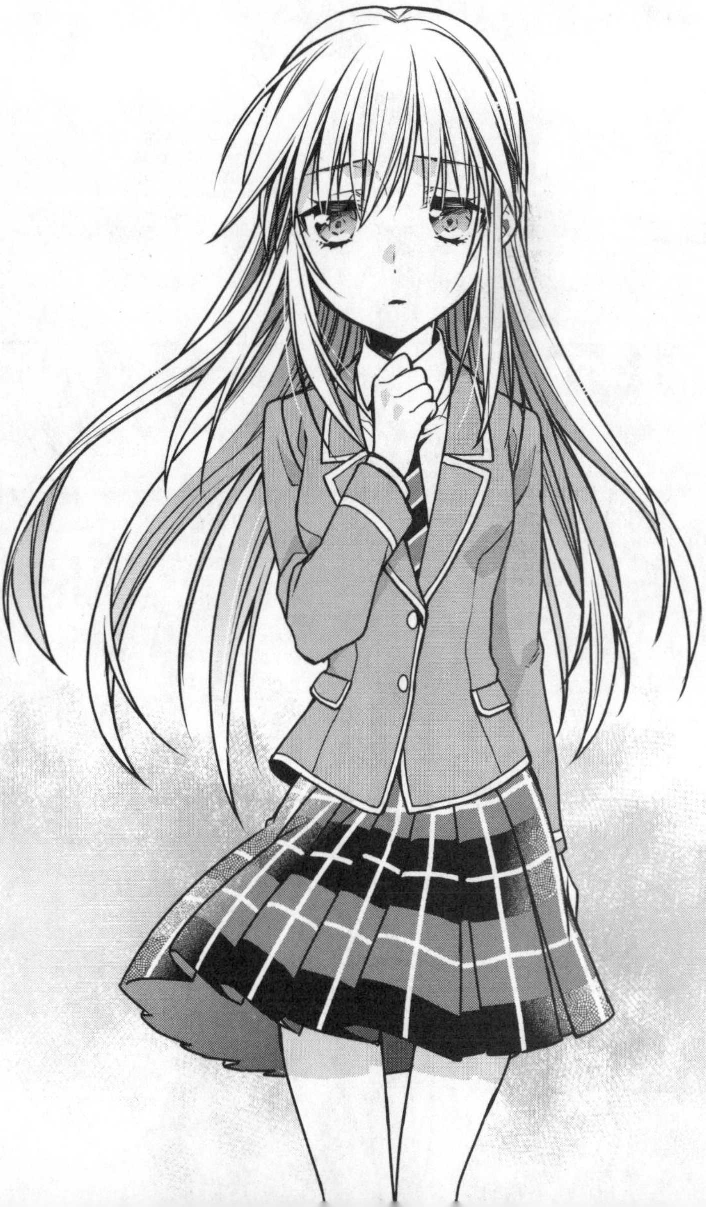

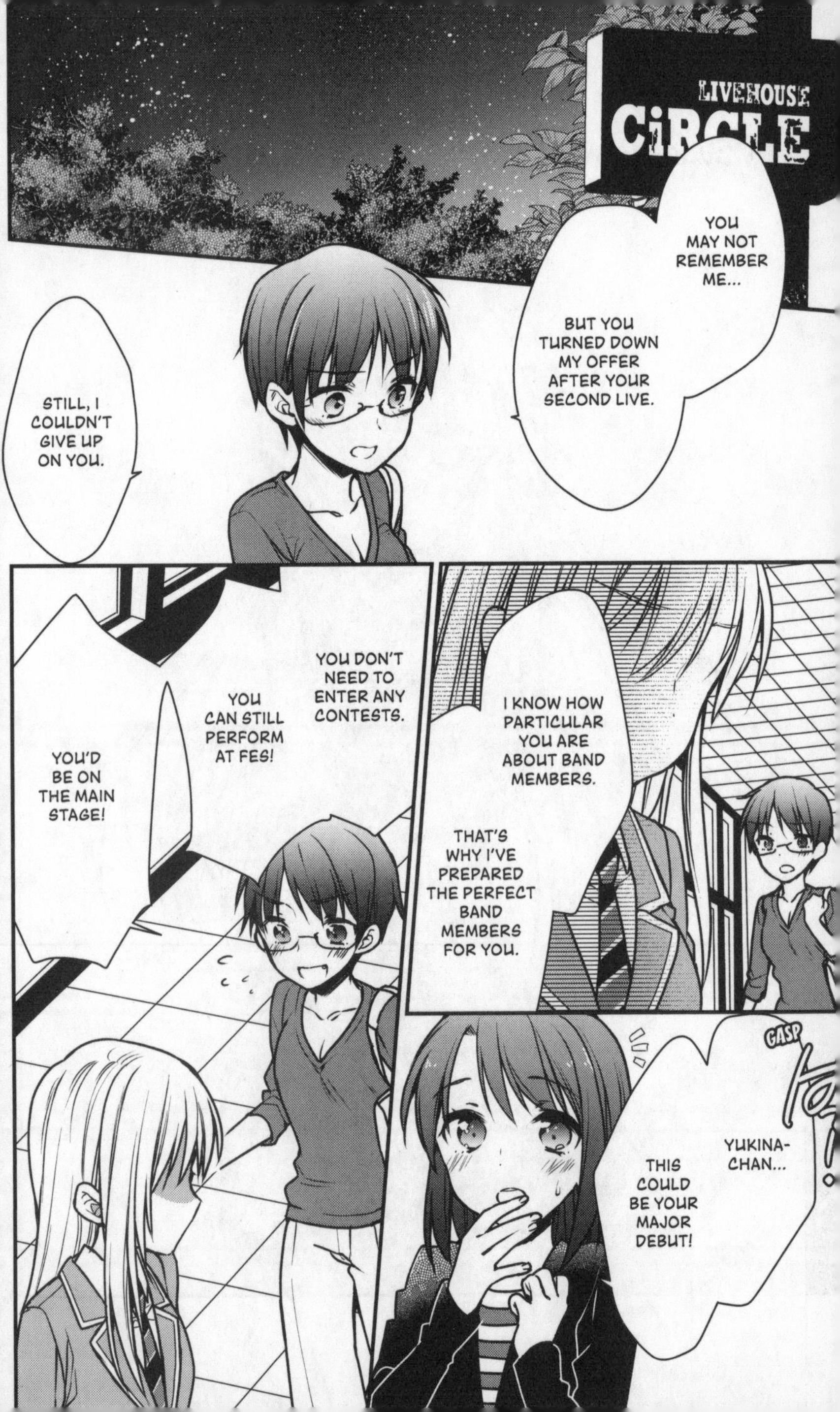
LIVEHOUSE
CiRCLE
YOU MAY NOT REMEMBER ME...
BUT YOU TURNED DOWN MY OFFER AFTER YOUR SECOND LIVE.
STILL, I COULDN'T GIVE UP ON YOU.
I KNOW HOW PARTICULAR YOU ARE ABOUT BAND MEMBERS.
THAT'S WHY I'VE PREPARED THE PERFECT BAND MEMBERS FOR YOU.
YOU DON'T NEED TO ENTER ANY CONTESTS.
YOU CAN STILL PERFORM AT FES!
YOU'D BE ON THE MAIN STAGE!
GASP
YUKINA-CHAN...
THIS COULD BE YOUR MAJOR DEBUT!

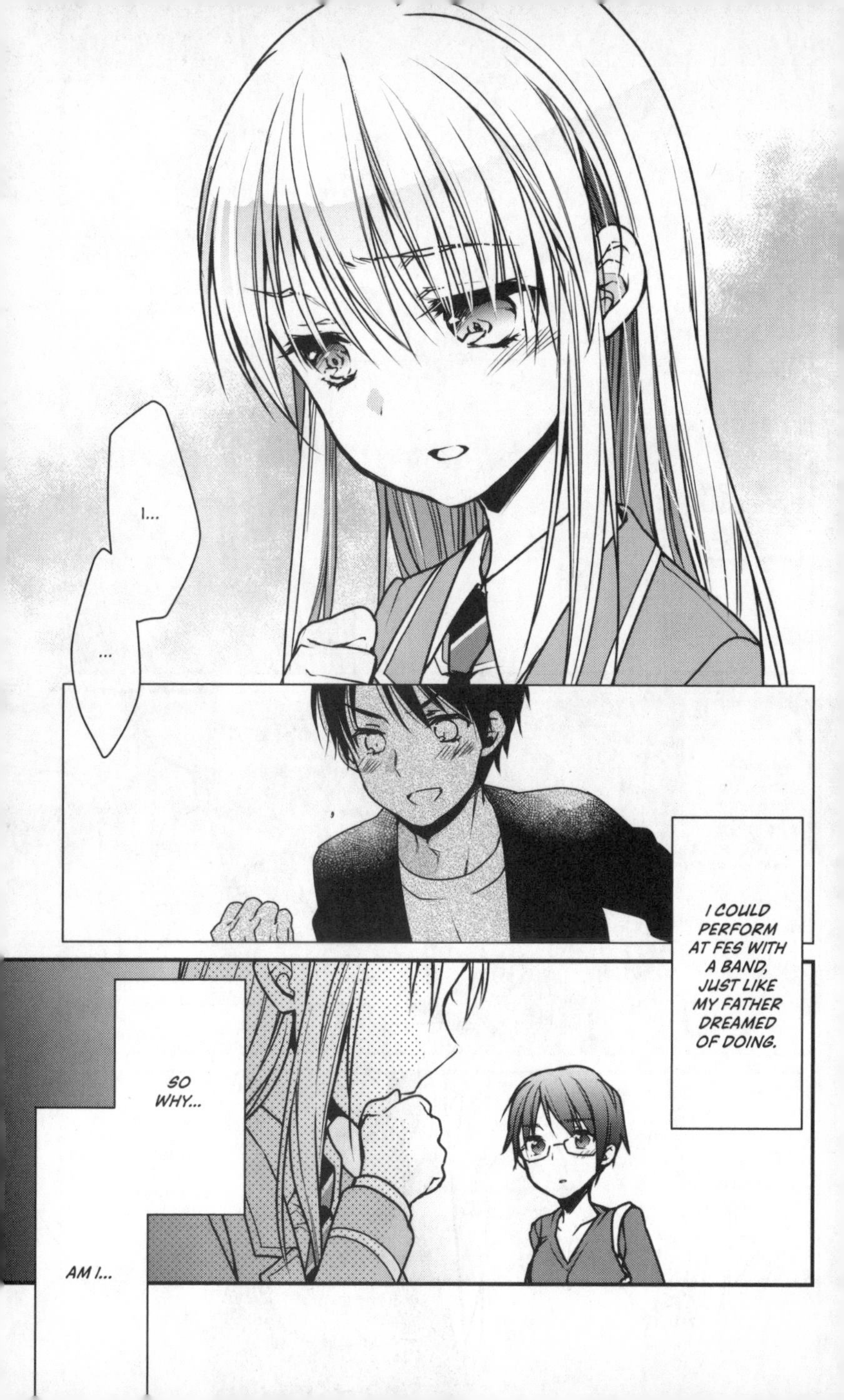
I...
...
I COULD PERFORM AT FES WITH A BAND, JUST LIKE MY FATHER DREAMED OF DOING.
SO WHY...
AM I...

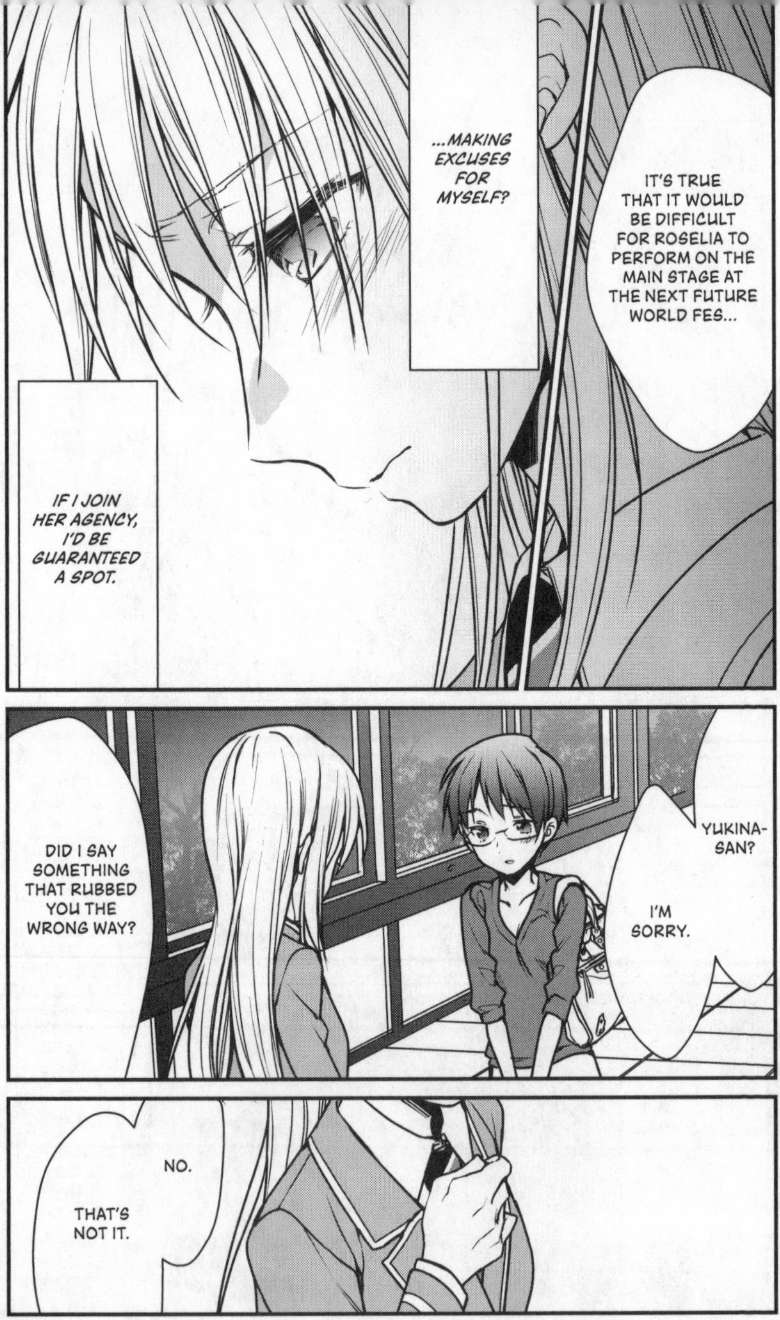
IT'S TRUE THAT IT WOULD BE DIFFICULT FOR ROSELIA TO PERFORM ON THE MAIN STAGE AT THE NEXT FUTURE WORLD FES...
IF I JOIN HER AGENCY, I'D BE GUARANTEED A SPOT.
...MAKING EXCUSES FOR MYSELF?
YUKINA-SAN?
I'M SORRY.
DID I SAY SOMETHING THAT RUBBED YOU THE WRONG WAY?
NO.
THAT'S NOT IT.

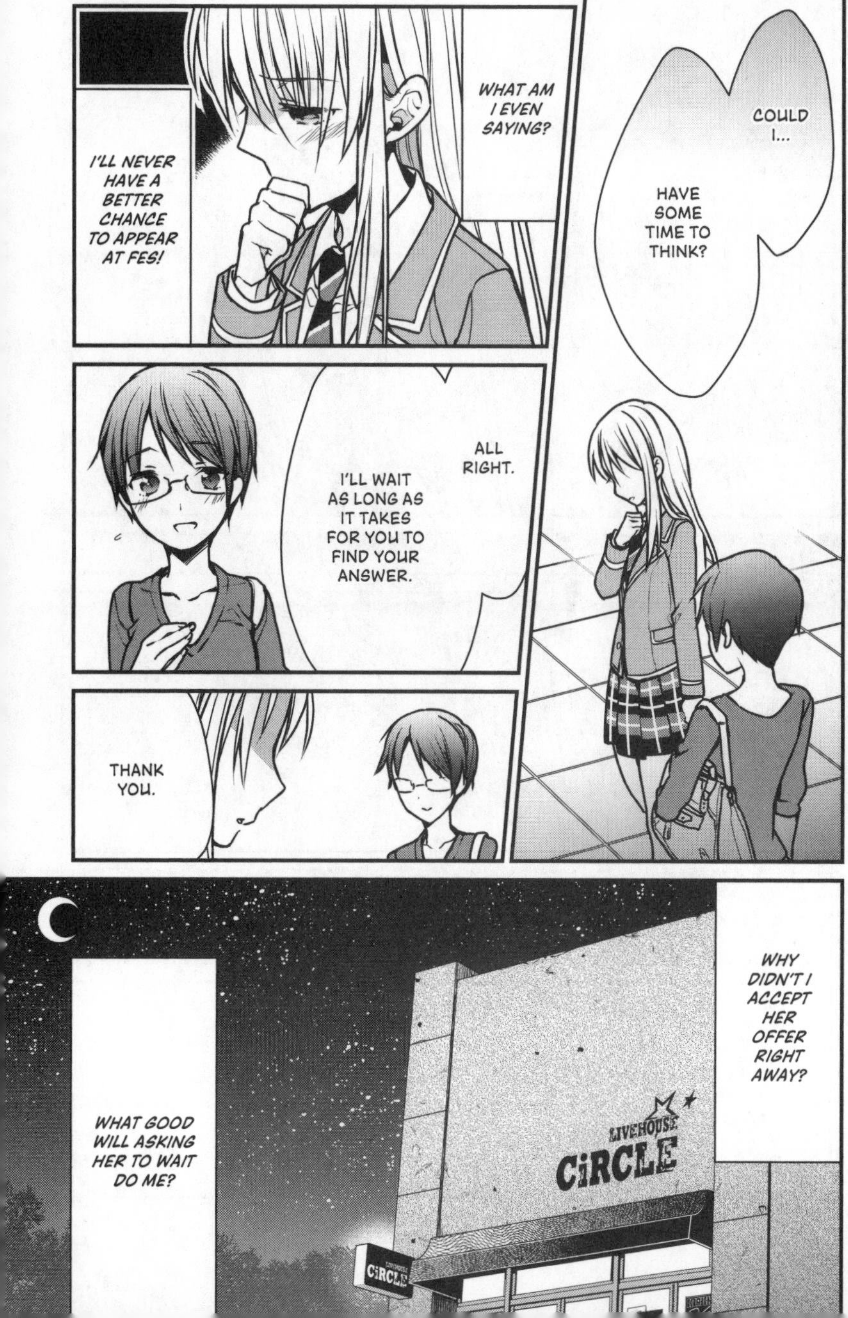
COULD I...
HAVE SOME TIME TO THINK?
WHAT AM I EVEN SAYING?
I'LL NEVER HAVE A BETTER CHANCE TO APPEAR AT FES!
ALL RIGHT.
I'LL WAIT AS LONG AS IT TAKES FOR YOU TO FIND YOUR ANSWER.
THANK YOU.
WHY DIDN'T I ACCEPT HER OFFER RIGHT AWAY?
LIVEHOUSE CiRCLE
WHAT GOOD WILL ASKING HER TO WAIT DO ME?

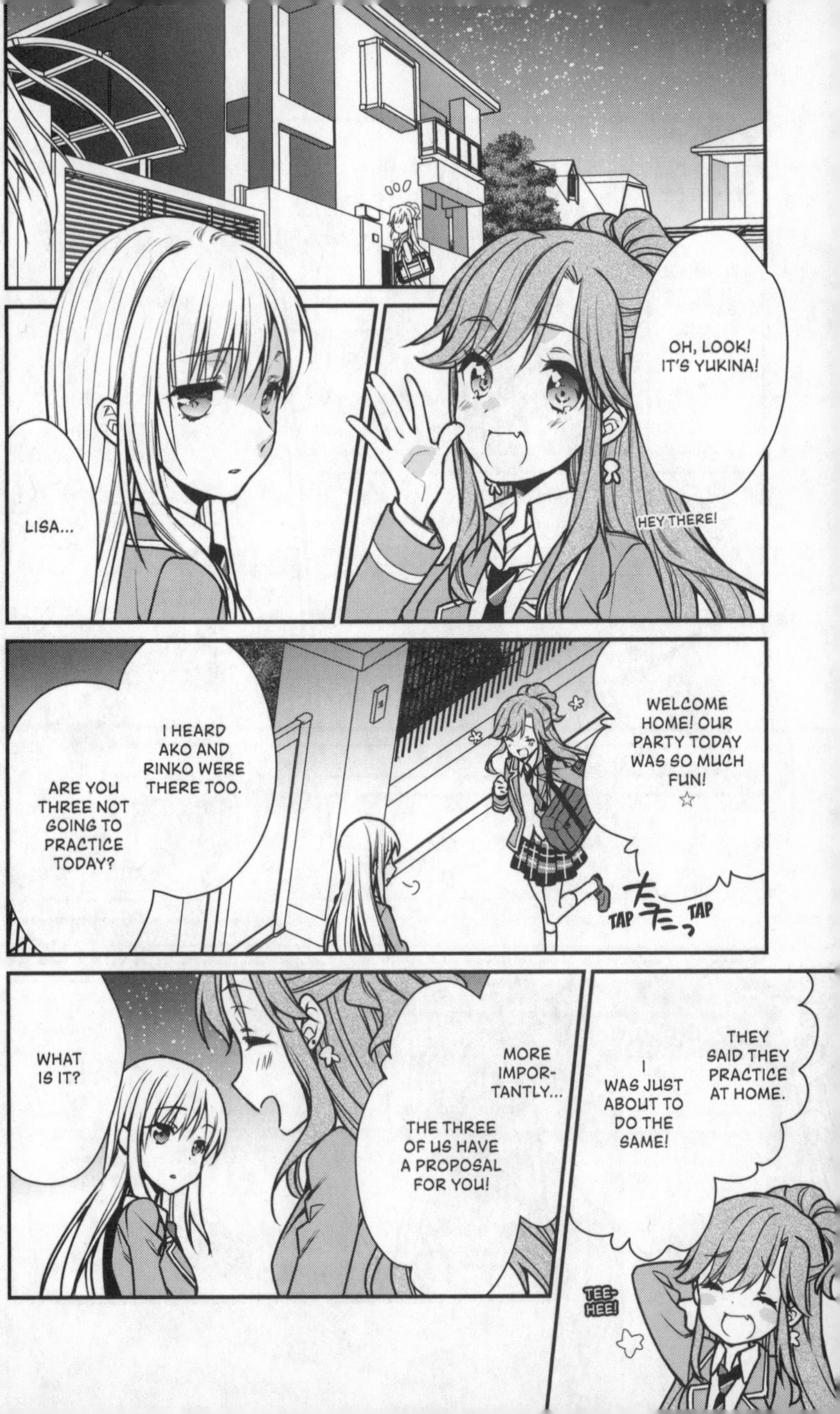
OH, LOOK! IT'S YUKINA!
HEY THERE!
LISA...
WELCOME HOME! OUR PARTY TODAY WAS SO MUCH FUN! ☆
TAP TAP
I HEARD AKO AND RINKO WERE THERE TOO.
ARE YOU THREE NOT GOING TO PRACTICE TODAY?
THEY SAID THEY PRACTICE AT HOME.
I WAS JUST ABOUT TO DO THE SAME!
TEE-HEE!
MORE IMPOR-TANTLY...
THE THREE OF US HAVE A PROPOSAL FOR YOU!
WHAT IS IT?

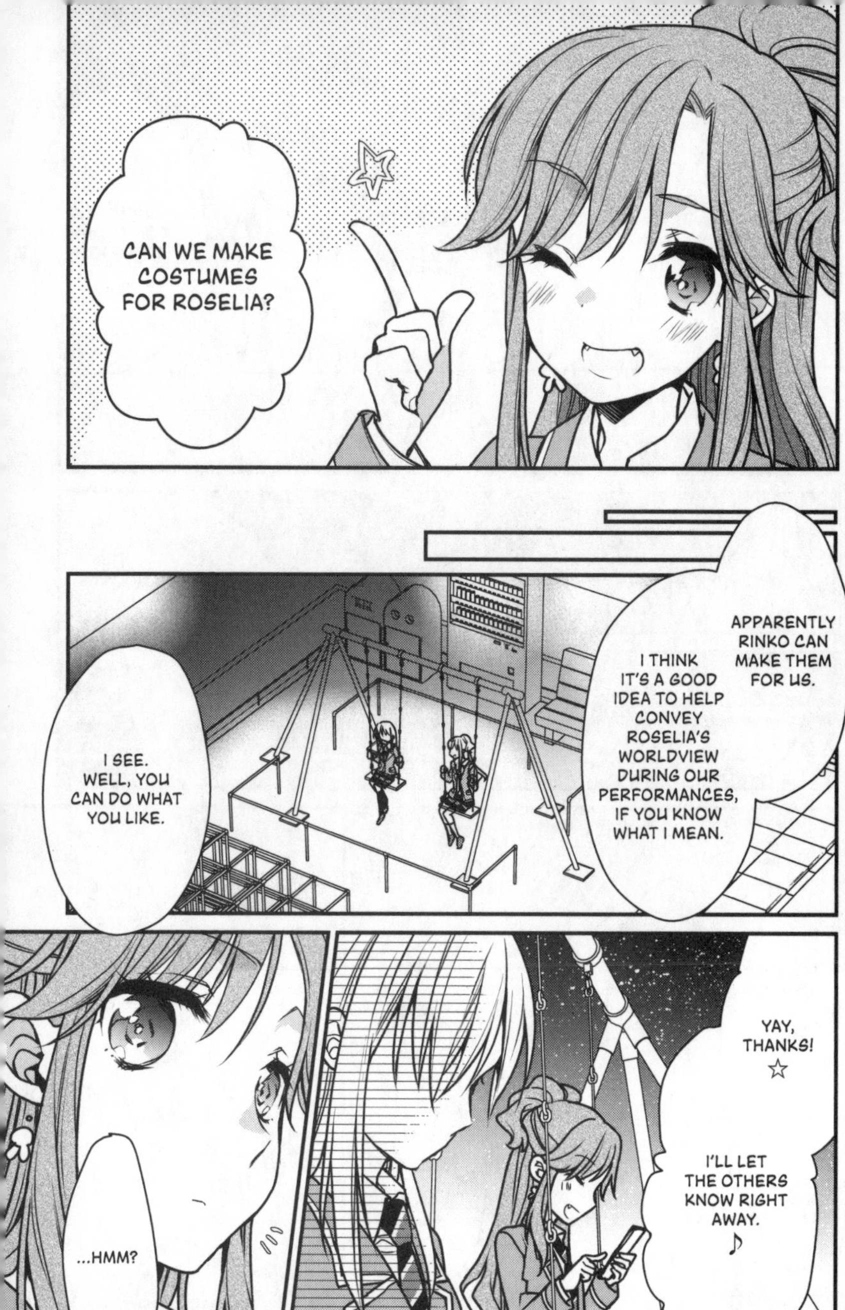
CAN WE MAKE COSTUMES FOR ROSELIA?
APPARENTLY RINKO CAN MAKE THEM FOR US.
I THINK IT'S A GOOD IDEA TO HELP CONVEY ROSELIA'S WORLDVIEW DURING OUR PERFORMANCES, IF YOU KNOW WHAT I MEAN.
I SEE. WELL, YOU CAN DO WHAT YOU LIKE.
YAY, THANKS! ☆
I'LL LET THE OTHERS KNOW RIGHT AWAY. ♪
...HMM?

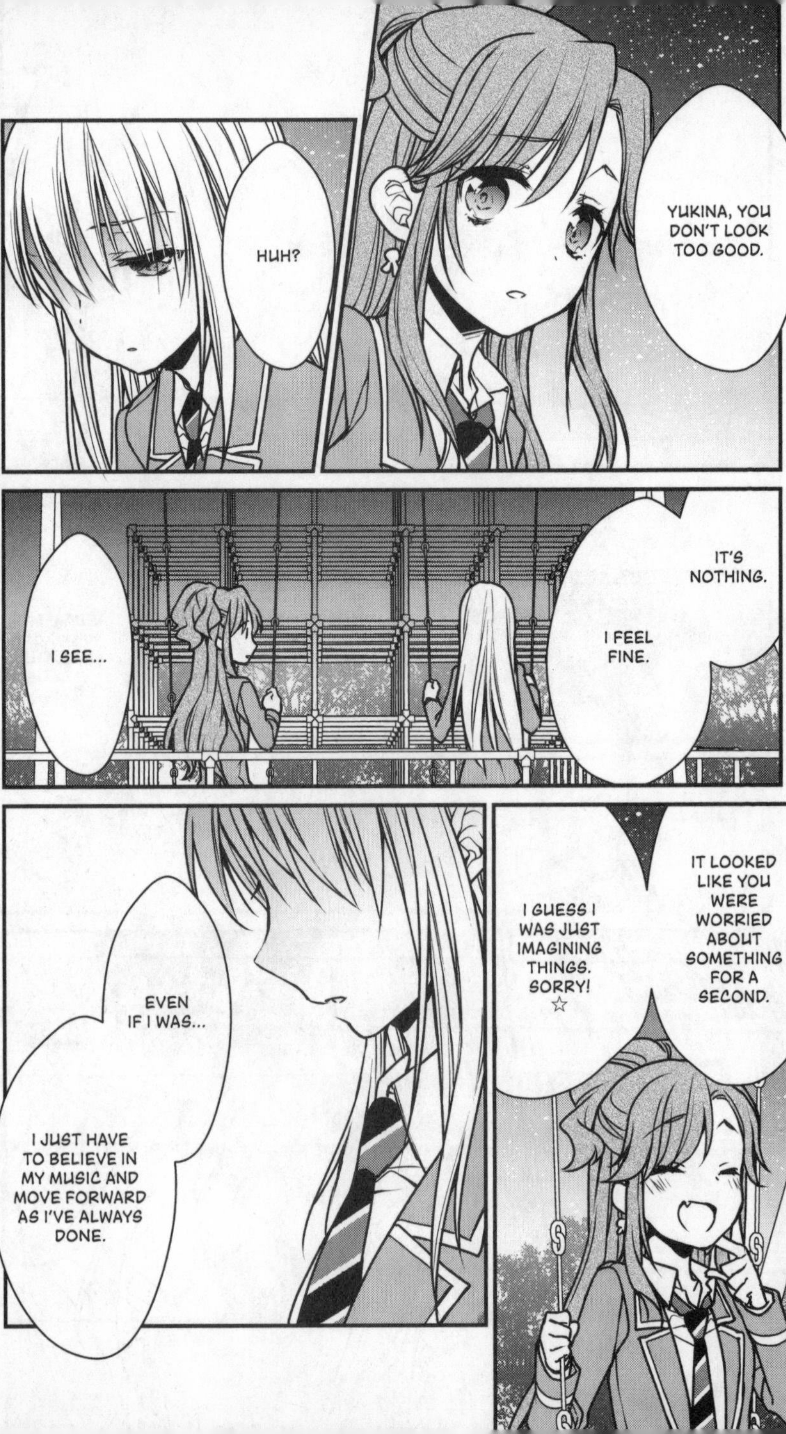
YUKINA, YOU DON'T LOOK TOO GOOD.
HUH?
IT'S NOTHING.
I FEEL FINE.
I SEE...
IT LOOKED LIKE YOU WERE WORRIED ABOUT SOMETHING FOR A SECOND.
I GUESS I WAS JUST IMAGINING THINGS. SORRY! ☆
EVEN IF I WAS...
I JUST HAVE TO BELIEVE IN MY MUSIC AND MOVE FORWARD AS I'VE ALWAYS DONE.

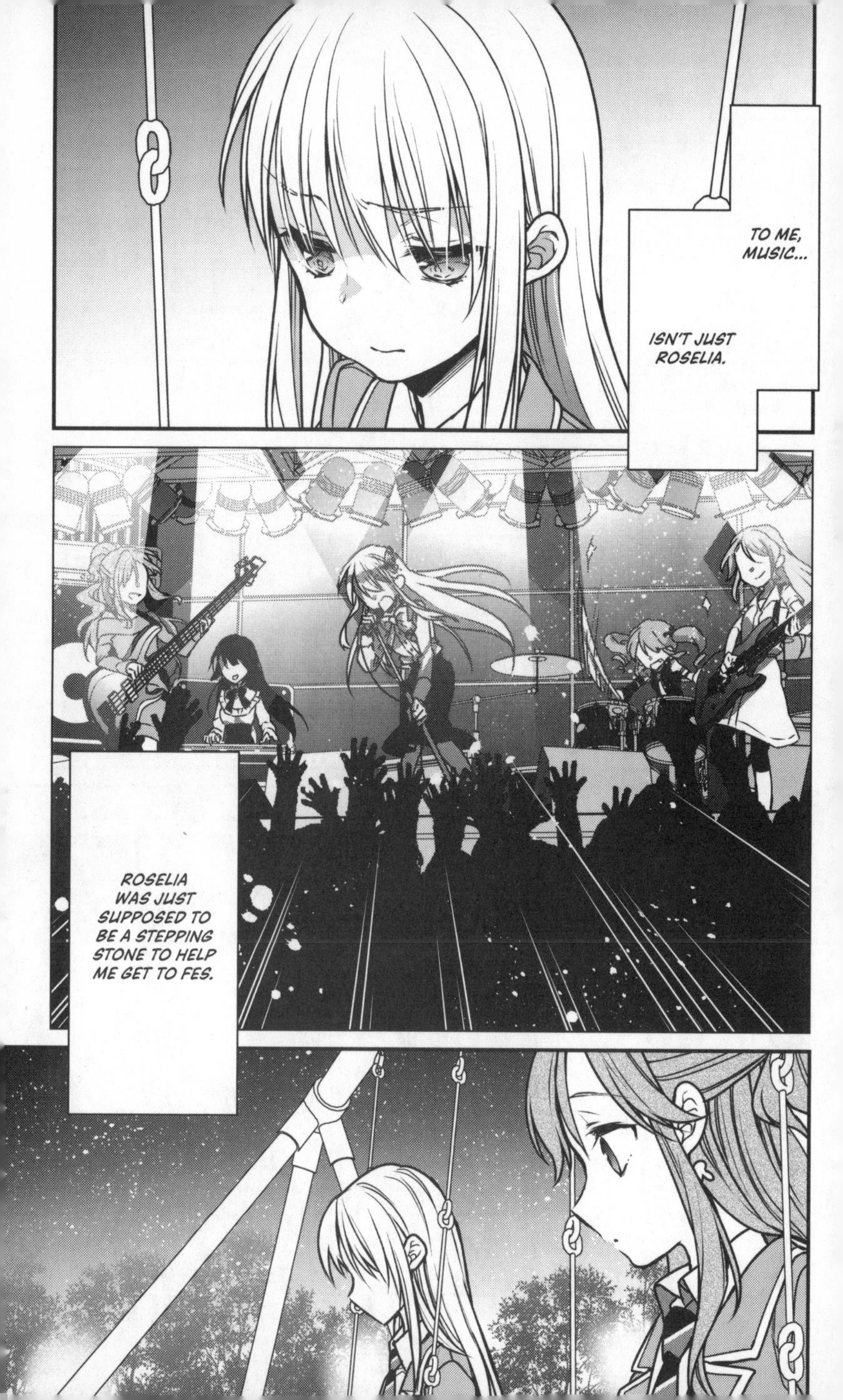
TO ME, MUSIC...
ISN'T JUST ROSELIA.
ROSELIA WAS JUST SUPPOSED TO BE A STEPPING STONE TO HELP ME GET TO FES.

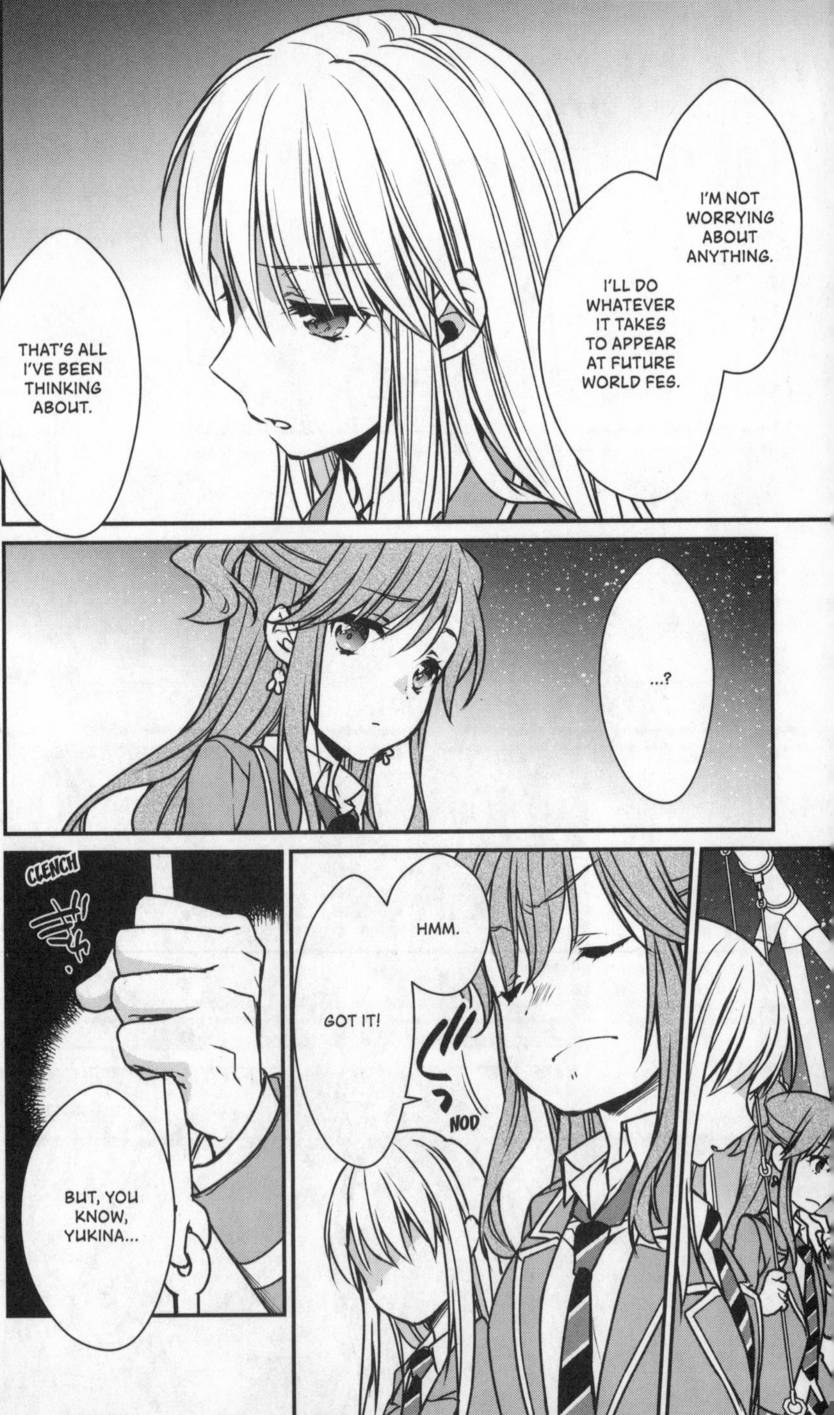
I'M NOT WORRYING ABOUT ANYTHING.
I'LL DO WHATEVER IT TAKES TO APPEAR AT FUTURE WORLD FES.
THAT'S ALL I'VE BEEN THINKING ABOUT.
...?
HMM.
GOT IT!
NOD
CLENCH
BUT, YOU KNOW, YUKINA...

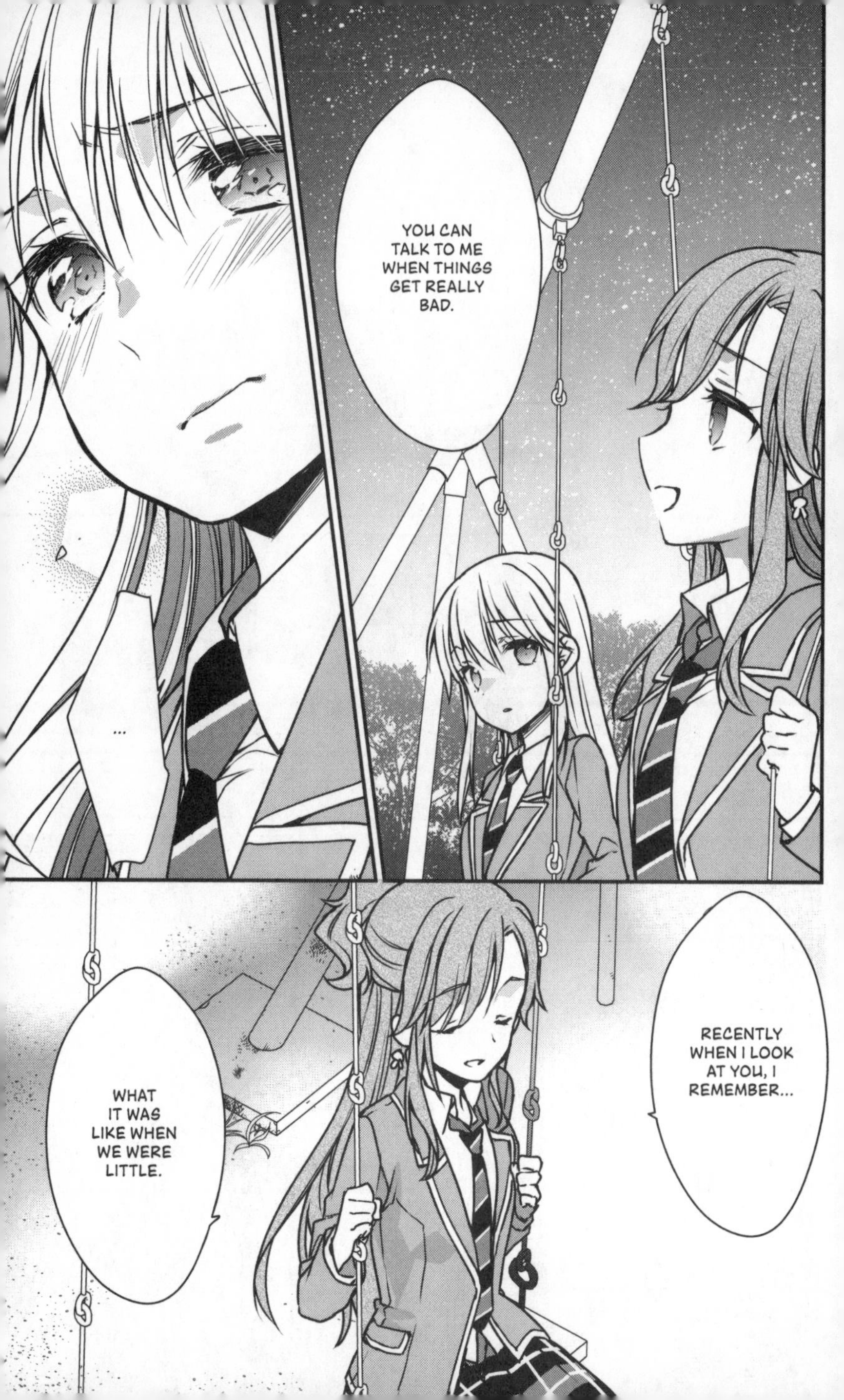
YOU CAN TALK TO ME WHEN THINGS GET REALLY BAD.
...
RECENTLY WHEN I LOOK AT YOU, I REMEMBER...
WHAT IT WAS LIKE WHEN WE WERE LITTLE.

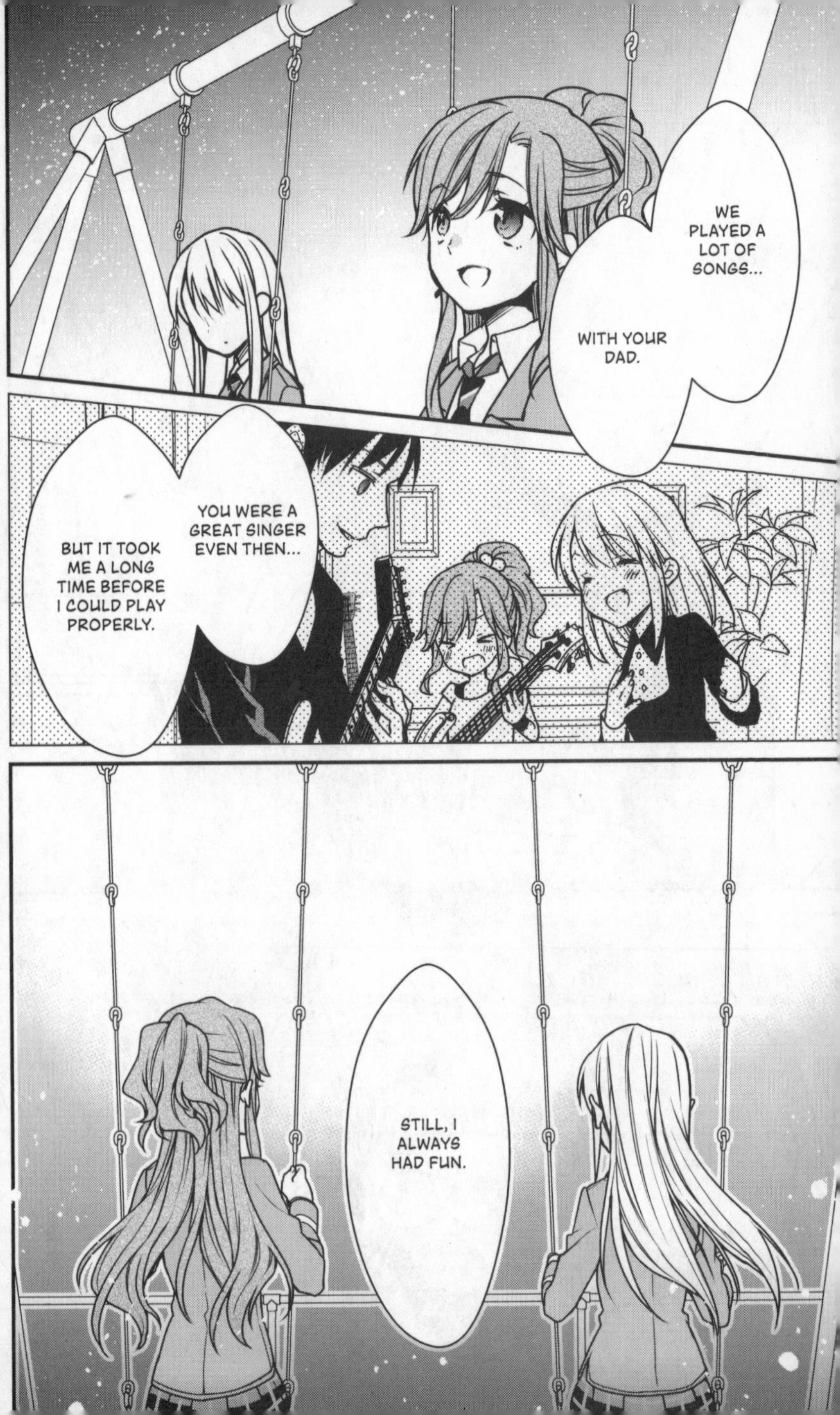
WE PLAYED A LOT OF SONGS...
WITH YOUR DAD.
YOU WERE A GREAT SINGER EVEN THEN...
BUT IT TOOK ME A LONG TIME BEFORE I COULD PLAY PROPERLY.
STILL, I ALWAYS HAD FUN.

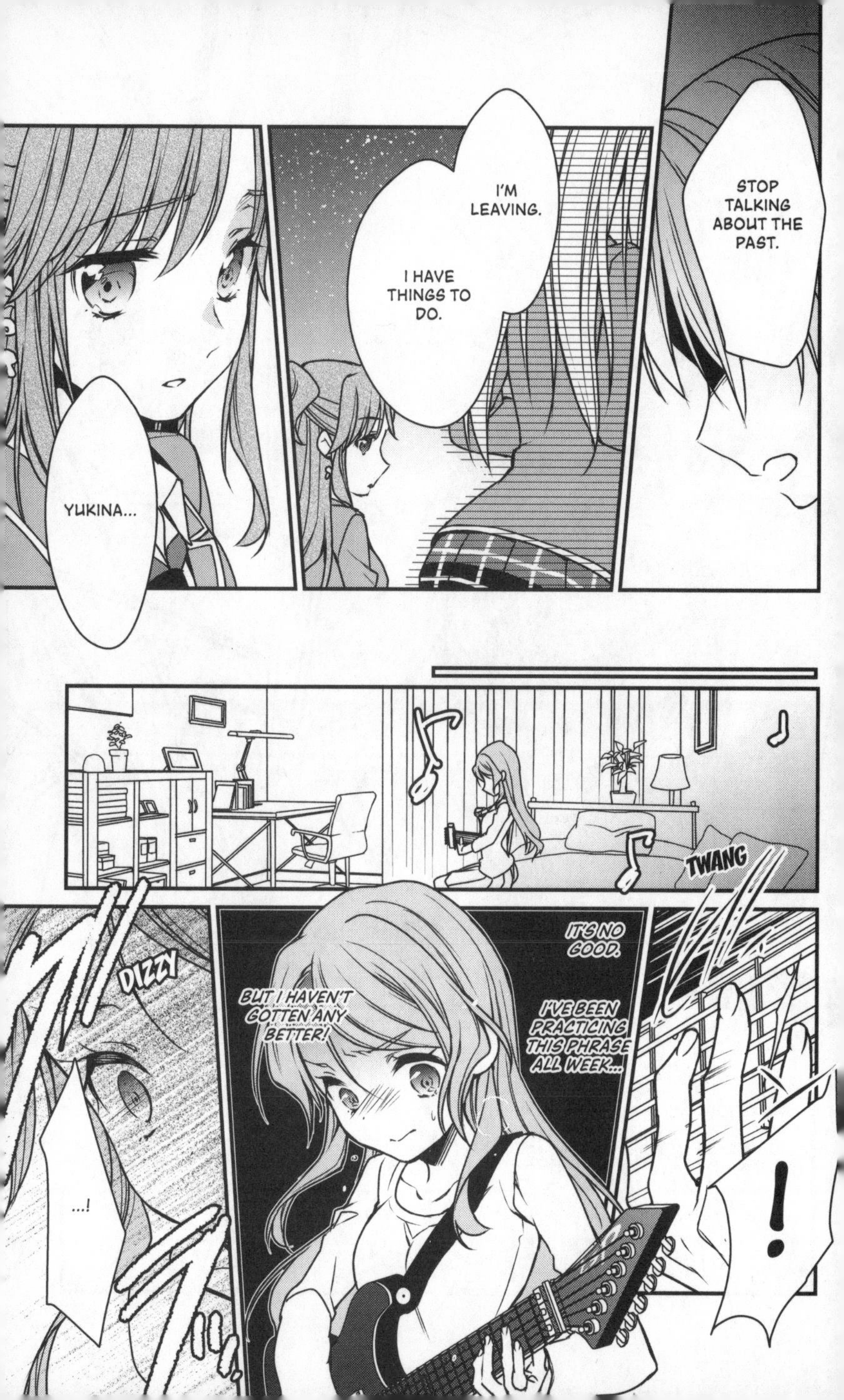
STOP TALKING ABOUT THE PAST.
I'M LEAVING.
I HAVE THINGS TO DO.
YUKINA...
TWANG
!
IT'S NO GOOD.
I'VE BEEN PRACTICING THIS PHRASE ALL WEEK...
BUT I HAVEN'T GOTTEN ANY BETTER!
DIZZY
...!

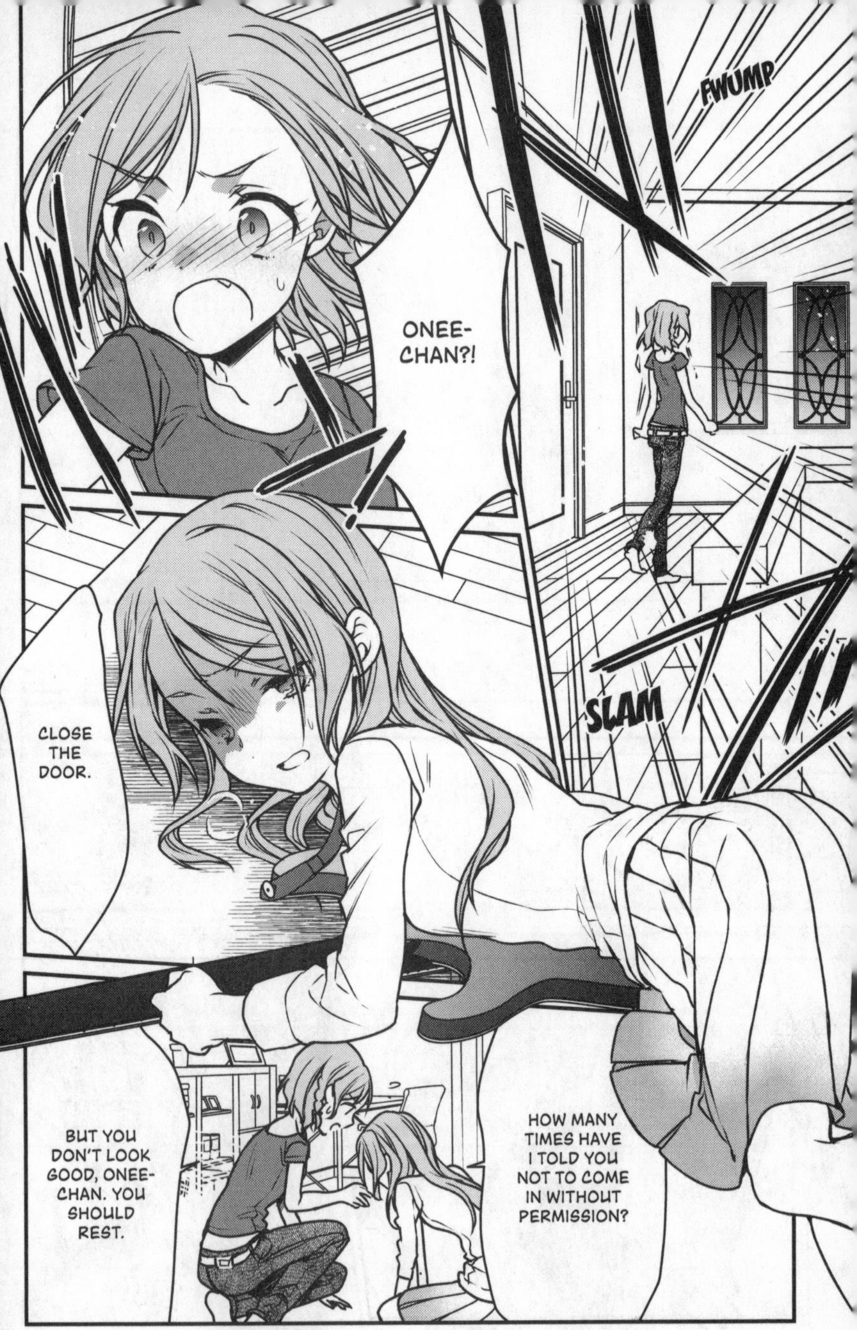
FWUMP
ONEE-CHAN?!
SLAM
CLOSE THE DOOR.
HOW MANY TIMES HAVE I TOLD YOU NOT TO COME IN WITHOUT PERMISSION?
BUT YOU DON'T LOOK GOOD, ONEE-CHAN. YOU SHOULD REST.

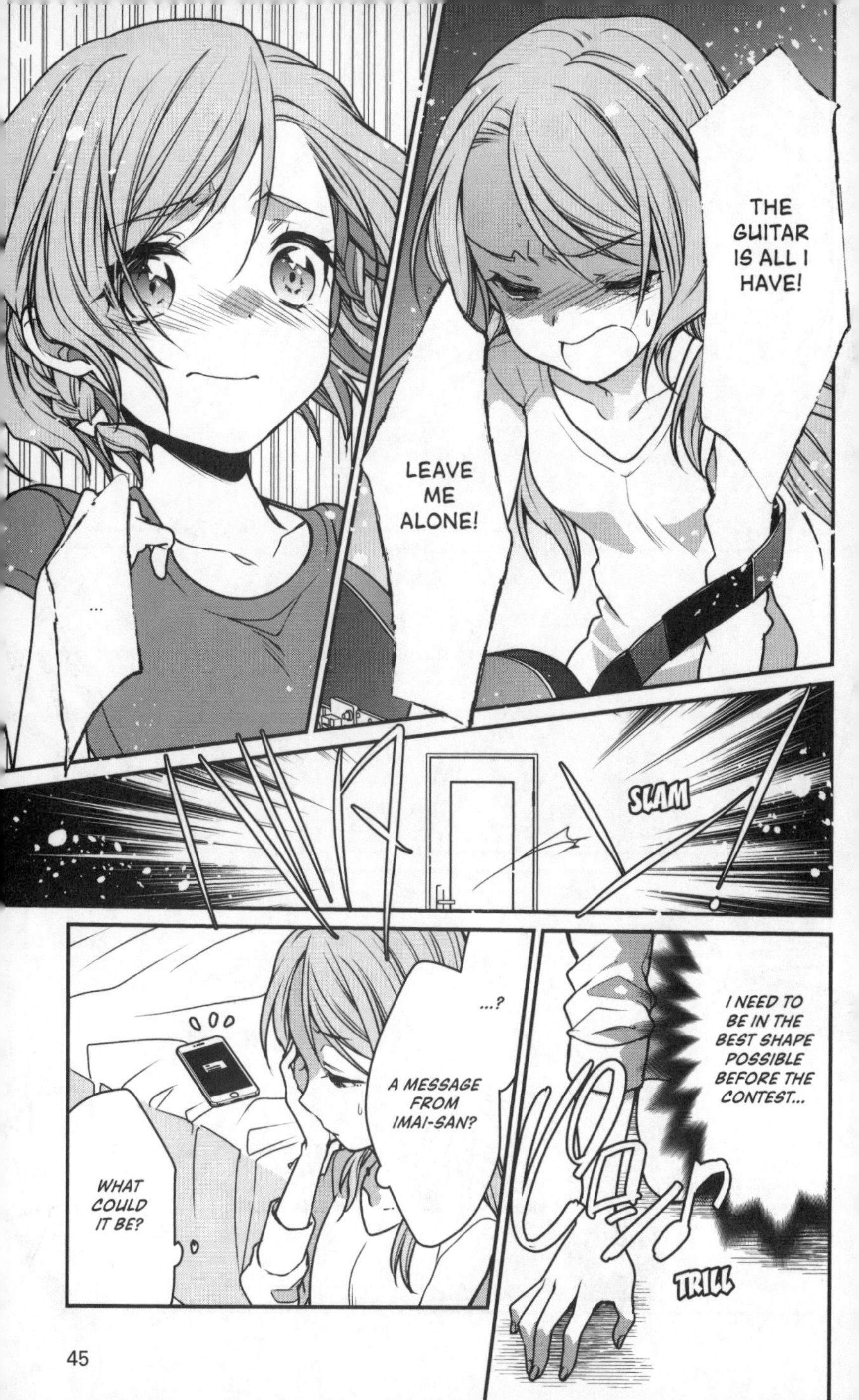
THE GUITAR IS ALL I HAVE!
LEAVE ME ALONE!
...
SLAM
I NEED TO BE IN THE BEST SHAPE POSSIBLE BEFORE THE CONTEST...
TRILL
...?
A MESSAGE FROM IMAI-SAN?
WHAT COULD IT BE?

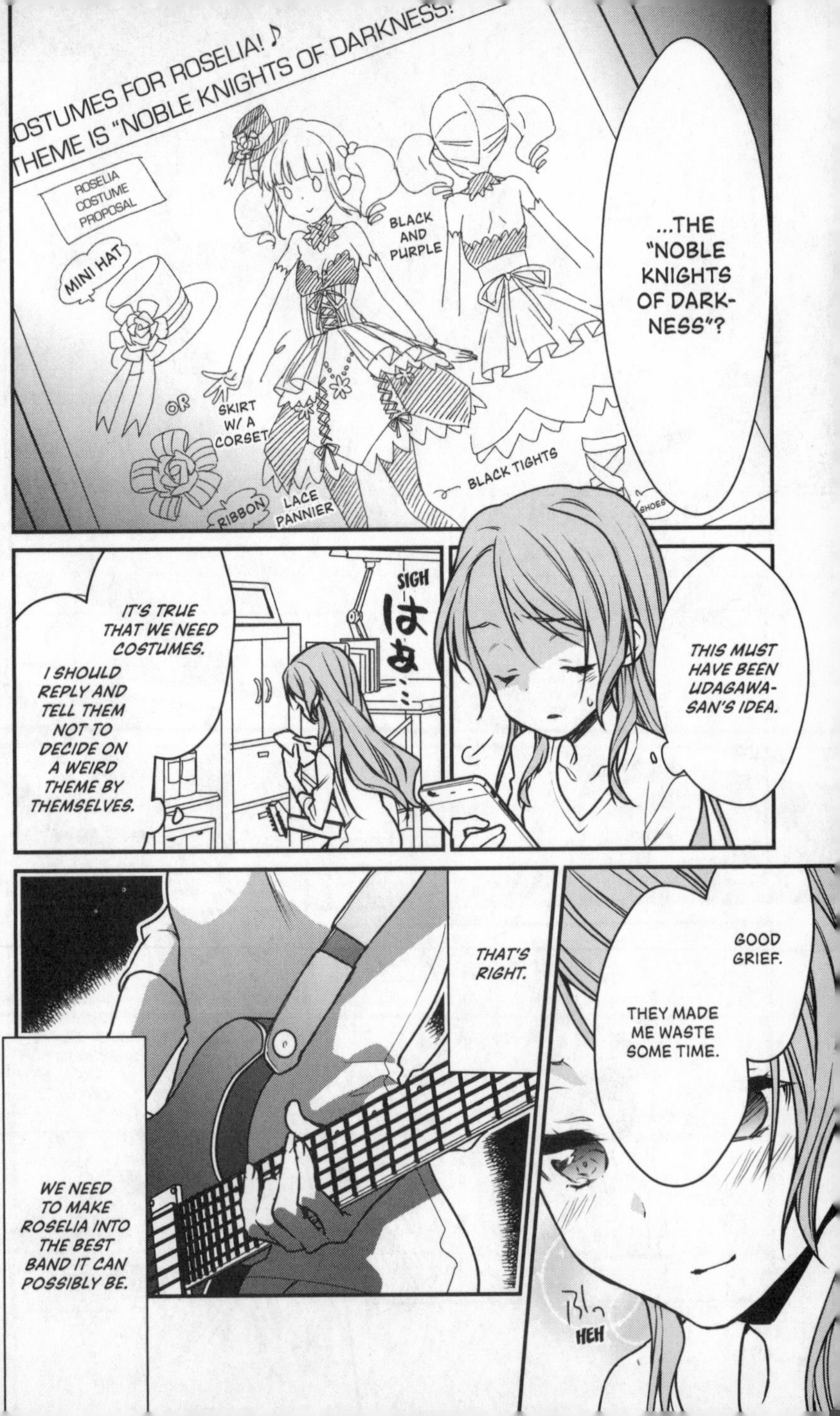
COSTUMES FOR ROSELIA! ♪
THEME IS "NOBLE KNIGHTS OF DARKNESS!
ROSELIA COSTUME PROPOSAL
MINI HAT
BLACK AND PURPLE
OR
SKIRT W/ A CORSET
BLACK TIGHTS
RIBBON
LACE PANNIER
SHOES
...THE "NOBLE KNIGHTS OF DARK-NESS"?
THIS MUST HAVE BEEN UDAGAWA-SAN'S IDEA.
SIGH
はぁ…
IT'S TRUE THAT WE NEED COSTUMES.
I SHOULD REPLY AND TELL THEM NOT TO DECIDE ON A WEIRD THEME BY THEMSELVES.
GOOD GRIEF.
THEY MADE ME WASTE SOME TIME.
ふっ
HEH
THAT'S RIGHT.
WE NEED TO MAKE ROSELIA INTO THE BEST BAND IT CAN POSSIBLY BE.

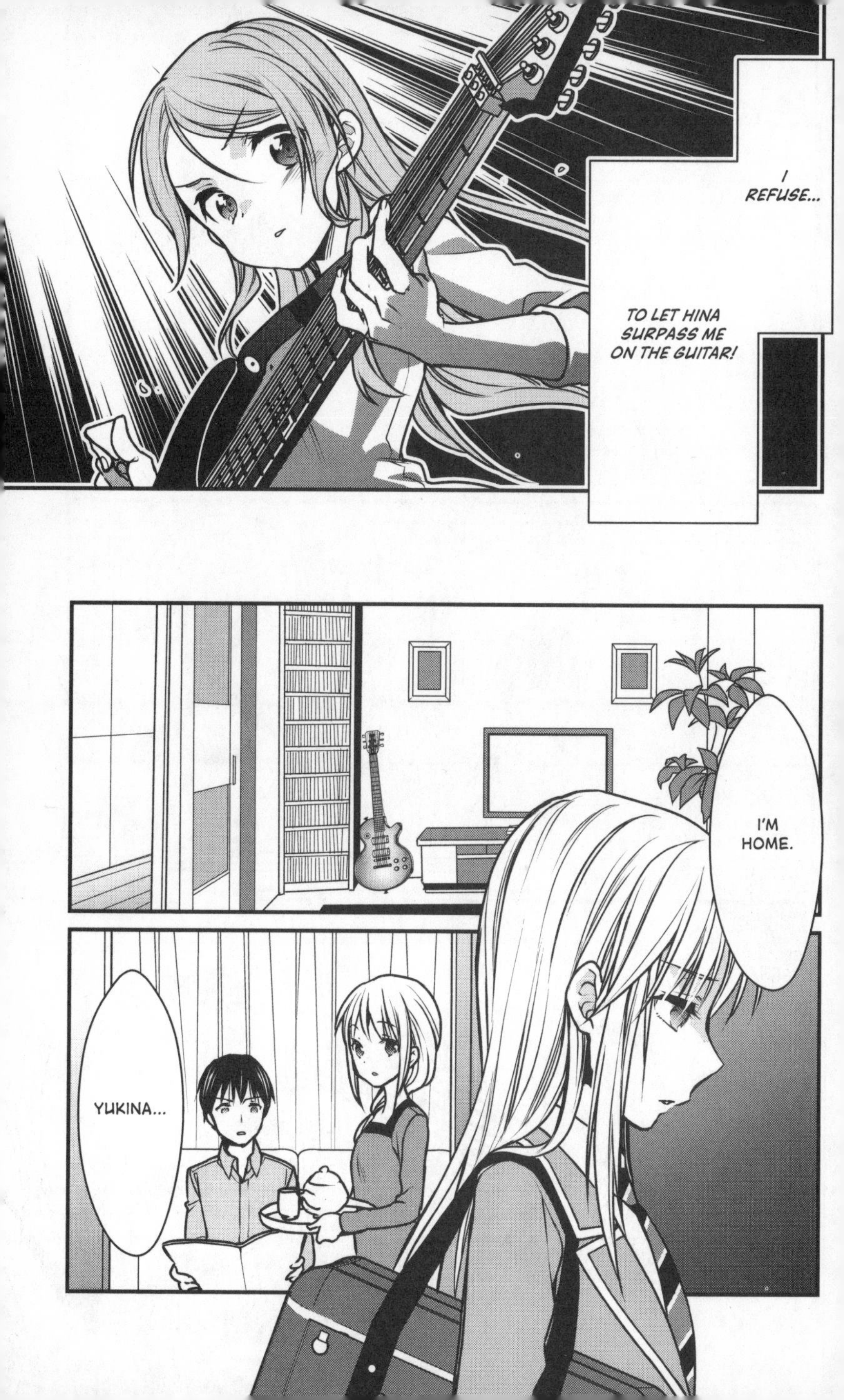
I REFUSE...
TO LET HINA SURPASS ME ON THE GUITAR!
I'M HOME.
YUKINA...

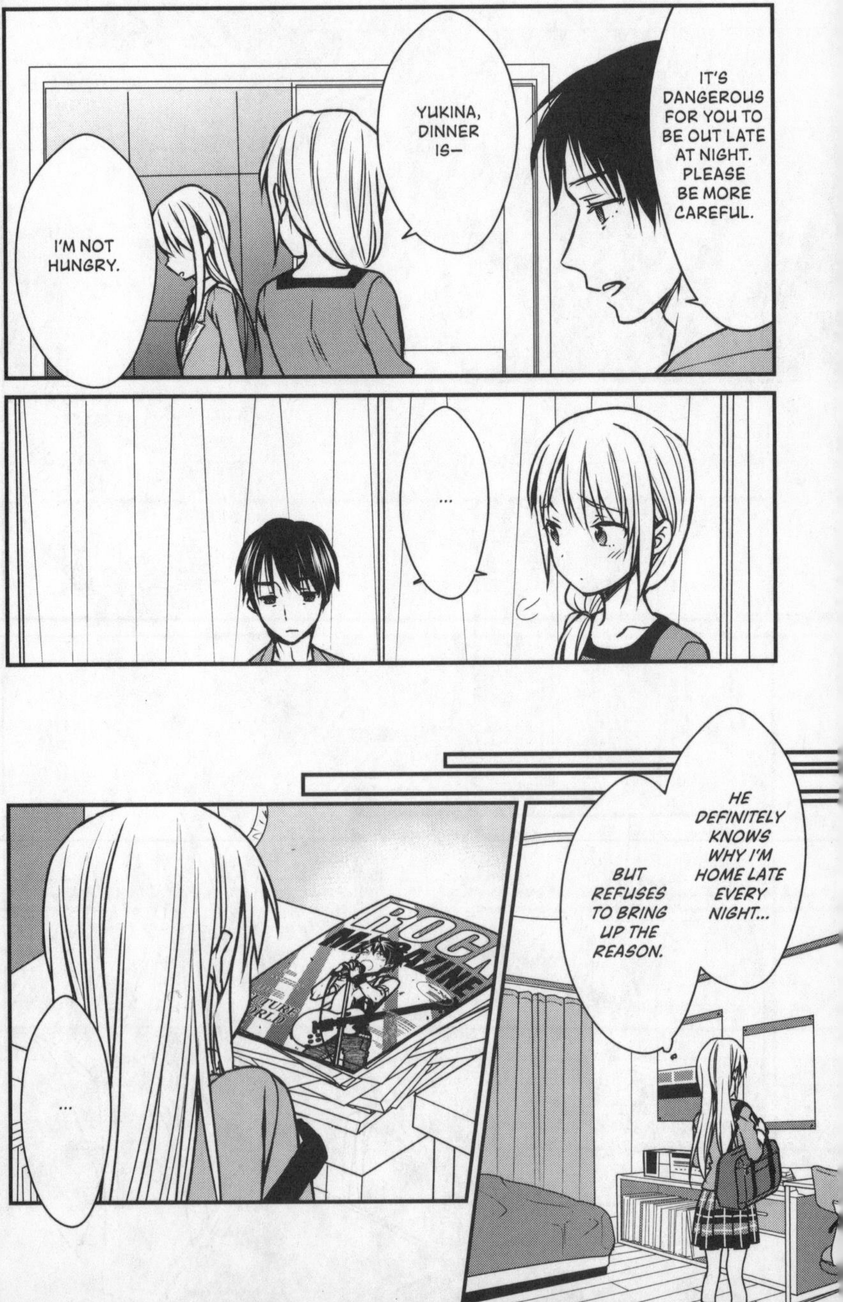
IT'S DANGEROUS FOR YOU TO BE OUT LATE AT NIGHT. PLEASE BE MORE CAREFUL.
YUKINA, DINNER IS—
I'M NOT HUNGRY.
...
HE DEFINITELY KNOWS WHY I'M HOME LATE EVERY NIGHT...
BUT REFUSES TO BRING UP THE REASON.
ROCK MAGAZINE
...

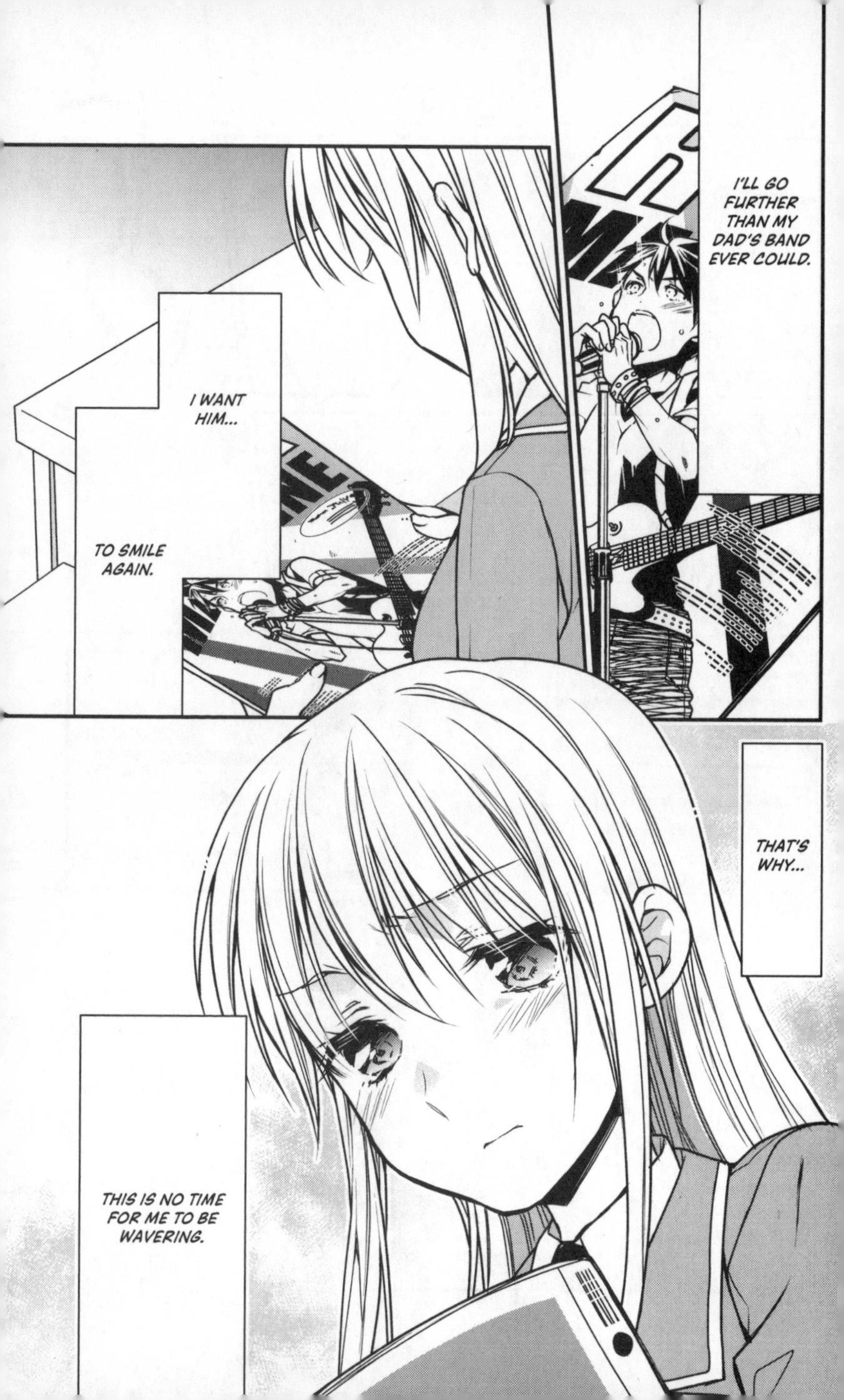
I'LL GO FURTHER THAN MY DAD'S BAND EVER COULD.
I WANT HIM...
TO SMILE AGAIN.
THAT'S WHY...
THIS IS NO TIME FOR ME TO BE WAVERING.

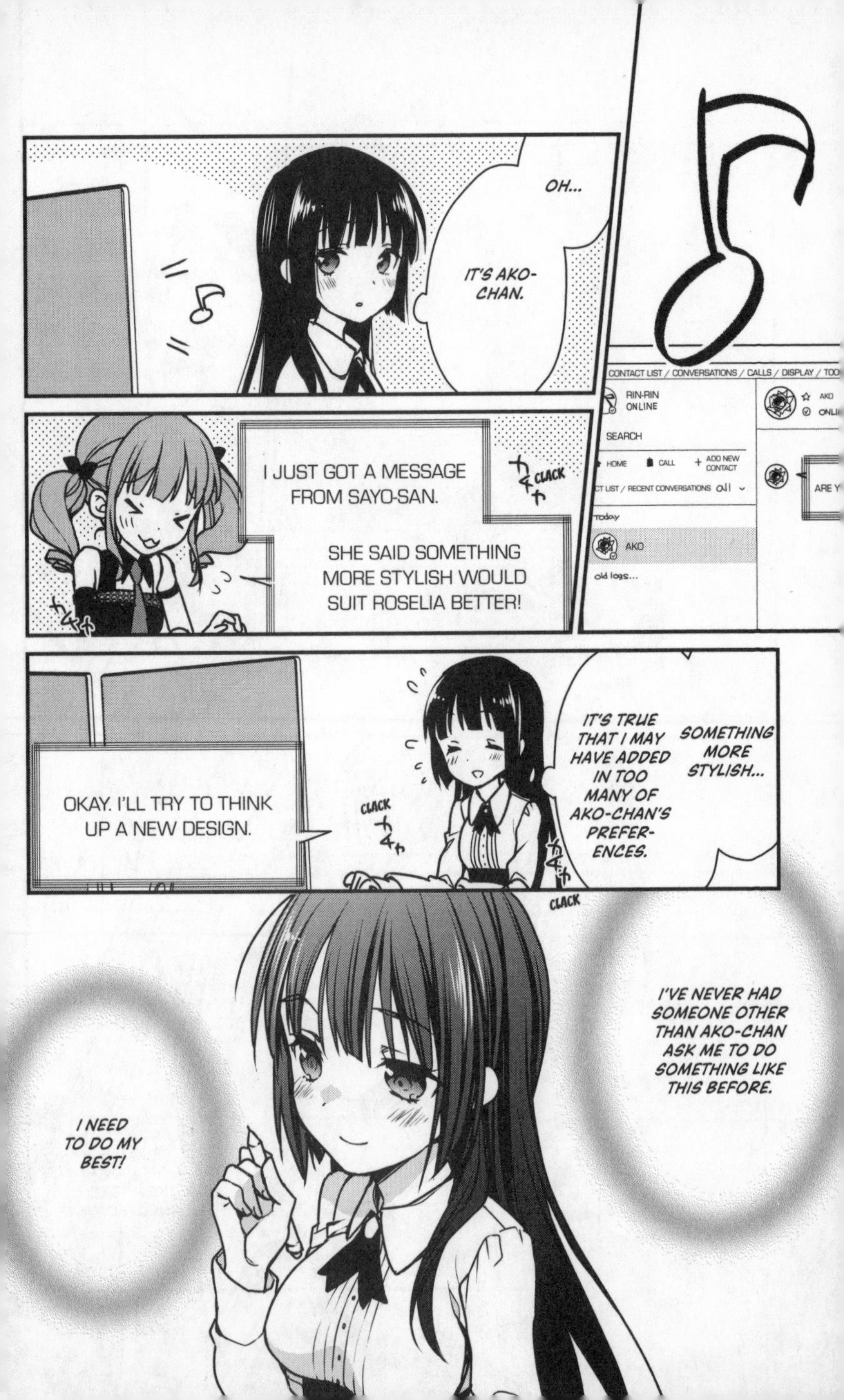
CONTACT LIST / CONVERSATIONS / CALLS / DISPLAY
RIN-RIN ONLINE
SEARCH
HOME
CALL
ADD NEW CONTACT
RECENT CONVERSATIONS all
Today
AKO
old logs...
AKO
OH...
IT'S AKO-CHAN.
CLACK
I JUST GOT A MESSAGE FROM SAYO-SAN.
SHE SAID SOMETHING MORE STYLISH WOULD SUIT ROSELIA BETTER!
SOMETHING MORE STYLISH...
IT'S TRUE THAT I MAY HAVE ADDED IN TOO MANY OF AKO-CHAN'S PREFER-ENCES.
CLACK
OKAY. I'LL TRY TO THINK UP A NEW DESIGN.
CLACK
I'VE NEVER HAD SOMEONE OTHER THAN AKO-CHAN ASK ME TO DO SOMETHING LIKE THIS BEFORE.
I NEED TO DO MY BEST!

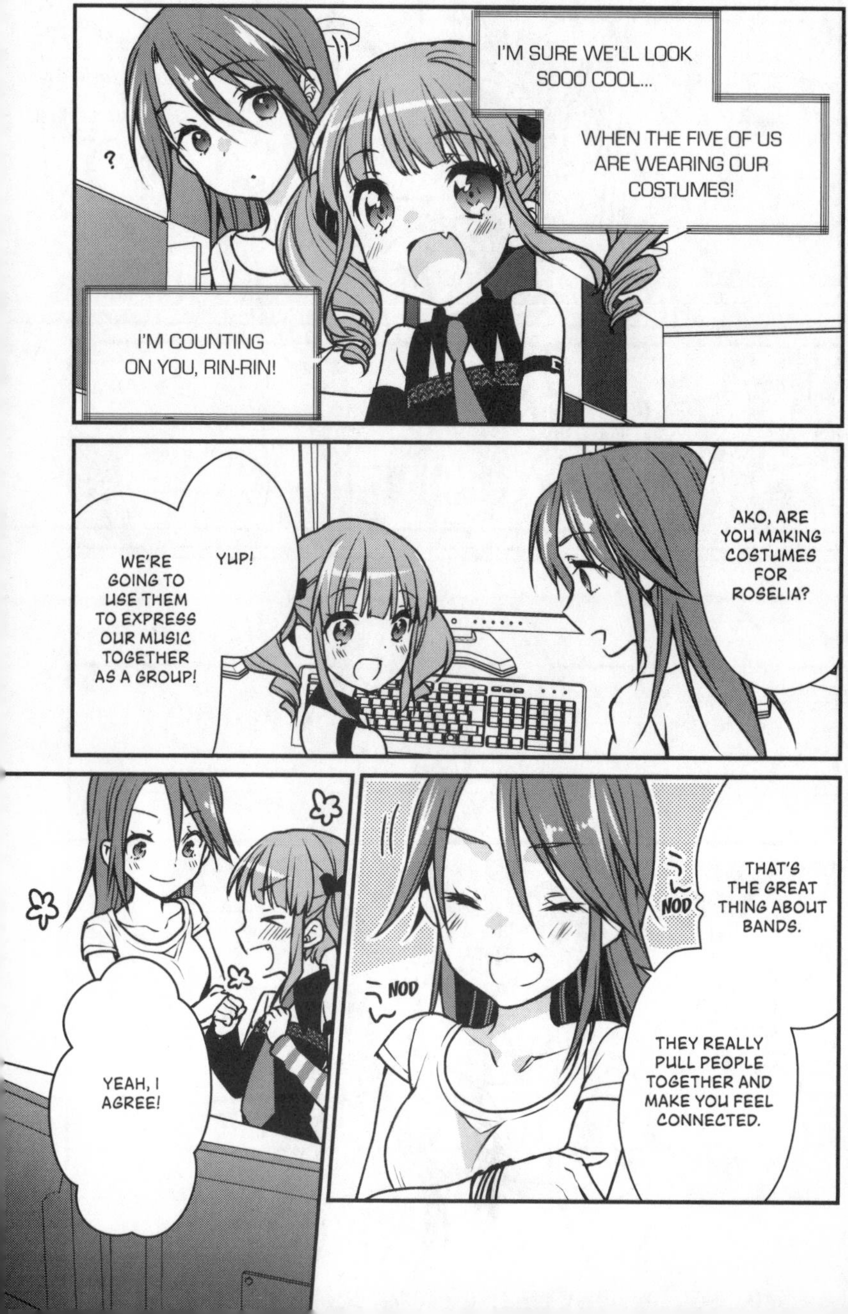
I'M SURE WE'LL LOOK SOOO COOL...
WHEN THE FIVE OF US ARE WEARING OUR COSTUMES!
?
I'M COUNTING ON YOU, RIN-RIN!
AKO, ARE YOU MAKING COSTUMES FOR ROSELIA?
YUP!
WE'RE GOING TO USE THEM TO EXPRESS OUR MUSIC TOGETHER AS A GROUP!
NOD
THAT'S THE GREAT THING ABOUT BANDS.
NOD
THEY REALLY PULL PEOPLE TOGETHER AND MAKE YOU FEEL CONNECTED.
YEAH, I AGREE!

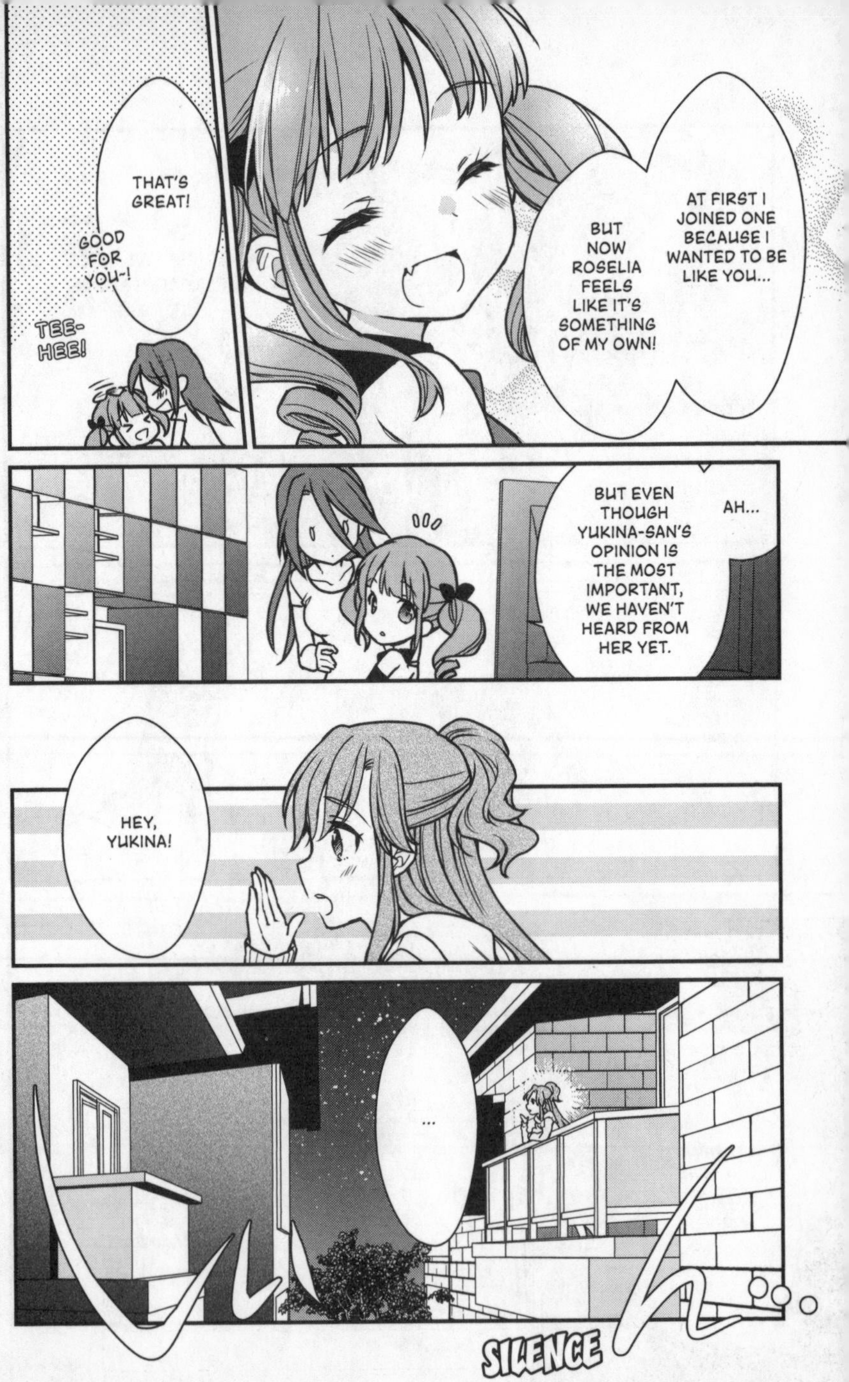
AT FIRST I JOINED ONE BECAUSE I WANTED TO BE LIKE YOU...
BUT NOW ROSELIA FEELS LIKE IT'S SOMETHING OF MY OWN!
THAT'S GREAT!
GOOD FOR YOU-!
TEE-HEE!
AH...
BUT EVEN THOUGH YUKINA-SAN'S OPINION IS THE MOST IMPORTANT, WE HAVEN'T HEARD FROM HER YET.
HEY, YUKINA!
...
SILENCE

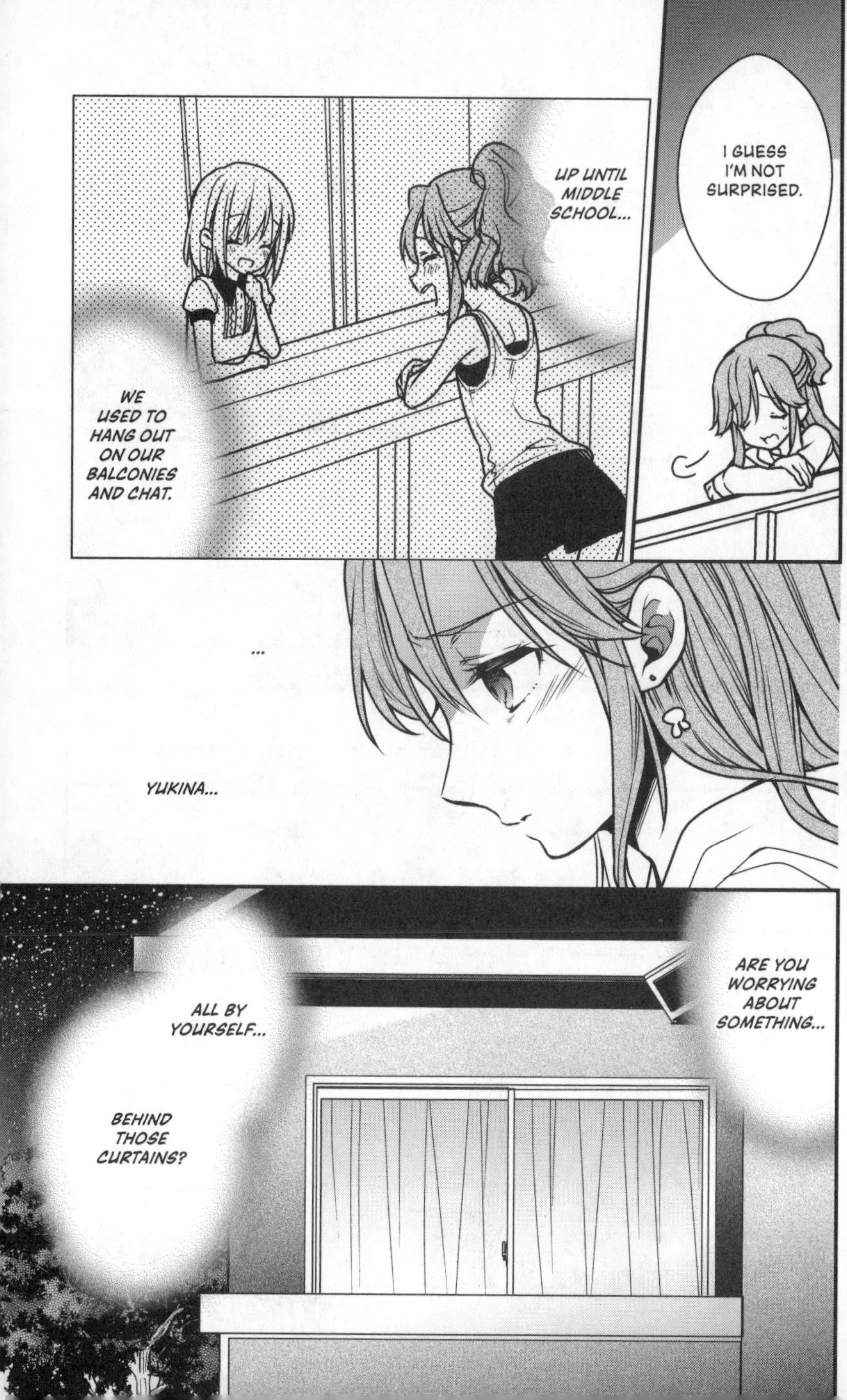
I GUESS I'M NOT SURPRISED.
UP UNTIL MIDDLE SCHOOL...
WE USED TO HANG OUT ON OUR BALCONIES AND CHAT.
...
YUKINA...
ARE YOU WORRYING ABOUT SOMETHING...
ALL BY YOURSELF...
BEHIND THOSE CURTAINS?

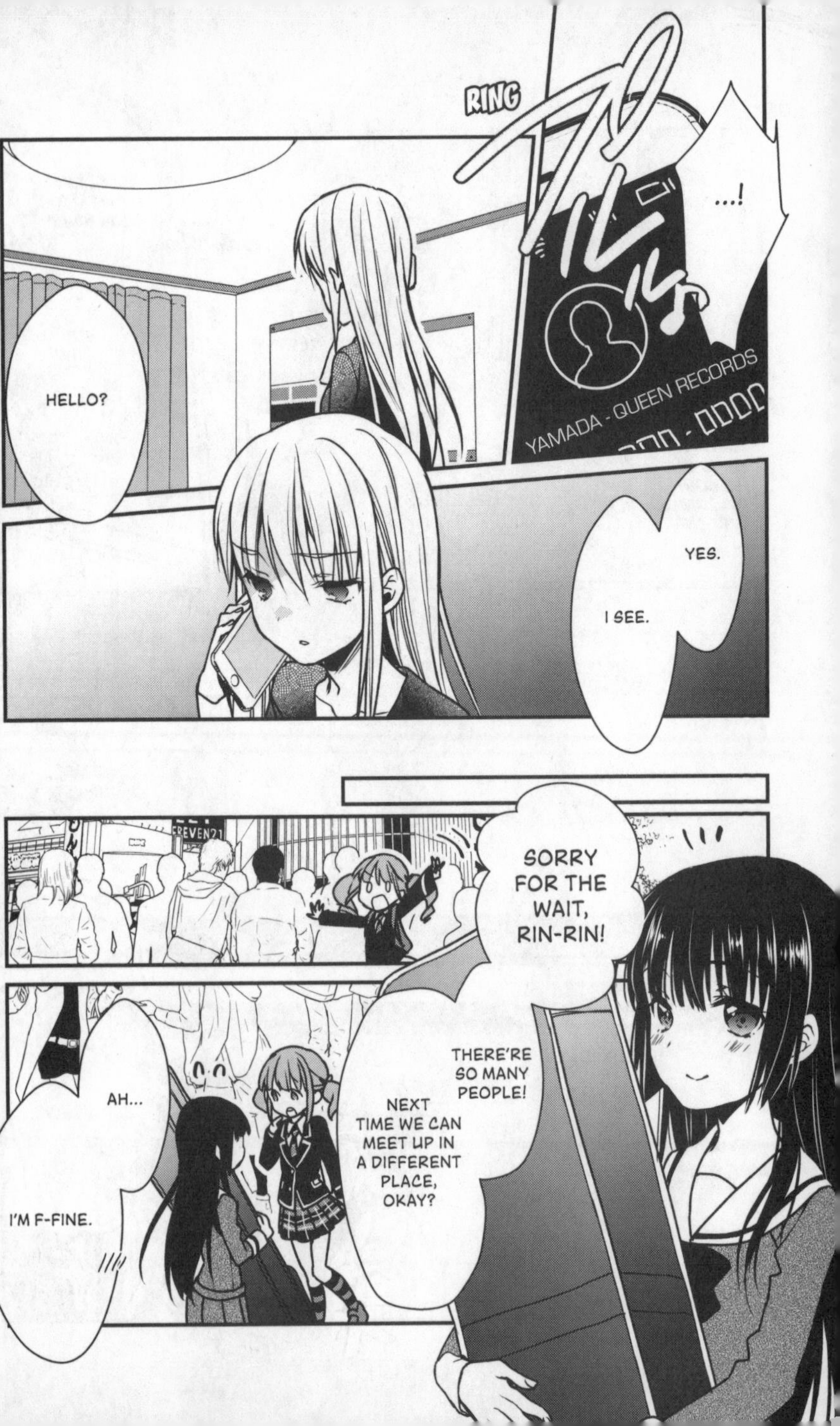
RING
...!
YAMADA - QUEEN RECORDS
HELLO?
YES.
I SEE.
SORRY FOR THE WAIT, RIN-RIN!
CREVEN21
THERE'RE SO MANY PEOPLE!
NEXT TIME WE CAN MEET UP IN A DIFFERENT PLACE, OKAY?
AH...
I'M F-FINE.

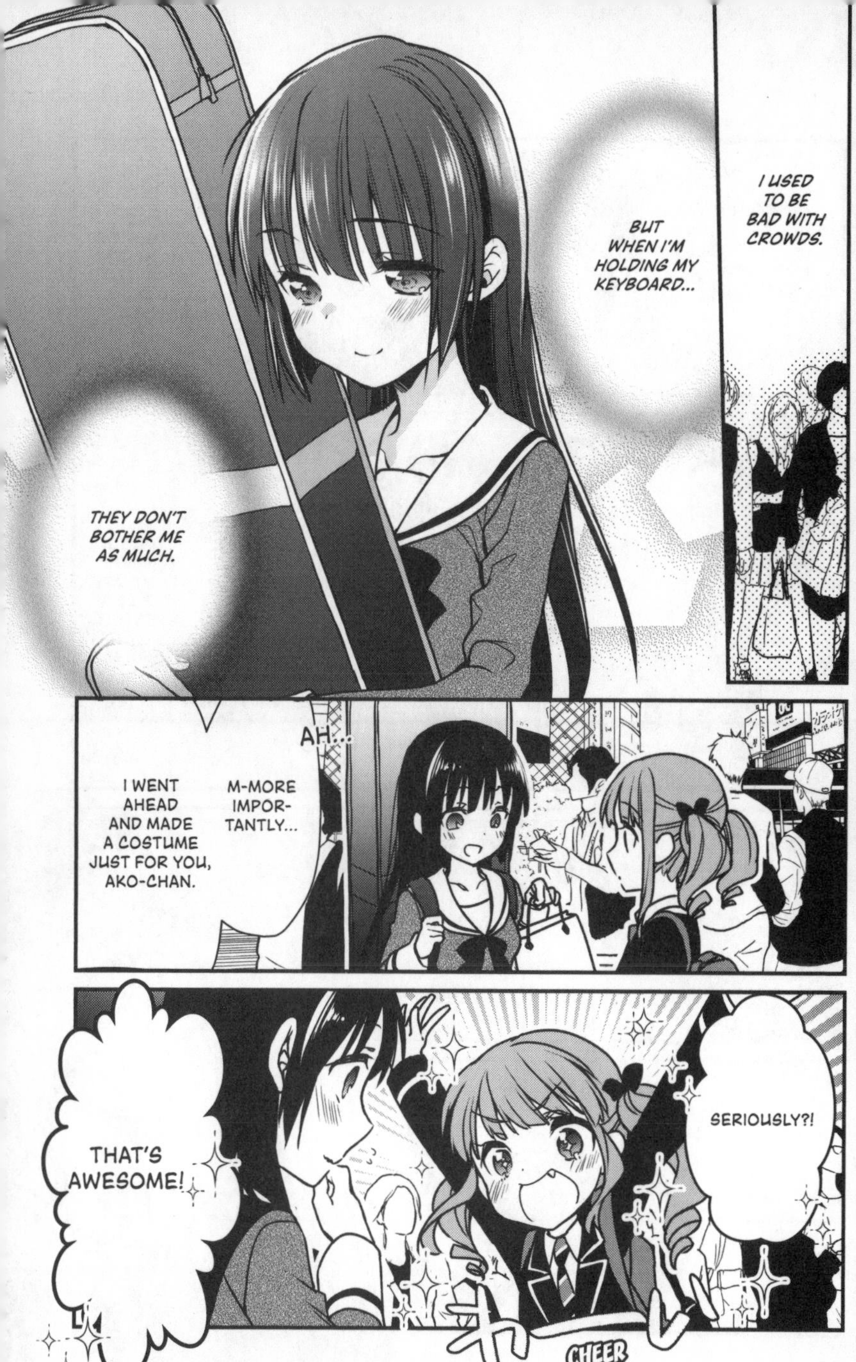
I USED TO BE BAD WITH CROWDS.
BUT WHEN I'M HOLDING MY KEYBOARD...
THEY DON'T BOTHER ME AS MUCH.
AH...
M-MORE IMPORTANTLY...
I WENT AHEAD AND MADE A COSTUME JUST FOR YOU, AKO-CHAN.
SERIOUSLY?!
THAT'S AWESOME!
CHEER

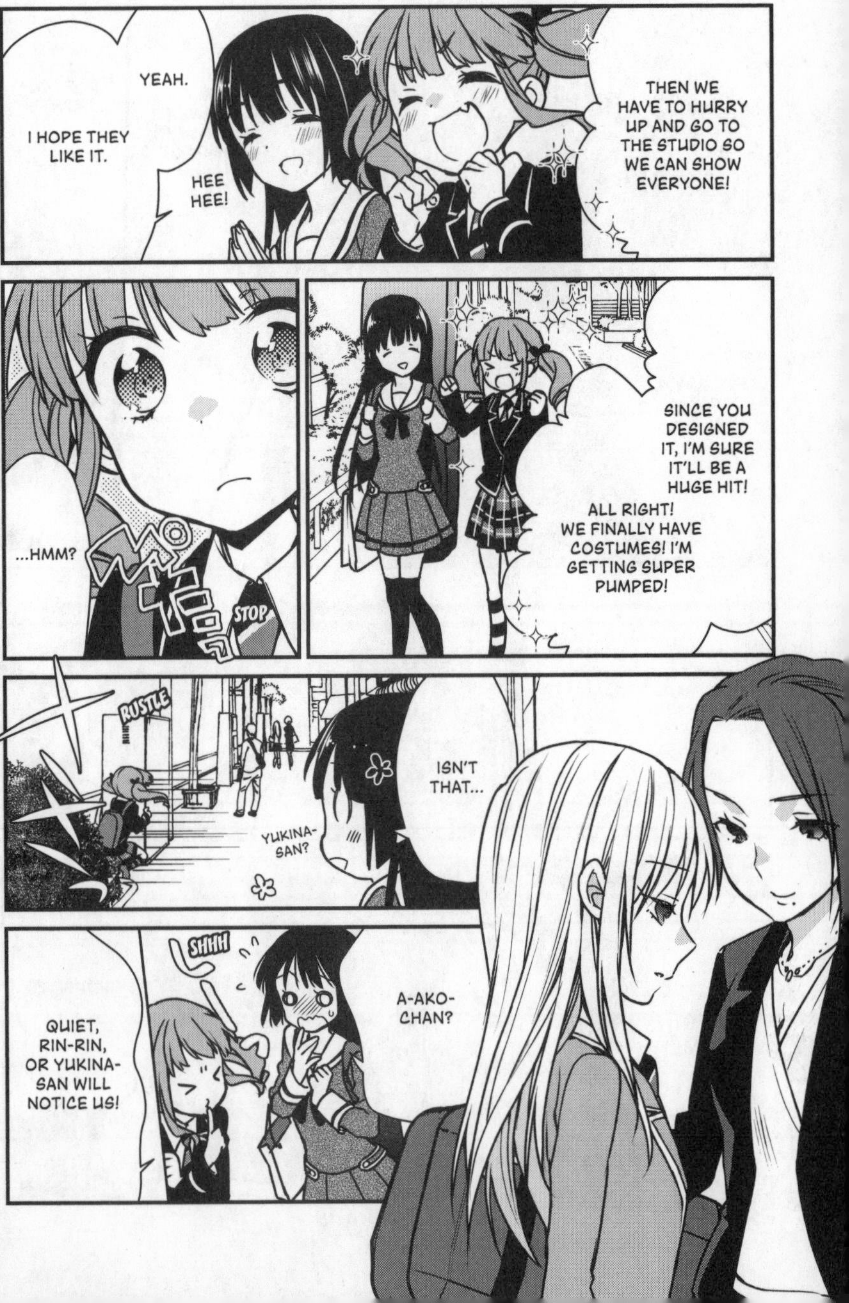
THEN WE HAVE TO HURRY UP AND GO TO THE STUDIO SO WE CAN SHOW EVERYONE!
HEE HEE!
YEAH.
I HOPE THEY LIKE IT.
SINCE YOU DESIGNED IT, I'M SURE IT'LL BE A HUGE HIT!
ALL RIGHT! WE FINALLY HAVE COSTUMES! I'M GETTING SUPER PUMPED!
STOP
...HMM?
ISN'T THAT...
YUKINA-SAN?
RUSTLE
A-AKO-CHAN?
SHHH
QUIET, RIN-RIN, OR YUKINA-SAN WILL NOTICE US!

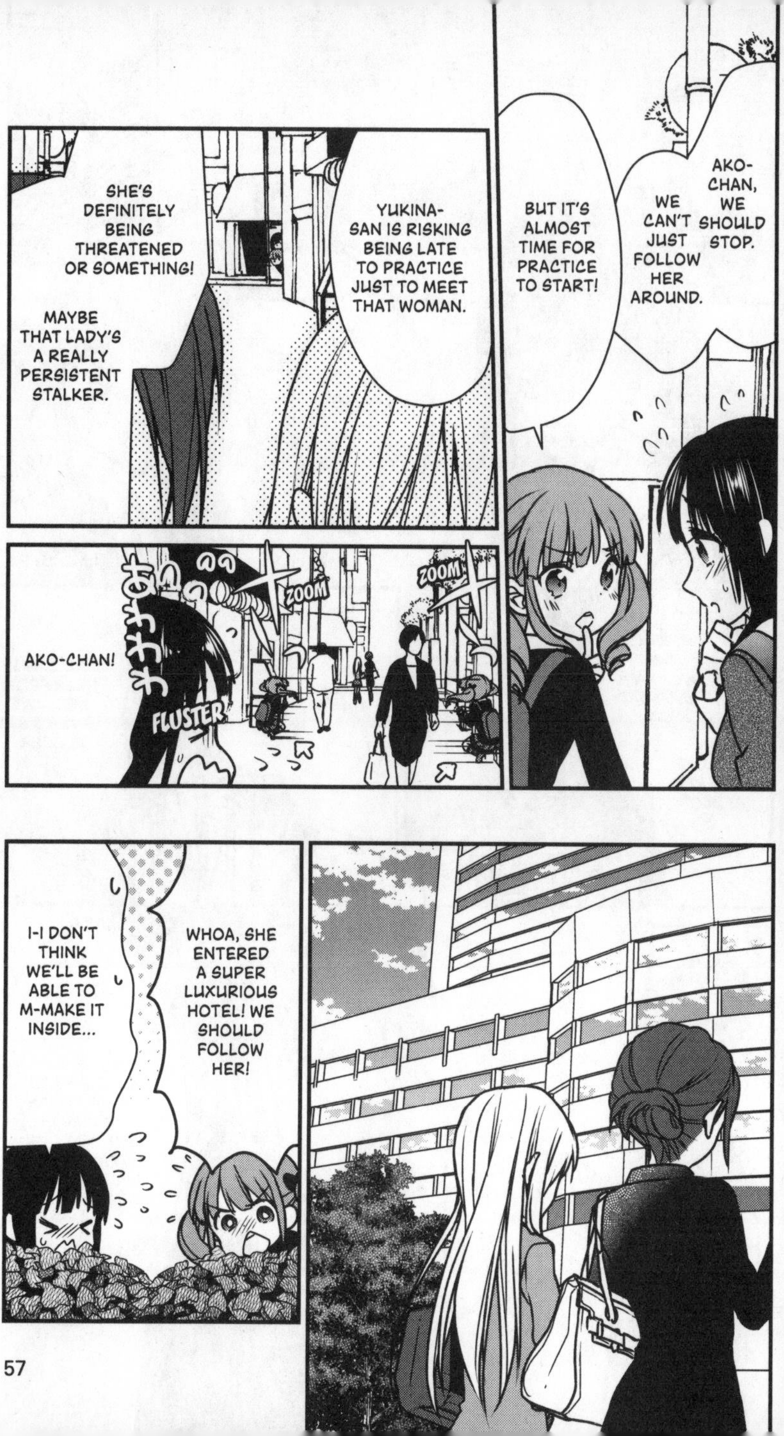
AKO-CHAN, WE SHOULD STOP.
WE CAN'T JUST FOLLOW HER AROUND.
BUT IT'S ALMOST TIME FOR PRACTICE TO START!
YUKINA-SAN IS RISKING BEING LATE TO PRACTICE JUST TO MEET THAT WOMAN.
SHE'S DEFINITELY BEING THREATENED OR SOMETHING!
MAYBE THAT LADY'S A REALLY PERSISTENT STALKER.
ZOOM
ZOOM
FLUSTER
AKO-CHAN!
WHOA, SHE ENTERED A SUPER LUXURIOUS HOTEL! WE SHOULD FOLLOW HER!
I-I DON'T THINK WE'LL BE ABLE TO M-MAKE IT INSIDE...

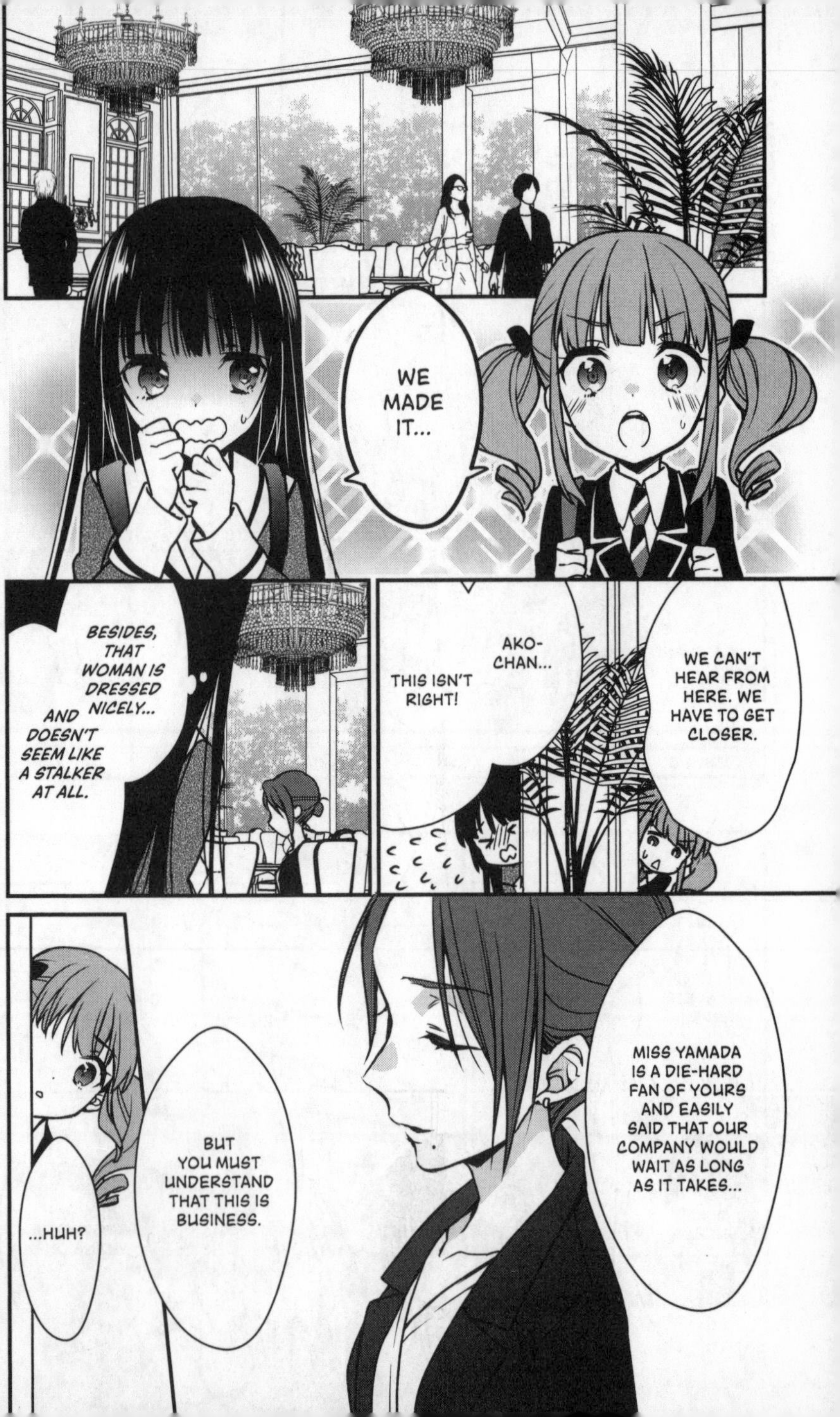
WE MADE IT...
WE CAN'T HEAR FROM HERE. WE HAVE TO GET CLOSER.
AKO-CHAN...
THIS ISN'T RIGHT!
BESIDES, THAT WOMAN IS DRESSED NICELY...
AND DOESN'T SEEM LIKE A STALKER AT ALL.
MISS YAMADA IS A DIE-HARD FAN OF YOURS AND EASILY SAID THAT OUR COMPANY WOULD WAIT AS LONG AS IT TAKES...
BUT YOU MUST UNDERSTAND THAT THIS IS BUSINESS.
...HUH?

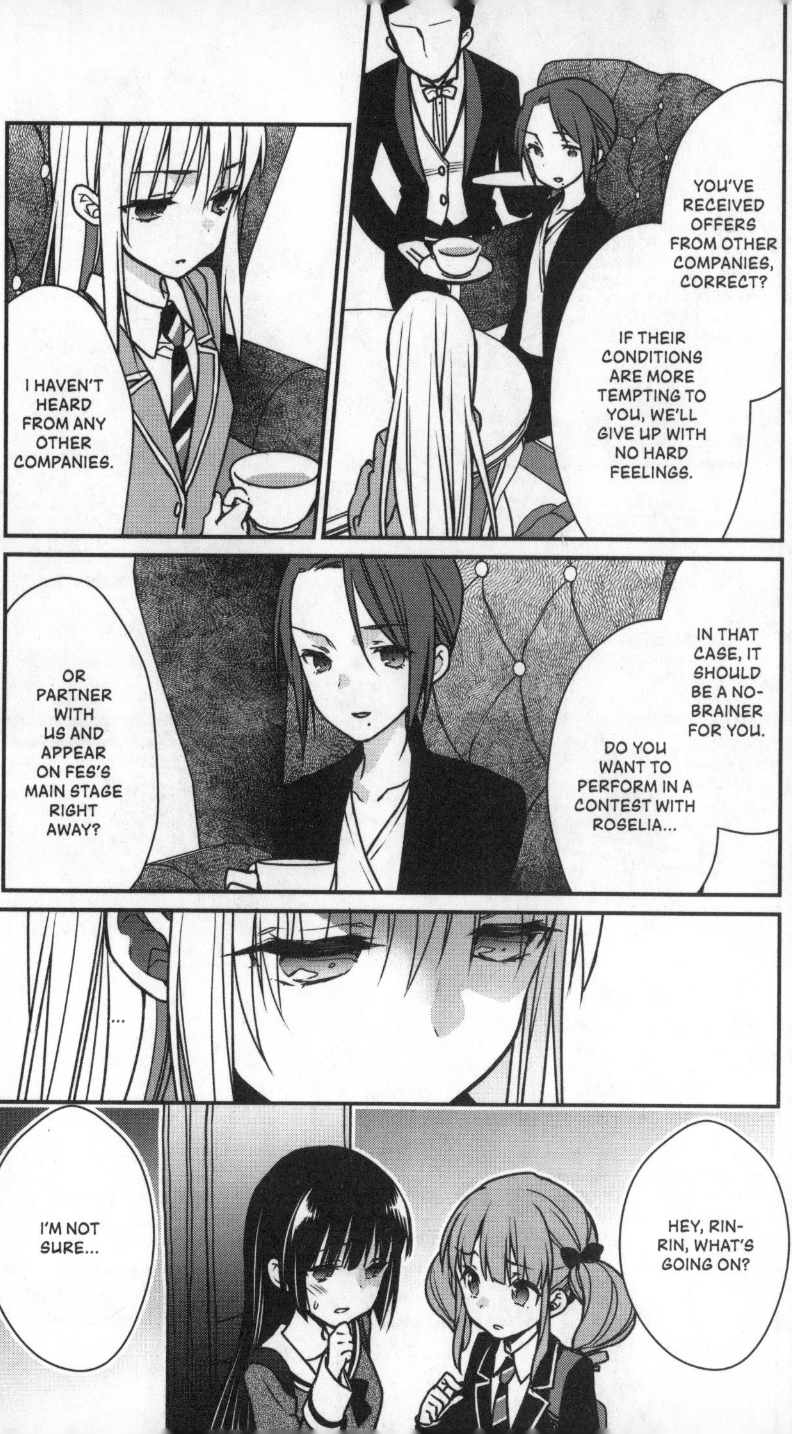
YOU'VE RECEIVED OFFERS FROM OTHER COMPANIES, CORRECT?
IF THEIR CONDITIONS ARE MORE TEMPTING TO YOU, WE'LL GIVE UP WITH NO HARD FEELINGS.
I HAVEN'T HEARD FROM ANY OTHER COMPANIES.
IN THAT CASE, IT SHOULD BE A NO-BRAINER FOR YOU.
DO YOU WANT TO PERFORM IN A CONTEST WITH ROSELIA...
OR PARTNER WITH US AND APPEAR ON FES'S MAIN STAGE RIGHT AWAY?
...
HEY, RIN-RIN, WHAT'S GOING ON?
I'M NOT SURE...

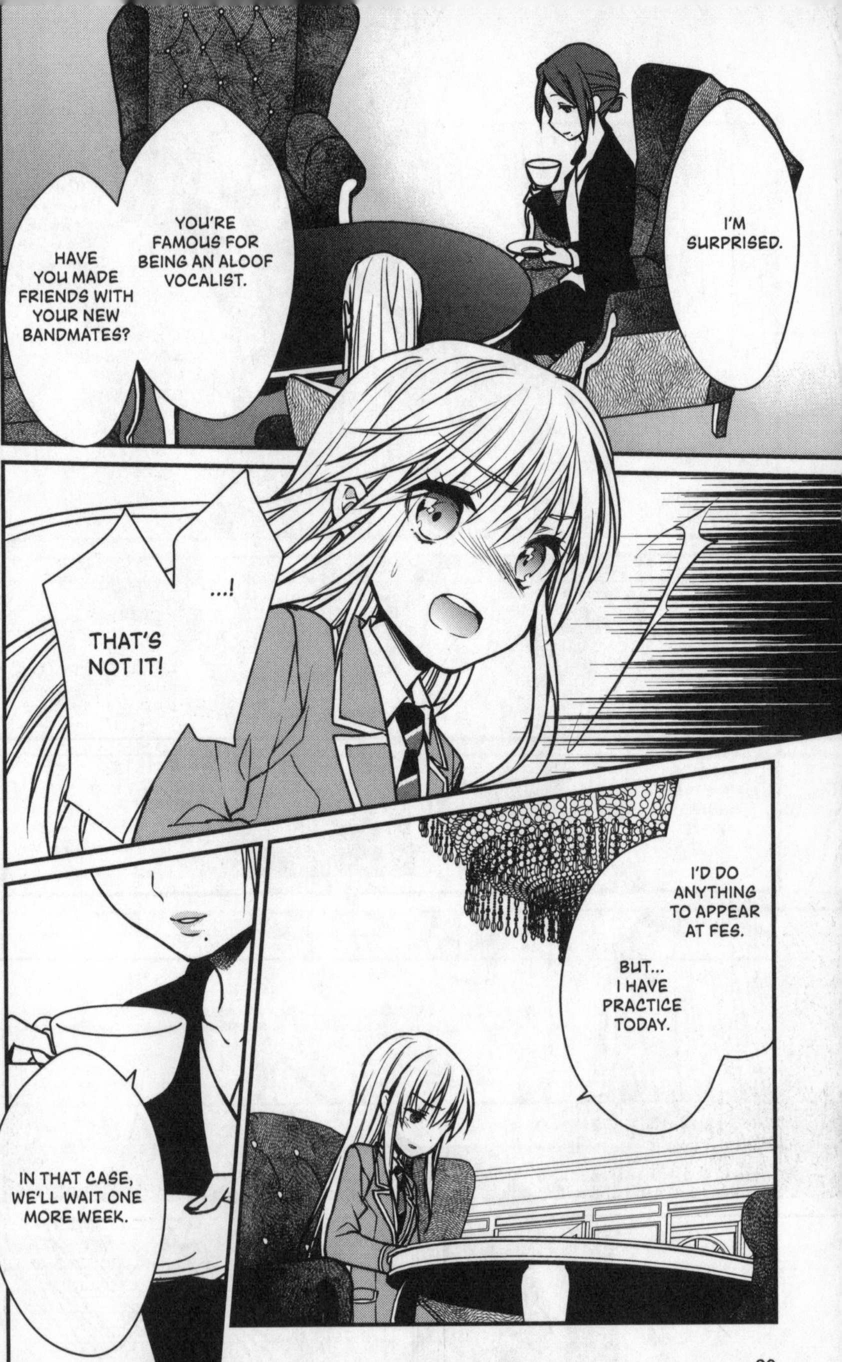
I'M SURPRISED.
YOU'RE FAMOUS FOR BEING AN ALOOF VOCALIST.
HAVE YOU MADE FRIENDS WITH YOUR NEW BANDMATES?
...!
THAT'S NOT IT!
I'D DO ANYTHING TO APPEAR AT FES.
BUT... I HAVE PRACTICE TODAY.
IN THAT CASE, WE'LL WAIT ONE MORE WEEK.

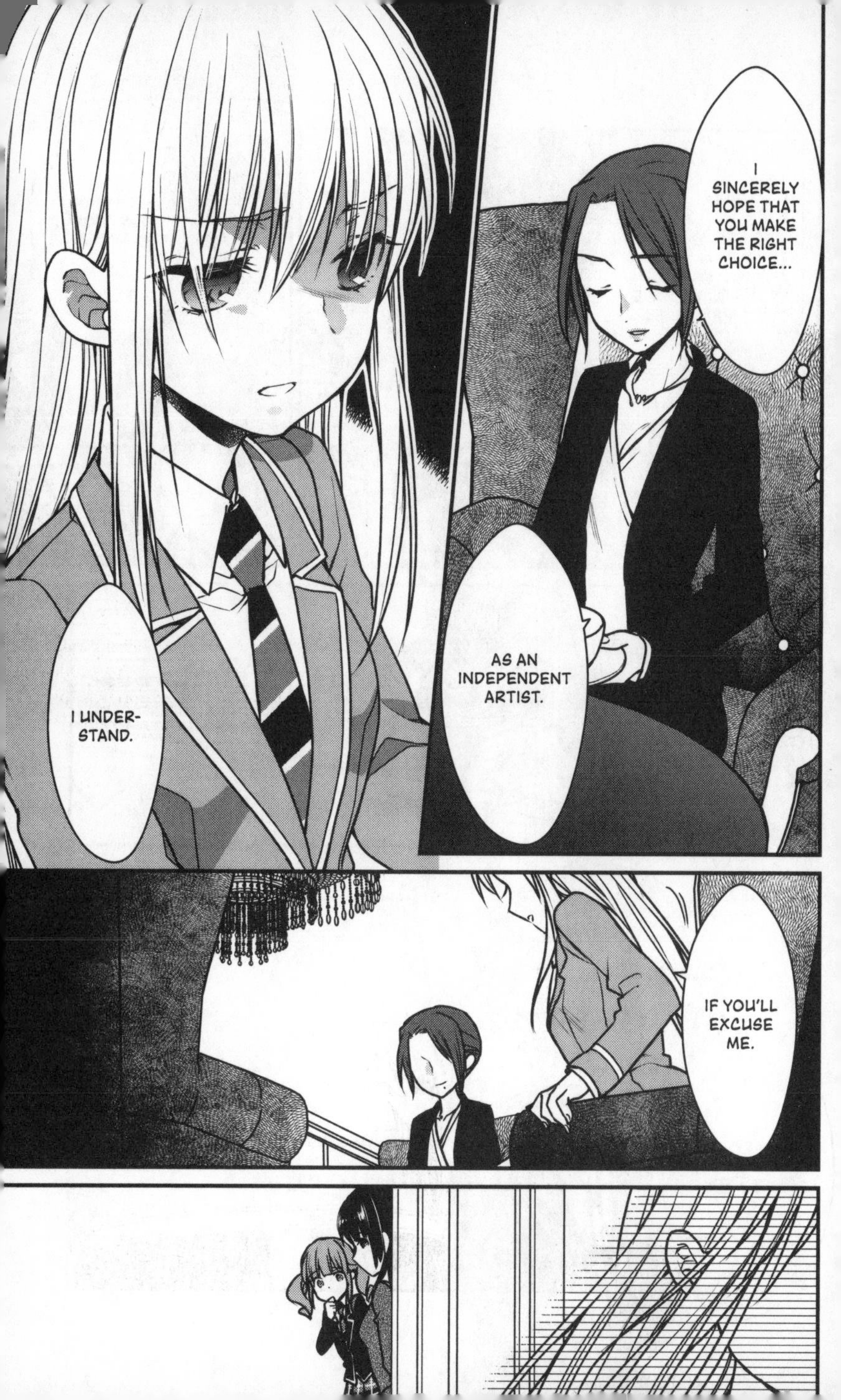
I SINCERELY HOPE THAT YOU MAKE THE RIGHT CHOICE...
AS AN INDEPENDENT ARTIST.
I UNDER-STAND.
IF YOU'LL EXCUSE ME.

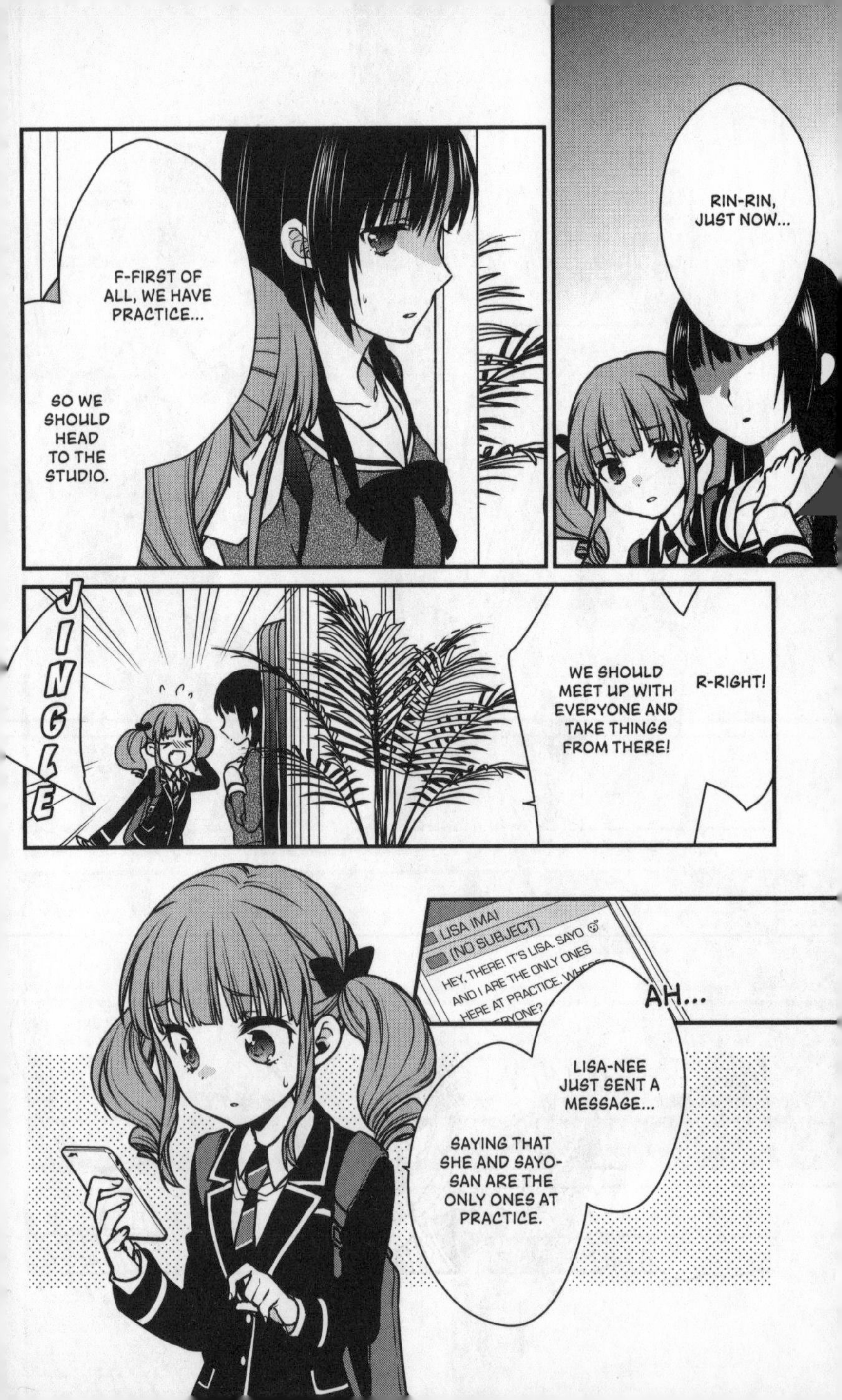
RIN-RIN, JUST NOW...
F-FIRST OF ALL, WE HAVE PRACTICE...
SO WE SHOULD HEAD TO THE STUDIO.
R-RIGHT!
WE SHOULD MEET UP WITH EVERYONE AND TAKE THINGS FROM THERE!
JINGLE
LISA IMAI
(NO SUBJECT)
HEY, THERE! IT'S LISA. SAYO
AND I ARE THE ONLY ONES
HERE AT PRACTICE.
AH...
LISA-NEE JUST SENT A MESSAGE...
SAYING THAT SHE AND SAYO-SAN ARE THE ONLY ONES AT PRACTICE.

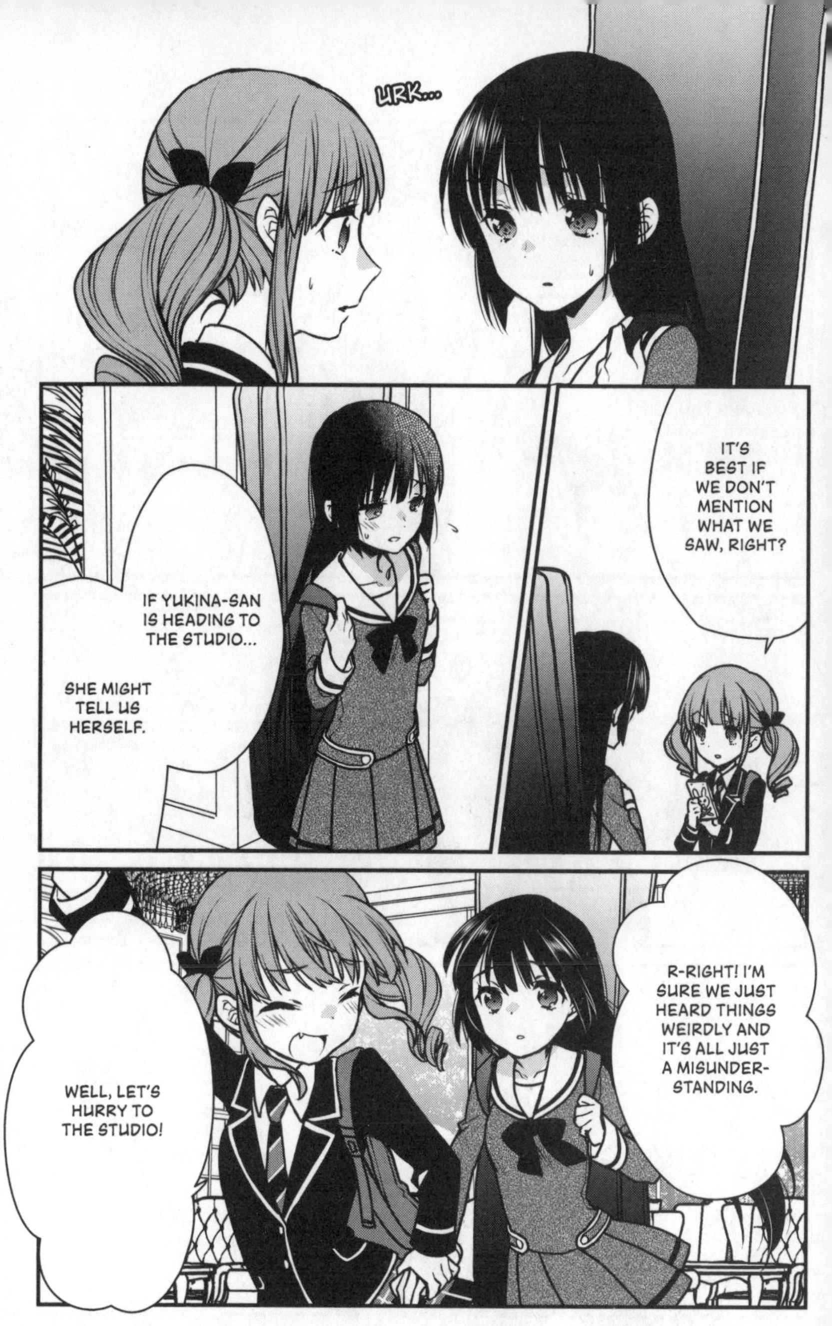
URK...
IT'S BEST IF WE DON'T MENTION WHAT WE SAW, RIGHT?
IF YUKINA-SAN IS HEADING TO THE STUDIO...
SHE MIGHT TELL US HERSELF.
R-RIGHT! I'M SURE WE JUST HEARD THINGS WEIRDLY AND IT'S ALL JUST A MISUNDER-STANDING.
WELL, LET'S HURRY TO THE STUDIO!

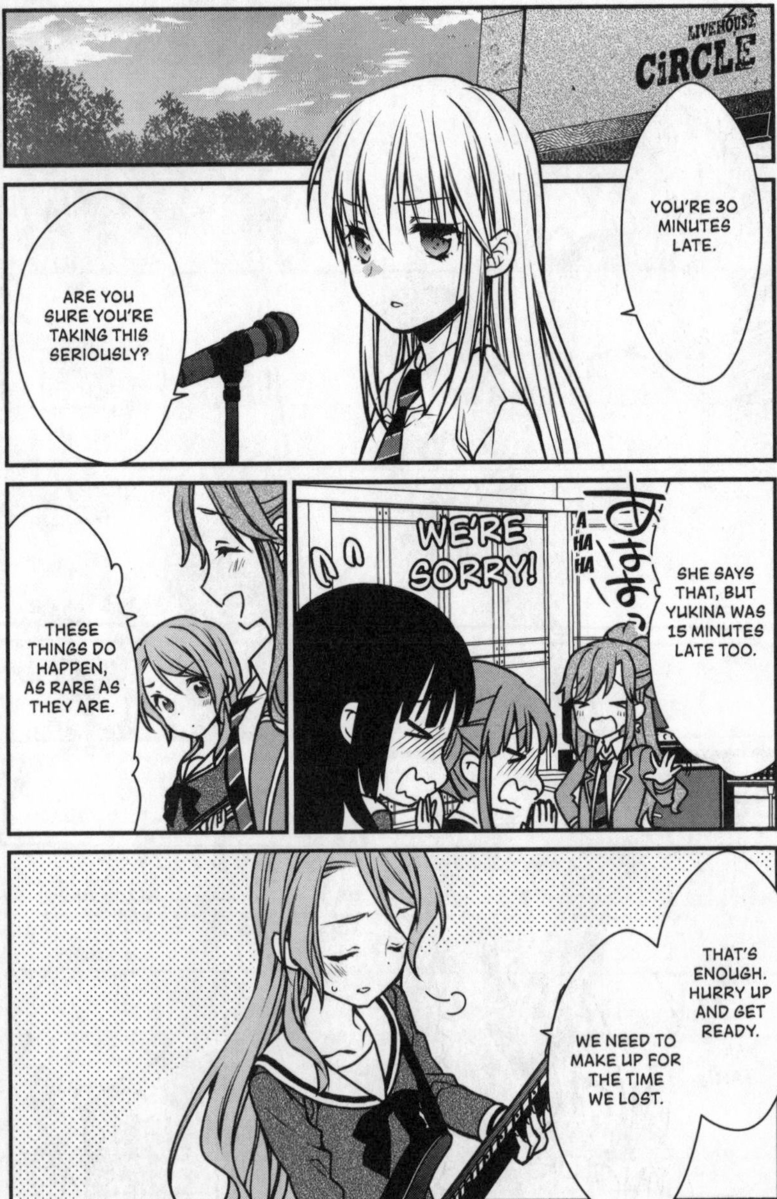
LIVEHOUSE
CiRCLE
YOU'RE 30 MINUTES LATE.
ARE YOU SURE YOU'RE TAKING THIS SERIOUSLY?
A HA HA
SHE SAYS THAT, BUT YUKINA WAS 15 MINUTES LATE TOO.
WE'RE SORRY!
THESE THINGS DO HAPPEN, AS RARE AS THEY ARE.
THAT'S ENOUGH. HURRY UP AND GET READY.
WE NEED TO MAKE UP FOR THE TIME WE LOST.

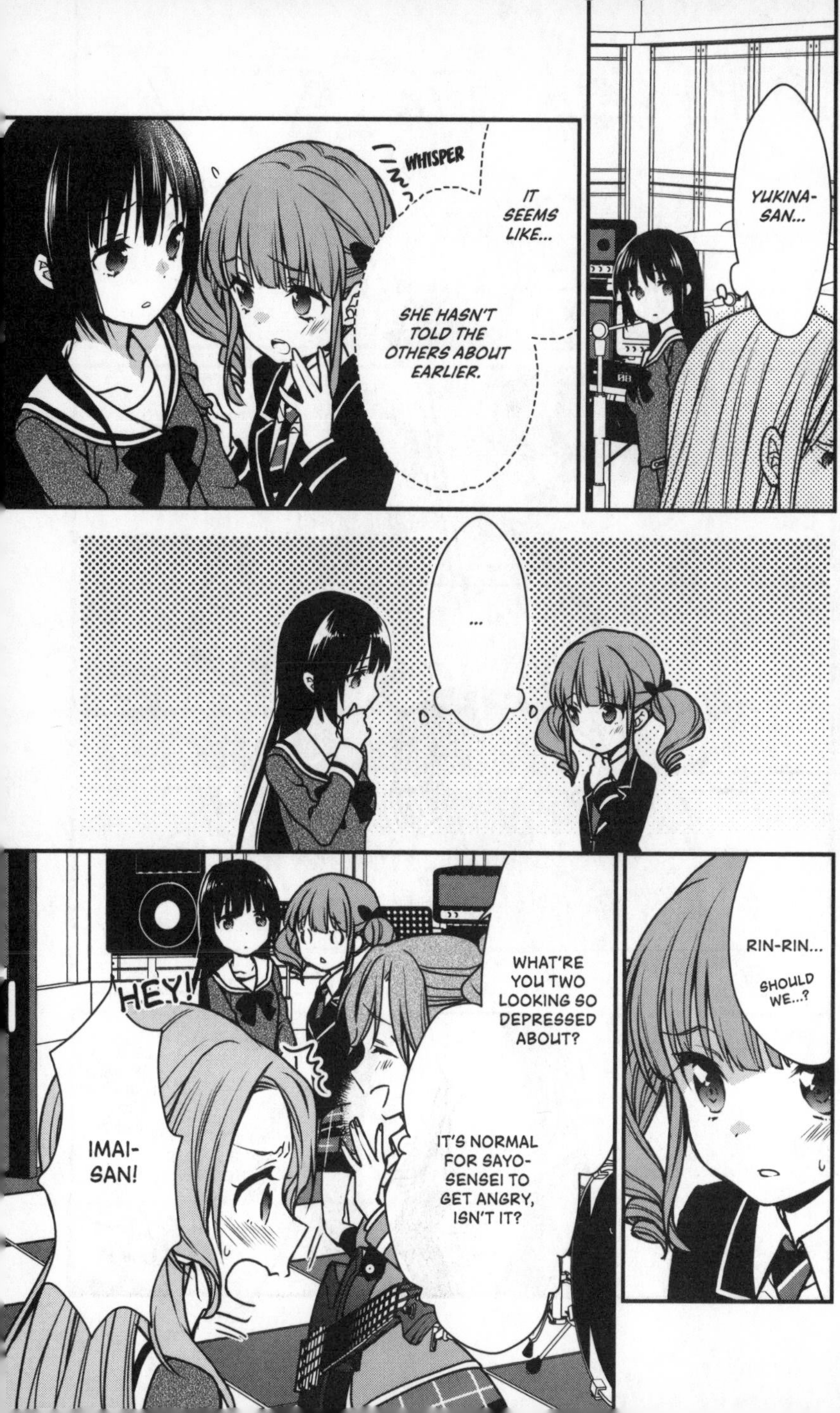
YUKINA-SAN...
WHISPER
IT SEEMS LIKE...
SHE HASN'T TOLD THE OTHERS ABOUT EARLIER.
...
RIN-RIN...
SHOULD WE...?
HEY!
WHAT'RE YOU TWO LOOKING SO DEPRESSED ABOUT?
IMAI-SAN!
IT'S NORMAL FOR SAYO-SENSEI TO GET ANGRY, ISN'T IT?

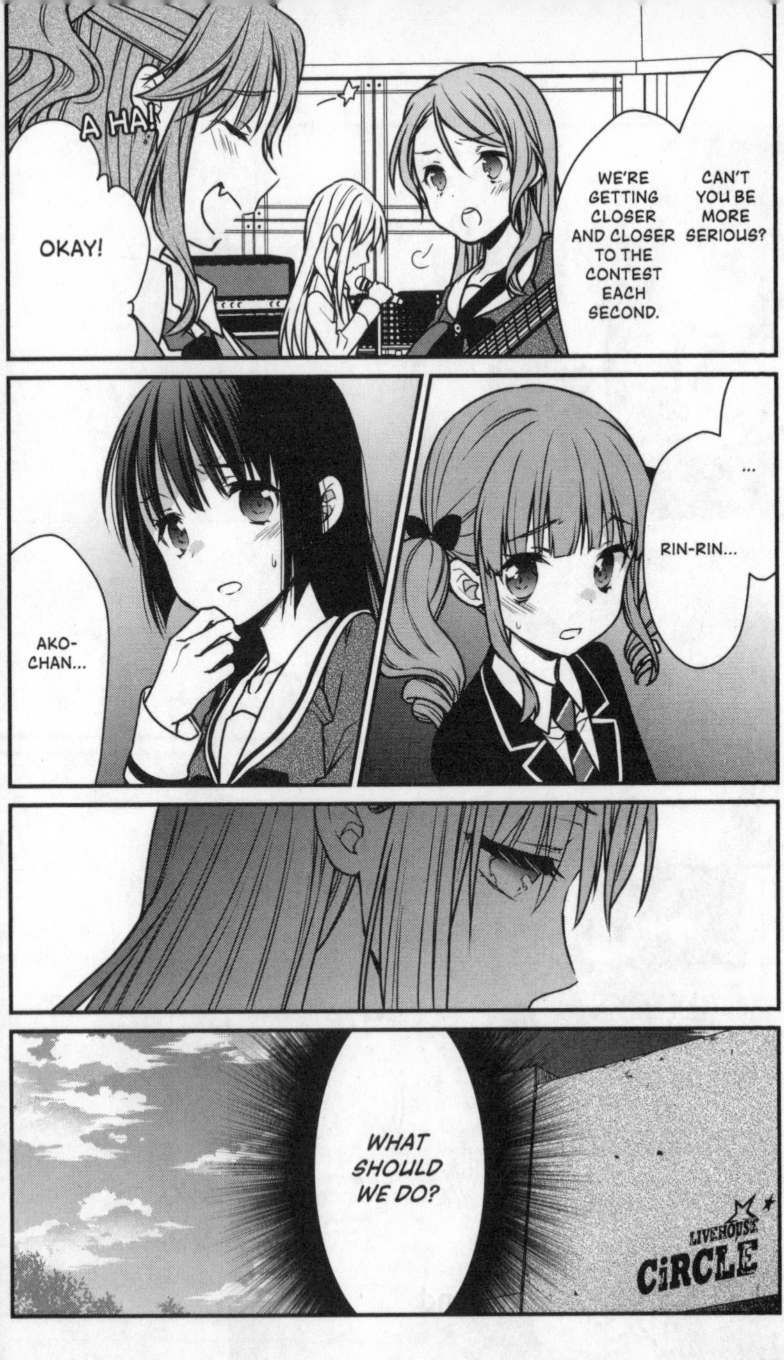
CAN'T YOU BE MORE SERIOUS?
WE'RE GETTING CLOSER AND CLOSER TO THE CONTEST EACH SECOND.
A HA!
OKAY!
...
RIN-RIN...
AKO-CHAN...
WHAT SHOULD WE DO?
LIVEHOUSE CiRCLE

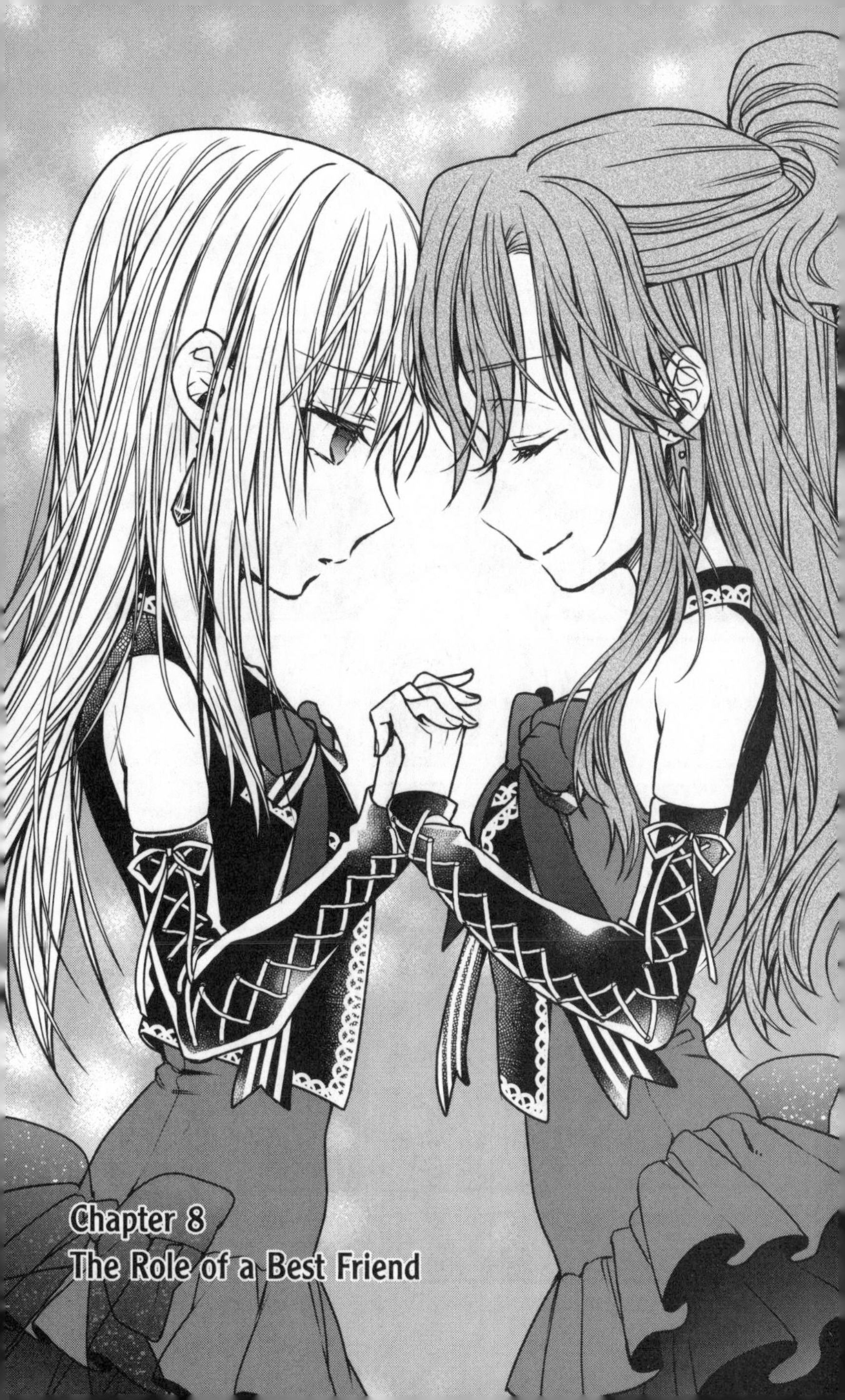

Chapter 8
The Role of a Best Friend

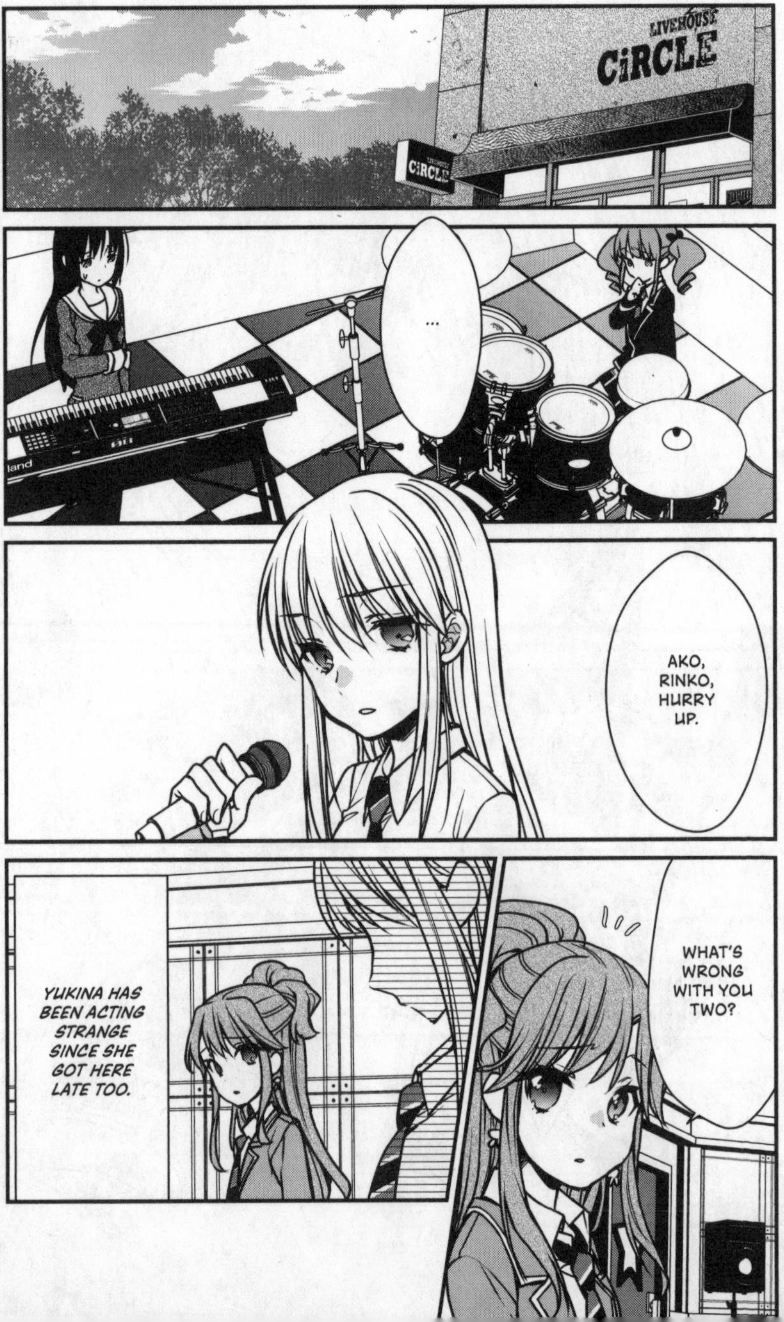
LIVEHOUSE
CiRCLE
CiRCLE
...
AKO, RINKO, HURRY UP.
WHAT'S WRONG WITH YOU TWO?
YUKINA HAS BEEN ACTING STRANGE SINCE SHE GOT HERE LATE TOO.

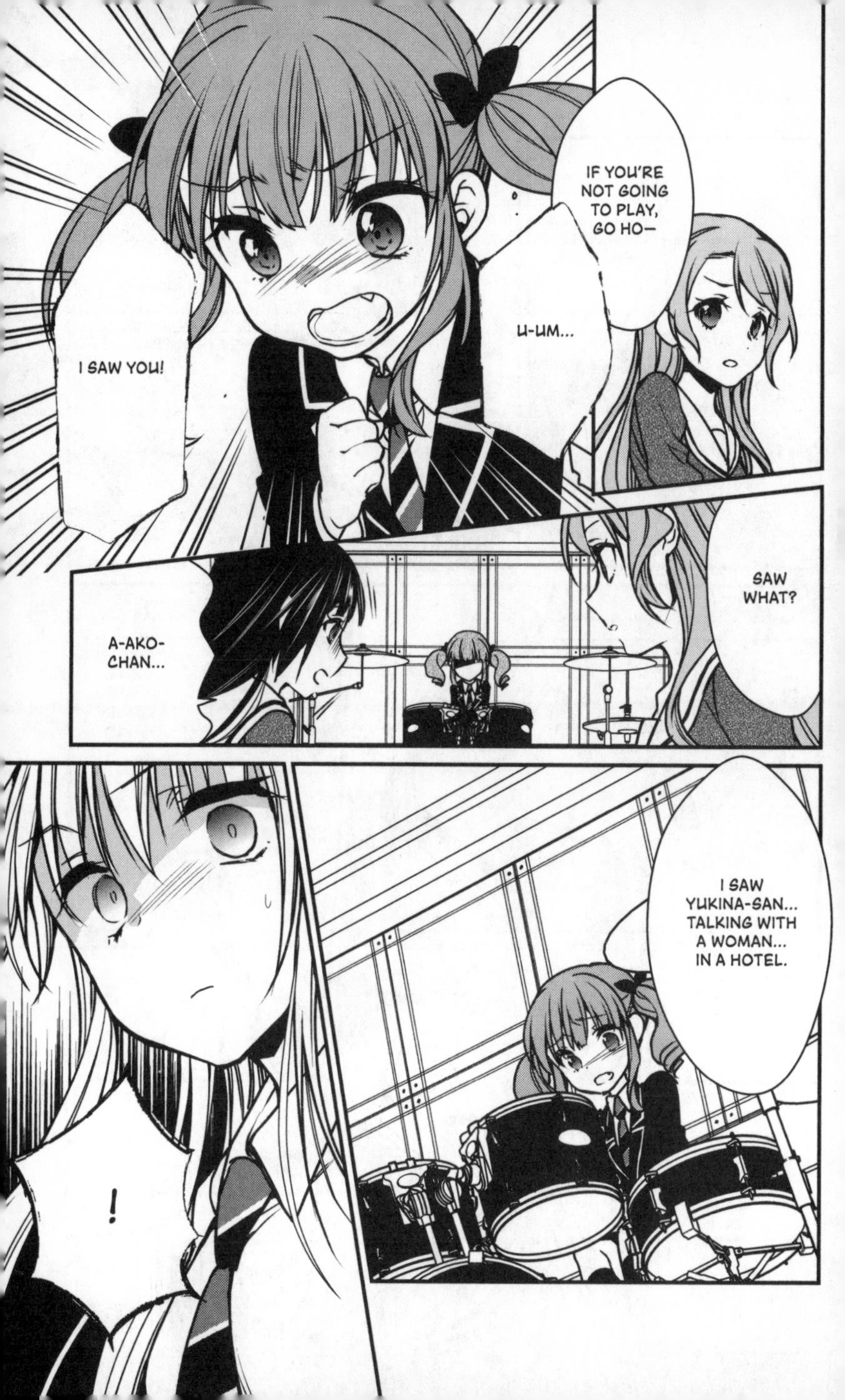
IF YOU'RE NOT GOING TO PLAY, GO HO—
U-UM...
I SAW YOU!
SAW WHAT?
A-AKO-CHAN...
I SAW YUKINA-SAN... TALKING WITH A WOMAN... IN A HOTEL.
!

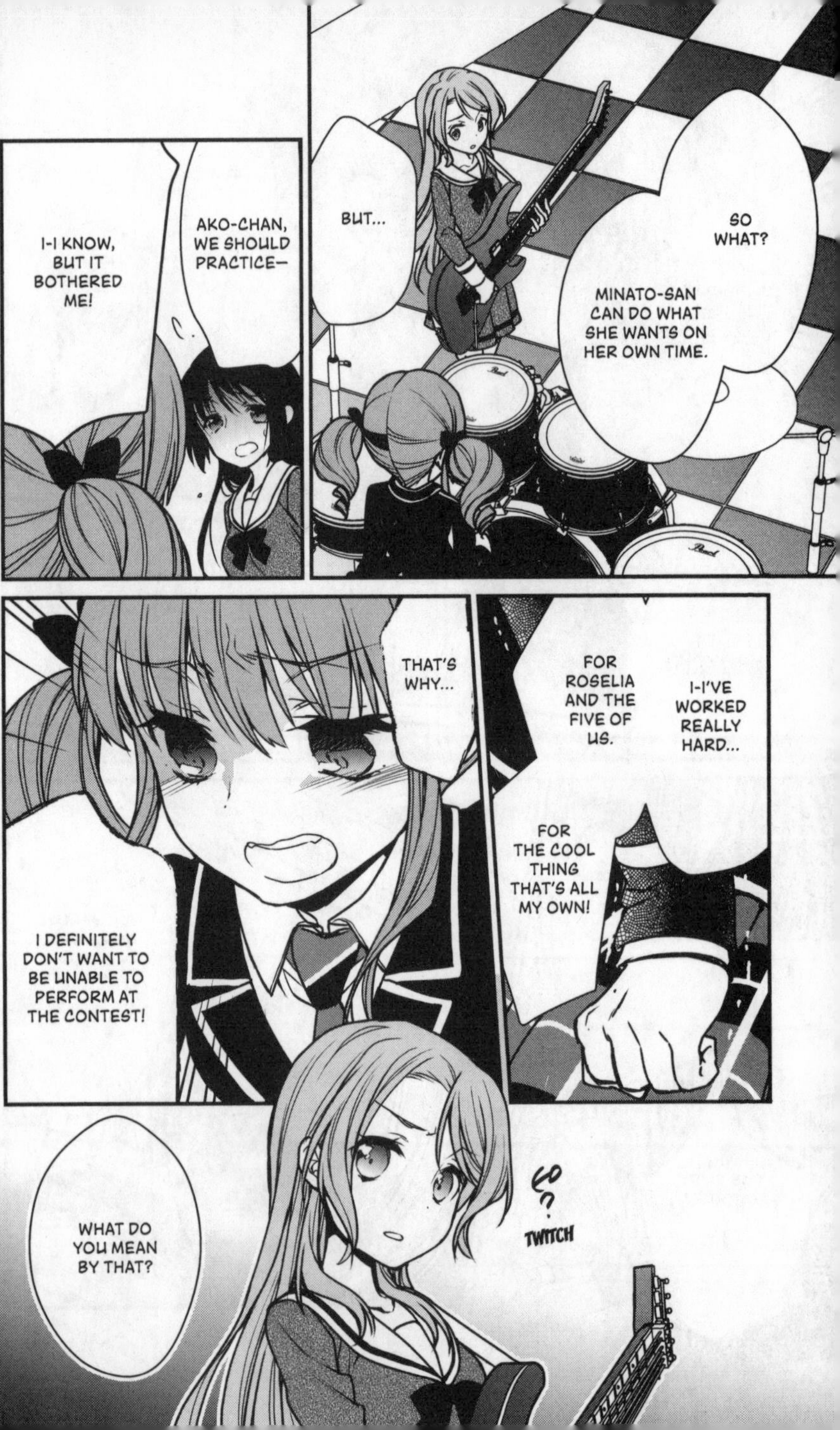
SO WHAT?
MINATO-SAN CAN DO WHAT SHE WANTS ON HER OWN TIME.
BUT...
AKO-CHAN, WE SHOULD PRACTICE—
I-I KNOW, BUT IT BOTHERED ME!
I-I'VE WORKED REALLY HARD...
FOR ROSELIA AND THE FIVE OF US.
FOR THE COOL THING THAT'S ALL MY OWN!
THAT'S WHY...
I DEFINITELY DON'T WANT TO BE UNABLE TO PERFORM AT THE CONTEST!
TWITCH
WHAT DO YOU MEAN BY THAT?

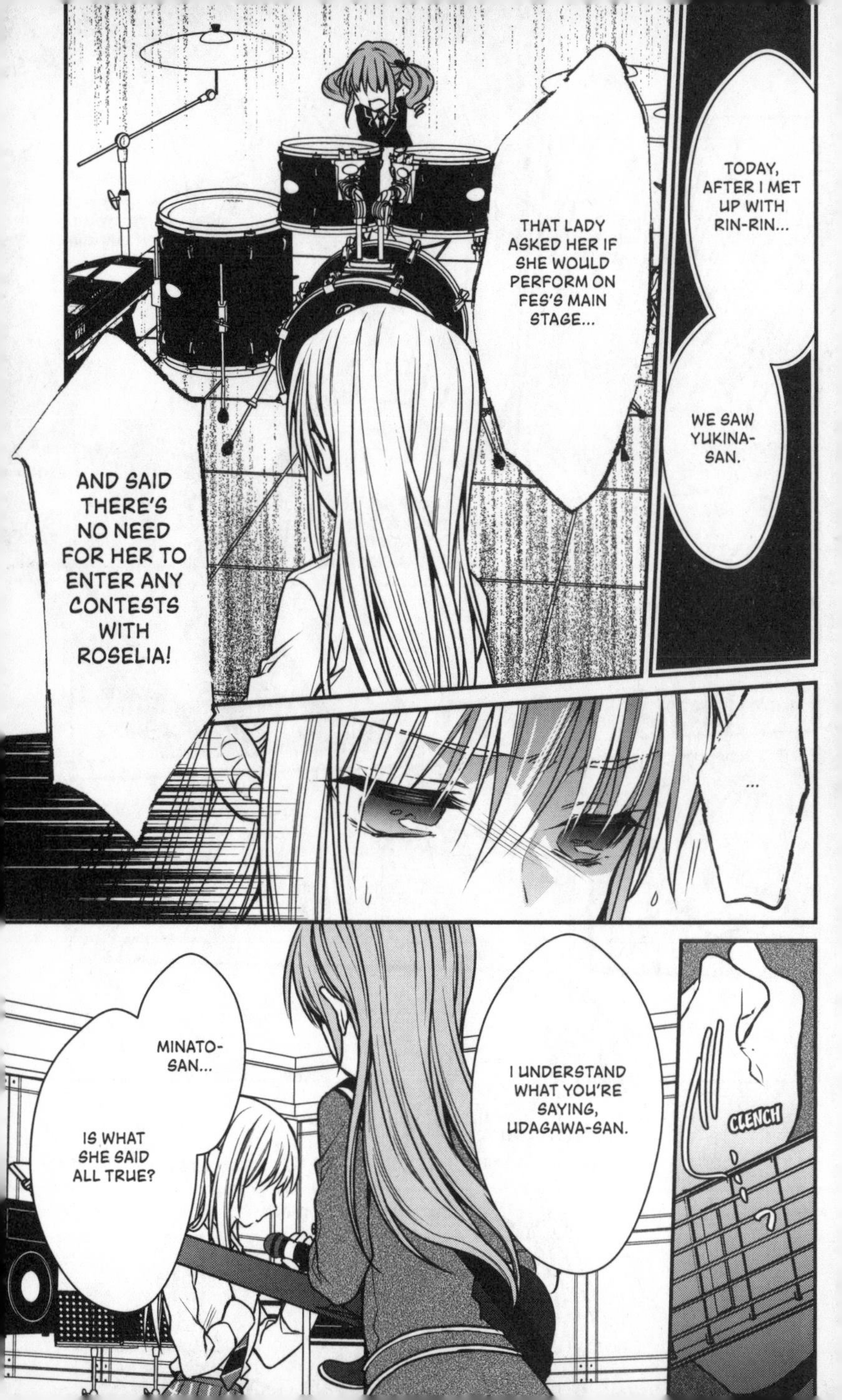
TODAY, AFTER I MET UP WITH RIN-RIN...
WE SAW YUKINA-SAN.
THAT LADY ASKED HER IF SHE WOULD PERFORM ON FES'S MAIN STAGE...
AND SAID THERE'S NO NEED FOR HER TO ENTER ANY CONTESTS WITH ROSELIA!
...
CLENCH
I UNDERSTAND WHAT YOU'RE SAYING, UDAGAWA-SAN.
MINATO-SAN...
IS WHAT SHE SAID ALL TRUE?

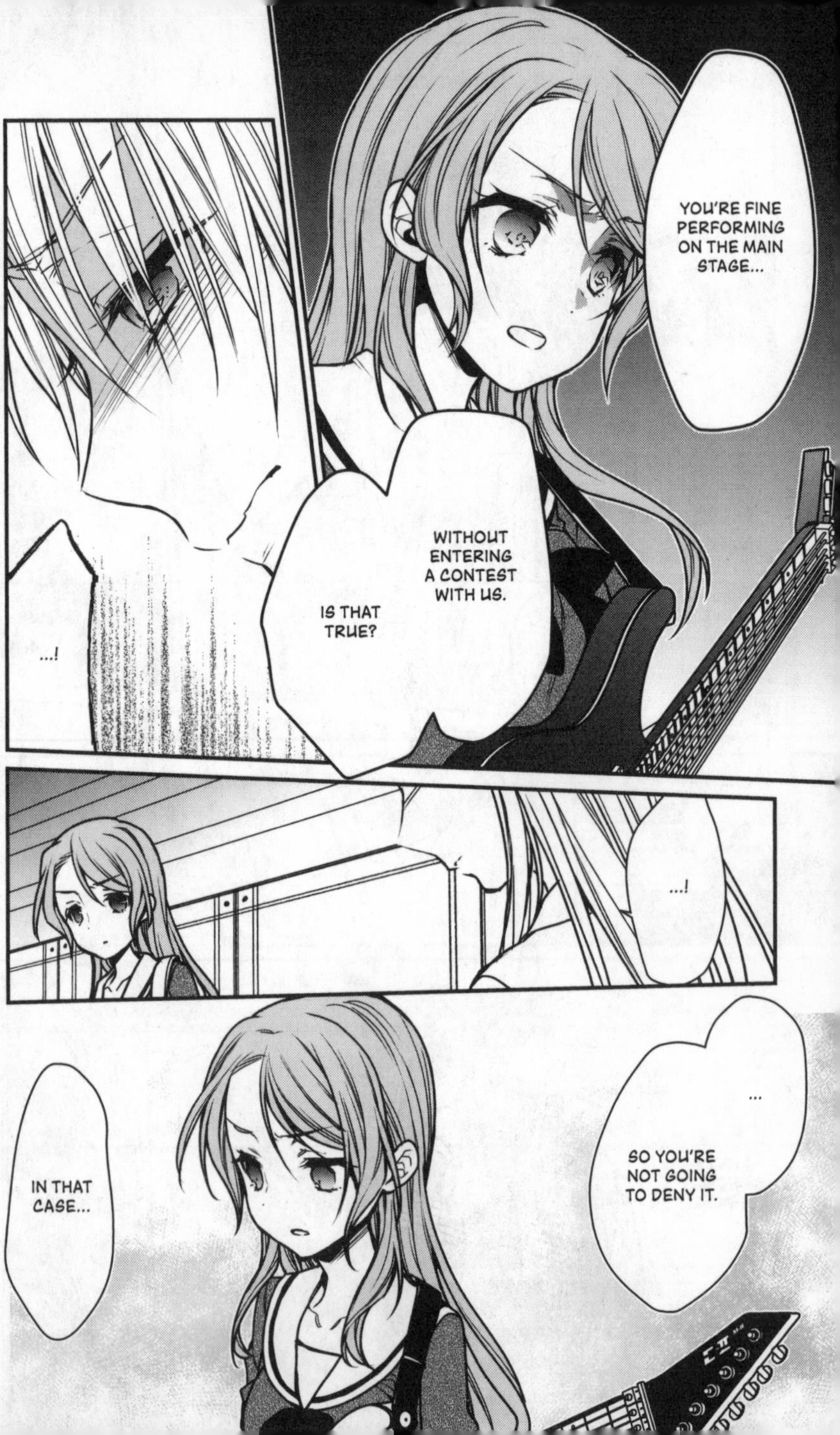
YOU'RE FINE PERFORMING ON THE MAIN STAGE...
WITHOUT ENTERING A CONTEST WITH US.
IS THAT TRUE?
...!
...!
...
SO YOU'RE NOT GOING TO DENY IT.
IN THAT CASE...

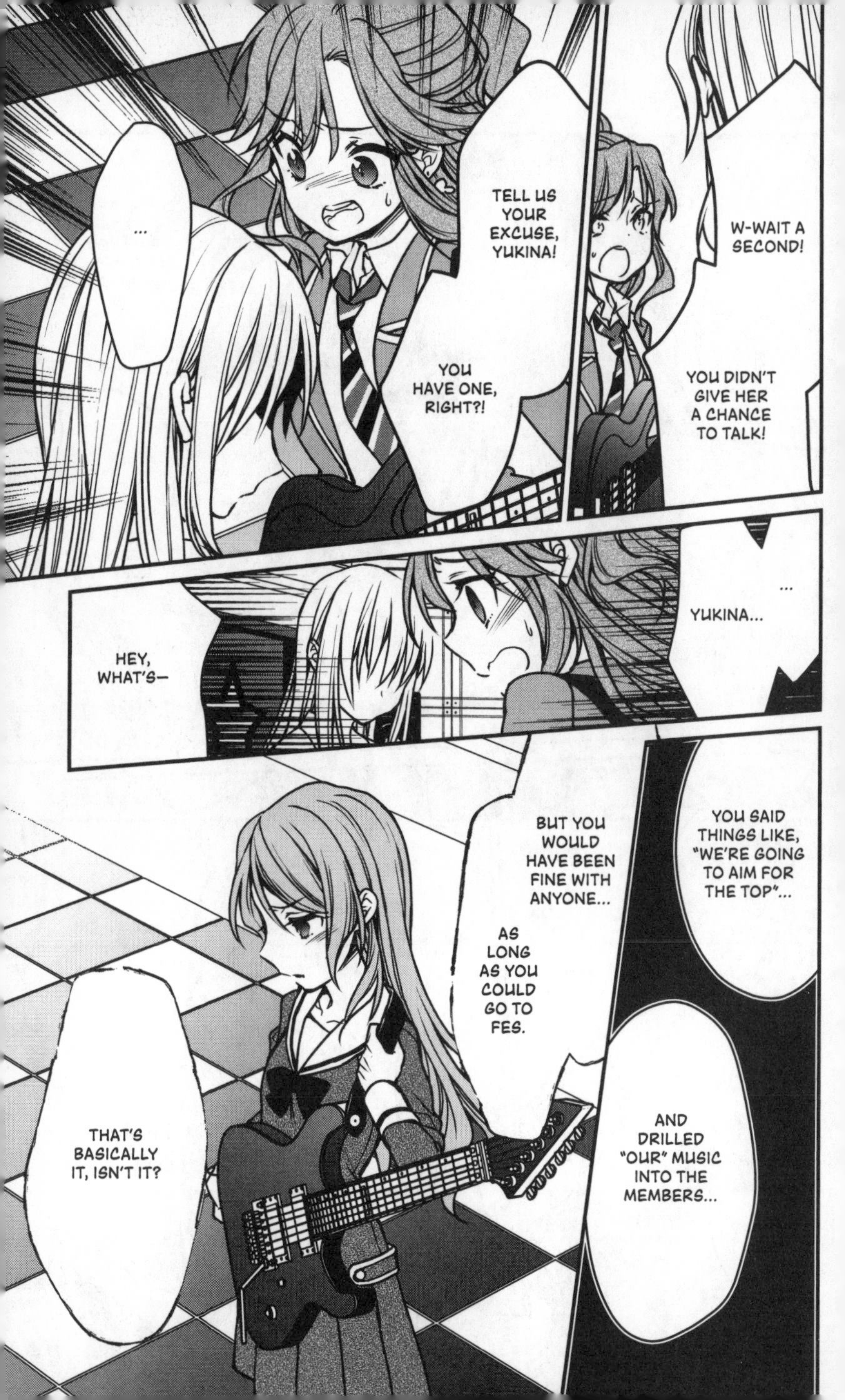
W-WAIT A SECOND!
YOU DIDN'T GIVE HER A CHANCE TO TALK!
TELL US YOUR EXCUSE, YUKINA!
YOU HAVE ONE, RIGHT?!
...
...
YUKINA...
HEY, WHAT'S—
YOU SAID THINGS LIKE, "WE'RE GOING TO AIM FOR THE TOP"...
AND DRILLED "OUR" MUSIC INTO THE MEMBERS...
BUT YOU WOULD HAVE BEEN FINE WITH ANYONE...
AS LONG AS YOU COULD GO TO FES.
THAT'S BASICALLY IT, ISN'T IT?

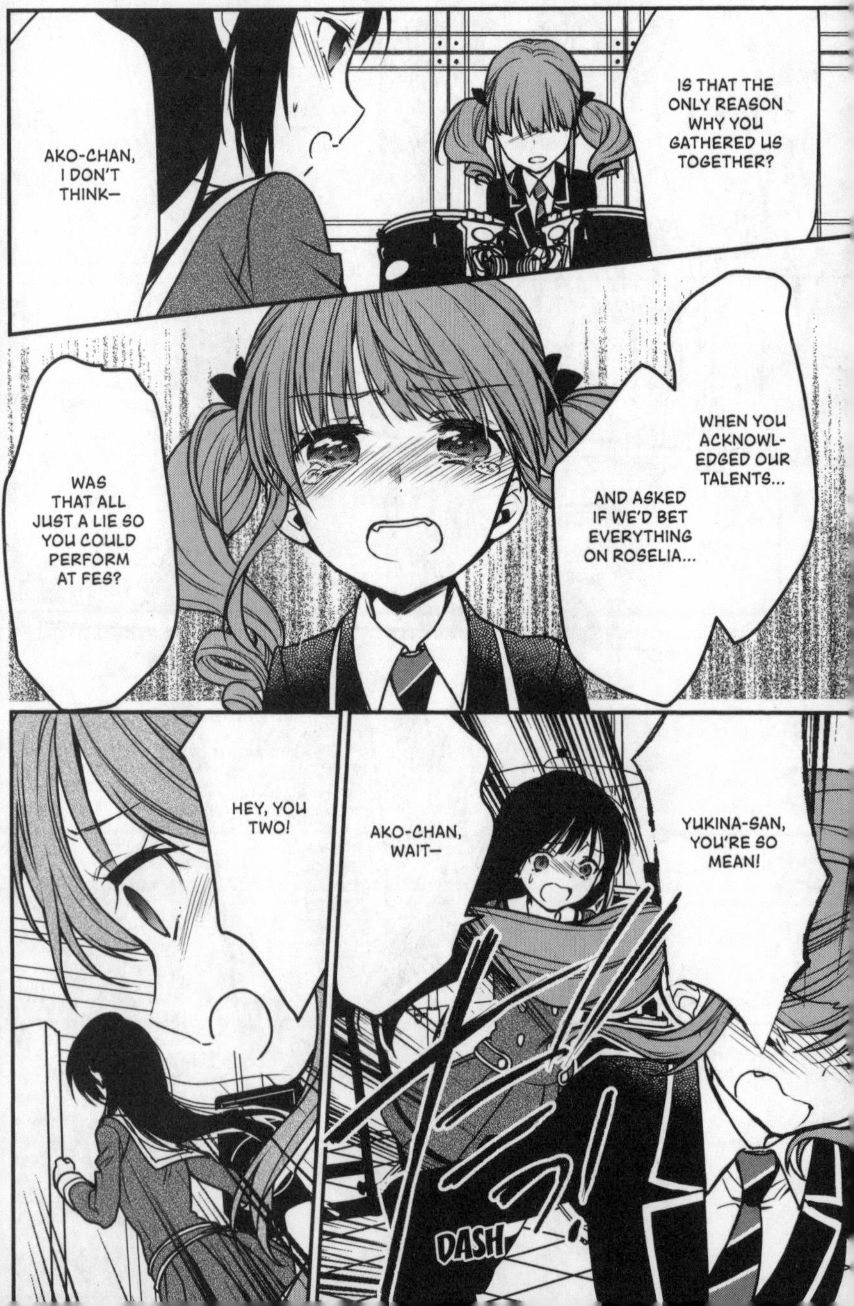
IS THAT THE ONLY REASON WHY YOU GATHERED US TOGETHER?
AKO-CHAN, I DON'T THINK—
WHEN YOU ACKNOWL-EDGED OUR TALENTS...
AND ASKED IF WE'D BET EVERYTHING ON ROSELIA...
WAS THAT ALL JUST A LIE SO YOU COULD PERFORM AT FES?
YUKINA-SAN, YOU'RE SO MEAN!
AKO-CHAN, WAIT—
HEY, YOU TWO!
DASH

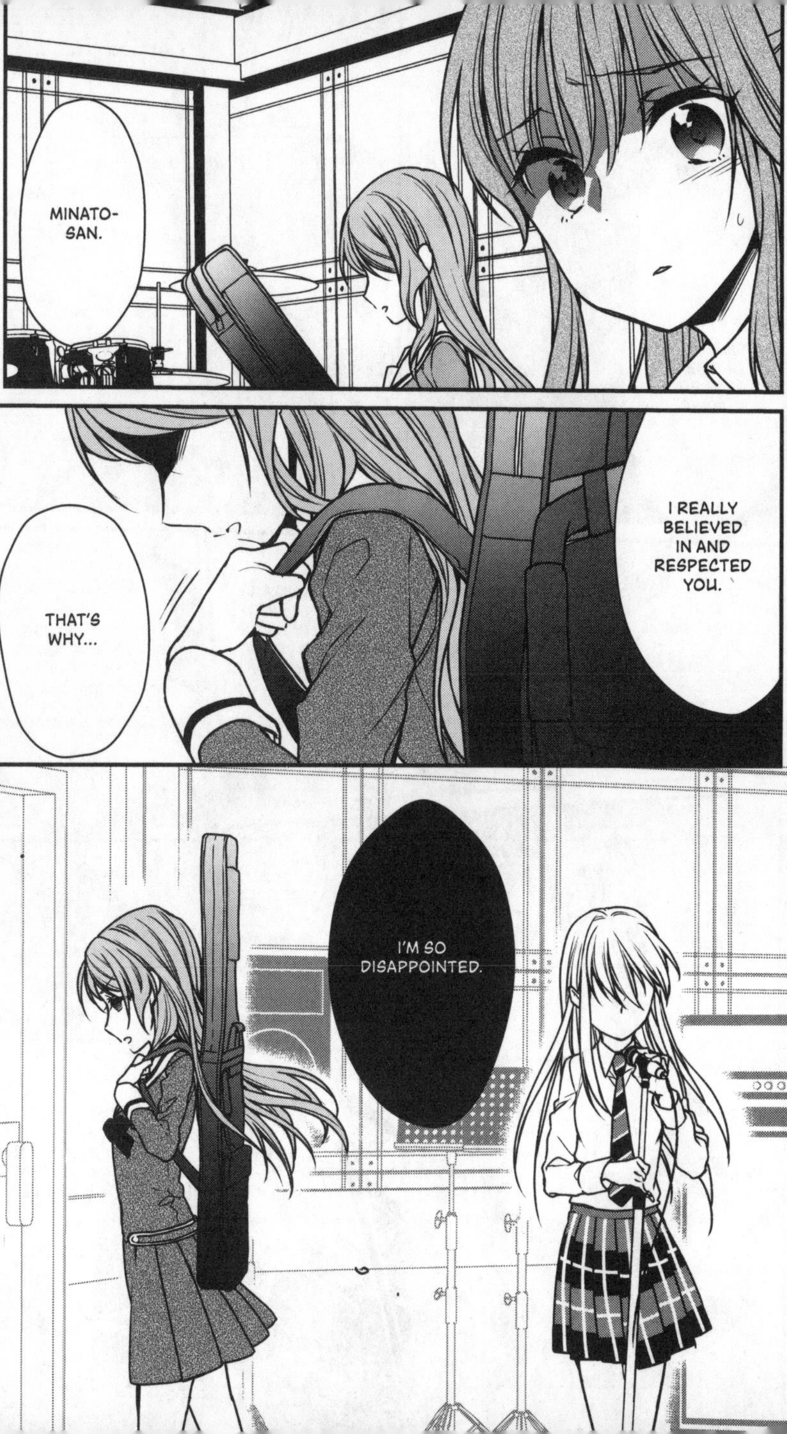
MINATO-SAN.
I REALLY BELIEVED IN AND RESPECTED YOU.
THAT'S WHY...
I'M SO DISAPPOINTED.

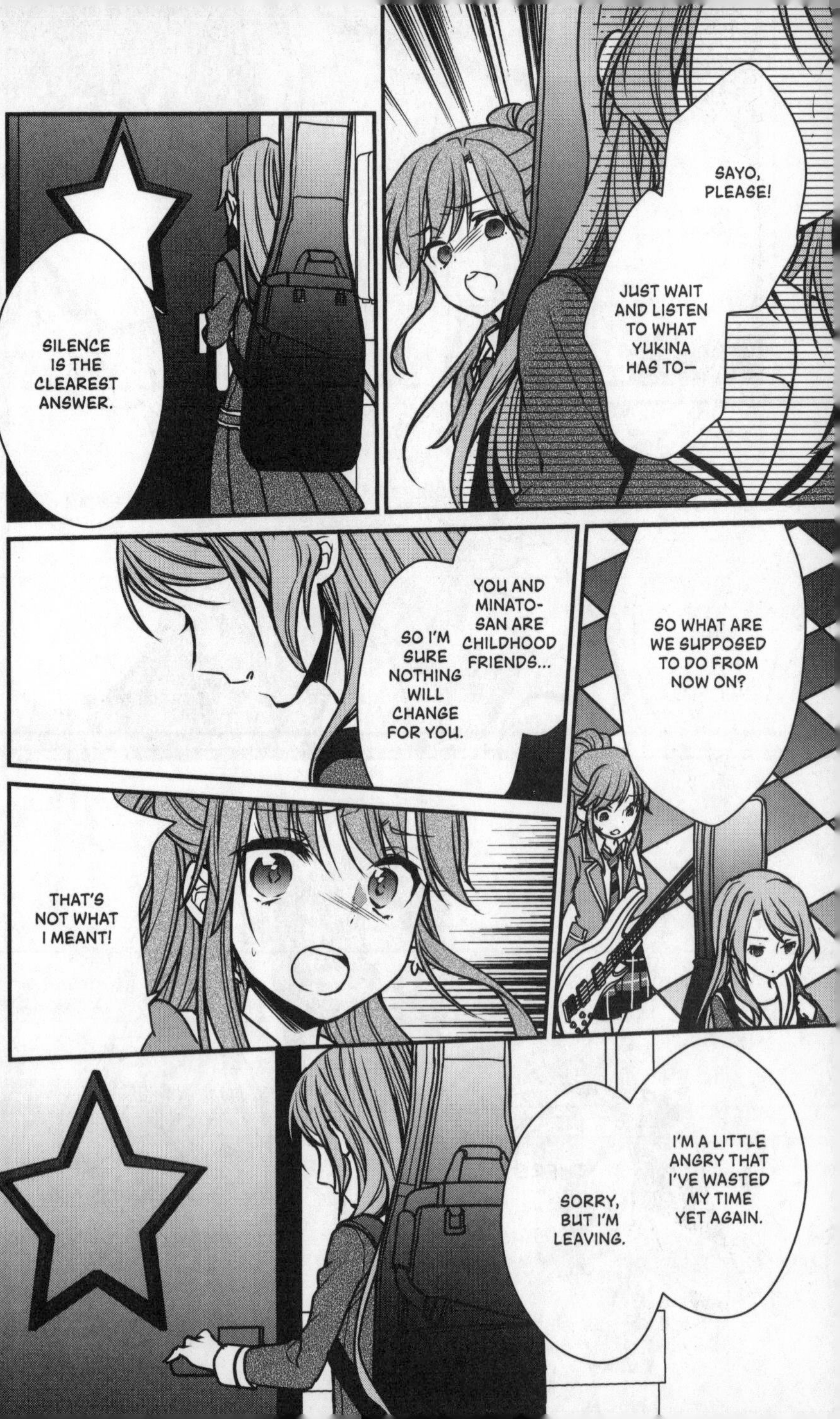
SAYO, PLEASE!
JUST WAIT AND LISTEN TO WHAT YUKINA HAS TO—
SILENCE IS THE CLEAREST ANSWER.
SO WHAT ARE WE SUPPOSED TO DO FROM NOW ON?
YOU AND MINATO-SAN ARE CHILDHOOD FRIENDS...
SO I'M SURE NOTHING WILL CHANGE FOR YOU.
THAT'S NOT WHAT I MEANT!
I'M A LITTLE ANGRY THAT I'VE WASTED MY TIME YET AGAIN.
SORRY, BUT I'M LEAVING.

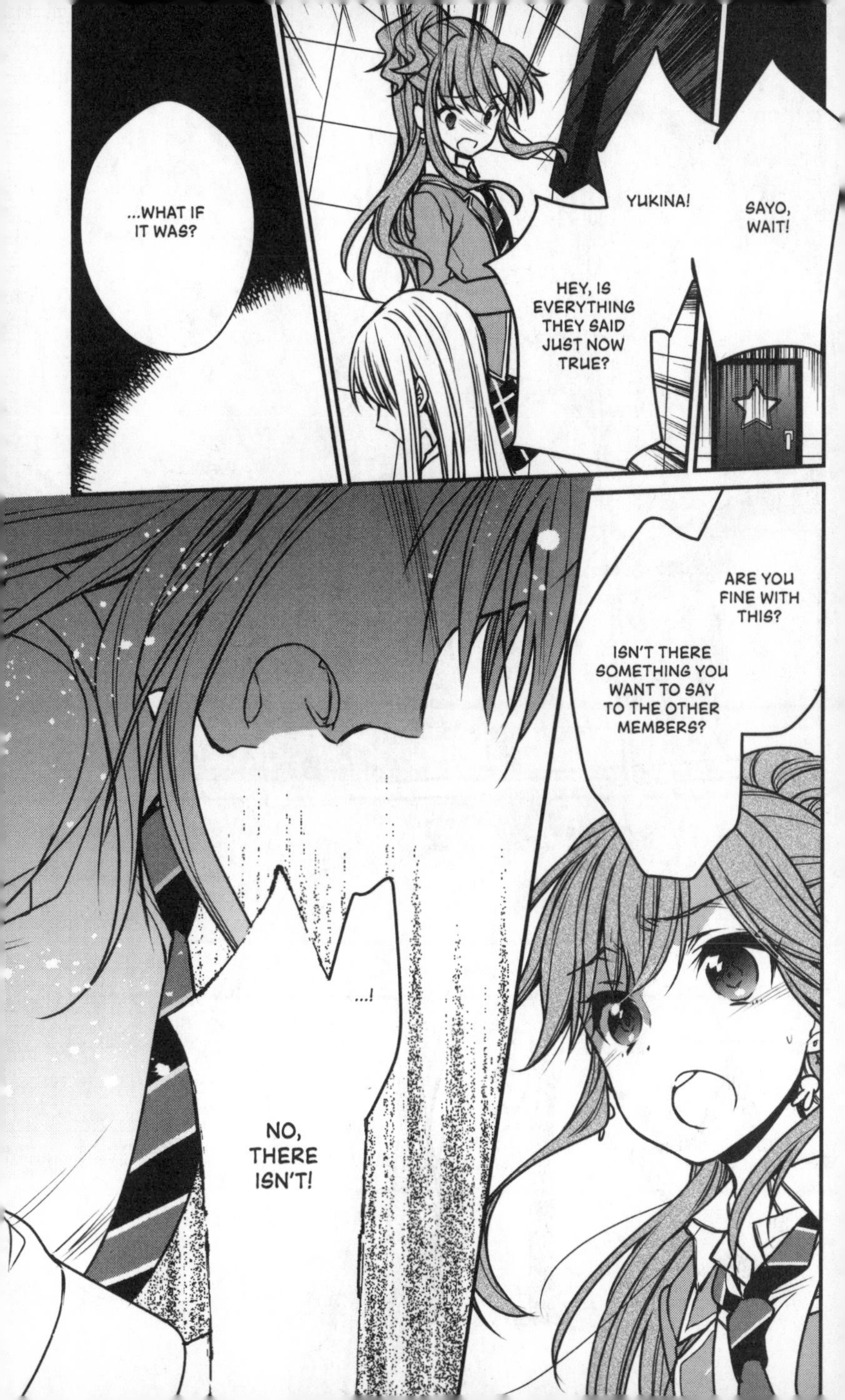
SAYO, WAIT!
YUKINA!
HEY, IS EVERYTHING THEY SAID JUST NOW TRUE?
...WHAT IF IT WAS?
ARE YOU FINE WITH THIS?
ISN'T THERE SOMETHING YOU WANT TO SAY TO THE OTHER MEMBERS?
...!
NO, THERE ISN'T!

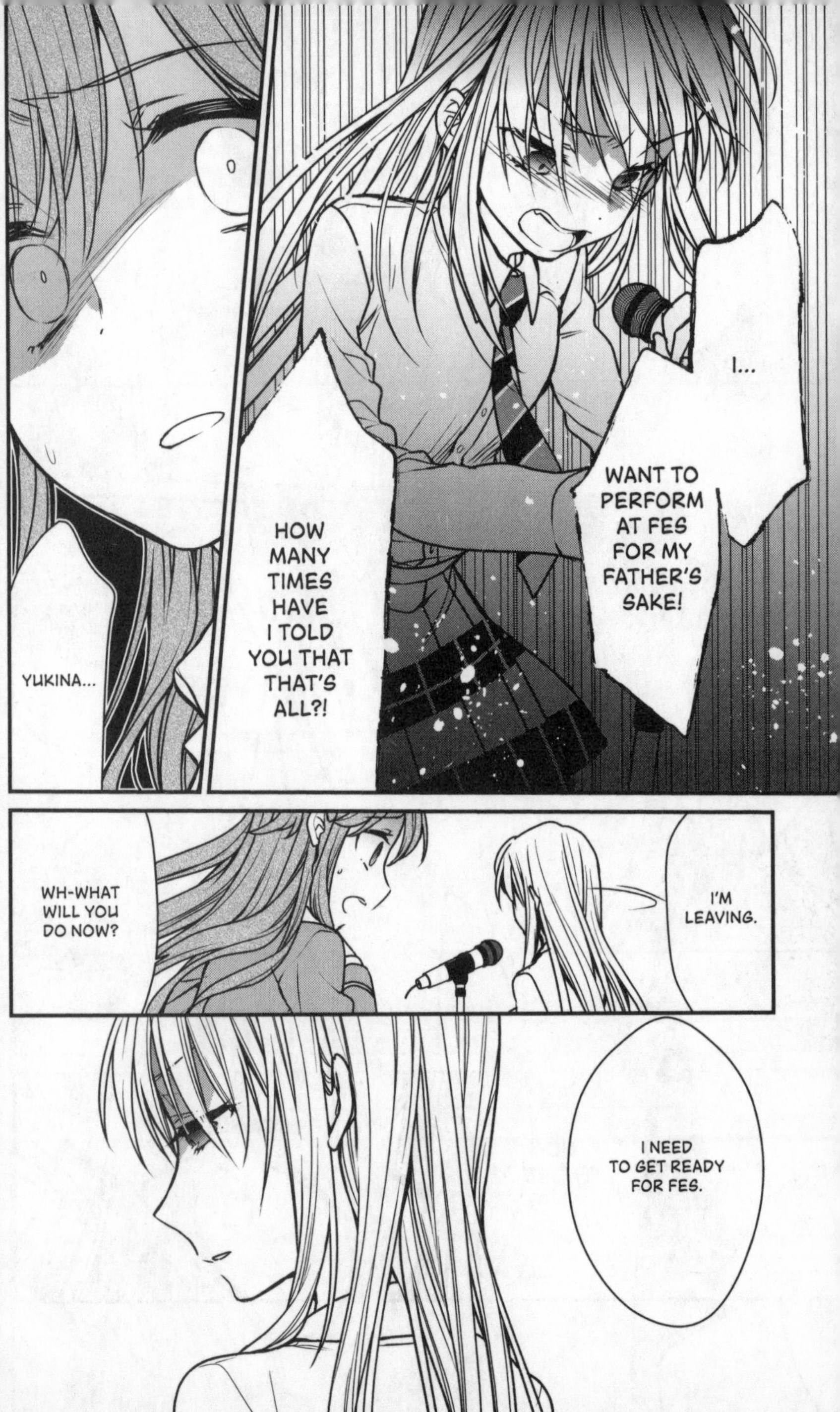
I...
WANT TO PERFORM AT FES FOR MY FATHER'S SAKE!
HOW MANY TIMES HAVE I TOLD YOU THAT THAT'S ALL?!
YUKINA...
I'M LEAVING.
WH-WHAT WILL YOU DO NOW?
I NEED TO GET READY FOR FES.

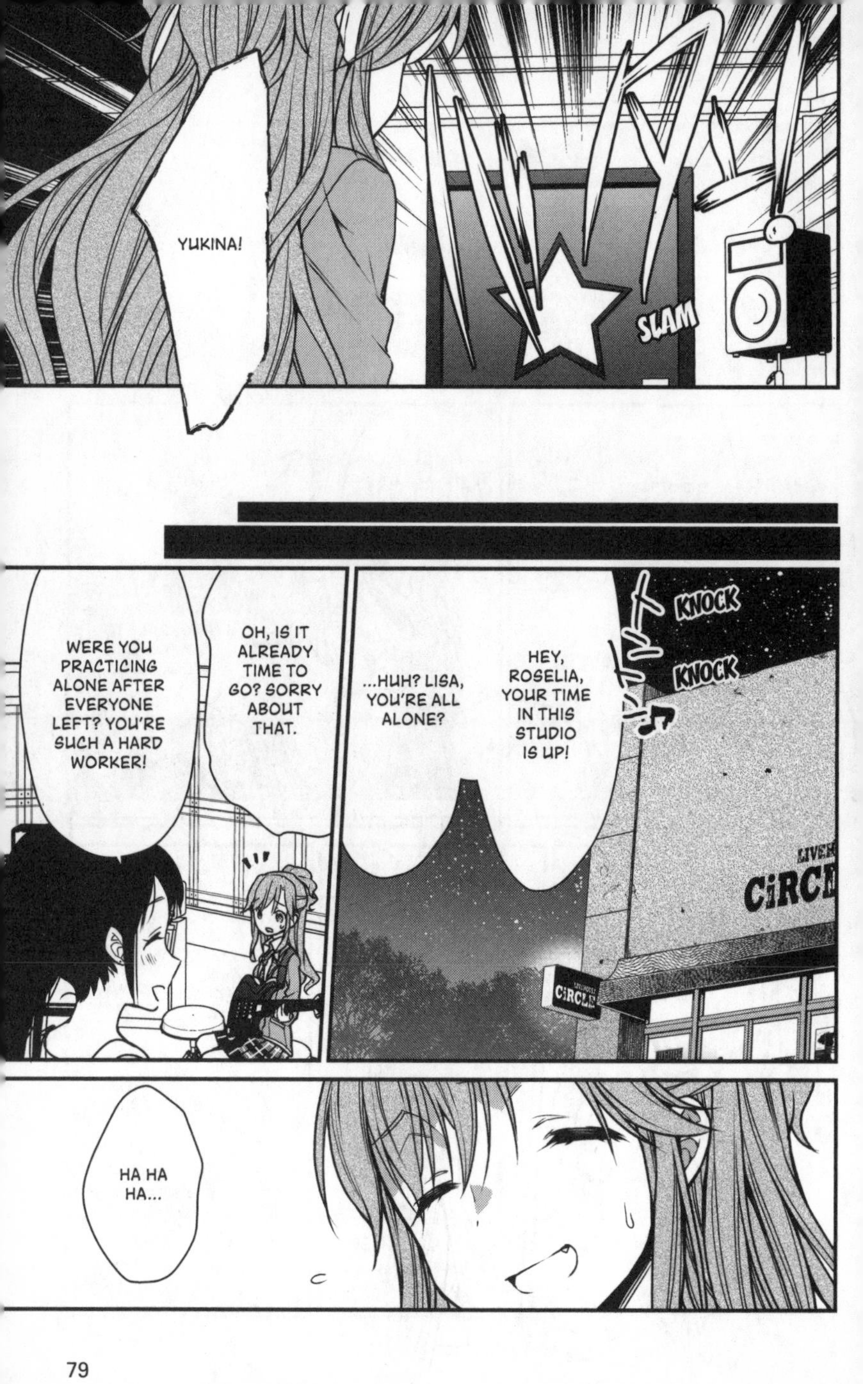
SLAM
YUKINA!
KNOCK
KNOCK
HEY, ROSELIA, YOUR TIME IN THIS STUDIO IS UP!
...HUH? LISA, YOU'RE ALL ALONE?
CiRCLE
CiRCLE
OH, IS IT ALREADY TIME TO GO? SORRY ABOUT THAT.
WERE YOU PRACTICING ALONE AFTER EVERYONE LEFT? YOU'RE SUCH A HARD WORKER!
HA HA HA...

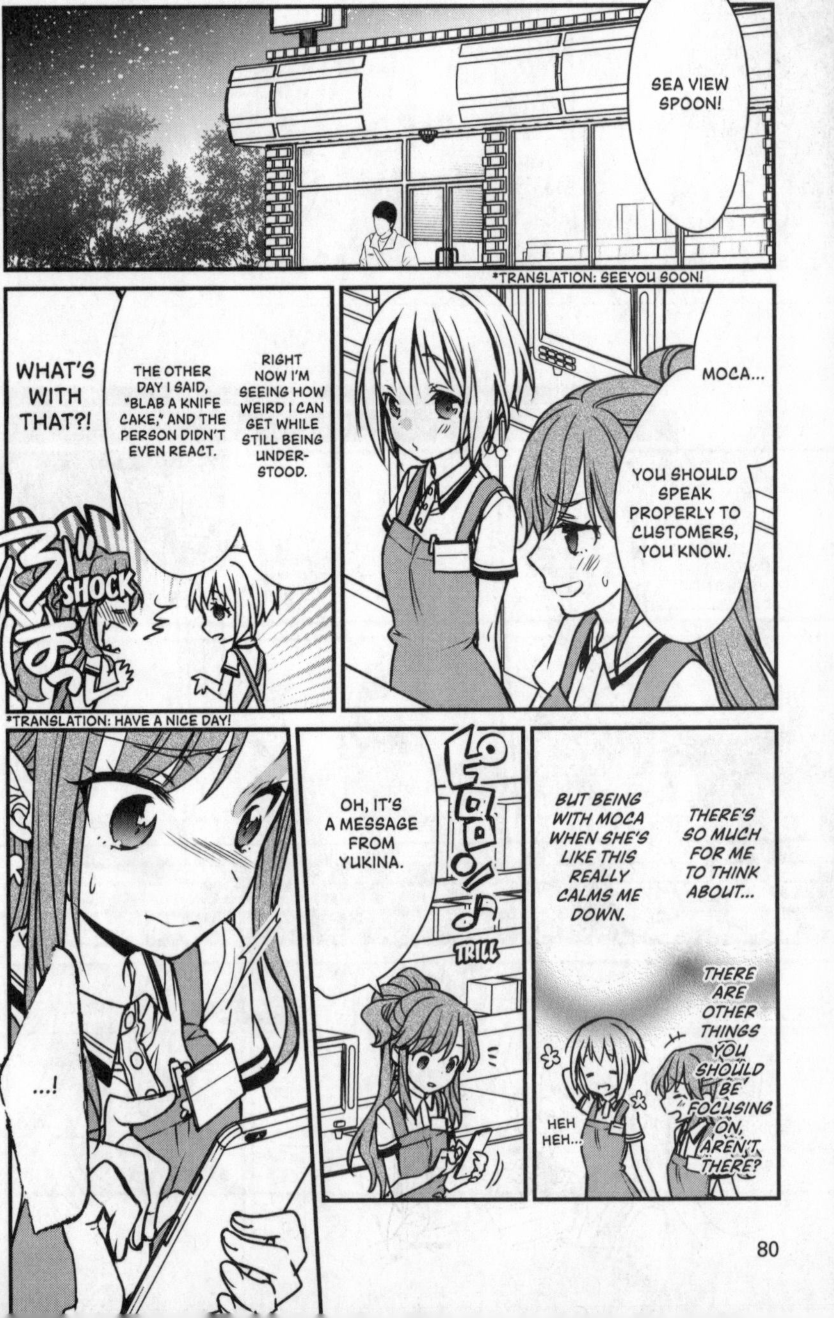
SEA VIEW SPOON!
*TRANSLATION: SEEYOU SOON!
MOCA...
YOU SHOULD SPEAK PROPERLY TO CUSTOMERS, YOU KNOW.
RIGHT NOW I'M SEEING HOW WEIRD I CAN GET WHILE STILL BEING UNDER-STOOD.
THE OTHER DAY I SAID, "BLAB A KNIFE CAKE," AND THE PERSON DIDN'T EVEN REACT.
WHAT'S WITH THAT?!
SHOCK
*TRANSLATION: HAVE A NICE DAY!
THERE'S SO MUCH FOR ME TO THINK ABOUT...
BUT BEING WITH MOCA WHEN SHE'S LIKE THIS REALLY CALMS ME DOWN.
THERE ARE OTHER THINGS YOU SHOULD BE FOCUSING ON, AREN'T THERE?
HEH HEH...
TRILL
OH, IT'S A MESSAGE FROM YUKINA.
...!

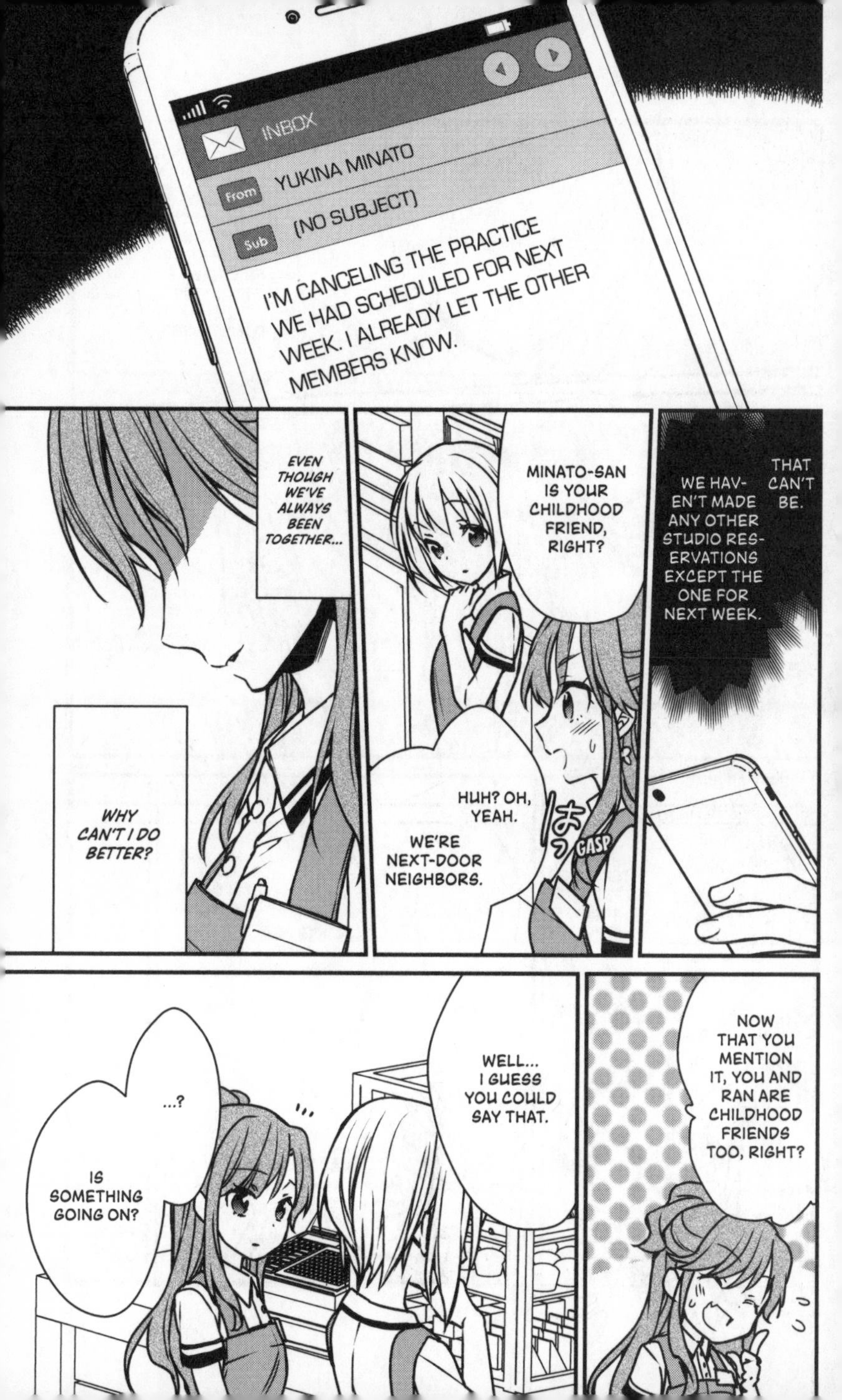
INBOX
From YUKINA MINATO
Sub (NO SUBJECT)
I'M CANCELING THE PRACTICE WE HAD SCHEDULED FOR NEXT WEEK. I ALREADY LET THE OTHER MEMBERS KNOW.
THAT CAN'T BE.
WE HAVEN'T MADE ANY OTHER STUDIO RESERVATIONS EXCEPT THE ONE FOR NEXT WEEK.
MINATO-SAN IS YOUR CHILDHOOD FRIEND, RIGHT?
はっ GASP
HUH? OH, YEAH.
WE'RE NEXT-DOOR NEIGHBORS.
EVEN THOUGH WE'VE ALWAYS BEEN TOGETHER...
WHY CAN'T I DO BETTER?
NOW THAT YOU MENTION IT, YOU AND RAN ARE CHILDHOOD FRIENDS TOO, RIGHT?
WELL... I GUESS YOU COULD SAY THAT.
...?
IS SOMETHING GOING ON?

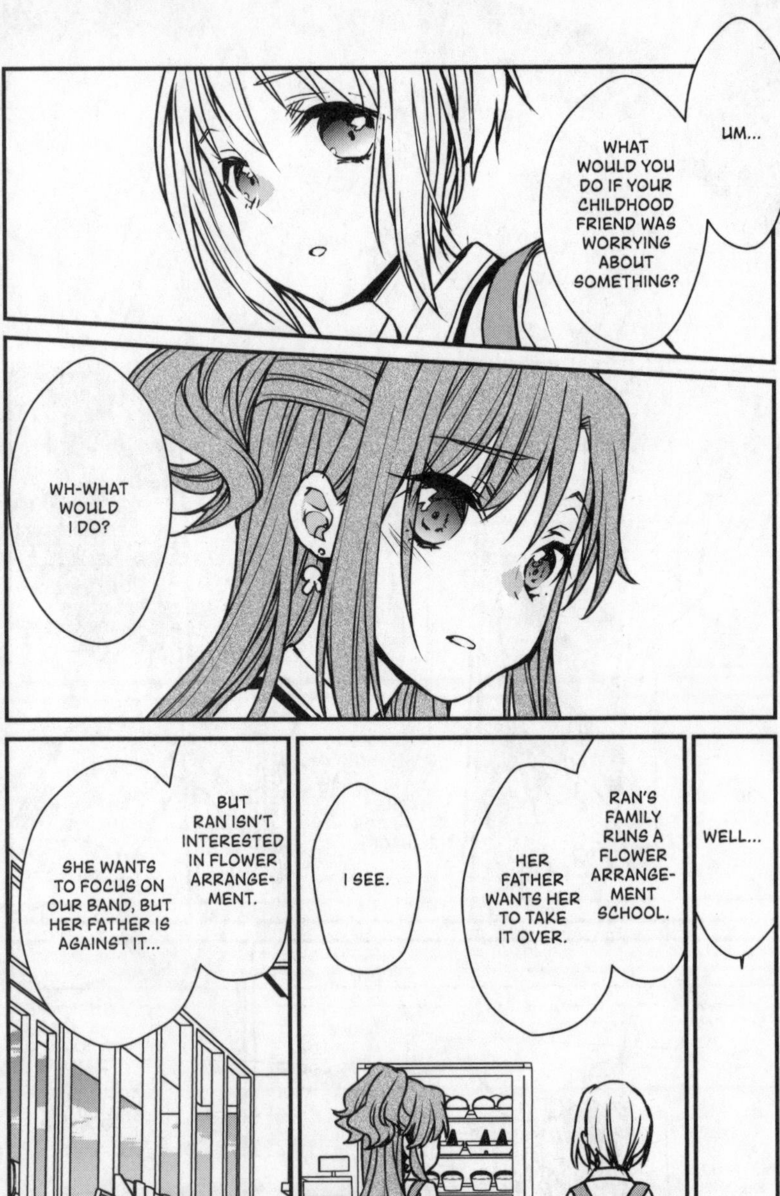
UM...
WHAT WOULD YOU DO IF YOUR CHILDHOOD FRIEND WAS WORRYING ABOUT SOMETHING?
WH-WHAT WOULD I DO?
WELL...
RAN'S FAMILY RUNS A FLOWER ARRANGE-MENT SCHOOL.
HER FATHER WANTS HER TO TAKE IT OVER.
I SEE.
BUT RAN ISN'T INTERESTED IN FLOWER ARRANGE-MENT.
SHE WANTS TO FOCUS ON OUR BAND, BUT HER FATHER IS AGAINST IT...

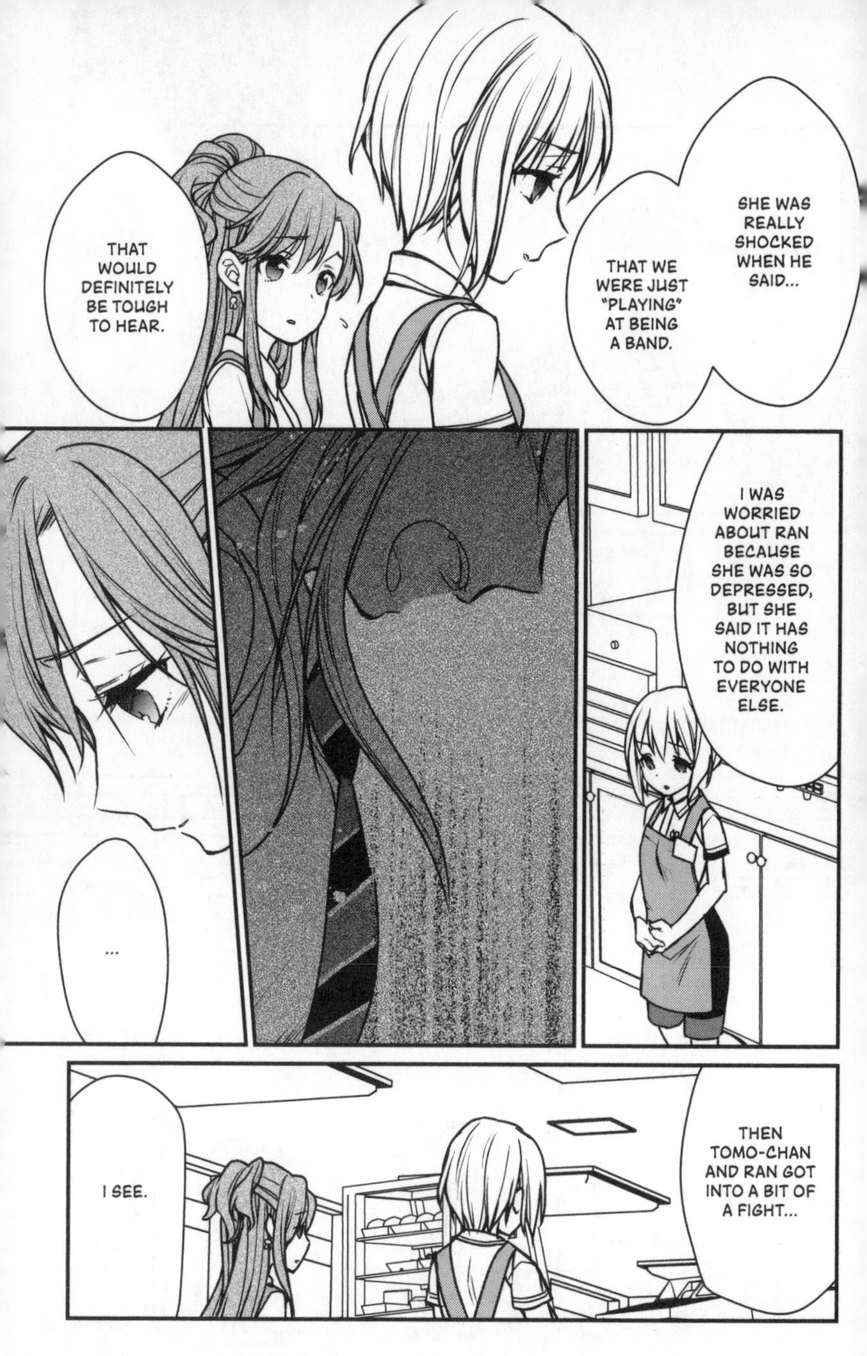
SHE WAS REALLY SHOCKED WHEN HE SAID...
THAT WE WERE JUST "PLAYING" AT BEING A BAND.
THAT WOULD DEFINITELY BE TOUGH TO HEAR.
I WAS WORRIED ABOUT RAN BECAUSE SHE WAS SO DEPRESSED, BUT SHE SAID IT HAS NOTHING TO DO WITH EVERYONE ELSE.
...
THEN TOMO-CHAN AND RAN GOT INTO A BIT OF A FIGHT...
I SEE.

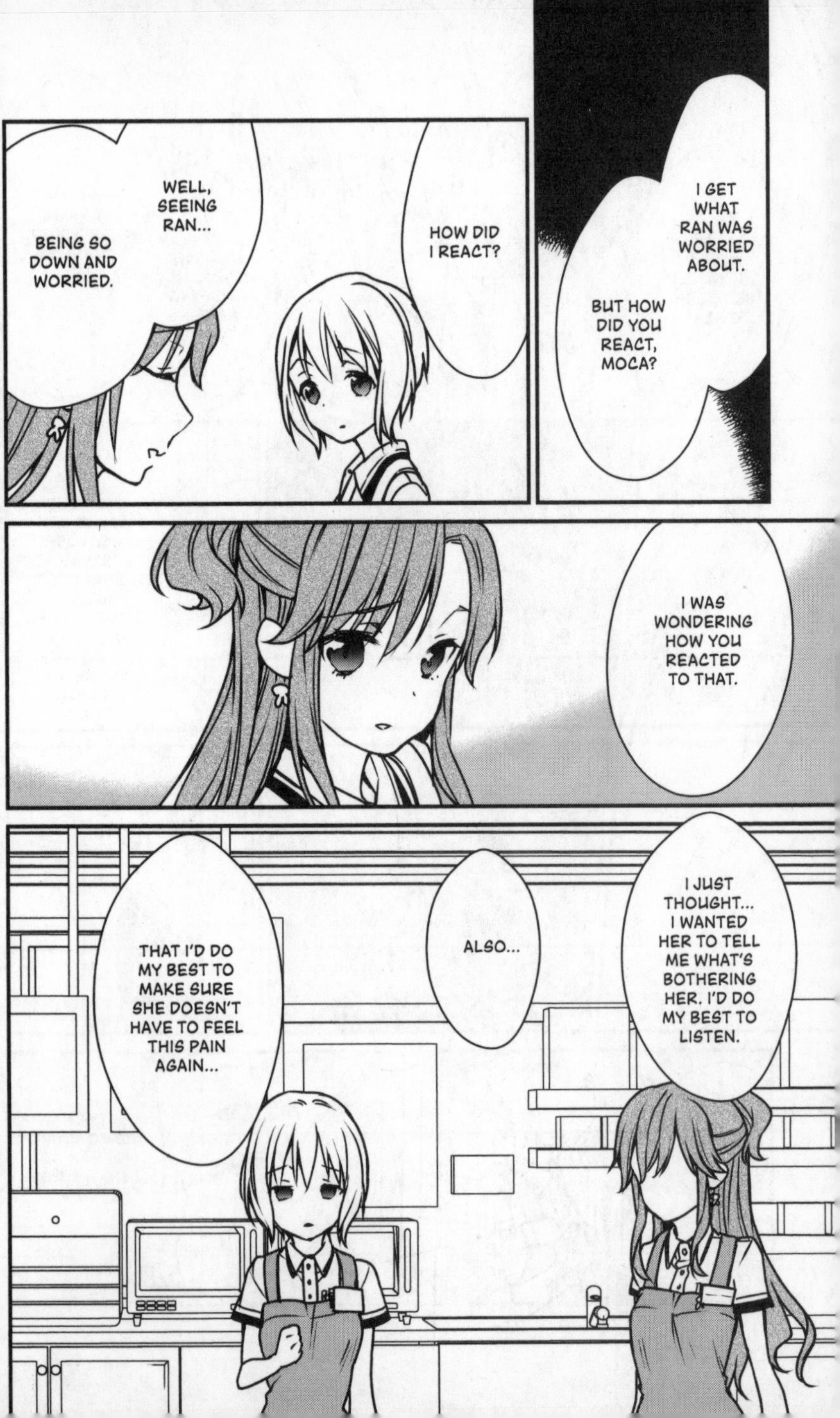
I GET WHAT RAN WAS WORRIED ABOUT.
BUT HOW DID YOU REACT, MOCA?
HOW DID I REACT?
WELL, SEEING RAN...
BEING SO DOWN AND WORRIED.
I WAS WONDERING HOW YOU REACTED TO THAT.
I JUST THOUGHT... I WANTED HER TO TELL ME WHAT'S BOTHERING HER. I'D DO MY BEST TO LISTEN.
ALSO...
THAT I'D DO MY BEST TO MAKE SURE SHE DOESN'T HAVE TO FEEL THIS PAIN AGAIN...

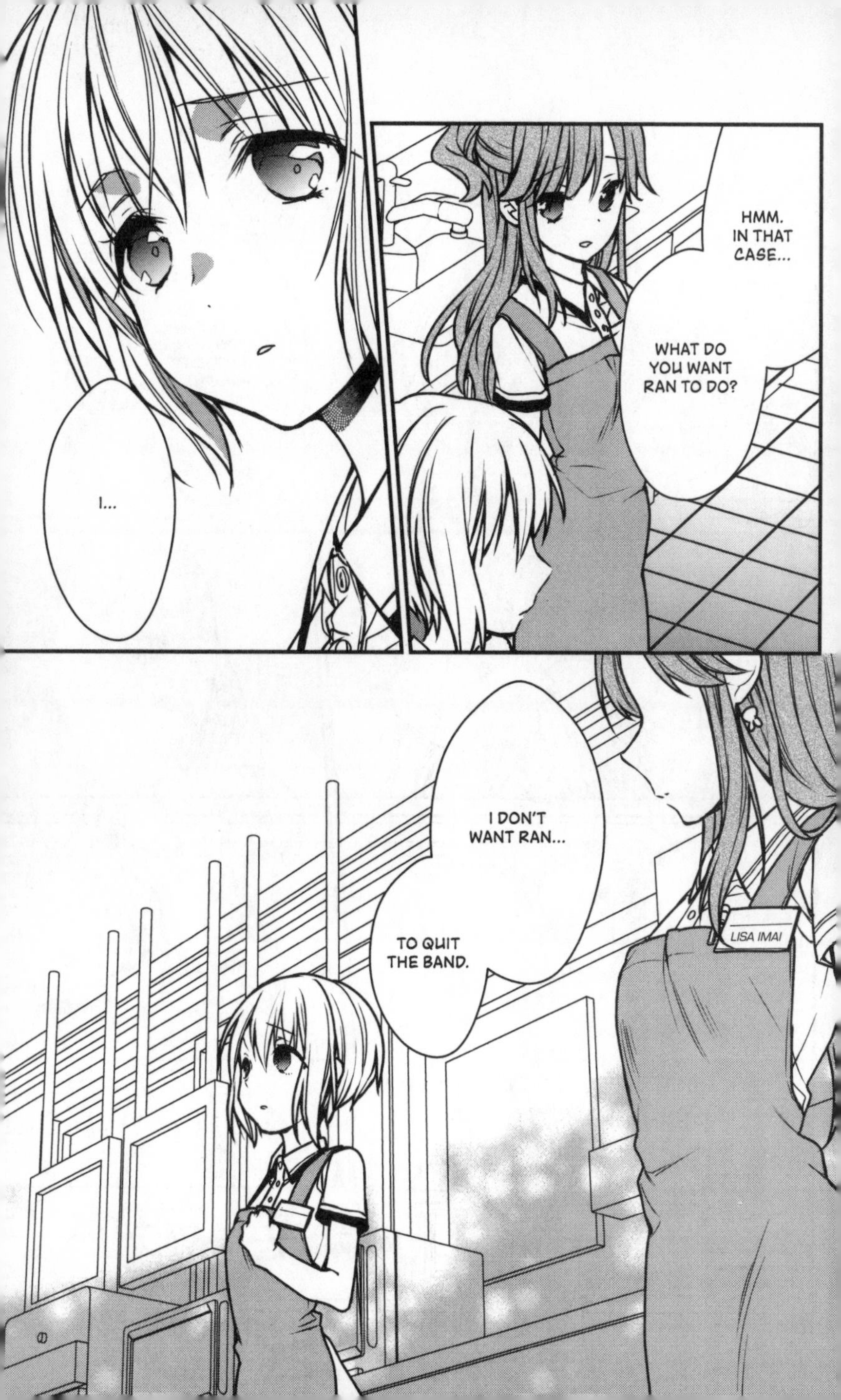
HMM. IN THAT CASE...
WHAT DO YOU WANT RAN TO DO?
I...
I DON'T WANT RAN...
TO QUIT THE BAND.
LISA IMAI

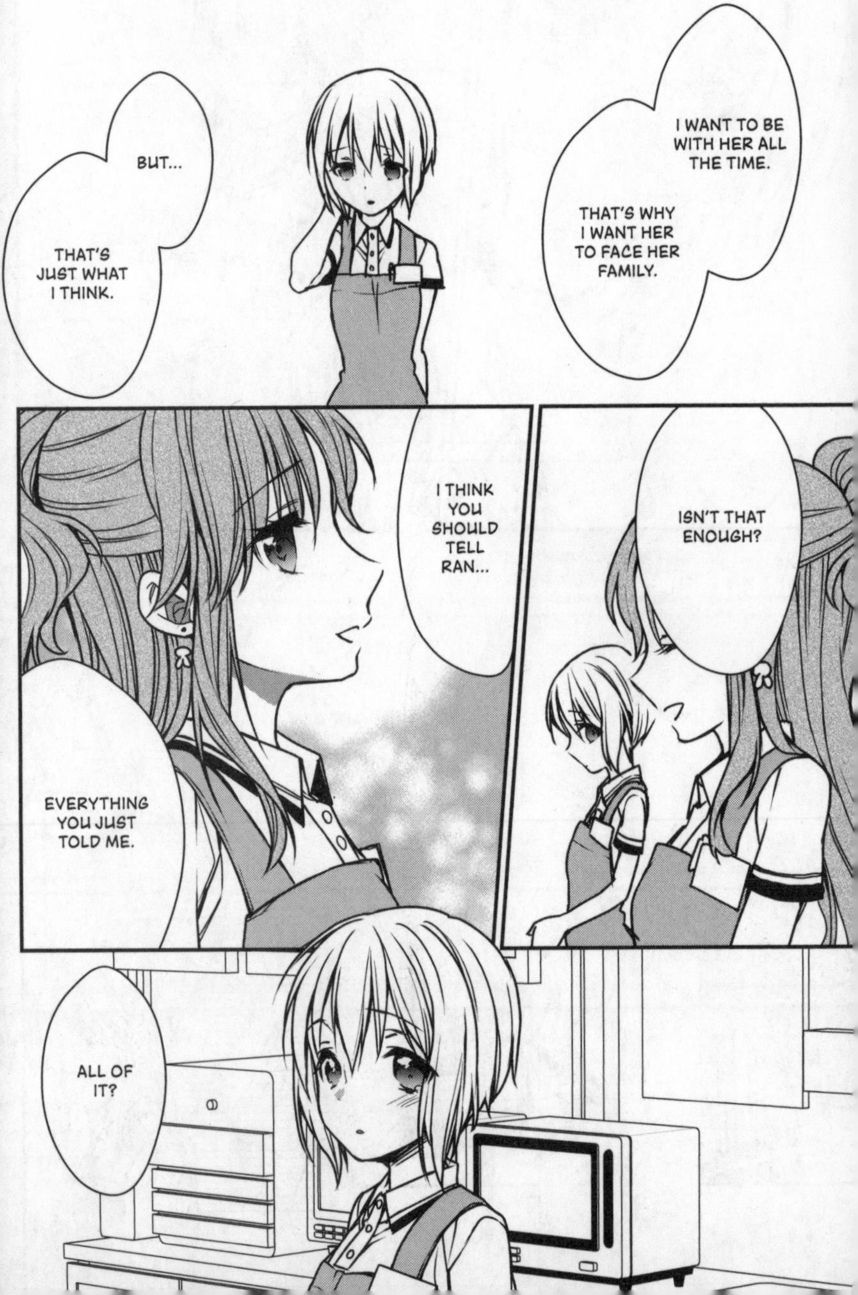
I WANT TO BE WITH HER ALL THE TIME.
THAT'S WHY I WANT HER TO FACE HER FAMILY.
BUT...
THAT'S JUST WHAT I THINK.
ISN'T THAT ENOUGH?
I THINK YOU SHOULD TELL RAN...
EVERYTHING YOU JUST TOLD ME.
ALL OF IT?

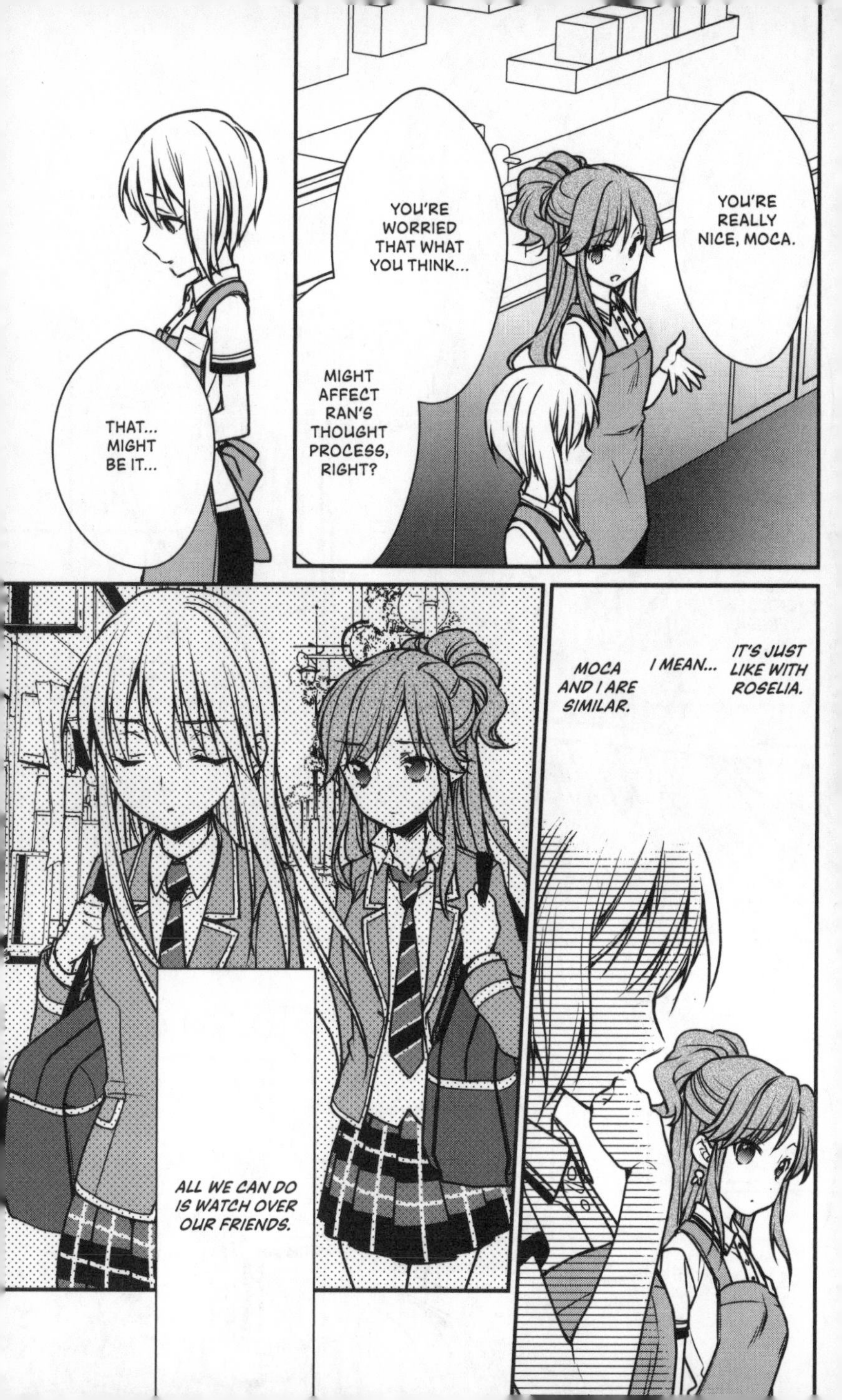
YOU'RE REALLY NICE, MOCA.
YOU'RE WORRIED THAT WHAT YOU THINK...
MIGHT AFFECT RAN'S THOUGHT PROCESS, RIGHT?
THAT... MIGHT BE IT...
IT'S JUST LIKE WITH ROSELIA.
I MEAN...
MOCA AND I ARE SIMILAR.
ALL WE CAN DO IS WATCH OVER OUR FRIENDS.

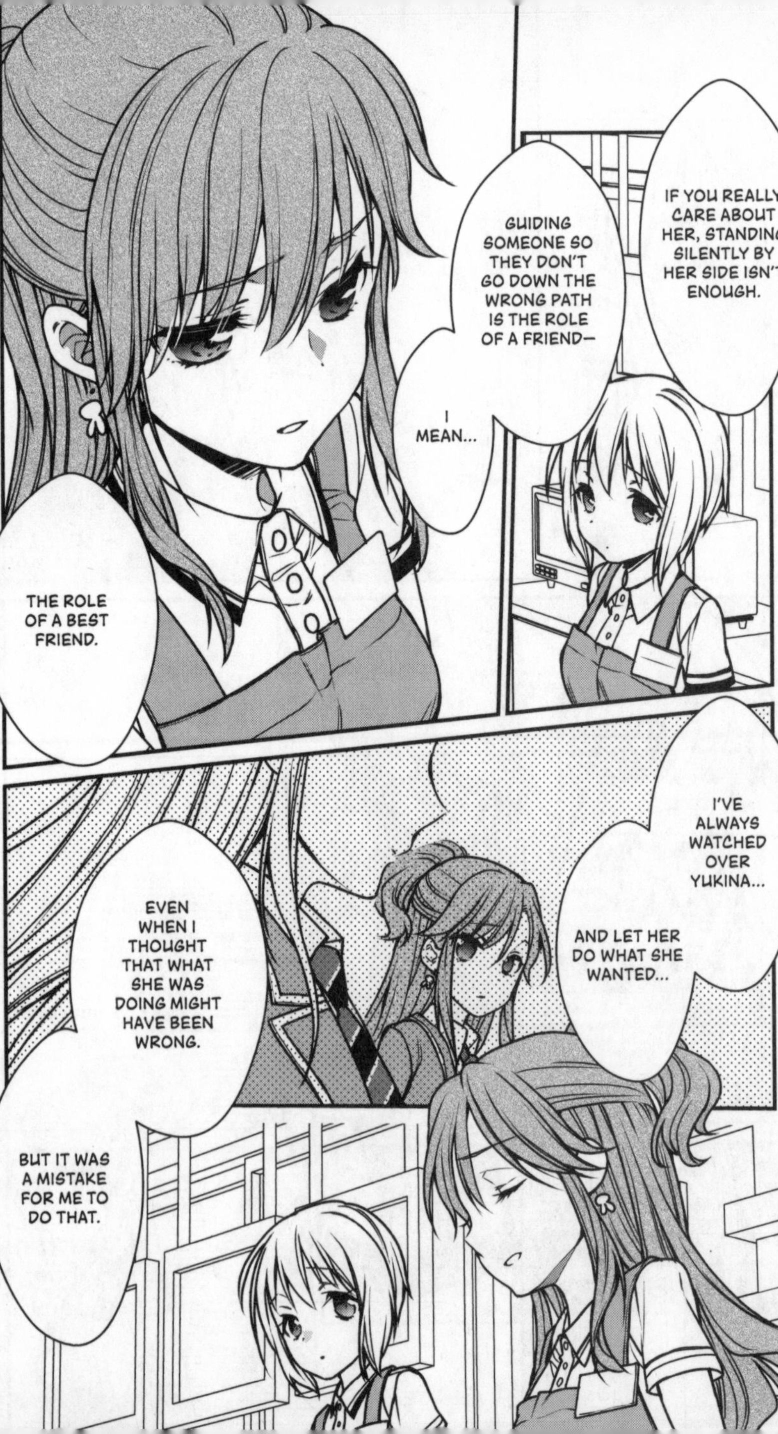
IF YOU REALLY CARE ABOUT HER, STANDING SILENTLY BY HER SIDE ISN'T ENOUGH.
GUIDING SOMEONE SO THEY DON'T GO DOWN THE WRONG PATH IS THE ROLE OF A FRIEND—
I MEAN...
THE ROLE OF A BEST FRIEND.
I'VE ALWAYS WATCHED OVER YUKINA...
AND LET HER DO WHAT SHE WANTED...
EVEN WHEN I THOUGHT THAT WHAT SHE WAS DOING MIGHT HAVE BEEN WRONG.
BUT IT WAS A MISTAKE FOR ME TO DO THAT.

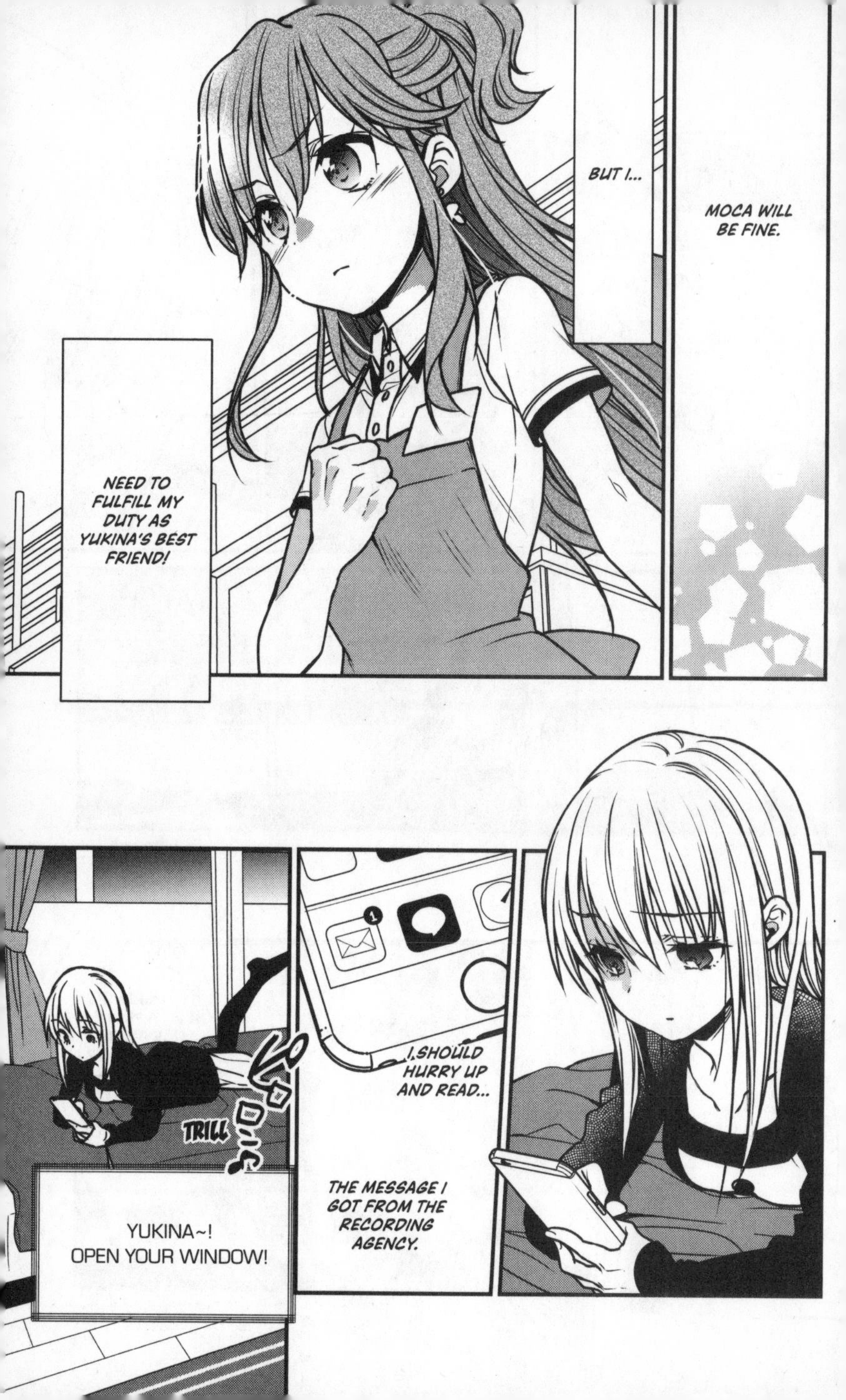

MOCA WILL BE FINE.
BUT I...
NEED TO FULFILL MY DUTY AS YUKINA'S BEST FRIEND!
I SHOULD HURRY UP AND READ...
THE MESSAGE I GOT FROM THE RECORDING AGENCY.
TRILL
YUKINA~! OPEN YOUR WINDOW!

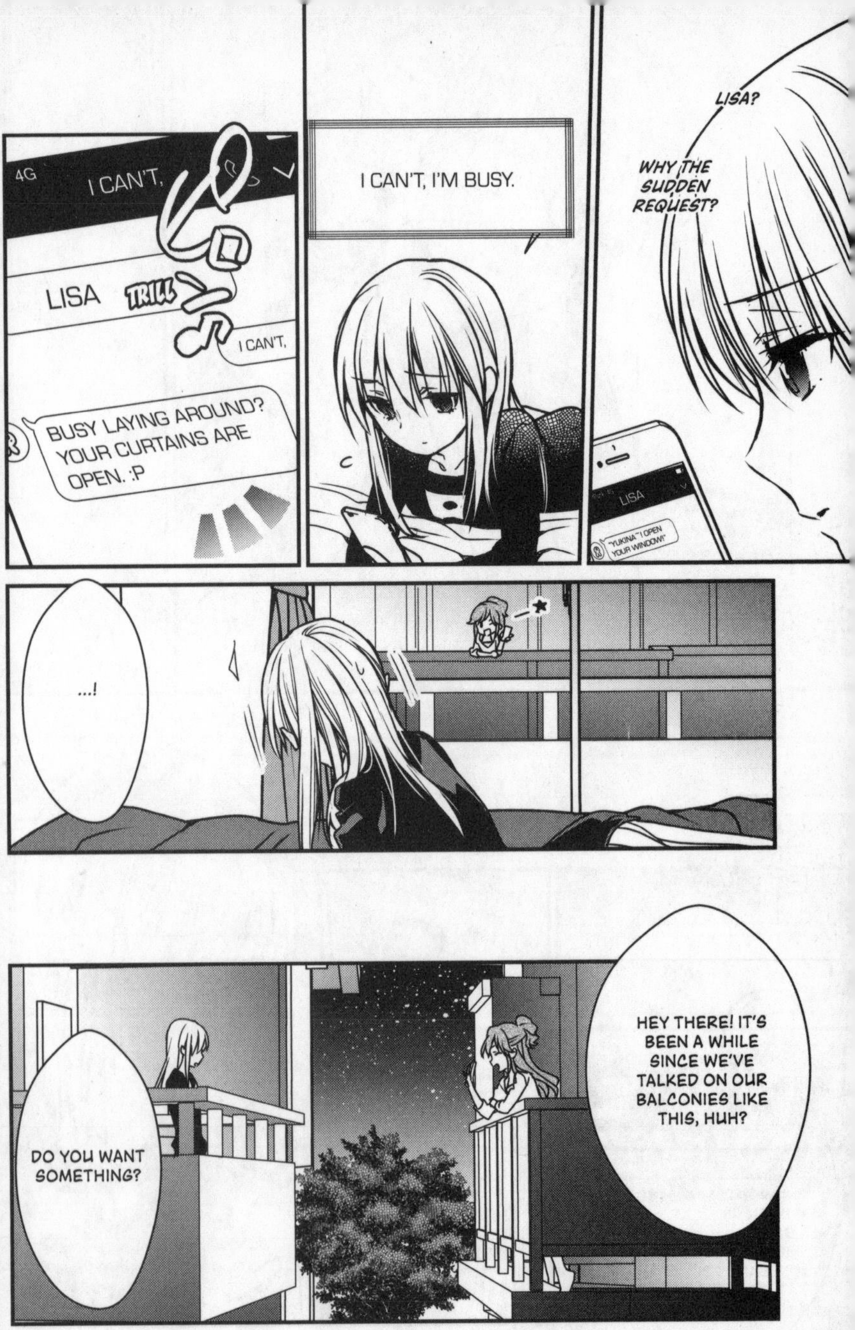
LISA?
WHY THE SUDDEN REQUEST?
LISA
"YUKINA~! OPEN YOUR WINDOW!"
I CAN'T, I'M BUSY.
4G
I CAN'T,
LISA
TRILL
I CAN'T,
BUSY LAYING AROUND? YOUR CURTAINS ARE OPEN. :P
...!
HEY THERE! IT'S BEEN A WHILE SINCE WE'VE TALKED ON OUR BALCONIES LIKE THIS, HUH?
DO YOU WANT SOMETHING?

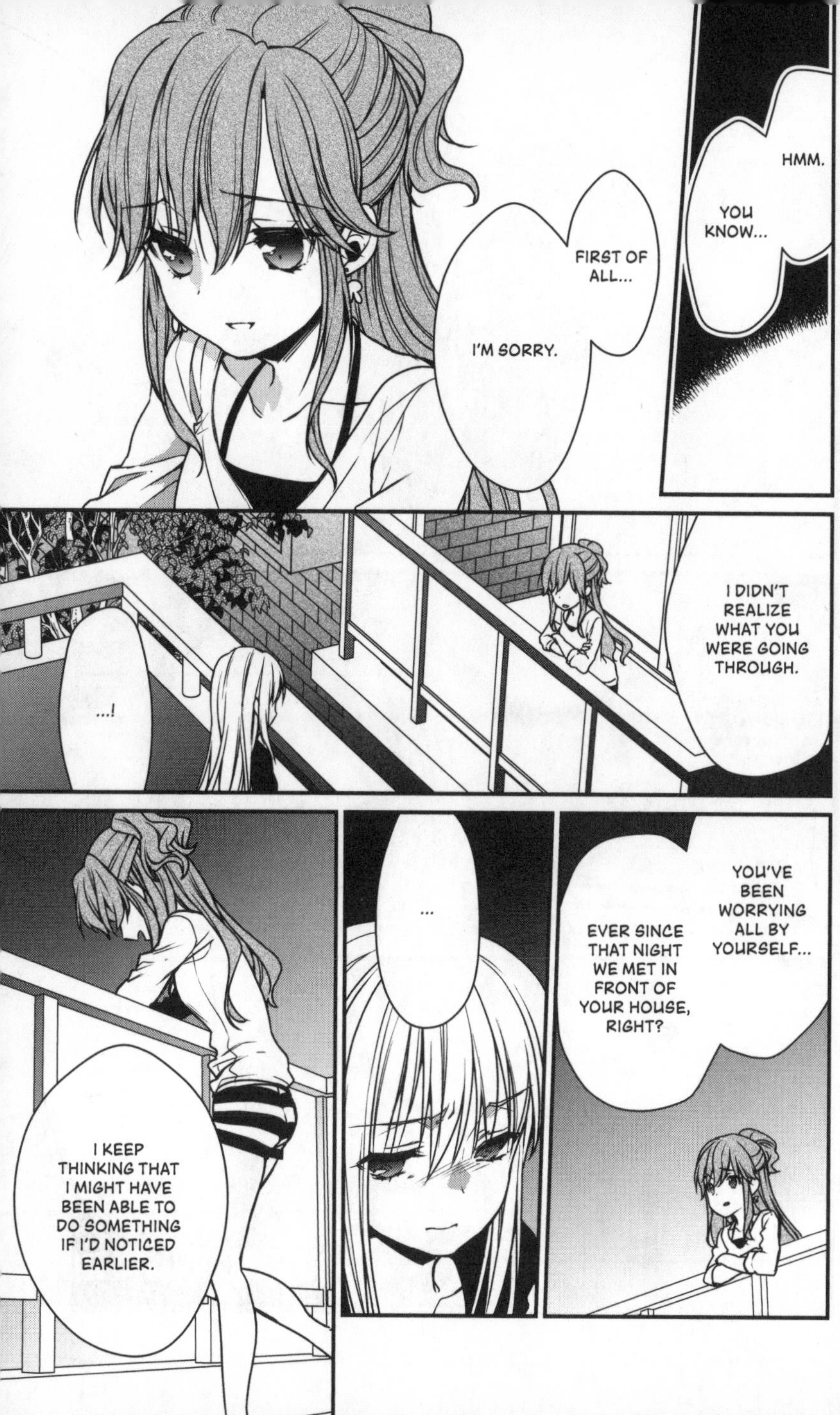
HMM.
YOU KNOW...
FIRST OF ALL...
I'M SORRY.
I DIDN'T REALIZE WHAT YOU WERE GOING THROUGH.
...!
YOU'VE BEEN WORRYING ALL BY YOURSELF...
EVER SINCE THAT NIGHT WE MET IN FRONT OF YOUR HOUSE, RIGHT?
...
I KEEP THINKING THAT I MIGHT HAVE BEEN ABLE TO DO SOMETHING IF I'D NOTICED EARLIER.

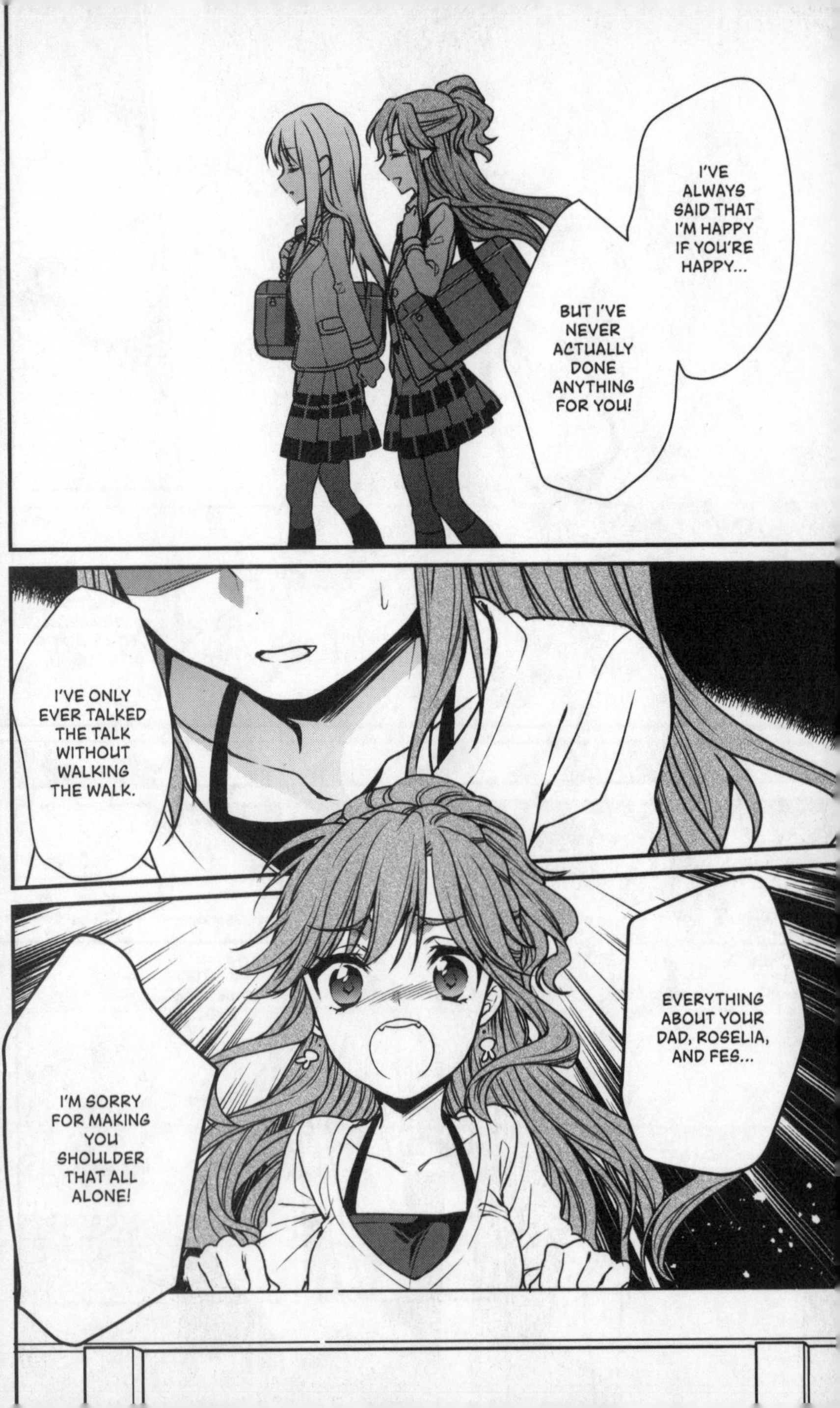
I'VE ALWAYS SAID THAT I'M HAPPY IF YOU'RE HAPPY...
BUT I'VE NEVER ACTUALLY DONE ANYTHING FOR YOU!
I'VE ONLY EVER TALKED THE TALK WITHOUT WALKING THE WALK.
EVERYTHING ABOUT YOUR DAD, ROSELIA, AND FES...
I'M SORRY FOR MAKING YOU SHOULDER THAT ALL ALONE!

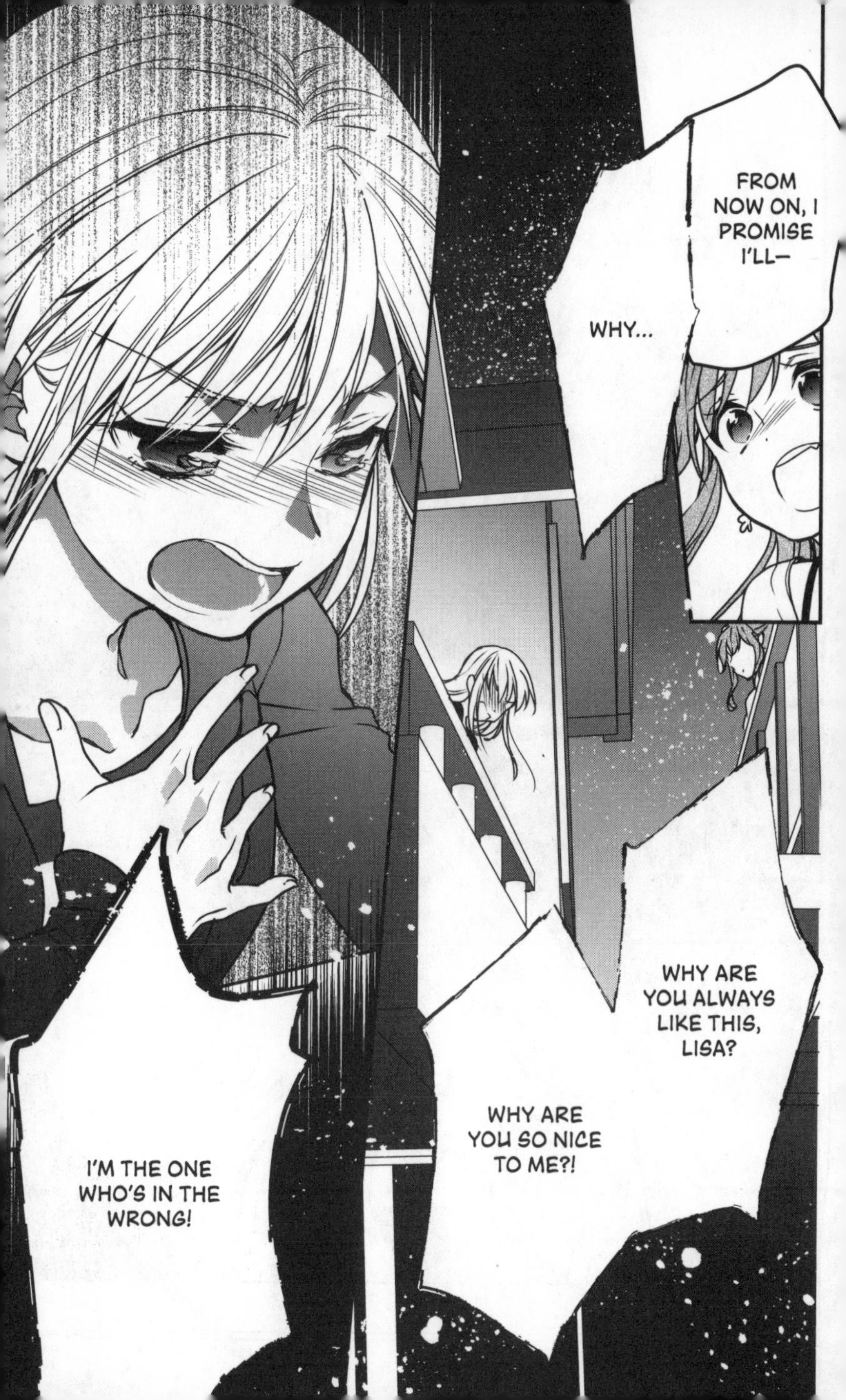
FROM NOW ON, I PROMISE I'LL—
WHY...
WHY ARE YOU ALWAYS LIKE THIS, LISA?
WHY ARE YOU SO NICE TO ME?!
I'M THE ONE WHO'S IN THE WRONG!

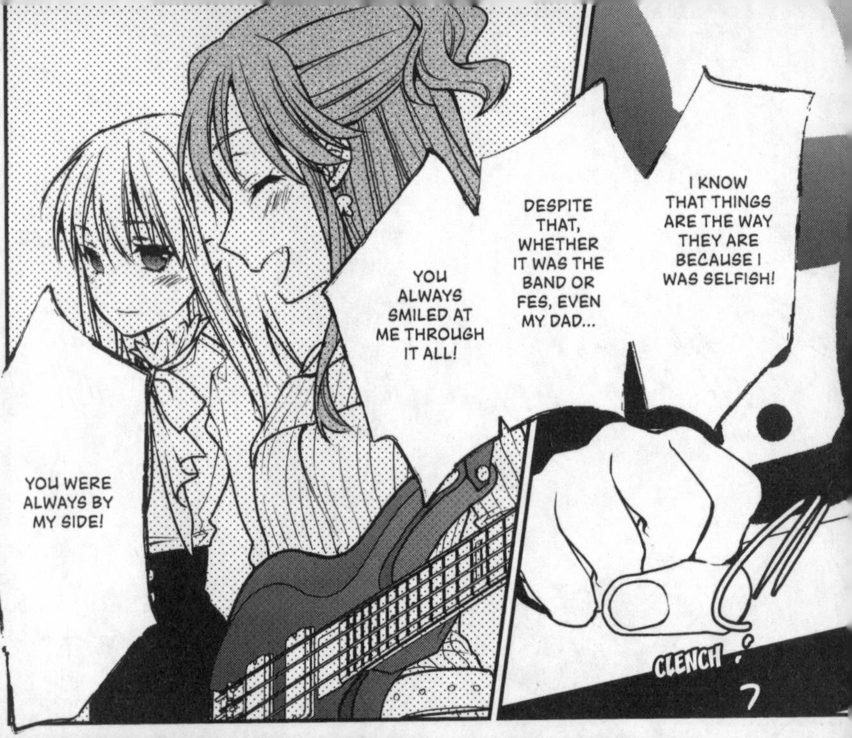
I KNOW THAT THINGS ARE THE WAY THEY ARE BECAUSE I WAS SELFISH!
DESPITE THAT, WHETHER IT WAS THE BAND OR FES, EVEN MY DAD...
YOU ALWAYS SMILED AT ME THROUGH IT ALL!
YOU WERE ALWAYS BY MY SIDE!
CLENCH

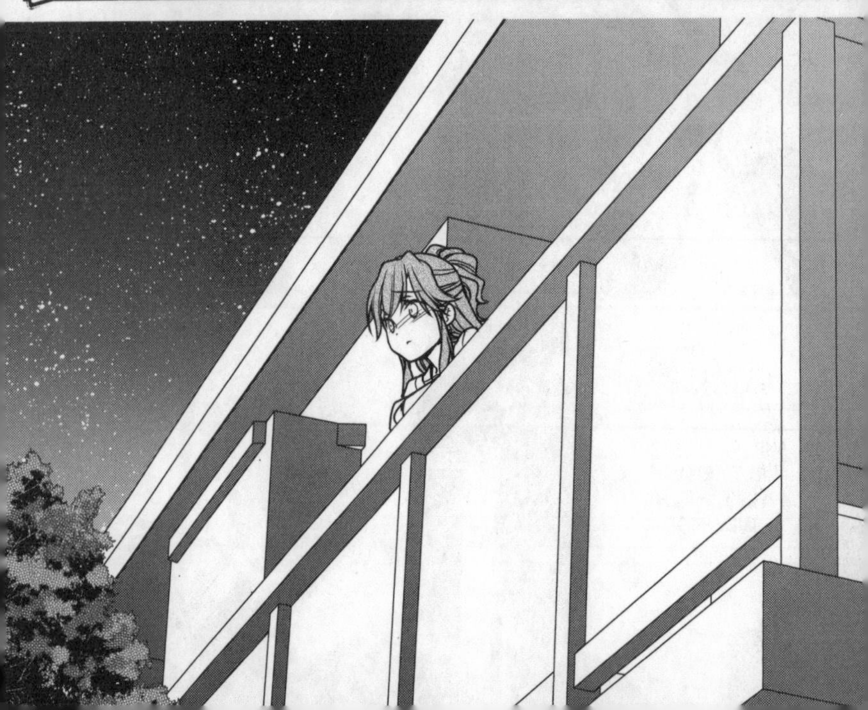

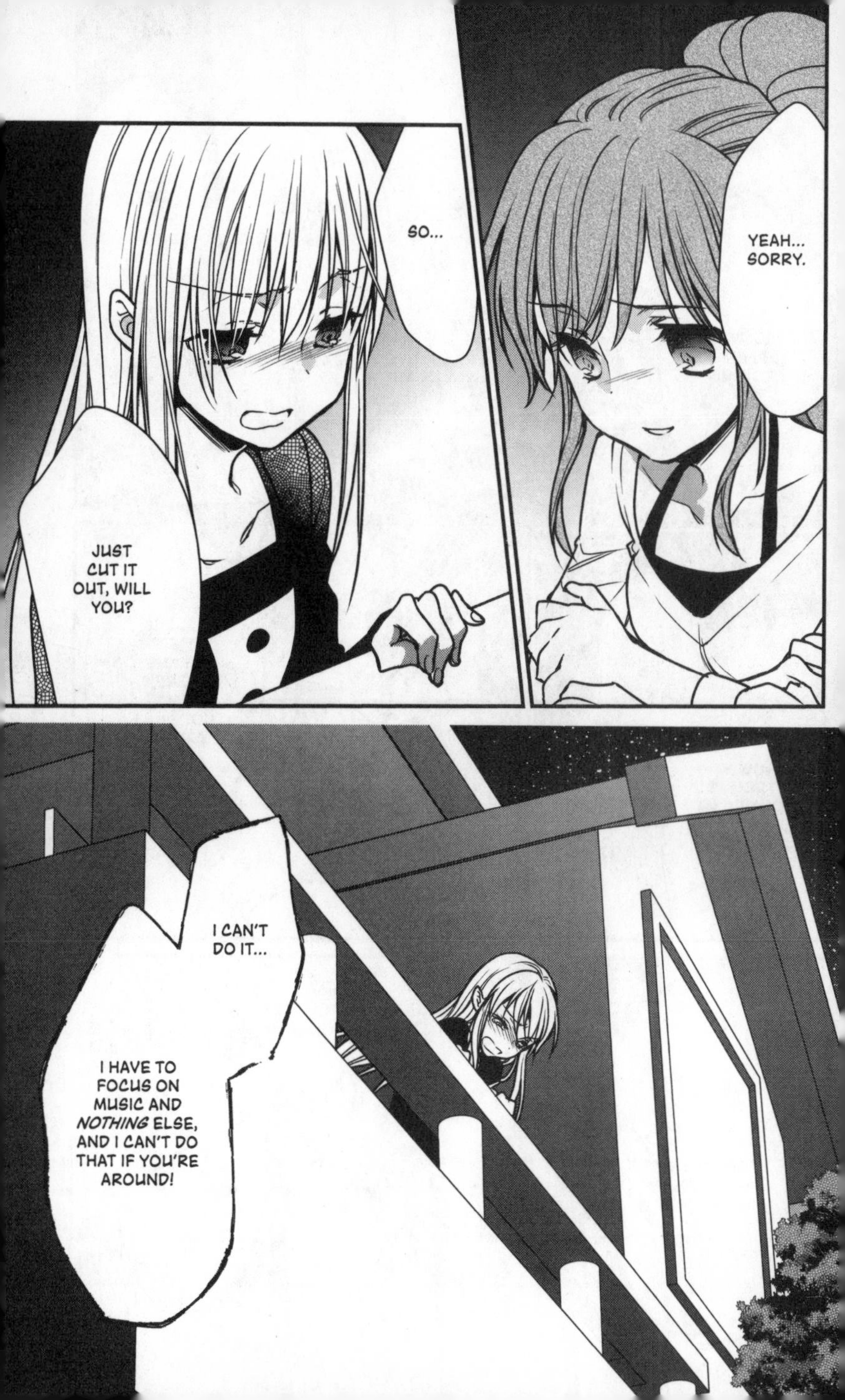
YEAH... SORRY.
SO...
JUST CUT IT OUT, WILL YOU?
I CAN'T DO IT...
I HAVE TO FOCUS ON MUSIC AND *NOTHING* ELSE, AND I CAN'T DO THAT IF YOU'RE AROUND!

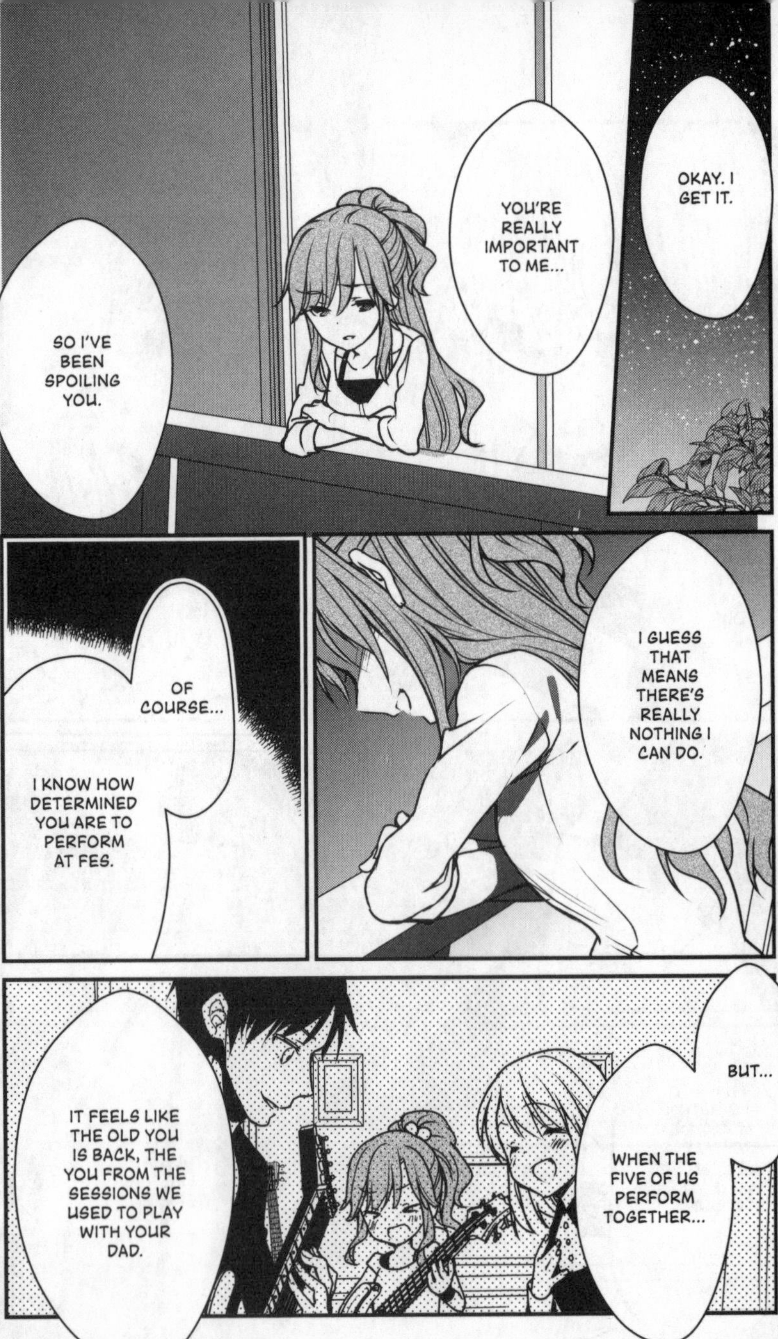
OKAY. I GET IT.
YOU'RE REALLY IMPORTANT TO ME...
SO I'VE BEEN SPOILING YOU.
I GUESS THAT MEANS THERE'S REALLY NOTHING I CAN DO.
OF COURSE...
I KNOW HOW DETERMINED YOU ARE TO PERFORM AT FES.
BUT...
WHEN THE FIVE OF US PERFORM TOGETHER...
IT FEELS LIKE THE OLD YOU IS BACK, THE YOU FROM THE SESSIONS WE USED TO PLAY WITH YOUR DAD.

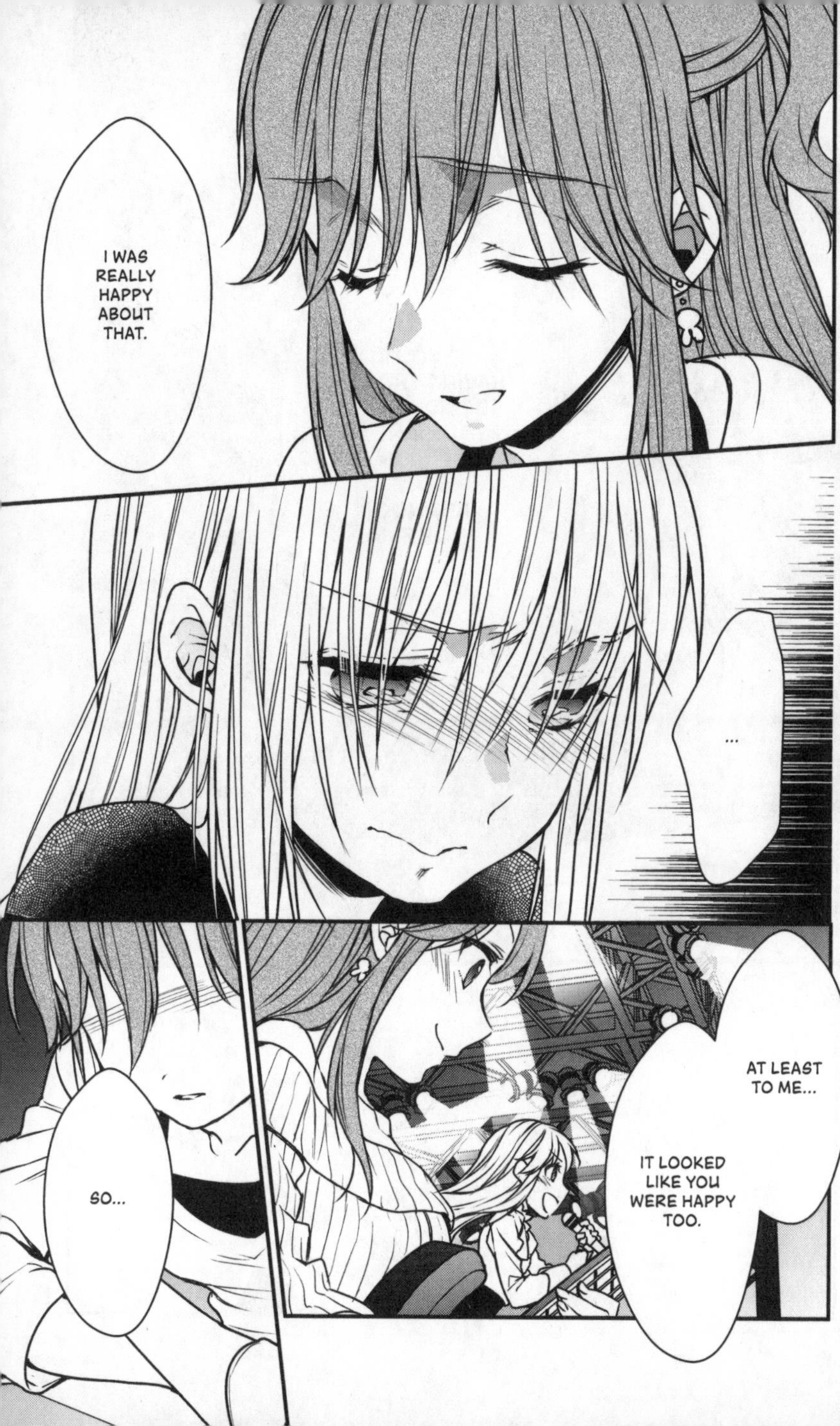
I WAS REALLY HAPPY ABOUT THAT.
...
AT LEAST TO ME...
IT LOOKED LIKE YOU WERE HAPPY TOO.
SO...

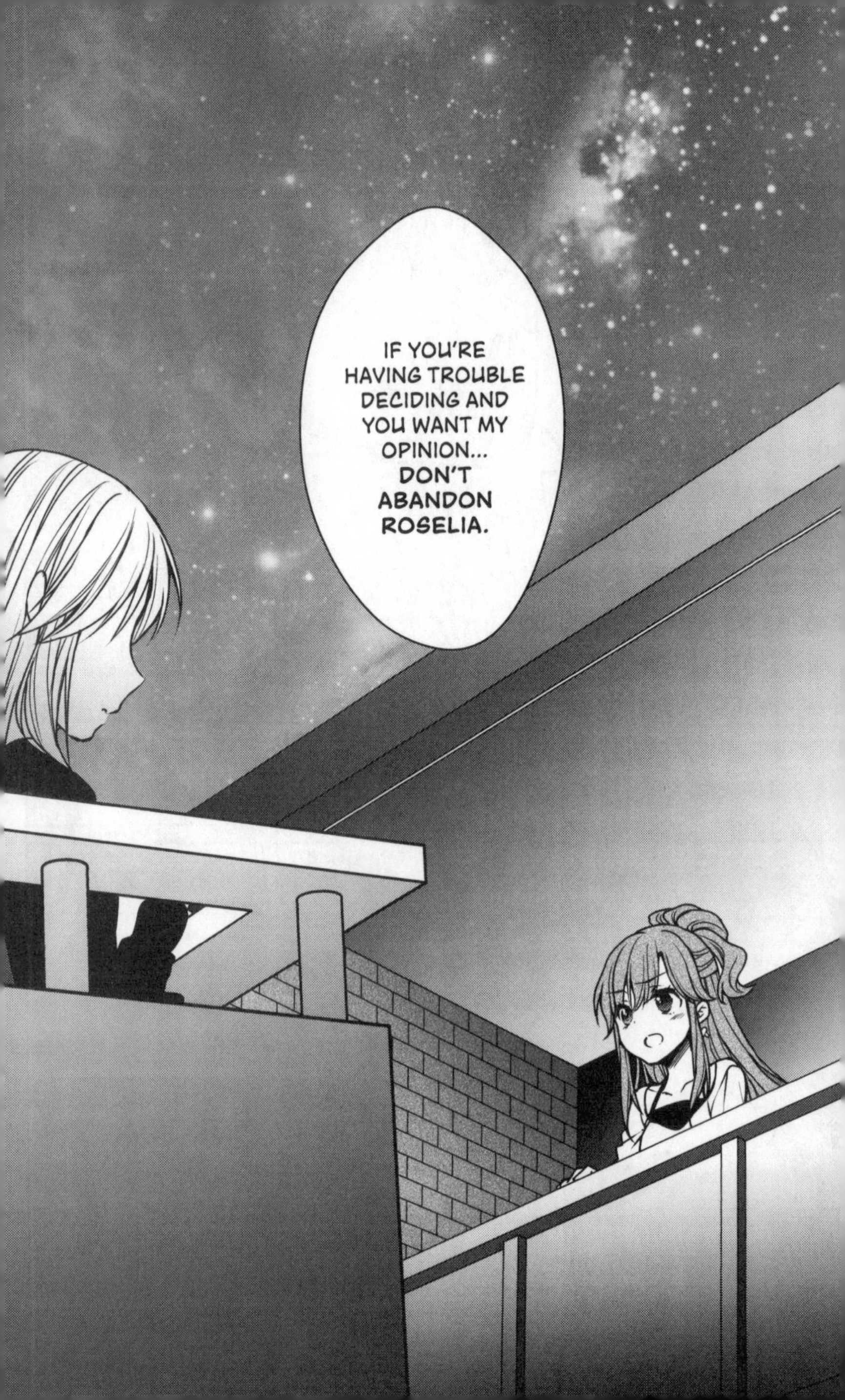
IF YOU'RE HAVING TROUBLE DECIDING AND YOU WANT MY OPINION... DON'T ABANDON ROSELIA.

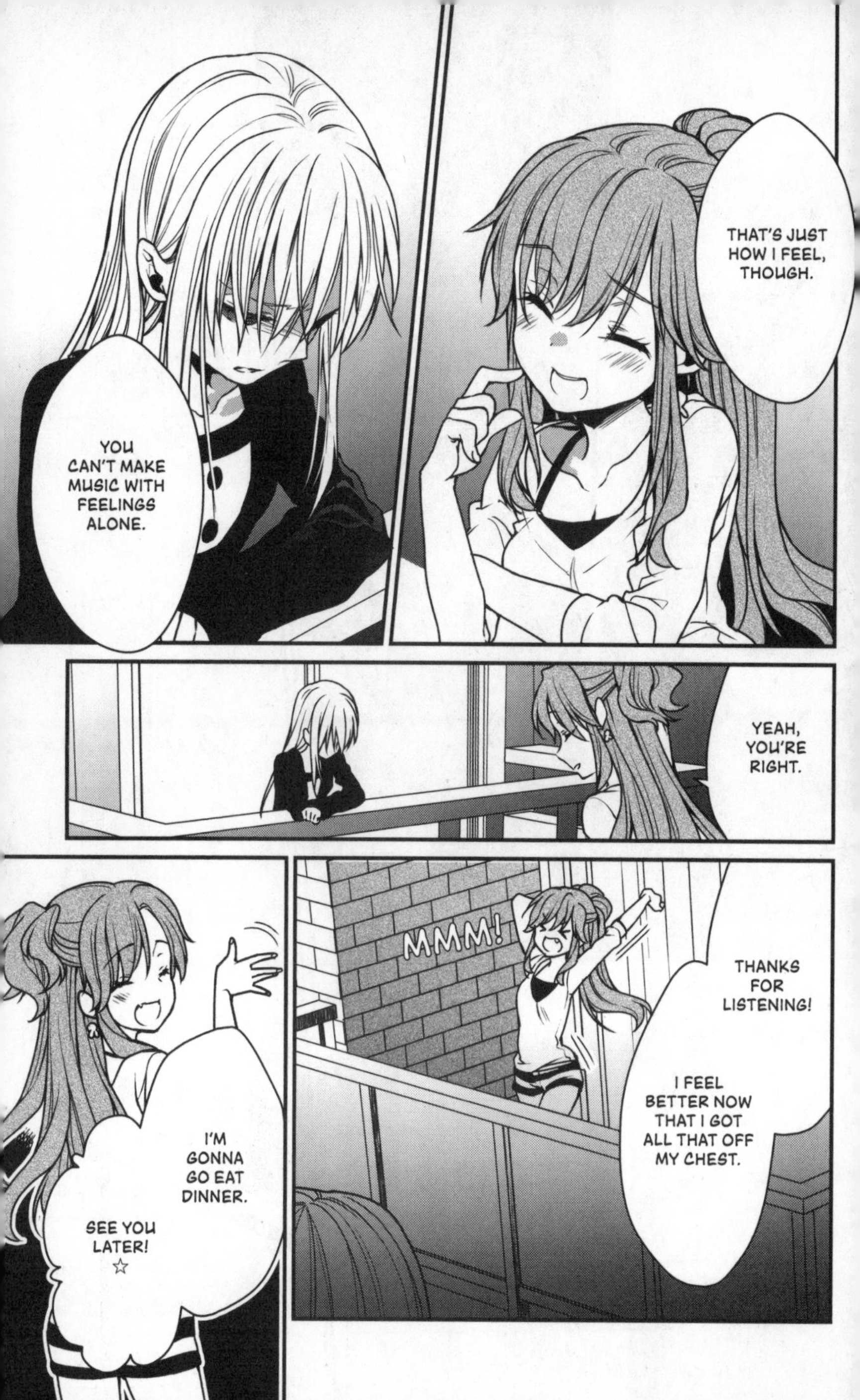
THAT'S JUST HOW I FEEL, THOUGH.
YOU CAN'T MAKE MUSIC WITH FEELINGS ALONE.
YEAH, YOU'RE RIGHT.
MMM!
THANKS FOR LISTENING!
I FEEL BETTER NOW THAT I GOT ALL THAT OFF MY CHEST.
I'M GONNA GO EAT DINNER.
SEE YOU LATER! ☆

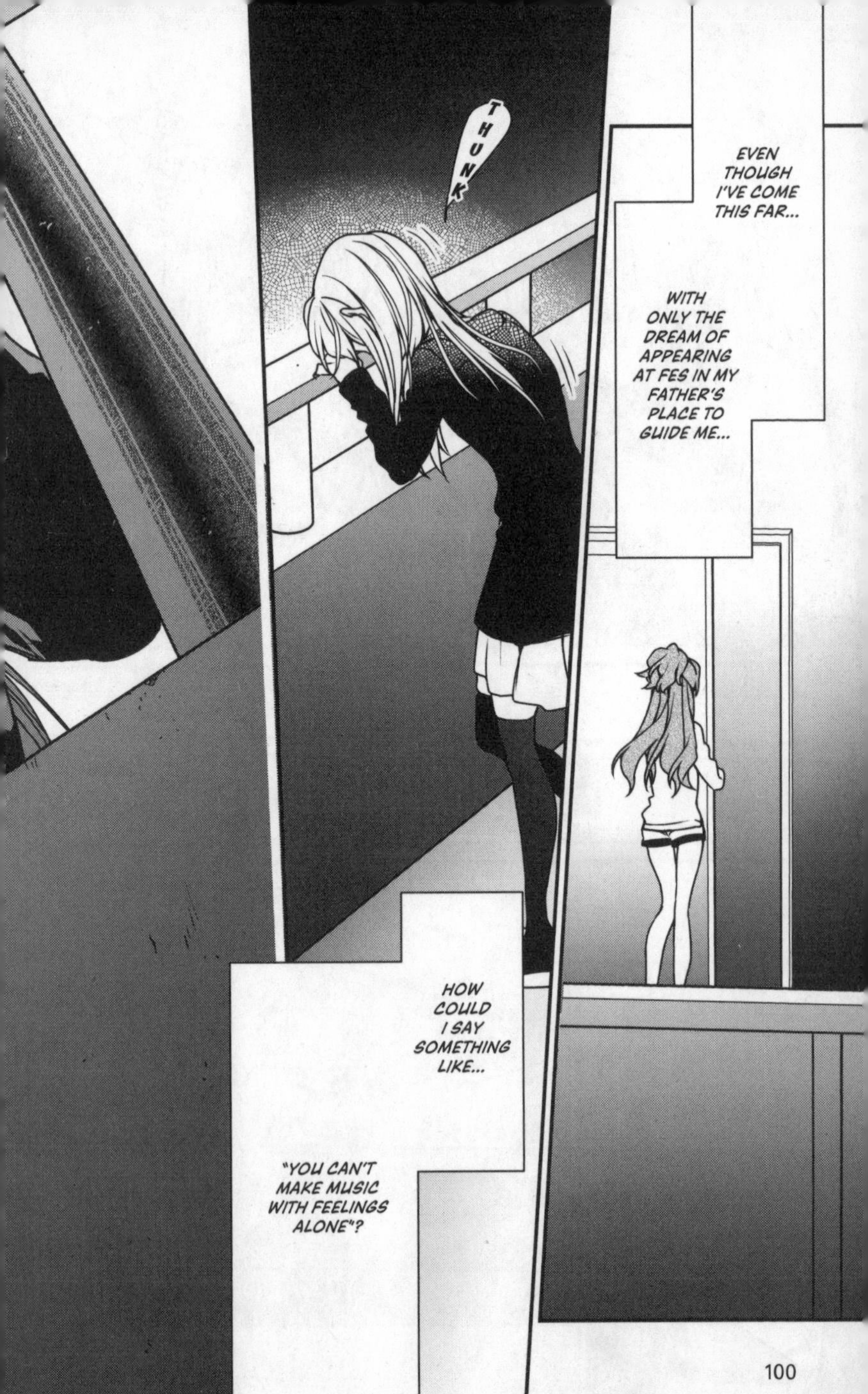
EVEN THOUGH I'VE COME THIS FAR...
WITH ONLY THE DREAM OF APPEARING AT FES IN MY FATHER'S PLACE TO GUIDE ME...
THUNK
HOW COULD I SAY SOMETHING LIKE...
"YOU CAN'T MAKE MUSIC WITH FEELINGS ALONE"?

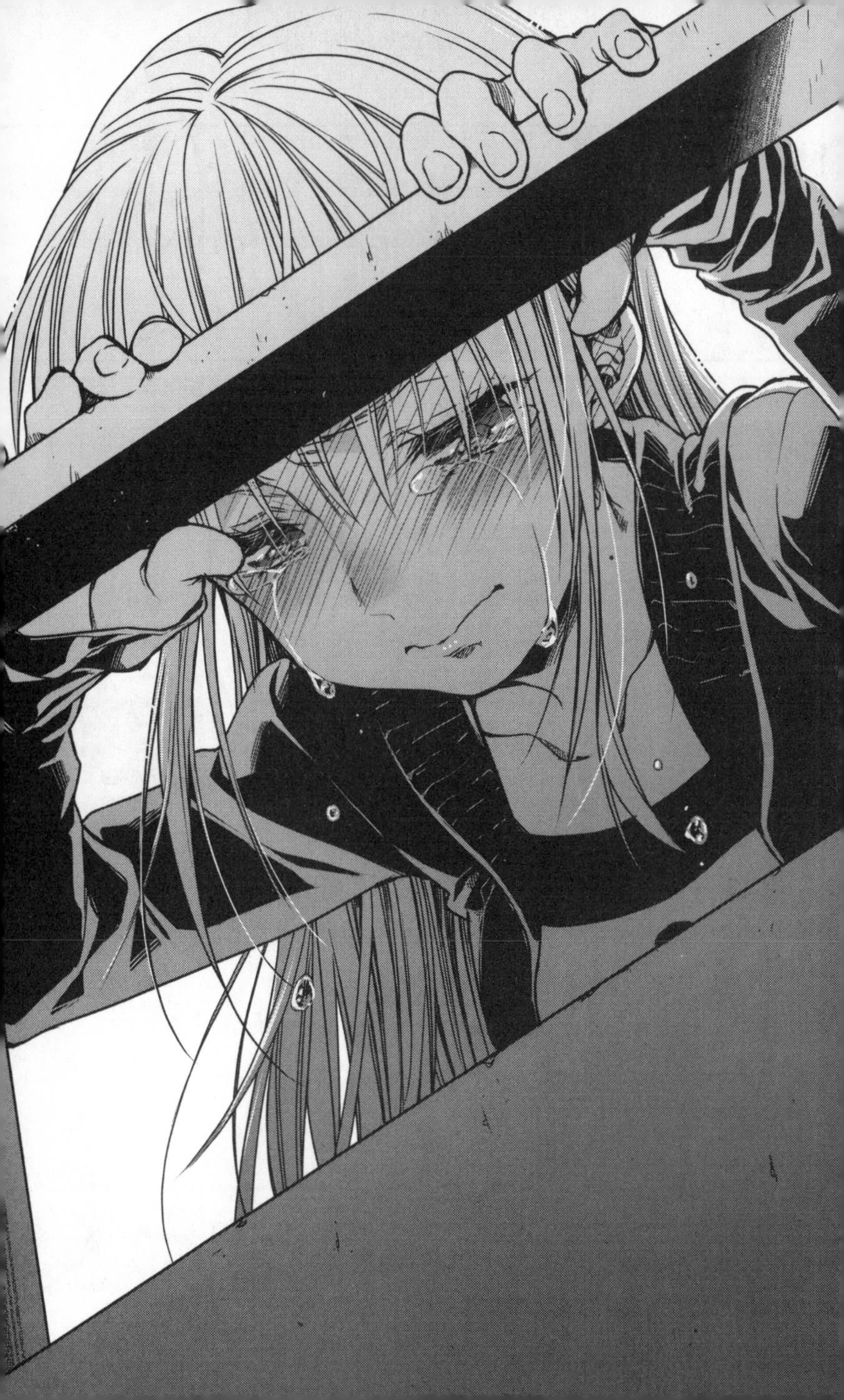

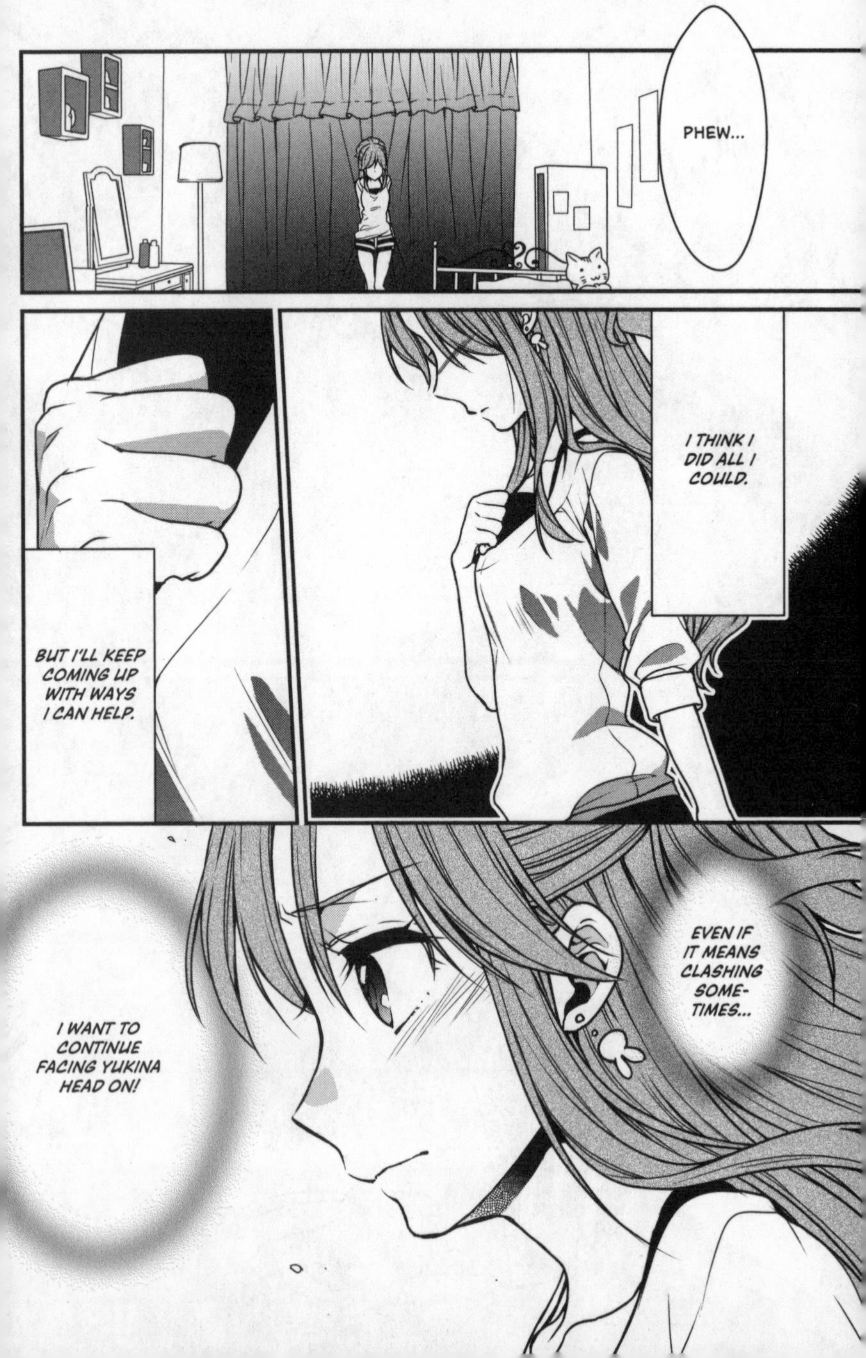
PHEW...
I THINK I DID ALL I COULD.
BUT I'LL KEEP COMING UP WITH WAYS I CAN HELP.
EVEN IF IT MEANS CLASHING SOME-TIMES...
I WANT TO CONTINUE FACING YUKINA HEAD ON!

Chapter 9
The Five of Us, Together Again

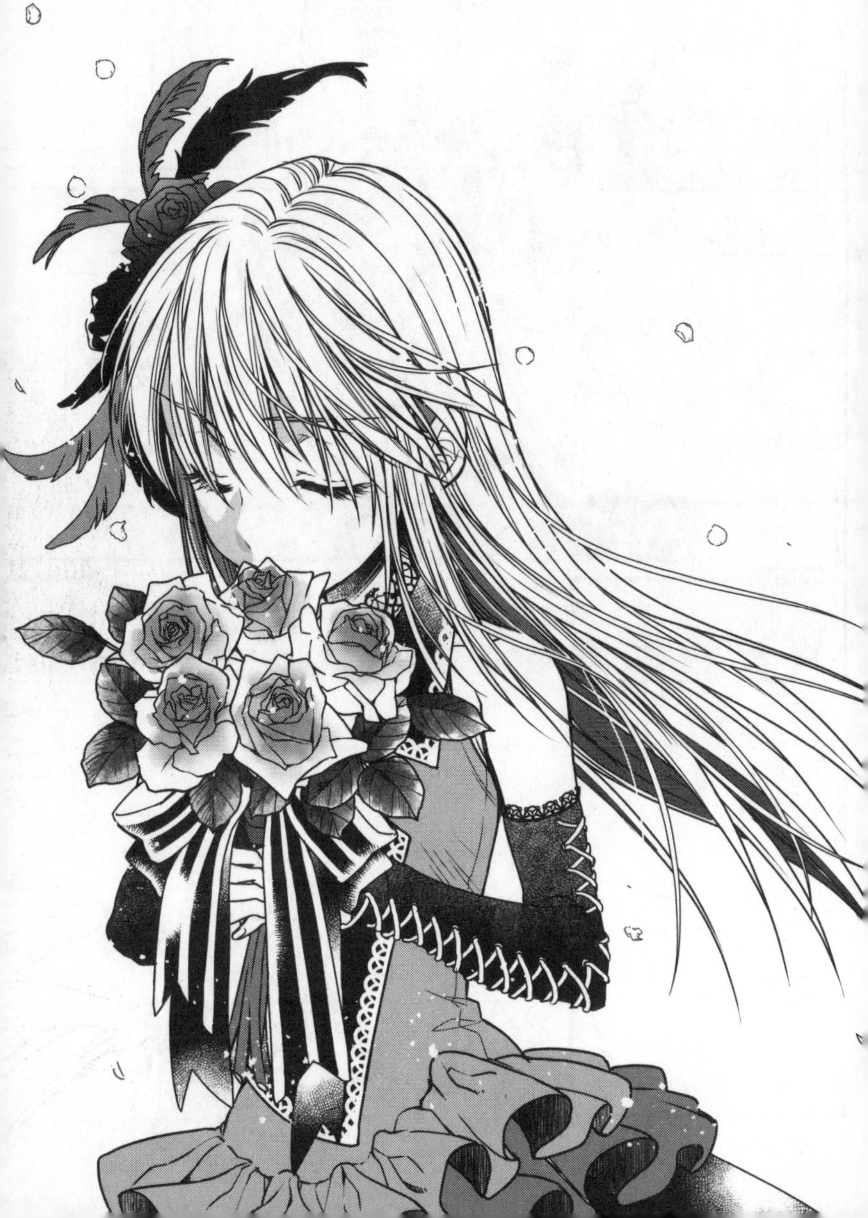

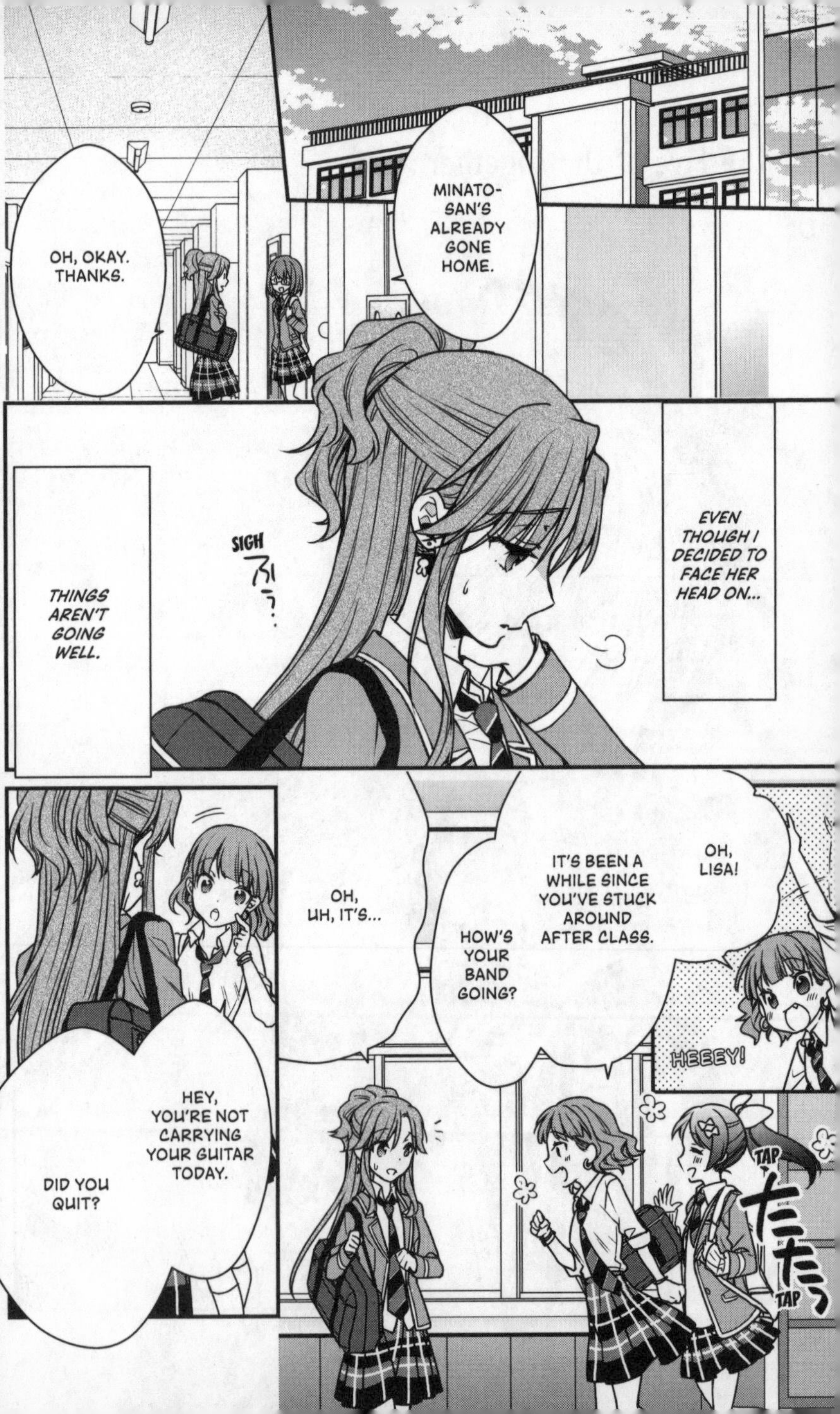
MINATO-SAN'S ALREADY GONE HOME.
OH, OKAY. THANKS.
EVEN THOUGH I DECIDED TO FACE HER HEAD ON...
SIGH
THINGS AREN'T GOING WELL.
OH, LISA!
HEEEY!
IT'S BEEN A WHILE SINCE YOU'VE STUCK AROUND AFTER CLASS.
HOW'S YOUR BAND GOING?
OH, UH, IT'S...
TAP TAP
HEY, YOU'RE NOT CARRYING YOUR GUITAR TODAY.
DID YOU QUIT?

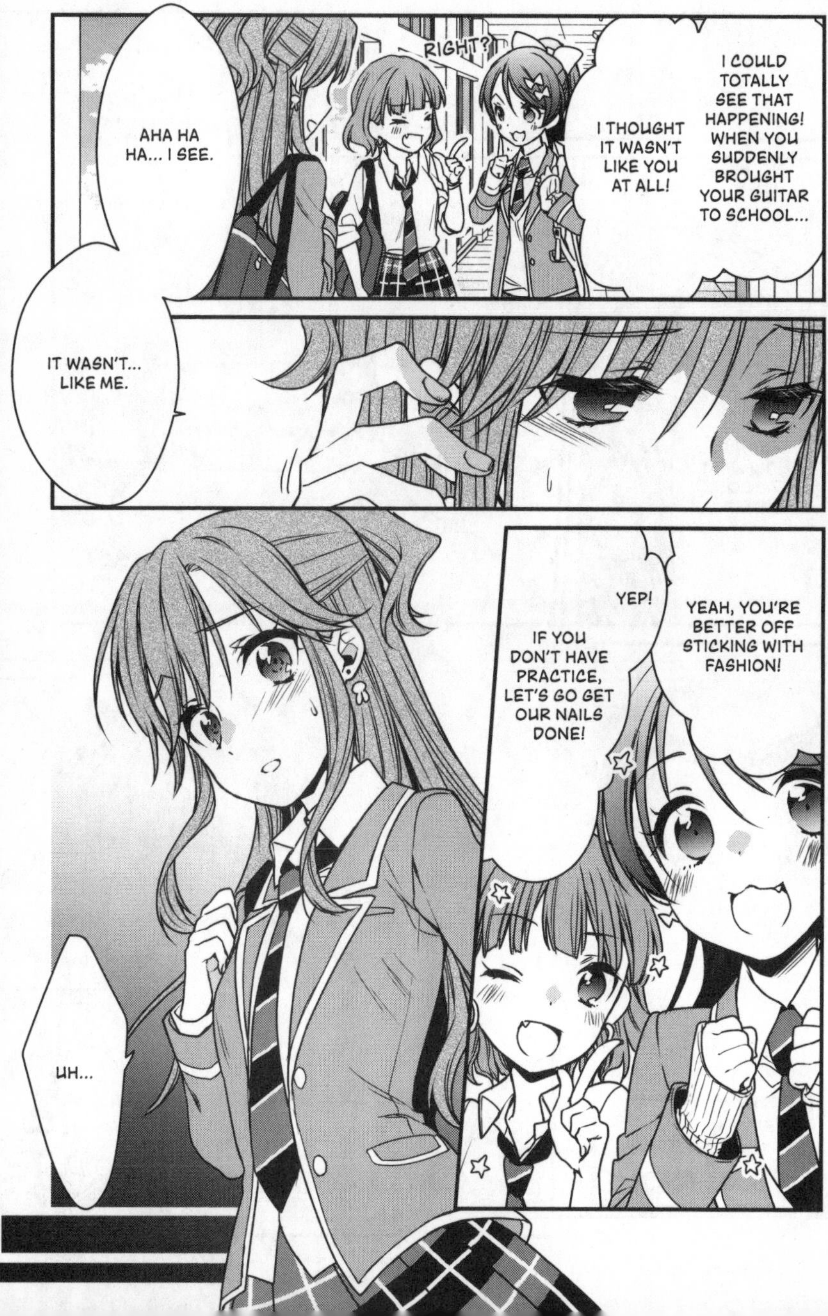
I COULD TOTALLY SEE THAT HAPPENING! WHEN YOU SUDDENLY BROUGHT YOUR GUITAR TO SCHOOL...
I THOUGHT IT WASN'T LIKE YOU AT ALL!
RIGHT?
AHA HA HA... I SEE.
IT WASN'T... LIKE ME.
YEAH, YOU'RE BETTER OFF STICKING WITH FASHION!
YEP!
IF YOU DON'T HAVE PRACTICE, LET'S GO GET OUR NAILS DONE!
UH...

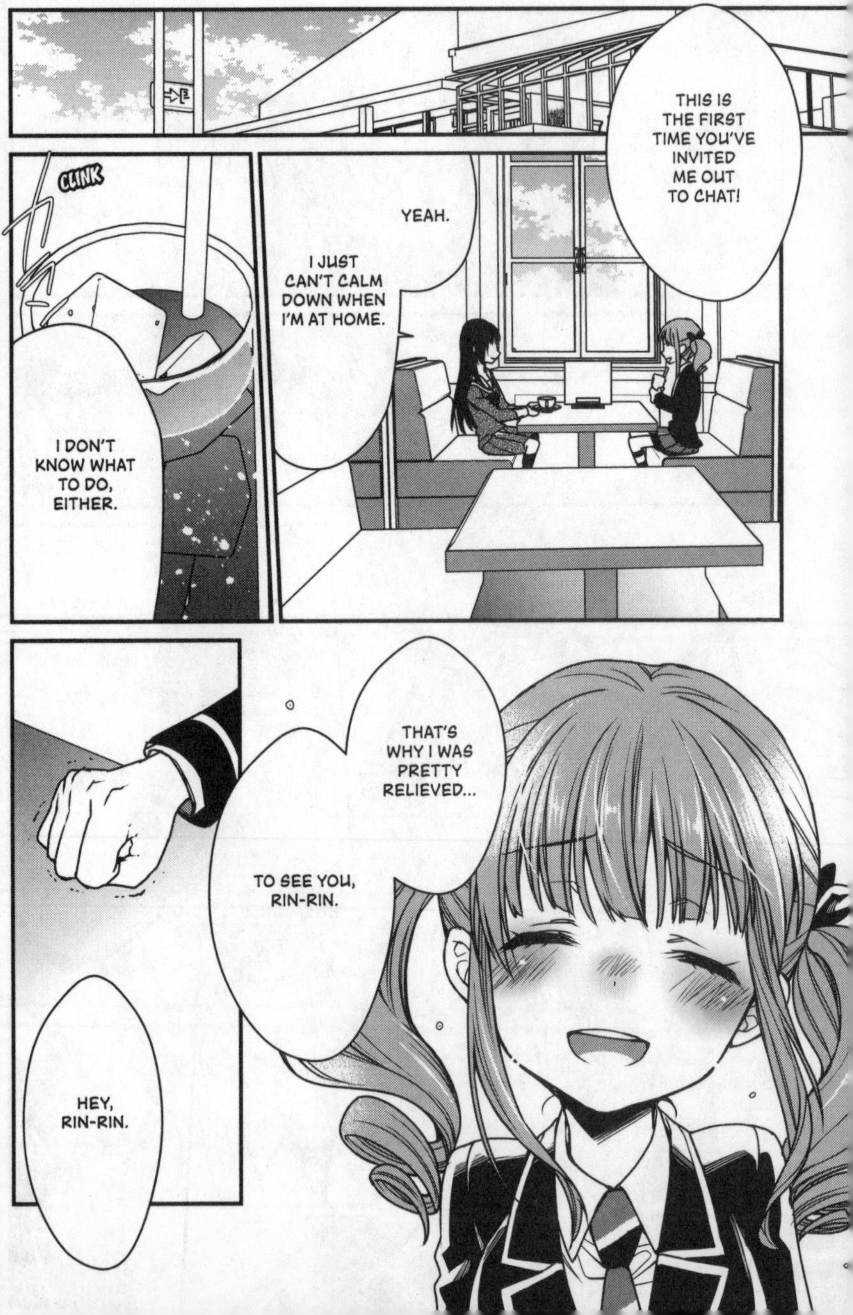
THIS IS THE FIRST TIME YOU'VE INVITED ME OUT TO CHAT!
YEAH.
I JUST CAN'T CALM DOWN WHEN I'M AT HOME.
CLINK
I DON'T KNOW WHAT TO DO, EITHER.
THAT'S WHY I WAS PRETTY RELIEVED...
TO SEE YOU, RIN-RIN.
HEY, RIN-RIN.

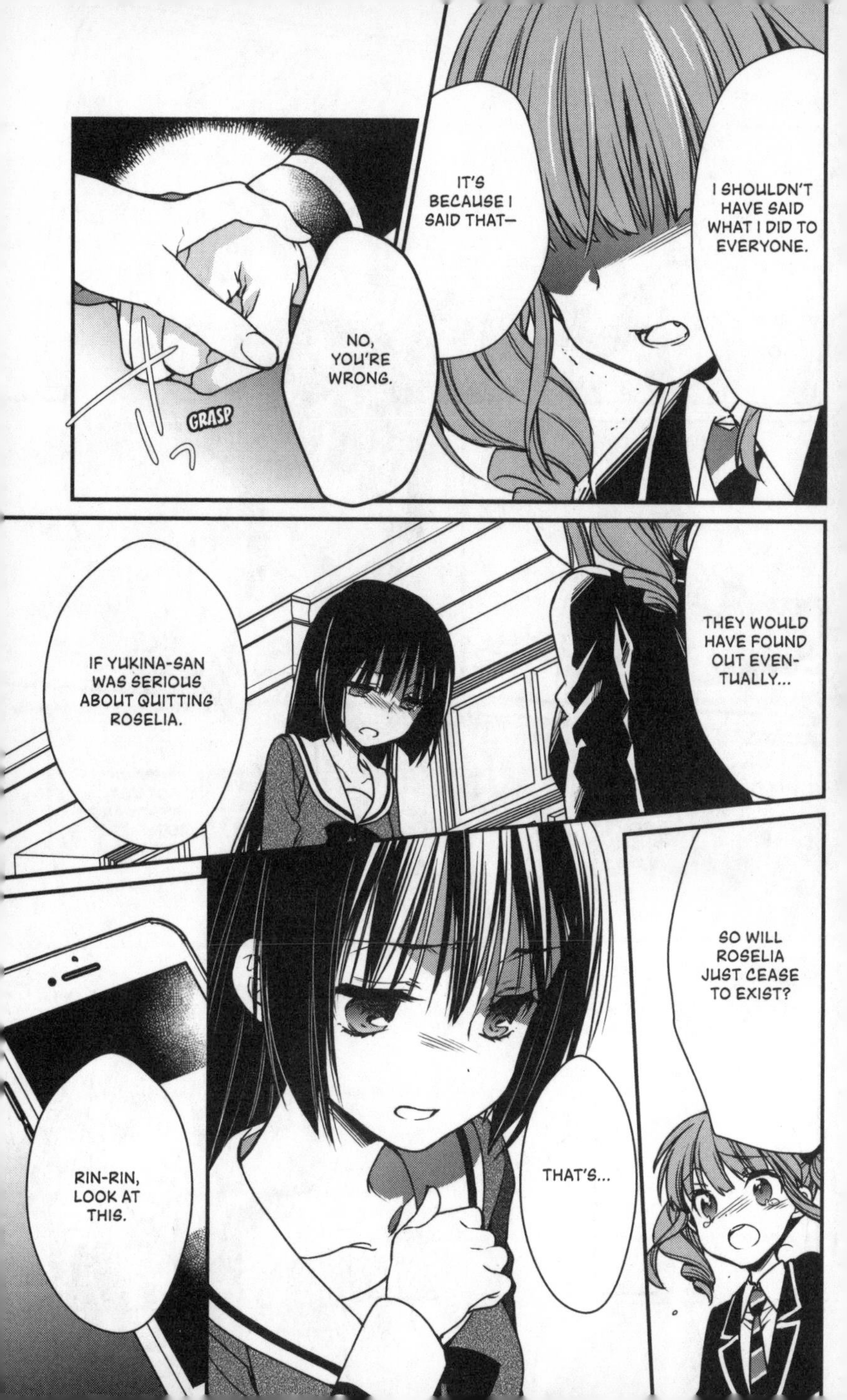

I SHOULDN'T HAVE SAID WHAT I DID TO EVERYONE.
IT'S BECAUSE I SAID THAT—
NO, YOU'RE WRONG.
GRASP
THEY WOULD HAVE FOUND OUT EVEN-TUALLY...
IF YUKINA-SAN WAS SERIOUS ABOUT QUITTING ROSELIA.
SO WILL ROSELIA JUST CEASE TO EXIST?
THAT'S...
RIN-RIN, LOOK AT THIS.

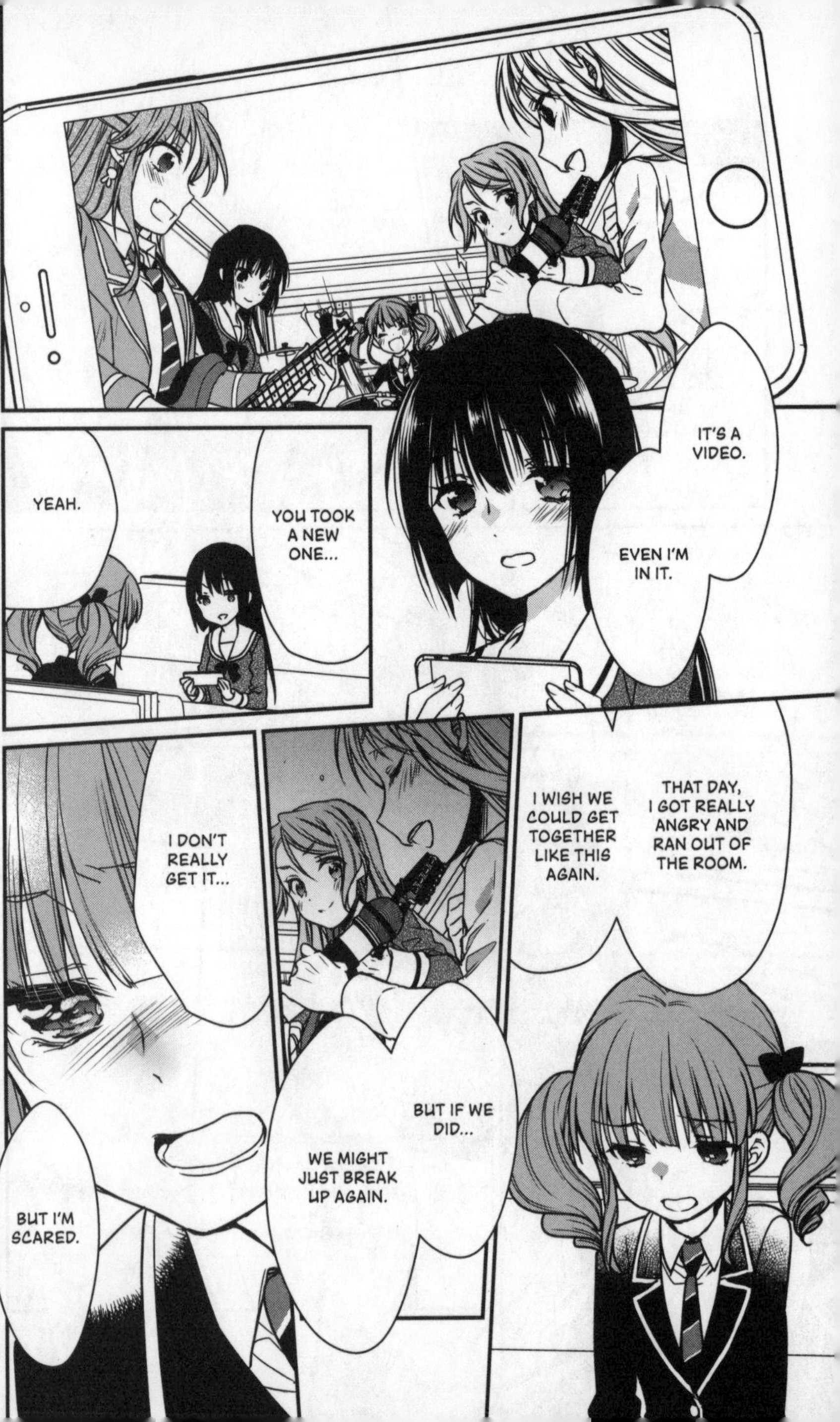
IT'S A VIDEO.
EVEN I'M IN IT.
YOU TOOK A NEW ONE...
YEAH.
THAT DAY, I GOT REALLY ANGRY AND RAN OUT OF THE ROOM.
I WISH WE COULD GET TOGETHER LIKE THIS AGAIN.
BUT IF WE DID...
WE MIGHT JUST BREAK UP AGAIN.
I DON'T REALLY GET IT...
BUT I'M SCARED.

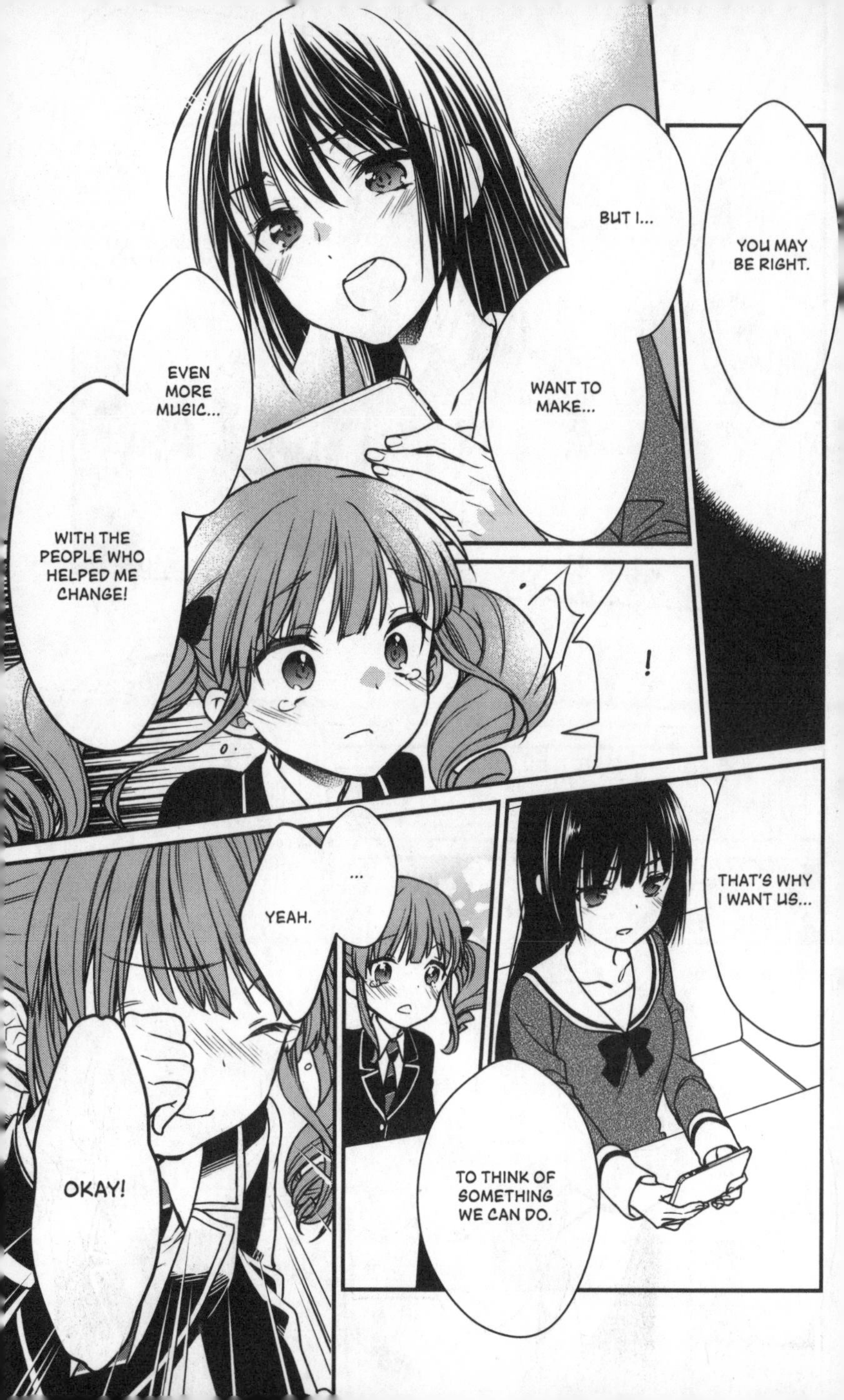
YOU MAY BE RIGHT.
BUT I... WANT TO MAKE...
EVEN MORE MUSIC...
WITH THE PEOPLE WHO HELPED ME CHANGE!
!
THAT'S WHY I WANT US...
TO THINK OF SOMETHING WE CAN DO.
... YEAH.
OKAY!

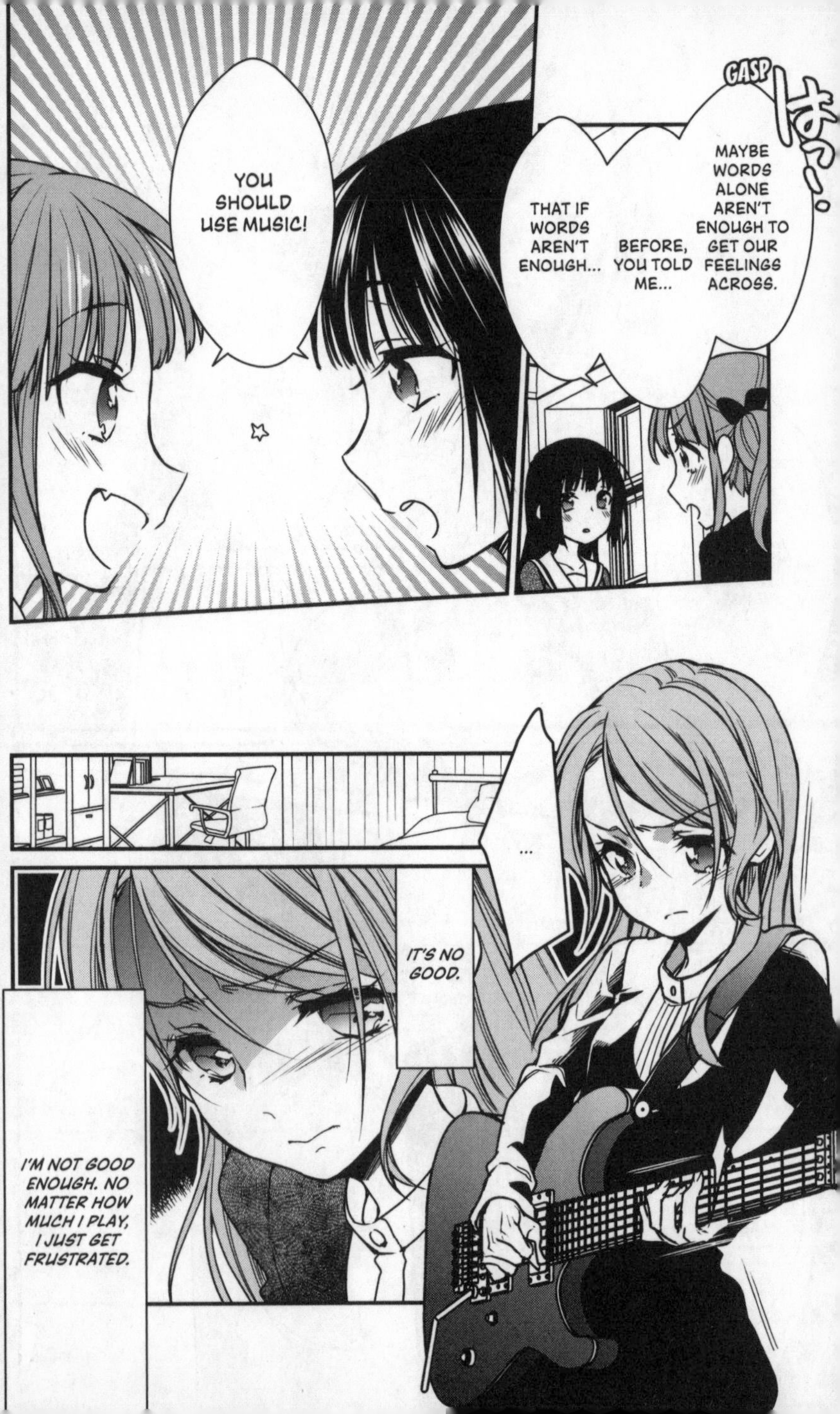
GASP
はっ。
MAYBE WORDS ALONE AREN'T ENOUGH TO GET OUR FEELINGS ACROSS.
BEFORE, YOU TOLD ME...
THAT IF WORDS AREN'T ENOUGH...
YOU SHOULD USE MUSIC!
...
IT'S NO GOOD.
I'M NOT GOOD ENOUGH. NO MATTER HOW MUCH I PLAY, I JUST GET FRUSTRATED.

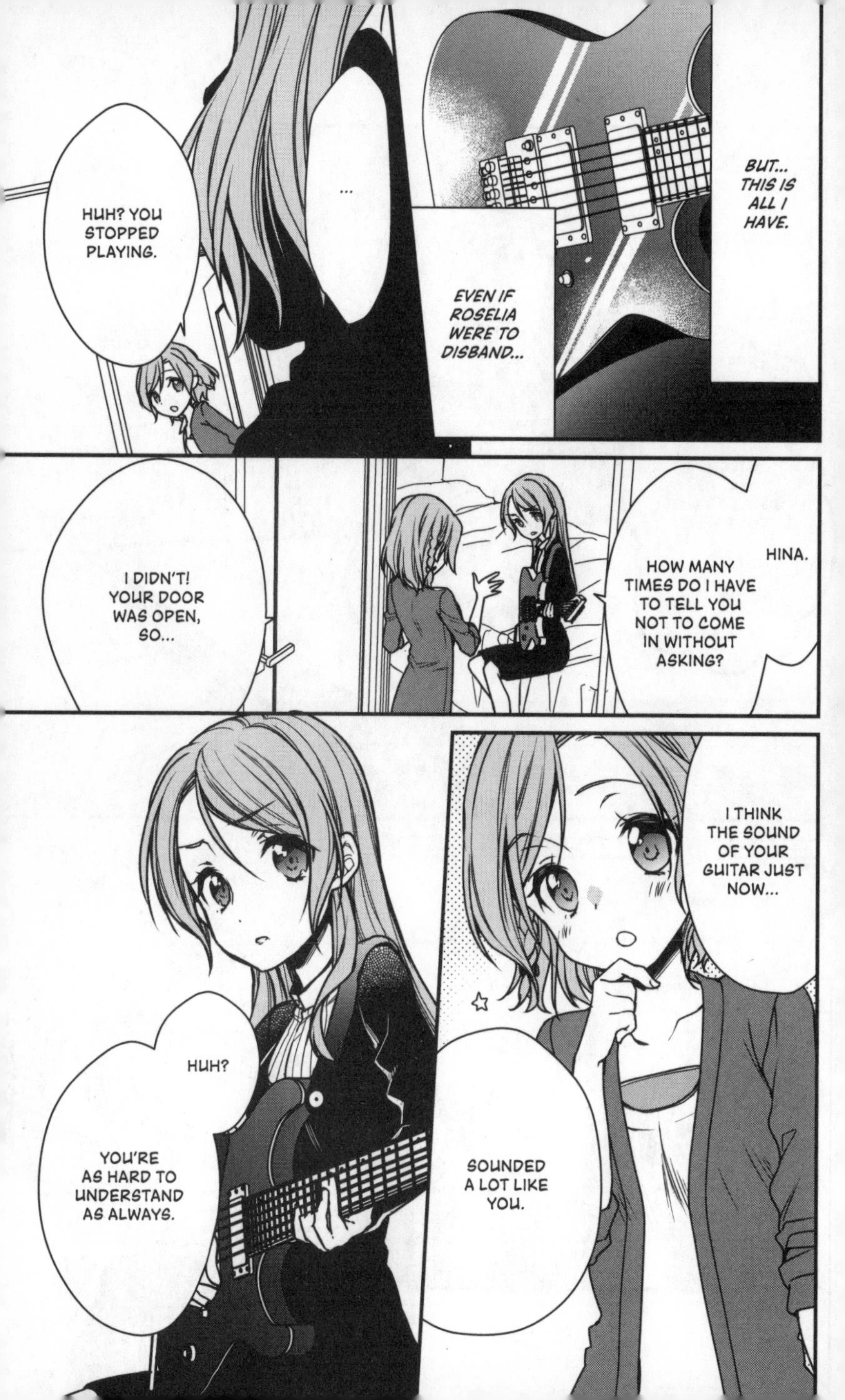
BUT... THIS IS ALL I HAVE.
EVEN IF ROSELIA WERE TO DISBAND...
...
HUH? YOU STOPPED PLAYING.
HINA.
HOW MANY TIMES DO I HAVE TO TELL YOU NOT TO COME IN WITHOUT ASKING?
I DIDN'T! YOUR DOOR WAS OPEN, SO...
I THINK THE SOUND OF YOUR GUITAR JUST NOW...
SOUNDED A LOT LIKE YOU.
HUH?
YOU'RE AS HARD TO UNDERSTAND AS ALWAYS.

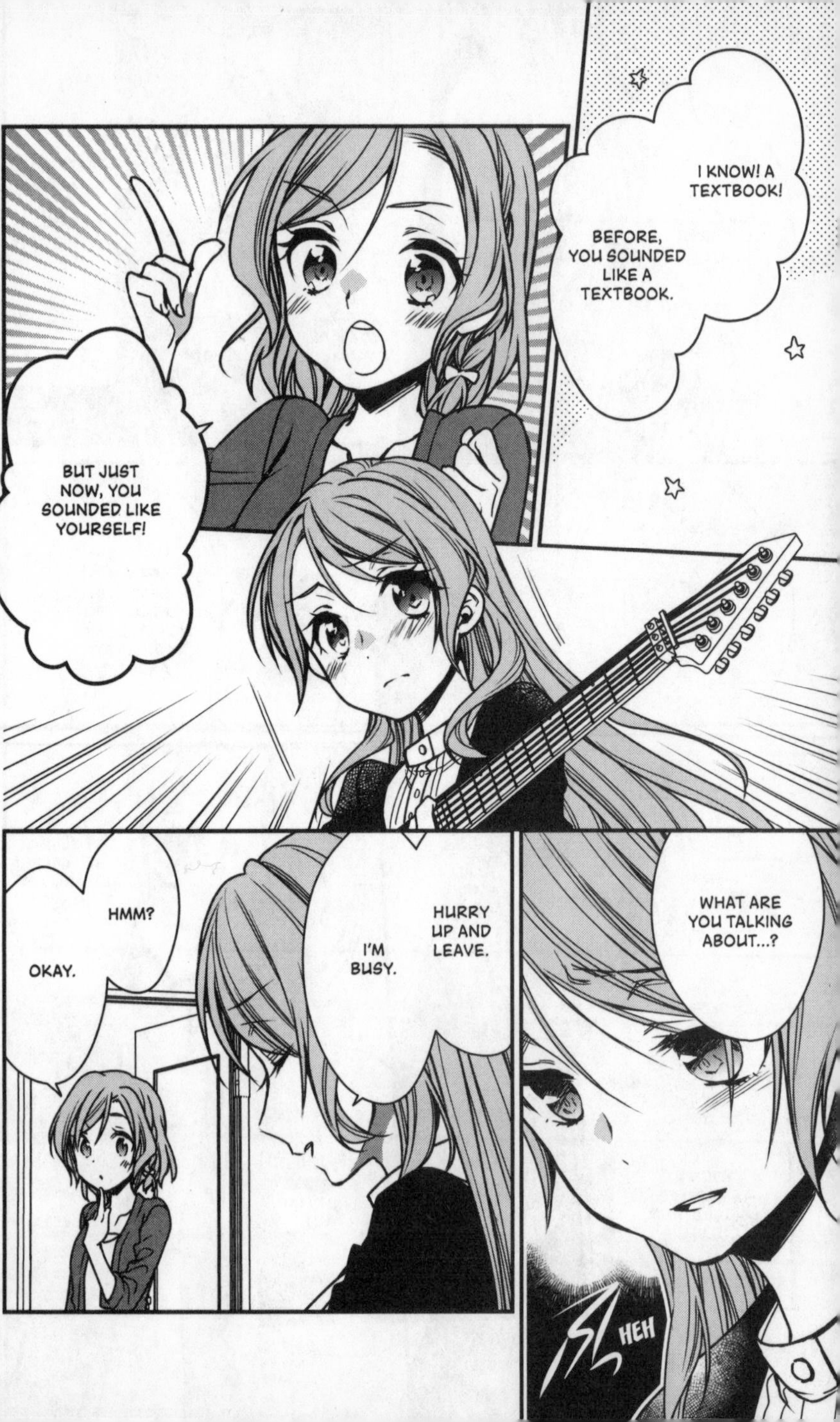
I KNOW! A TEXTBOOK!
BEFORE, YOU SOUNDED LIKE A TEXTBOOK.
BUT JUST NOW, YOU SOUNDED LIKE YOURSELF!
WHAT ARE YOU TALKING ABOUT...?
HEH
HURRY UP AND LEAVE.
I'M BUSY.
HMM?
OKAY.

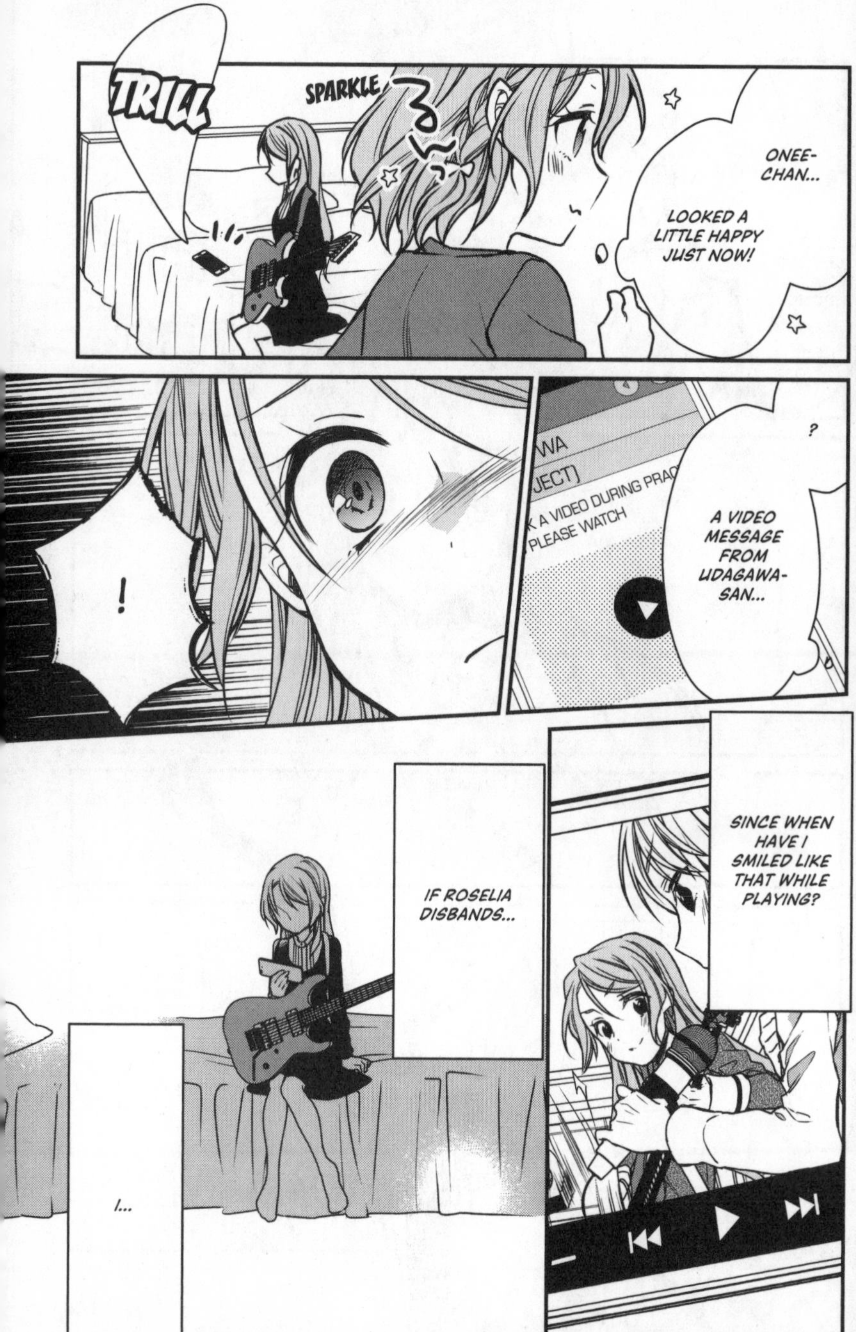
ONEE-CHAN... LOOKED A LITTLE HAPPY JUST NOW!
SPARKLE
TRILL
?
A VIDEO MESSAGE FROM UDAGAWA-SAN...
WA
JECT)
K A VIDEO DURING PRAC
PLEASE WATCH
!
SINCE WHEN HAVE I SMILED LIKE THAT WHILE PLAYING?
IF ROSELIA DISBANDS...
I...

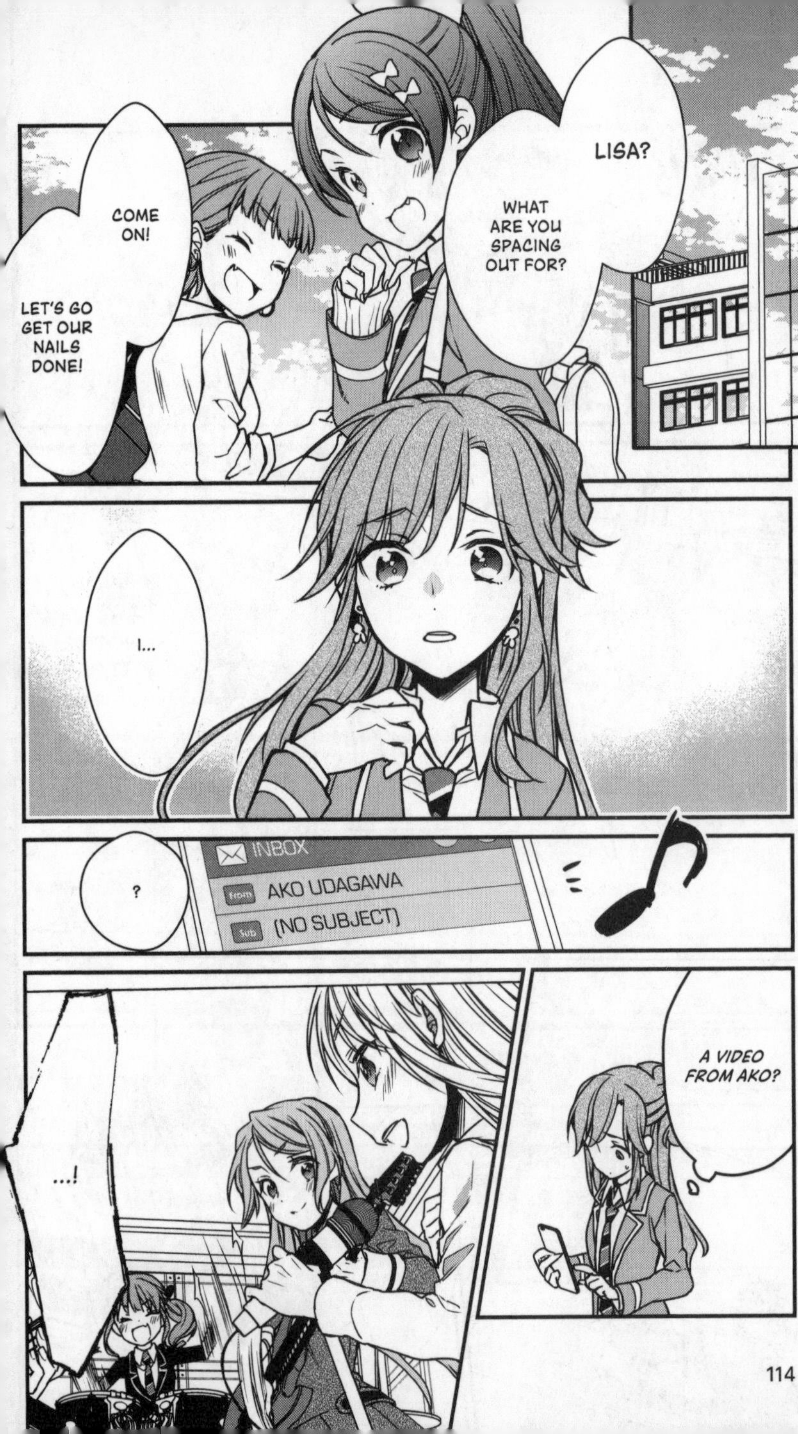
LISA?
WHAT ARE YOU SPACING OUT FOR?
COME ON! LET'S GO GET OUR NAILS DONE!
I...
INBOX
from AKO UDAGAWA
Sub (NO SUBJECT)
?
A VIDEO FROM AKO?
...!

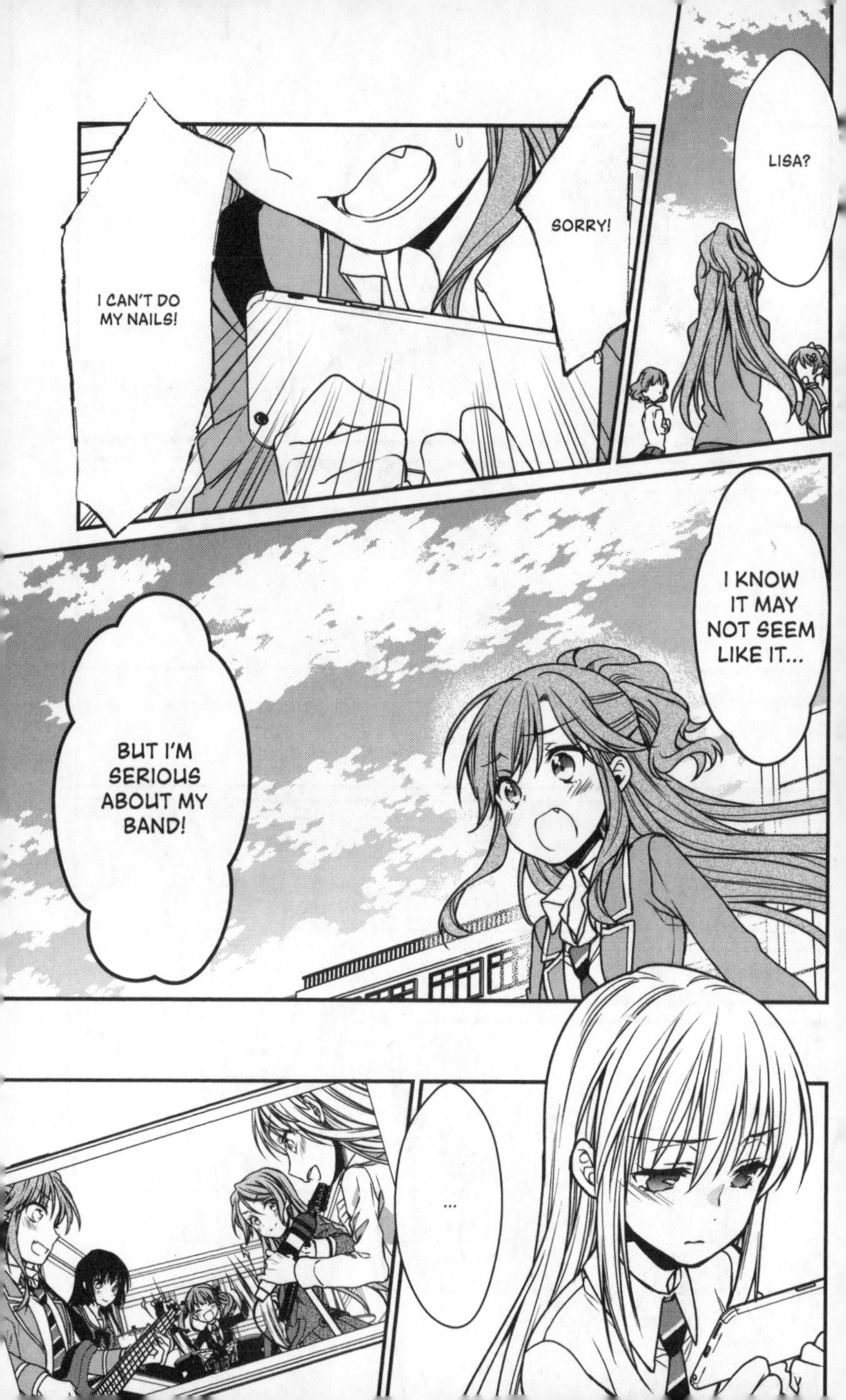
LISA?
SORRY!
I CAN'T DO MY NAILS!
I KNOW IT MAY NOT SEEM LIKE IT...
BUT I'M SERIOUS ABOUT MY BAND!
...

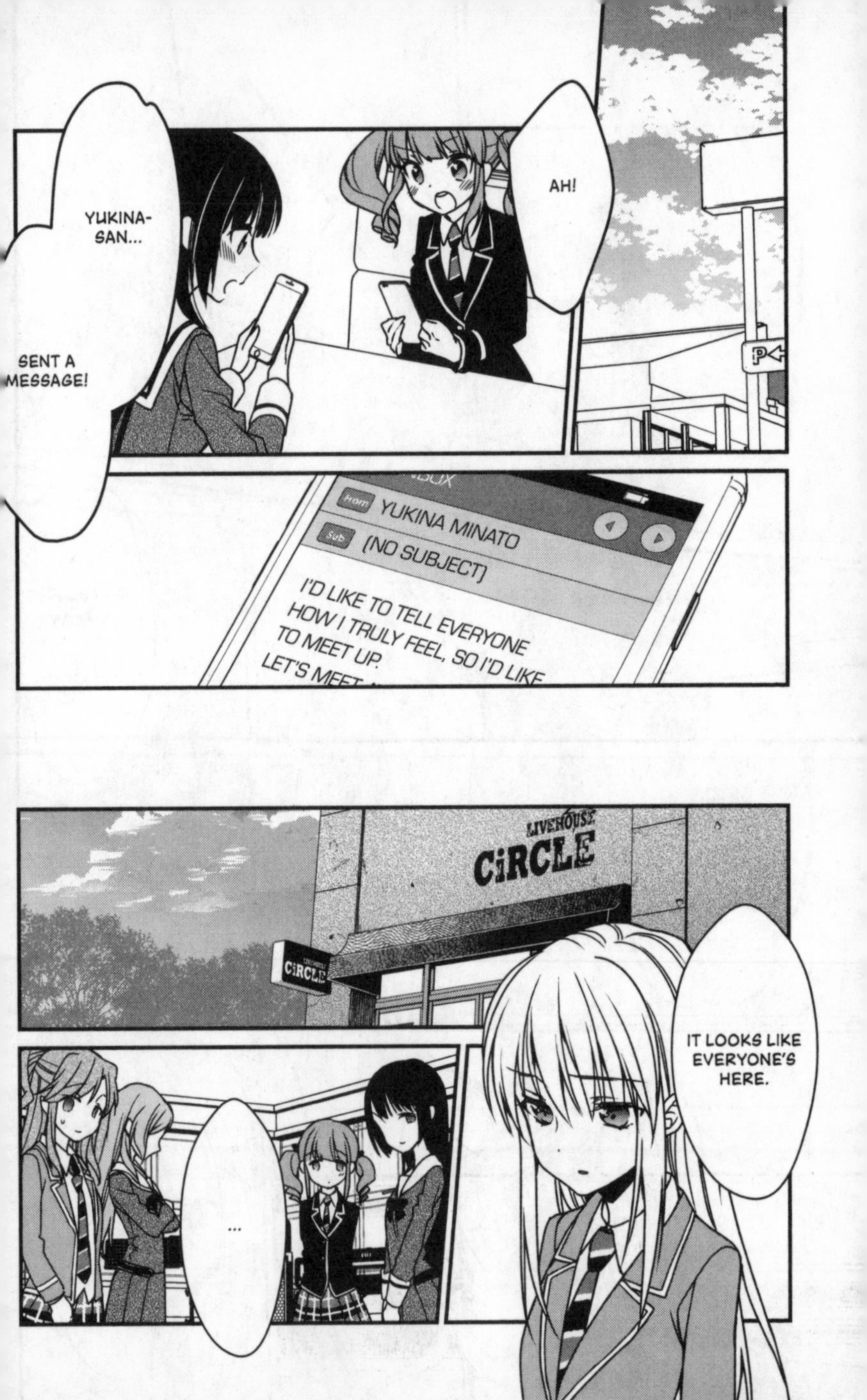
AH!
YUKINA-SAN... SENT A MESSAGE!
From
YUKINA MINATO
Sub
(NO SUBJECT)
I'D LIKE TO TELL EVERYONE HOW I TRULY FEEL, SO I'D LIKE TO MEET UP.
LET'S MEET
LIVEHOUSE CiRCLE
CiRCLE
IT LOOKS LIKE EVERYONE'S HERE.
...

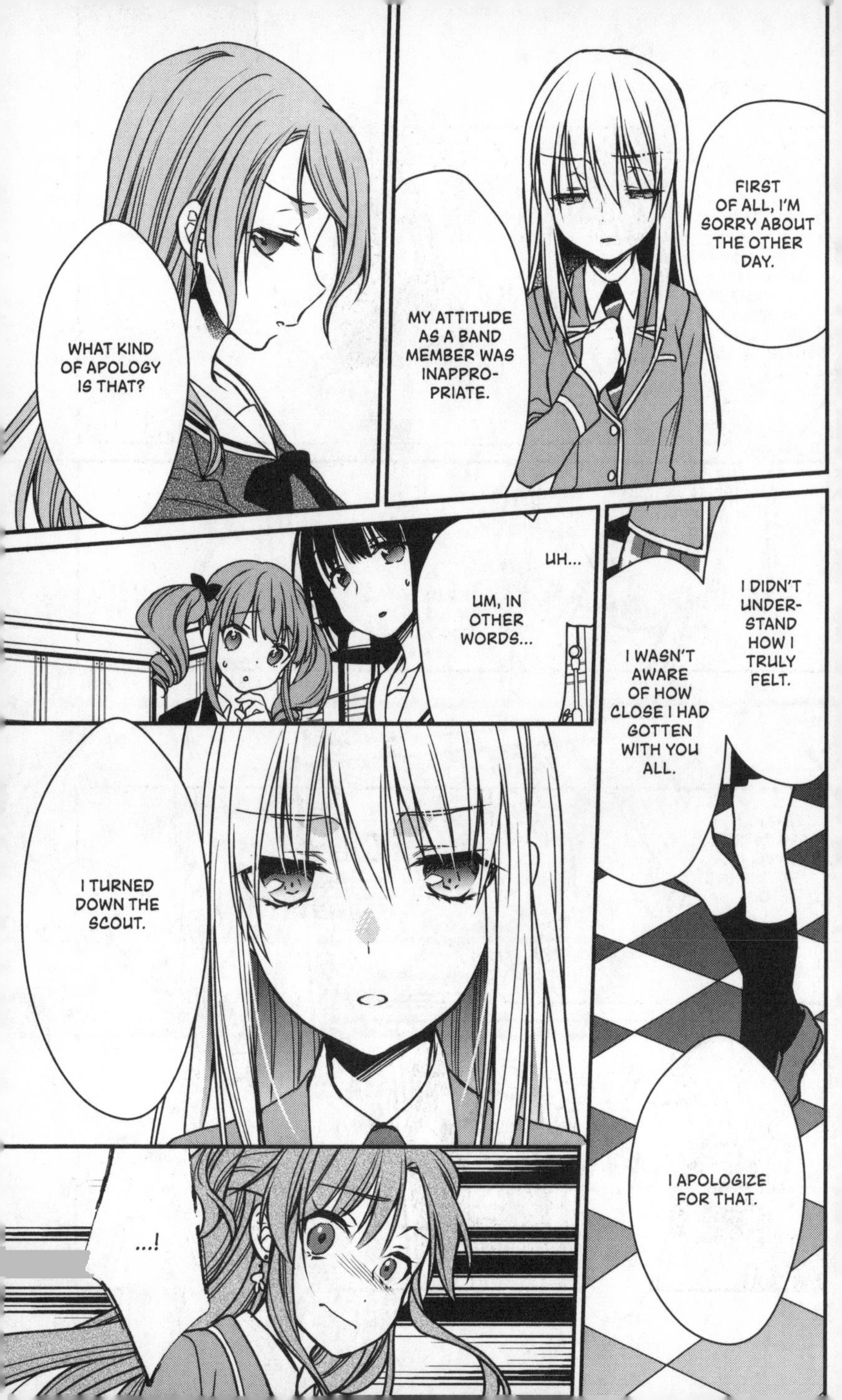
FIRST OF ALL, I'M SORRY ABOUT THE OTHER DAY.
MY ATTITUDE AS A BAND MEMBER WAS INAPPROPRIATE.
WHAT KIND OF APOLOGY IS THAT?
I DIDN'T UNDERSTAND HOW I TRULY FELT.
I WASN'T AWARE OF HOW CLOSE I HAD GOTTEN WITH YOU ALL.
I APOLOGIZE FOR THAT.
UH...
UM, IN OTHER WORDS...
I TURNED DOWN THE SCOUT.
...!

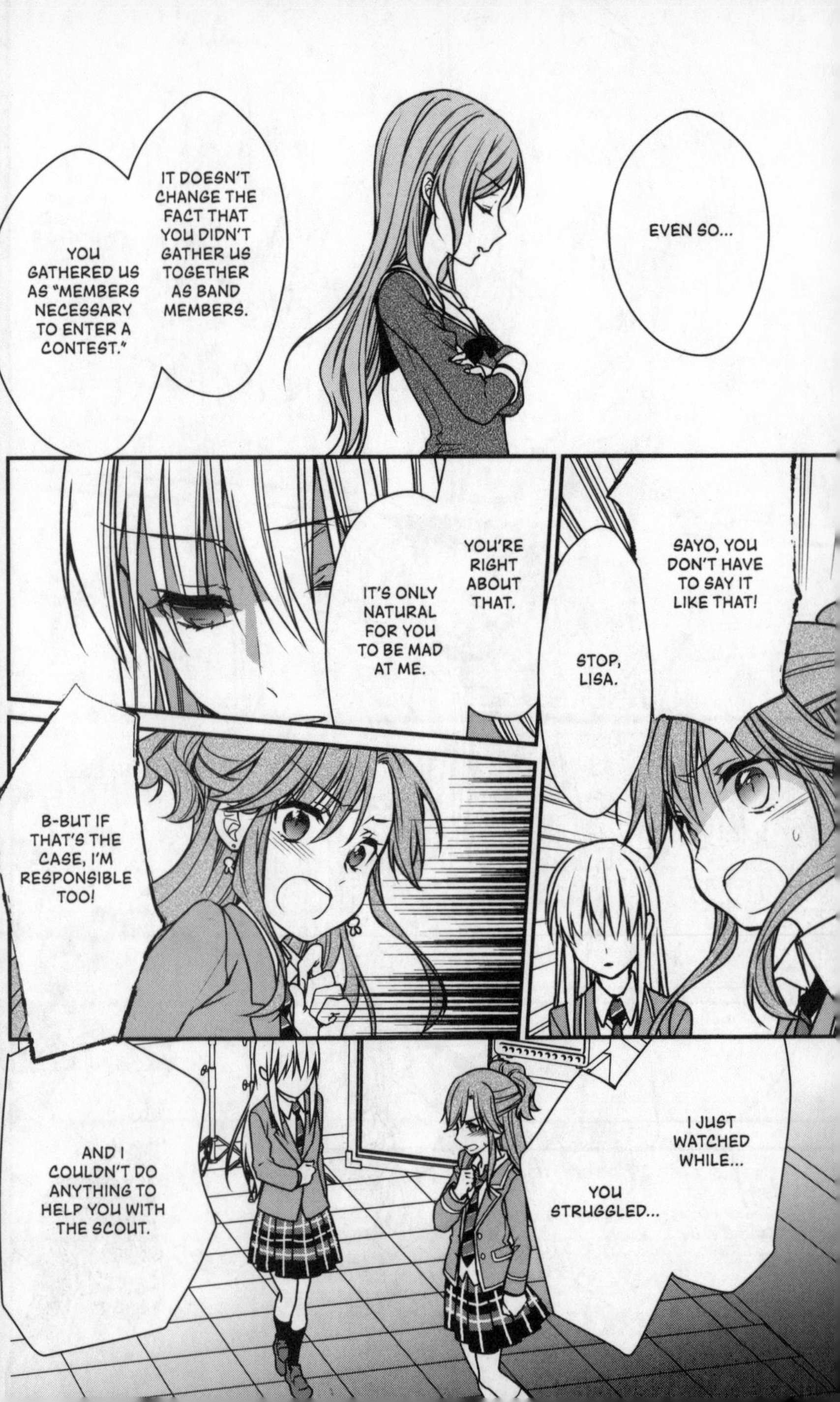
EVEN SO...
IT DOESN'T CHANGE THE FACT THAT YOU DIDN'T GATHER US TOGETHER AS BAND MEMBERS.
YOU GATHERED US AS "MEMBERS NECESSARY TO ENTER A CONTEST."
SAYO, YOU DON'T HAVE TO SAY IT LIKE THAT!
STOP, LISA.
YOU'RE RIGHT ABOUT THAT.
IT'S ONLY NATURAL FOR YOU TO BE MAD AT ME.
B-BUT IF THAT'S THE CASE, I'M RESPONSIBLE TOO!
I JUST WATCHED WHILE...
YOU STRUGGLED...
AND I COULDN'T DO ANYTHING TO HELP YOU WITH THE SCOUT.

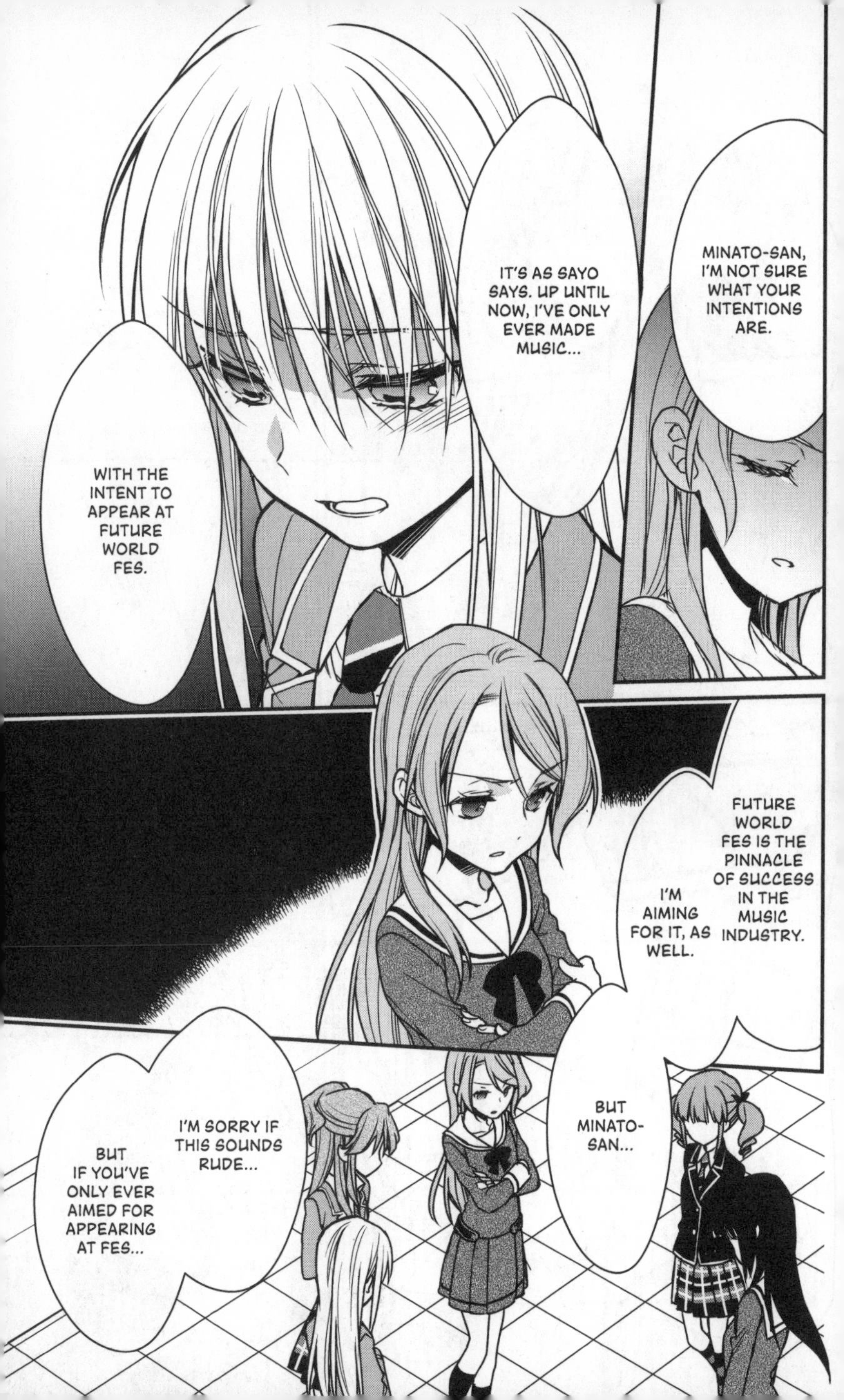
MINATO-SAN, I'M NOT SURE WHAT YOUR INTENTIONS ARE.
IT'S AS SAYO SAYS. UP UNTIL NOW, I'VE ONLY EVER MADE MUSIC...
WITH THE INTENT TO APPEAR AT FUTURE WORLD FES.
FUTURE WORLD FES IS THE PINNACLE OF SUCCESS IN THE MUSIC INDUSTRY.
I'M AIMING FOR IT, AS WELL.
BUT MINATO-SAN...
I'M SORRY IF THIS SOUNDS RUDE...
BUT IF YOU'VE ONLY EVER AIMED FOR APPEARING AT FES...

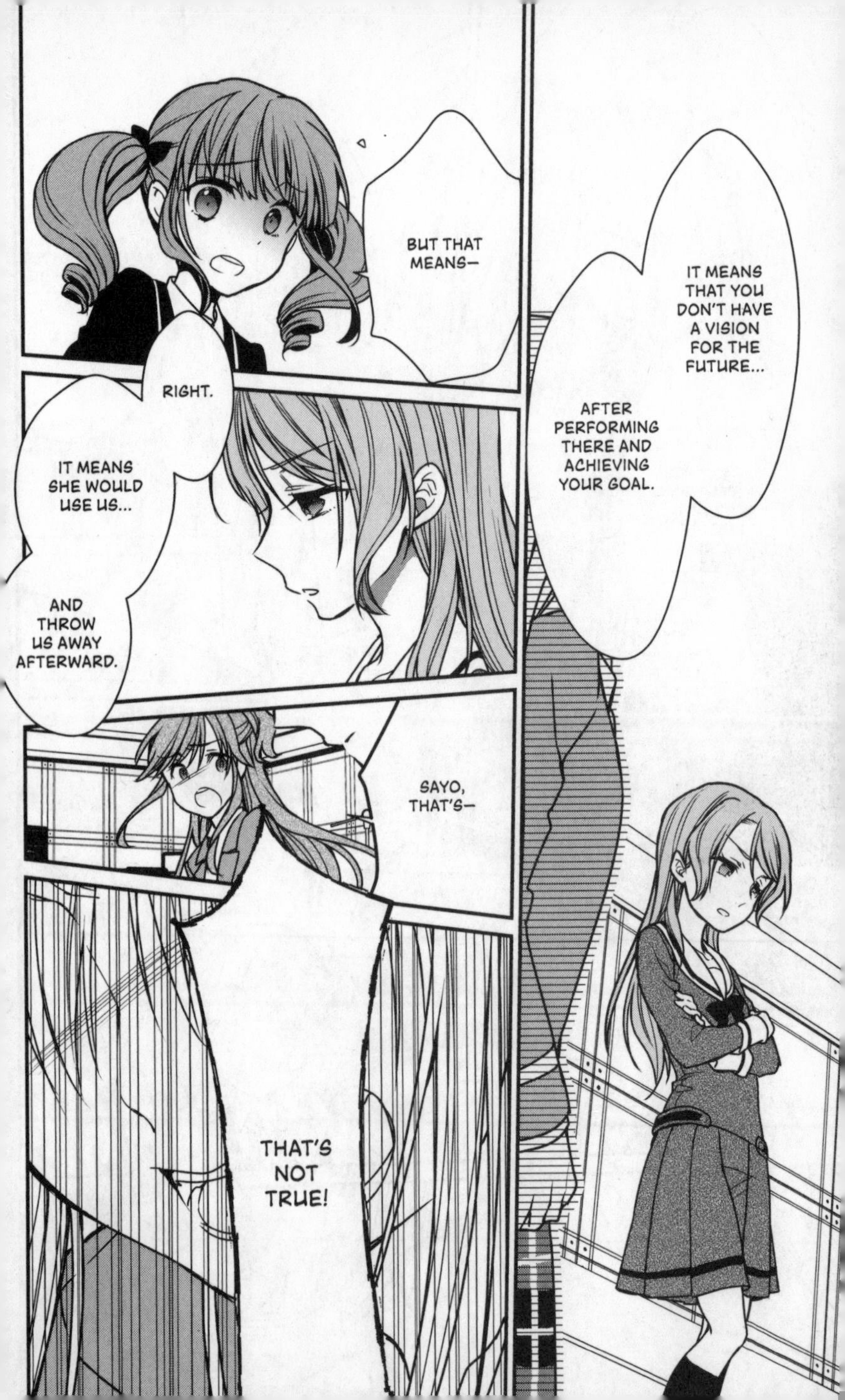
IT MEANS THAT YOU DON'T HAVE A VISION FOR THE FUTURE...
AFTER PERFORMING THERE AND ACHIEVING YOUR GOAL.
BUT THAT MEANS—
RIGHT.
IT MEANS SHE WOULD USE US...
AND THROW US AWAY AFTERWARD.
SAYO, THAT'S—
THAT'S NOT TRUE!

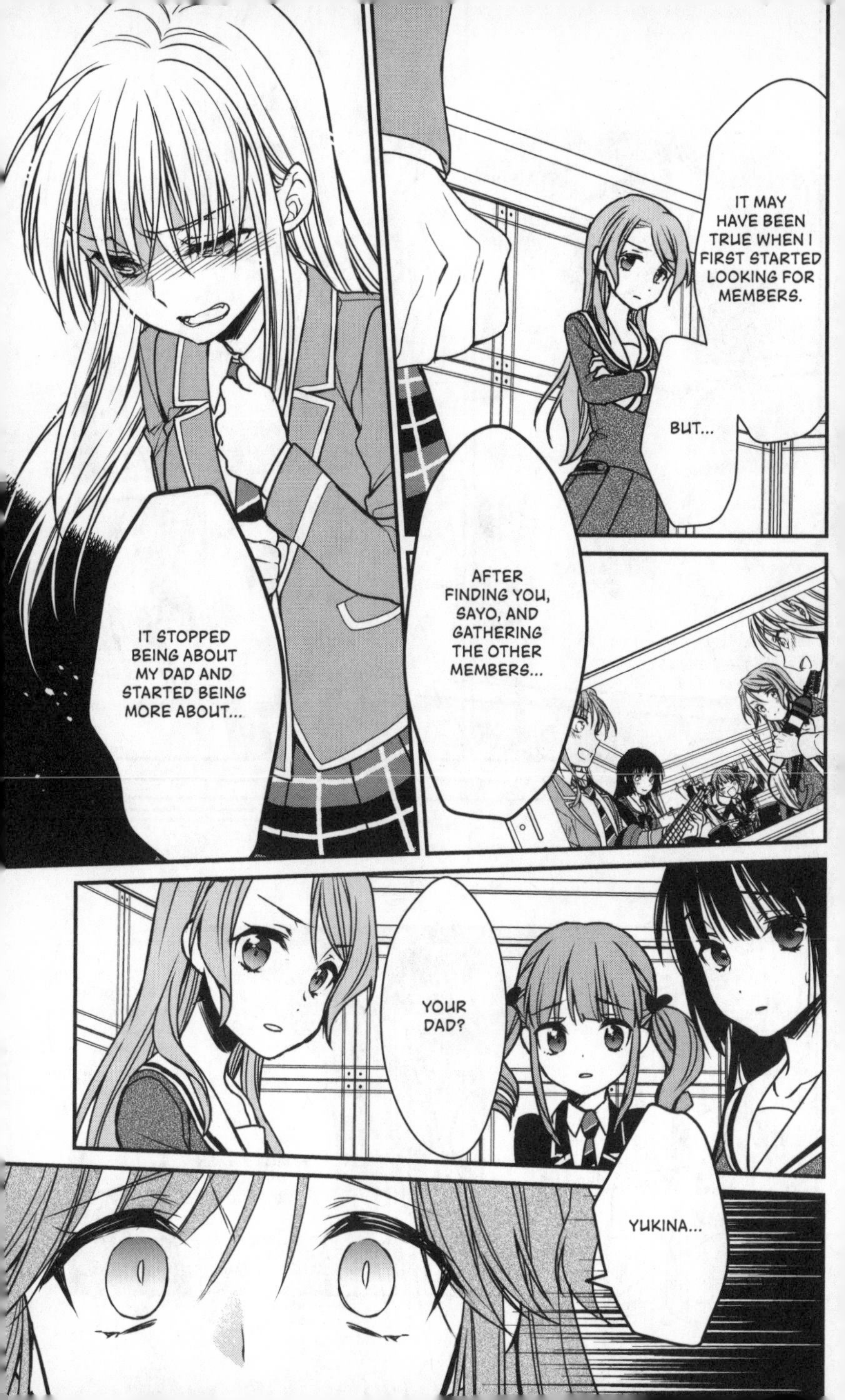
IT MAY HAVE BEEN TRUE WHEN I FIRST STARTED LOOKING FOR MEMBERS.
BUT...
AFTER FINDING YOU, SAYO, AND GATHERING THE OTHER MEMBERS...
IT STOPPED BEING ABOUT MY DAD AND STARTED BEING MORE ABOUT...
YOUR DAD?
YUKINA...

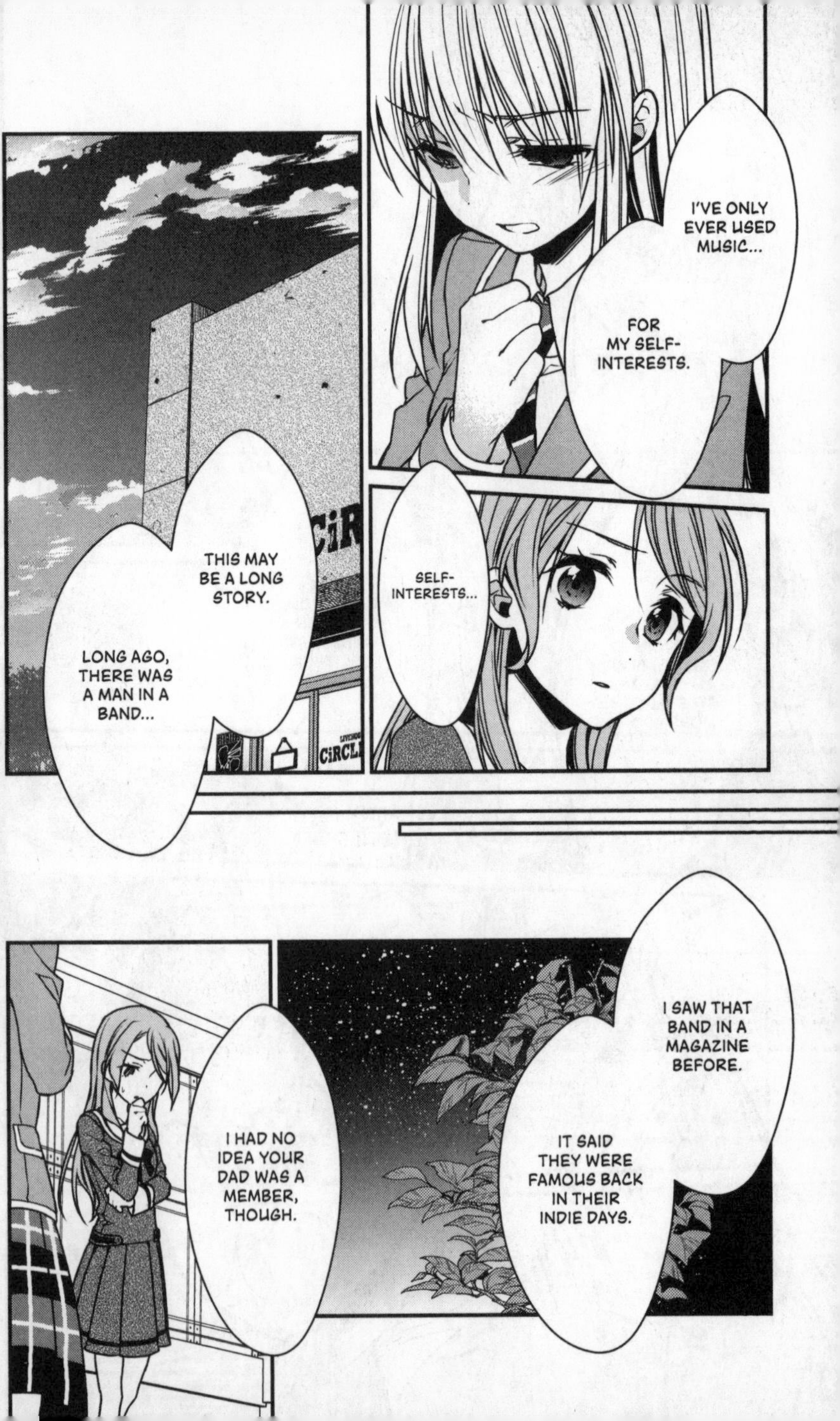
I'VE ONLY EVER USED MUSIC...
FOR MY SELF-INTERESTS.
SELF-INTERESTS...
THIS MAY BE A LONG STORY.
LONG AGO, THERE WAS A MAN IN A BAND...
I SAW THAT BAND IN A MAGAZINE BEFORE.
IT SAID THEY WERE FAMOUS BACK IN THEIR INDIE DAYS.
I HAD NO IDEA YOUR DAD WAS A MEMBER, THOUGH.

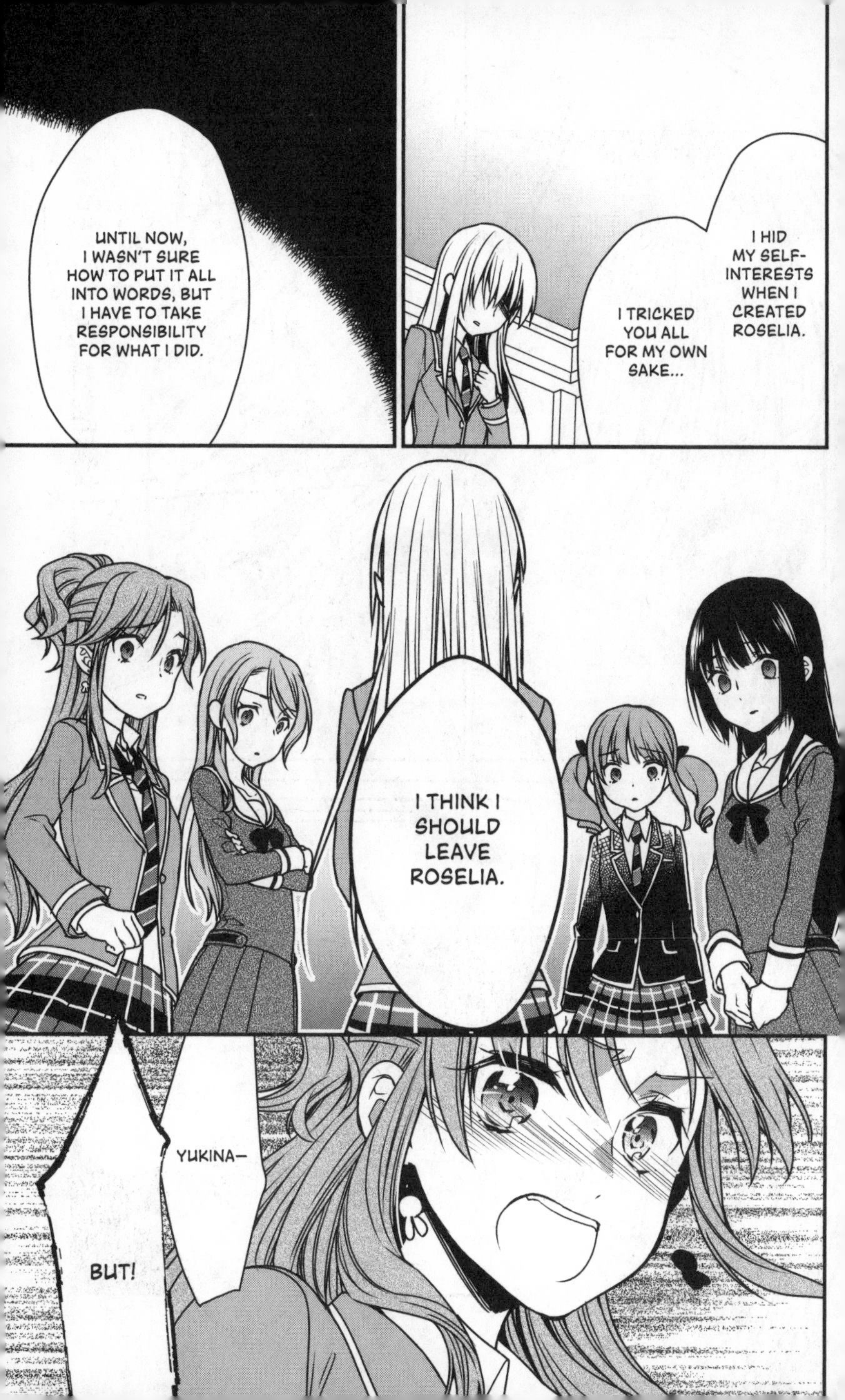
I HID MY SELF-INTERESTS WHEN I CREATED ROSELIA.
I TRICKED YOU ALL FOR MY OWN SAKE...
UNTIL NOW, I WASN'T SURE HOW TO PUT IT ALL INTO WORDS, BUT I HAVE TO TAKE RESPONSIBILITY FOR WHAT I DID.
I THINK I SHOULD LEAVE ROSELIA.
YUKINA—
BUT!

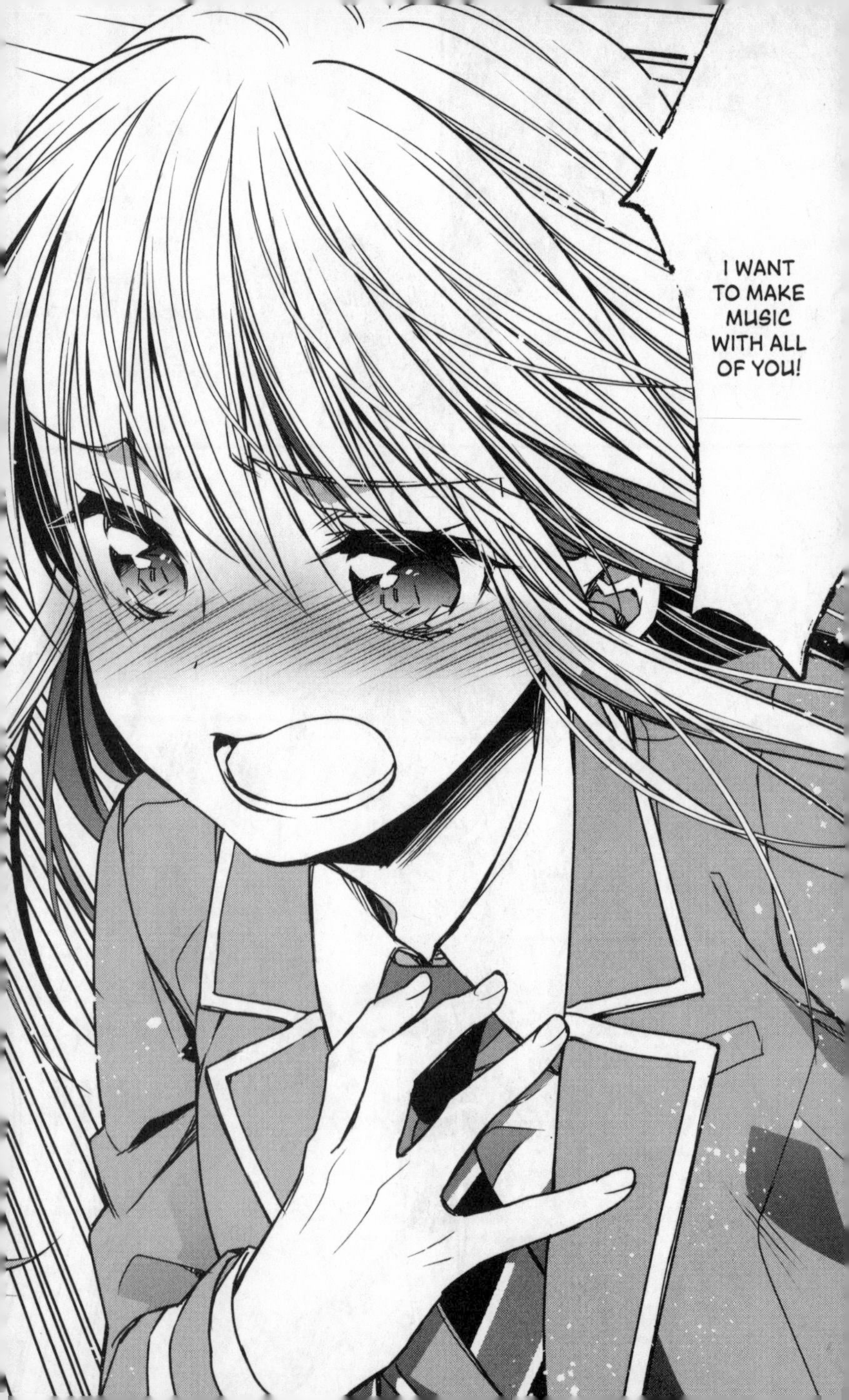
I WANT TO MAKE MUSIC WITH ALL OF YOU!

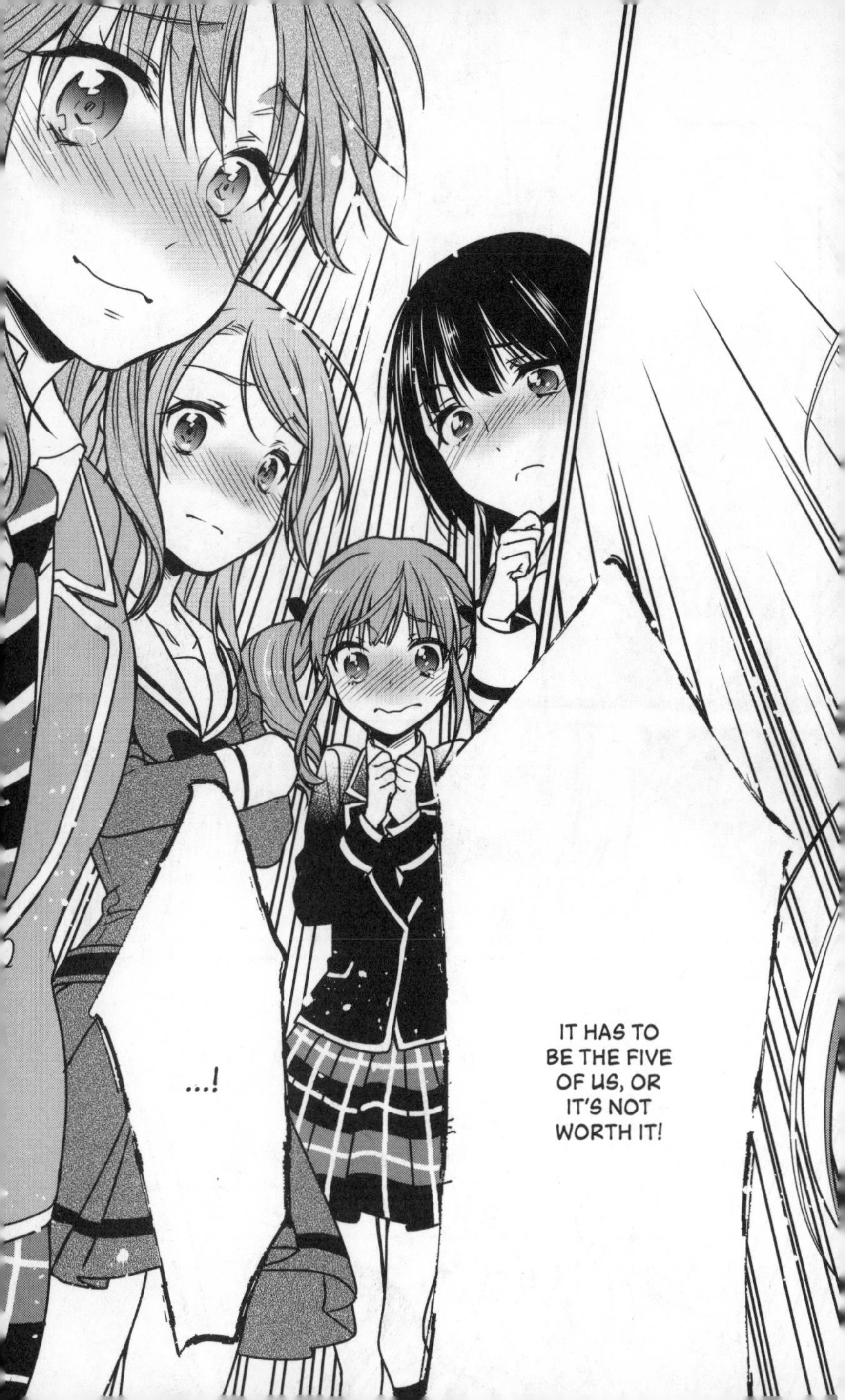
IT HAS TO BE THE FIVE OF US, OR IT'S NOT WORTH IT!
...!

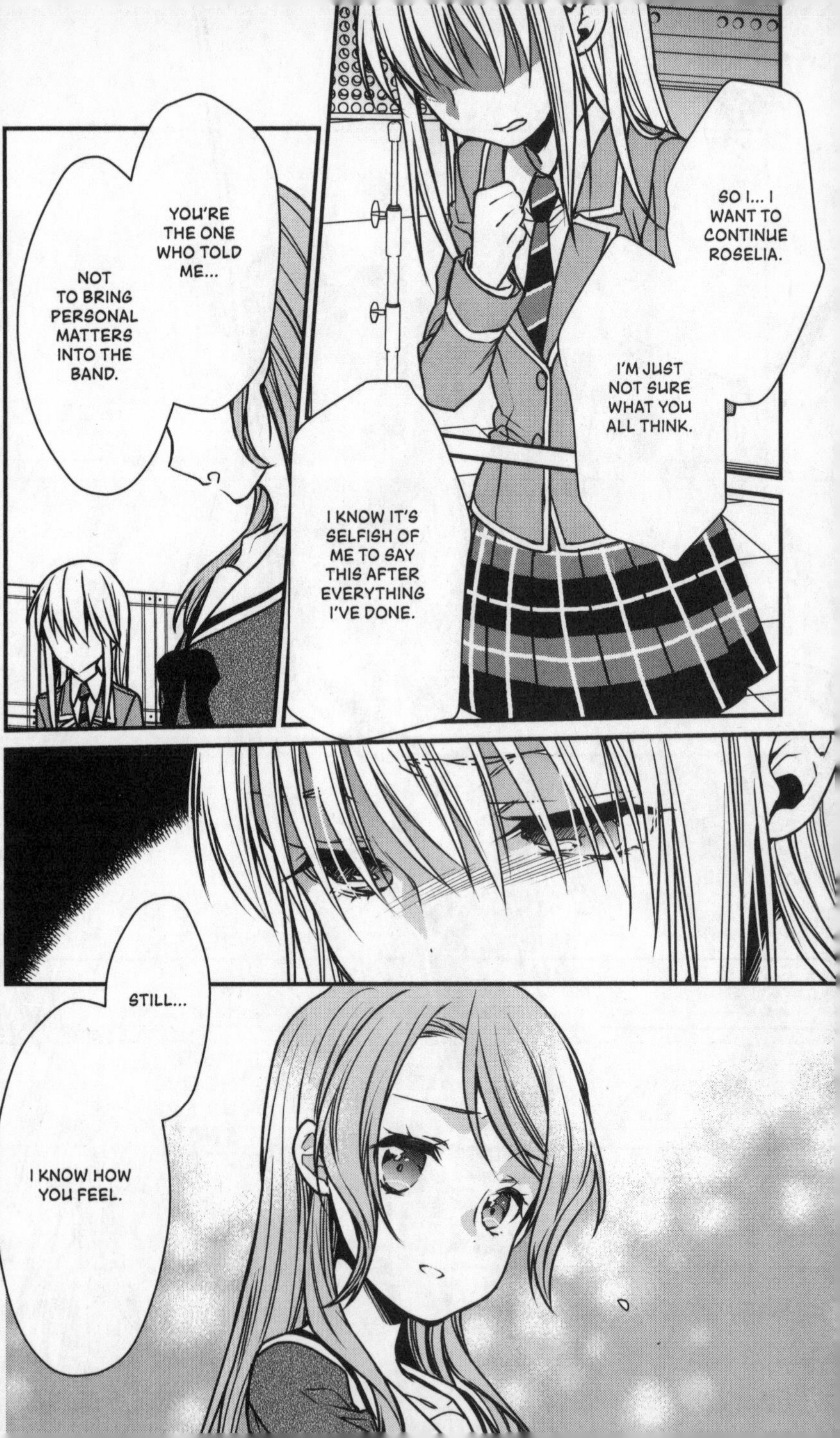
SO I... I WANT TO CONTINUE ROSELIA.
I'M JUST NOT SURE WHAT YOU ALL THINK.
I KNOW IT'S SELFISH OF ME TO SAY THIS AFTER EVERYTHING I'VE DONE.
YOU'RE THE ONE WHO TOLD ME...
NOT TO BRING PERSONAL MATTERS INTO THE BAND.
STILL...
I KNOW HOW YOU FEEL.

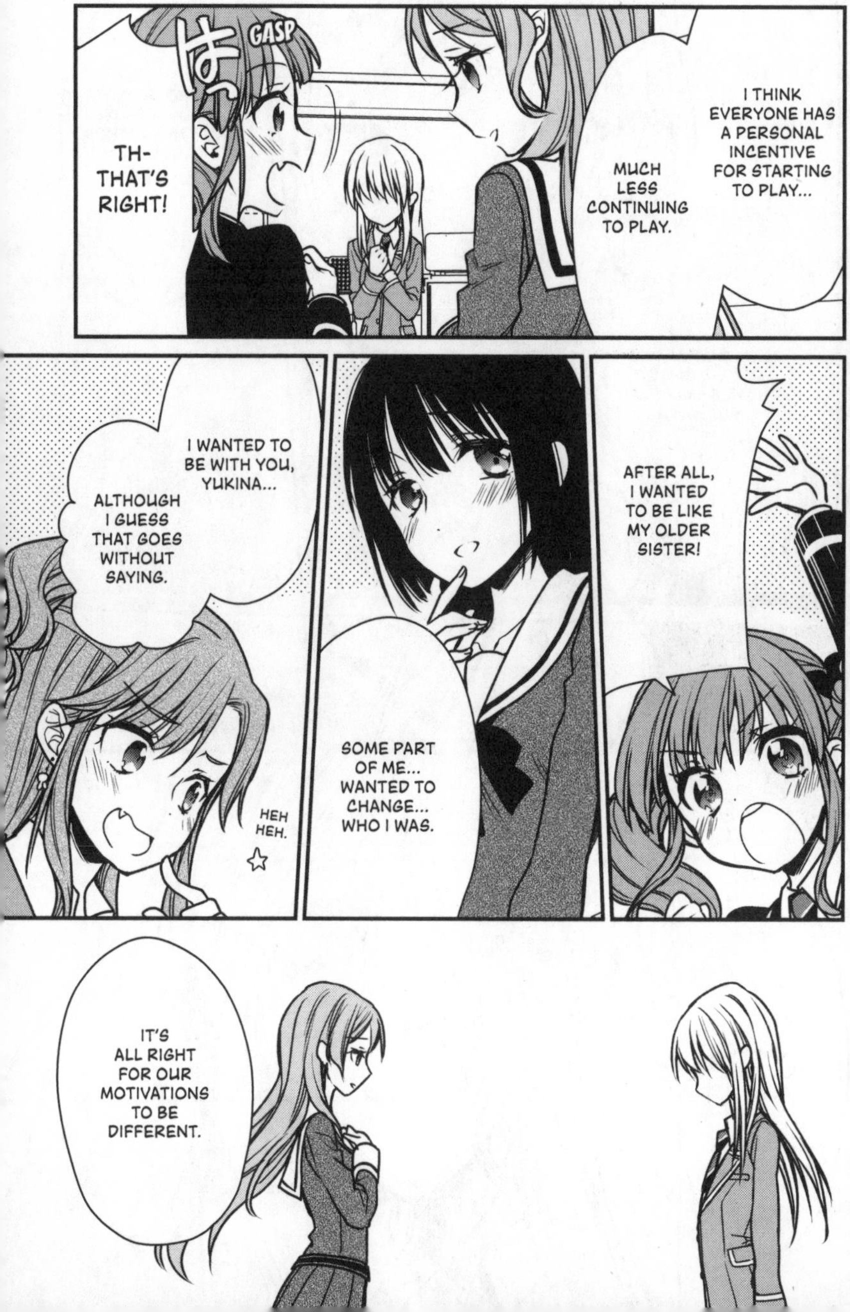
I THINK EVERYONE HAS A PERSONAL INCENTIVE FOR STARTING TO PLAY...
MUCH LESS CONTINUING TO PLAY.
はっ
GASP
TH- THAT'S RIGHT!
AFTER ALL, I WANTED TO BE LIKE MY OLDER SISTER!
SOME PART OF ME... WANTED TO CHANGE... WHO I WAS.
I WANTED TO BE WITH YOU, YUKINA...
ALTHOUGH I GUESS THAT GOES WITHOUT SAYING.
HEH HEH.
IT'S ALL RIGHT FOR OUR MOTIVATIONS TO BE DIFFERENT.

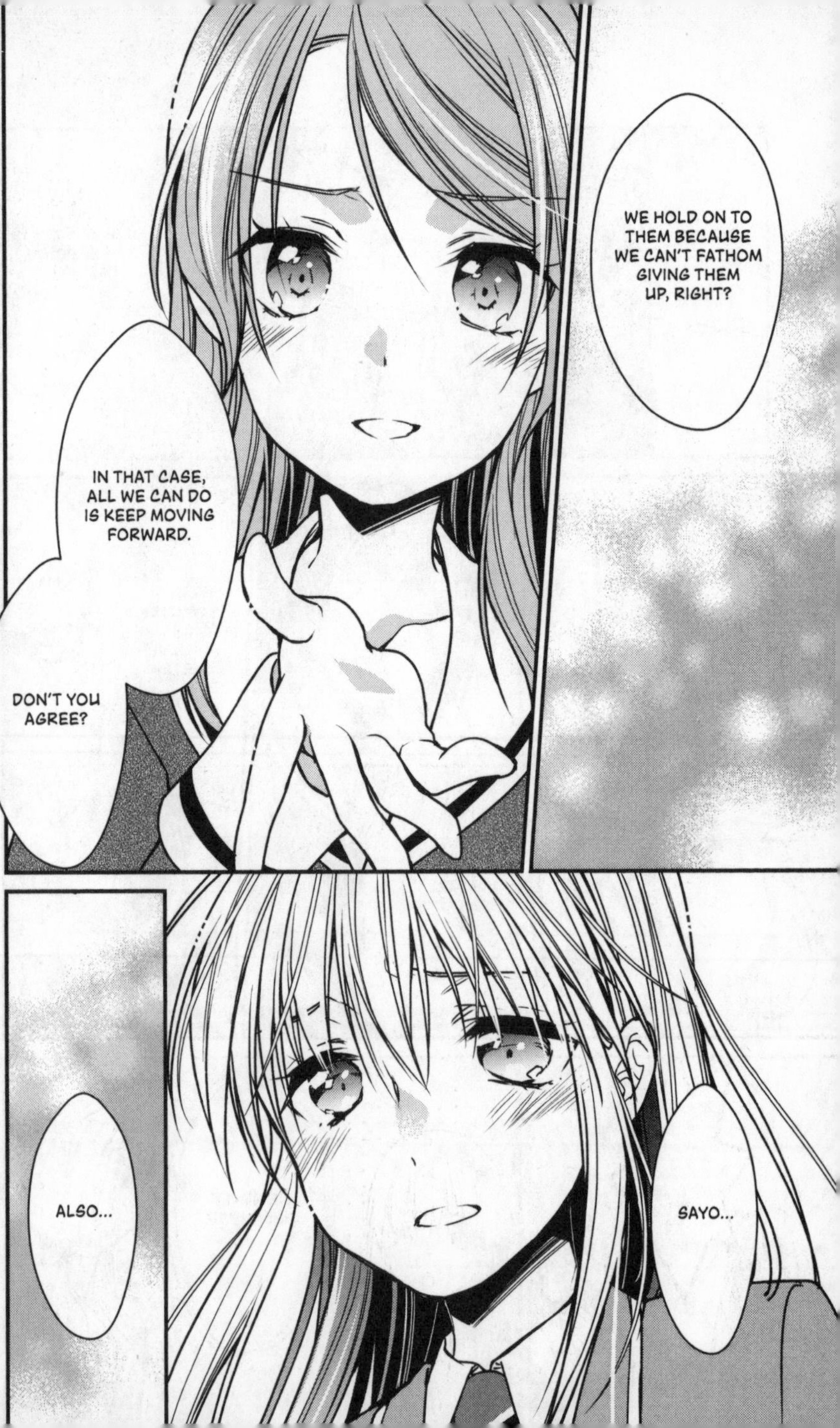
WE HOLD ON TO THEM BECAUSE WE CAN'T FATHOM GIVING THEM UP, RIGHT?
IN THAT CASE, ALL WE CAN DO IS KEEP MOVING FORWARD.
DON'T YOU AGREE?
SAYO...
ALSO...

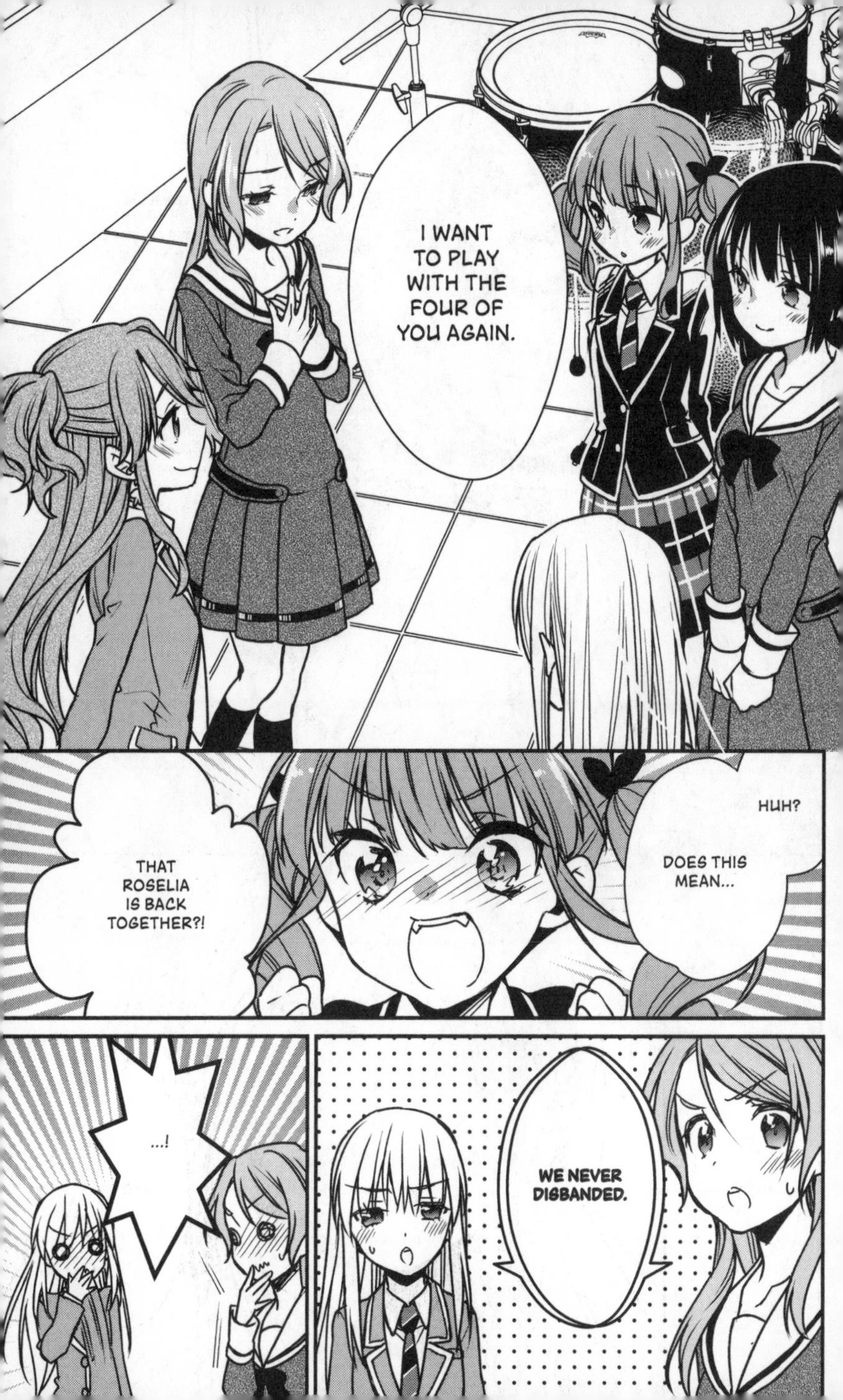
I WANT TO PLAY WITH THE FOUR OF YOU AGAIN.
HUH?
DOES THIS MEAN...
THAT ROSELIA IS BACK TOGETHER?!
WE NEVER DISBANDED.
...!

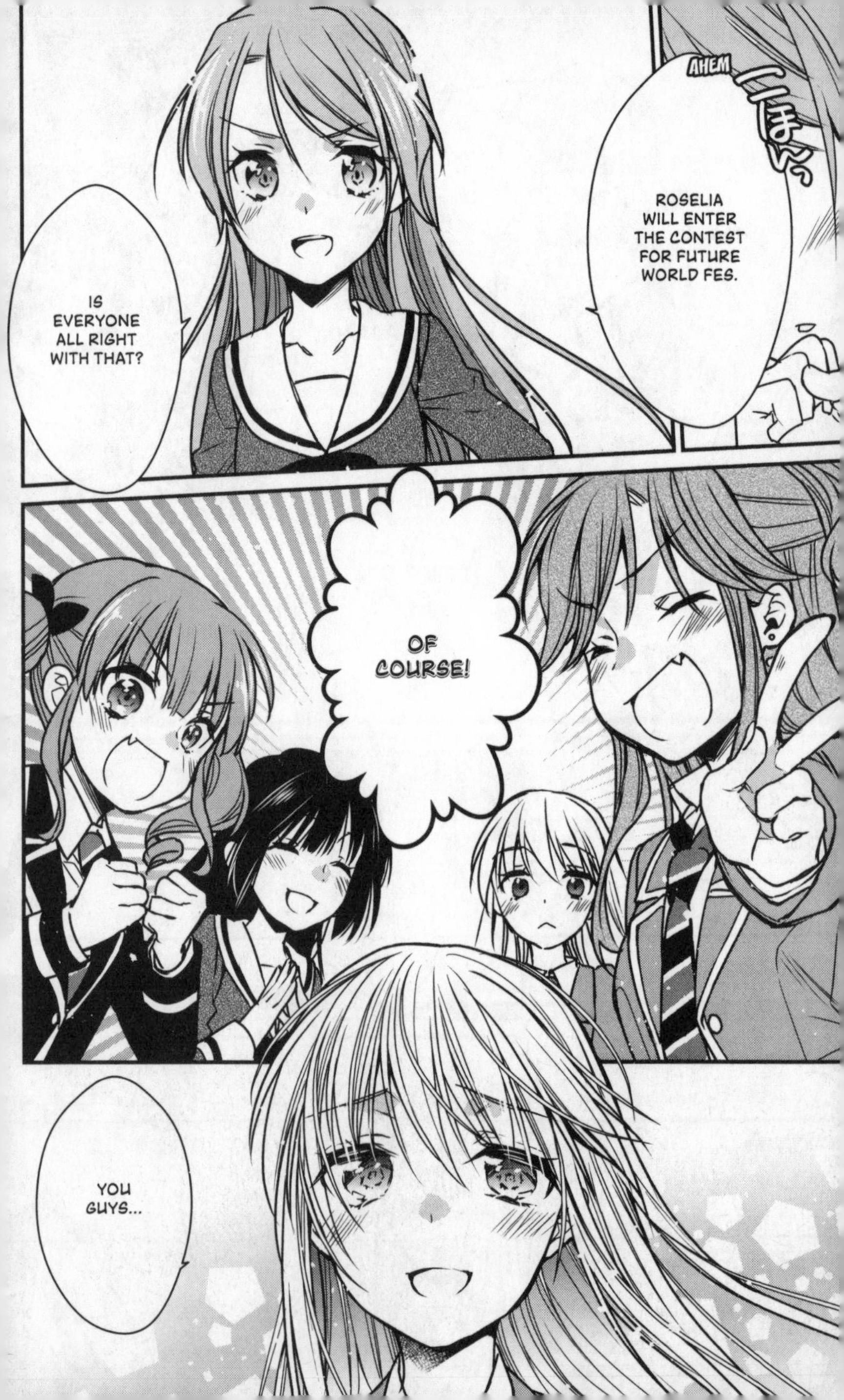
AHEM
こほんっ
ROSELIA WILL ENTER THE CONTEST FOR FUTURE WORLD FES.
IS EVERYONE ALL RIGHT WITH THAT?
OF COURSE!
YOU GUYS...

Chapter 10
Face Forward

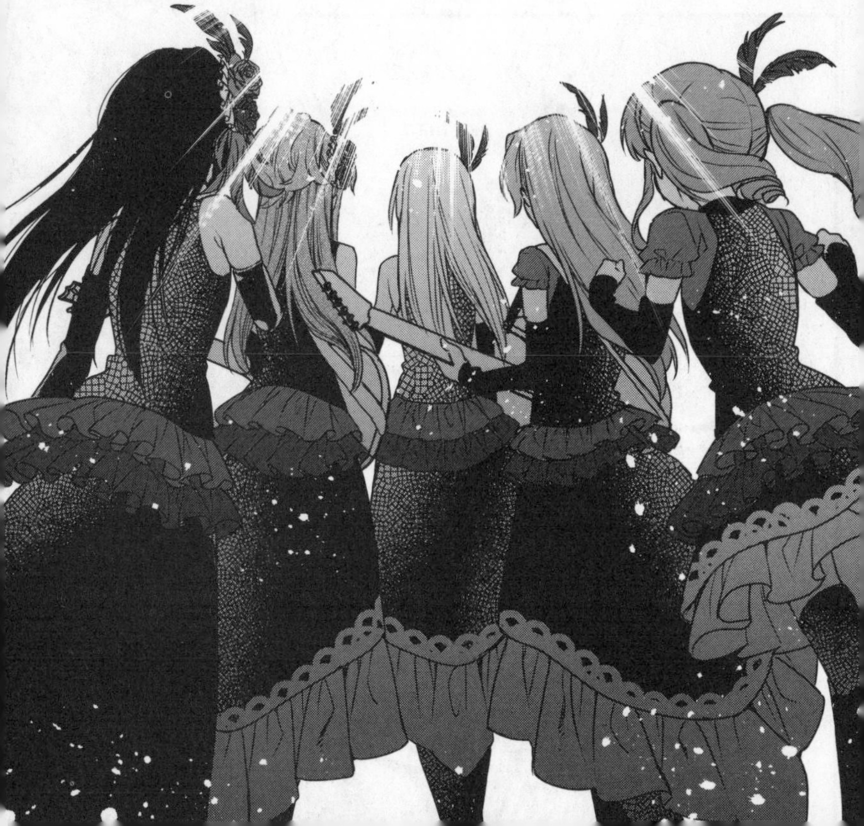

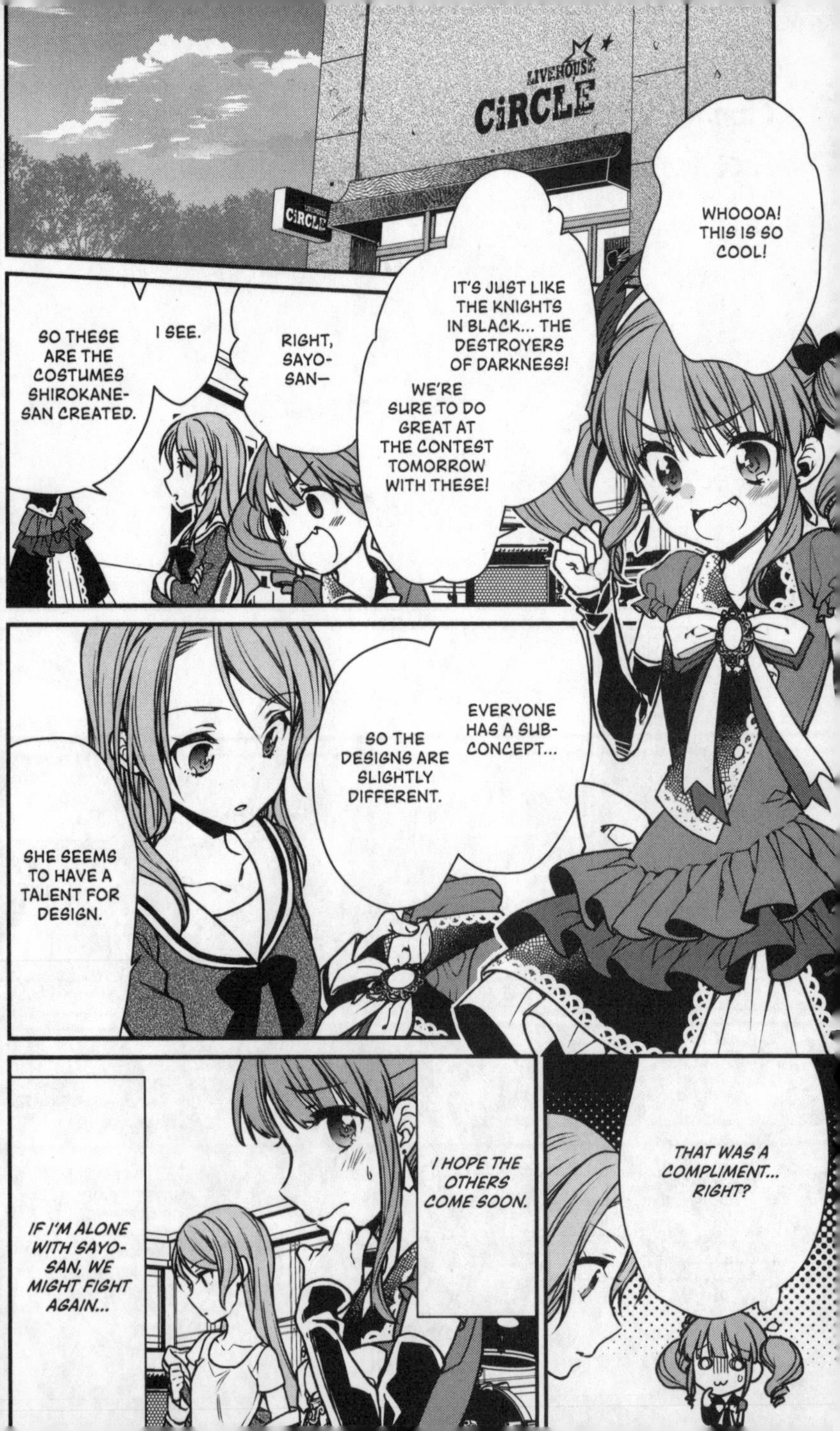
LIVEHOUSE CiRCLE
LIVEHOUSE CiRCLE
WHOOOA! THIS IS SO COOL!
IT'S JUST LIKE THE KNIGHTS IN BLACK... THE DESTROYERS OF DARKNESS!
WE'RE SURE TO DO GREAT AT THE CONTEST TOMORROW WITH THESE!
RIGHT, SAYO-SAN—
I SEE.
SO THESE ARE THE COSTUMES SHIROKANE-SAN CREATED.
EVERYONE HAS A SUB-CONCEPT...
SO THE DESIGNS ARE SLIGHTLY DIFFERENT.
SHE SEEMS TO HAVE A TALENT FOR DESIGN.
THAT WAS A COMPLIMENT... RIGHT?
I HOPE THE OTHERS COME SOON.
IF I'M ALONE WITH SAYO-SAN, WE MIGHT FIGHT AGAIN...

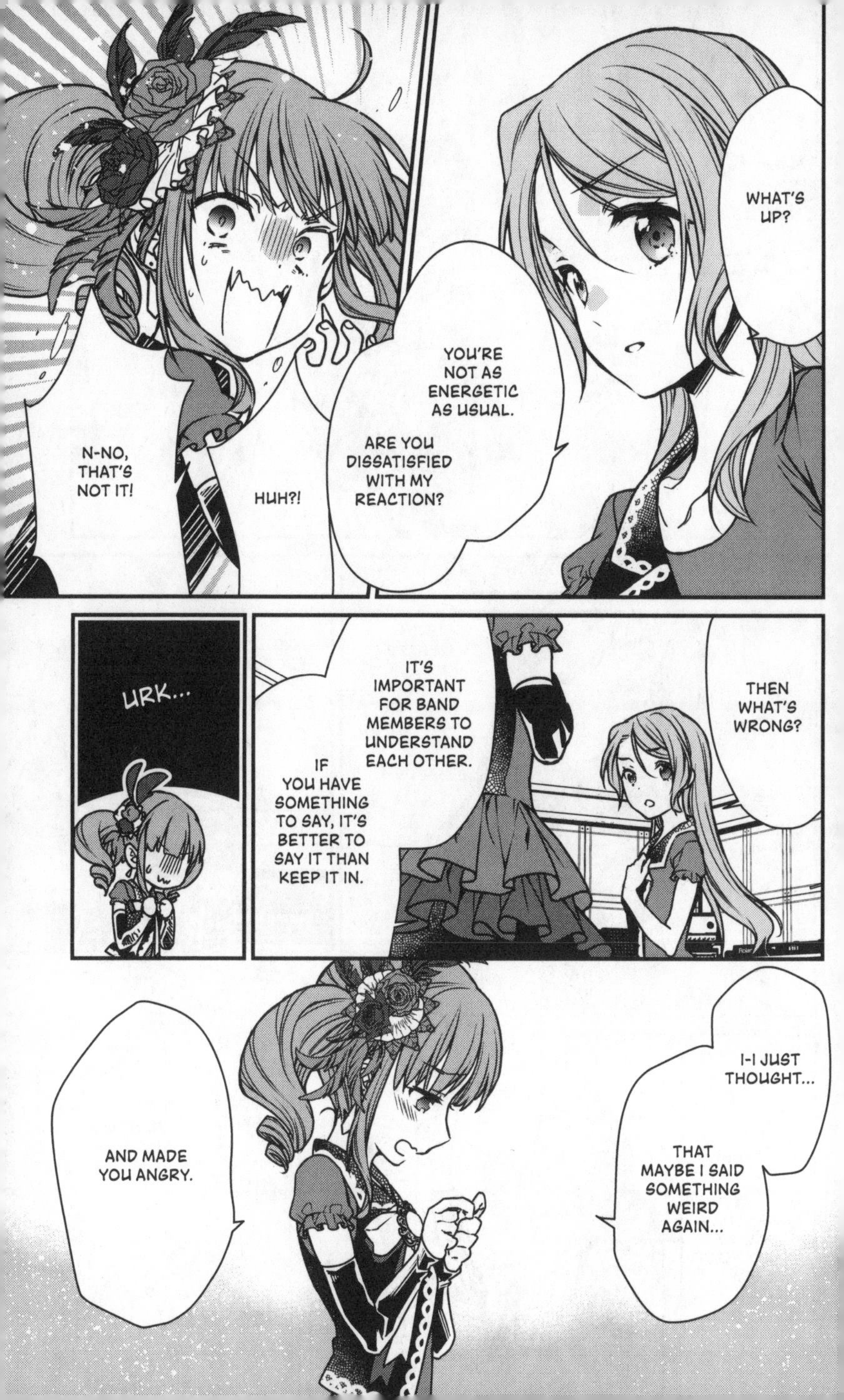
WHAT'S UP?
YOU'RE NOT AS ENERGETIC AS USUAL.
ARE YOU DISSATISFIED WITH MY REACTION?
HUH?!
N-NO, THAT'S NOT IT!
THEN WHAT'S WRONG?
IT'S IMPORTANT FOR BAND MEMBERS TO UNDERSTAND EACH OTHER.
IF YOU HAVE SOMETHING TO SAY, IT'S BETTER TO SAY IT THAN KEEP IT IN.
URK...
I-I JUST THOUGHT...
THAT MAYBE I SAID SOMETHING WEIRD AGAIN...
AND MADE YOU ANGRY.

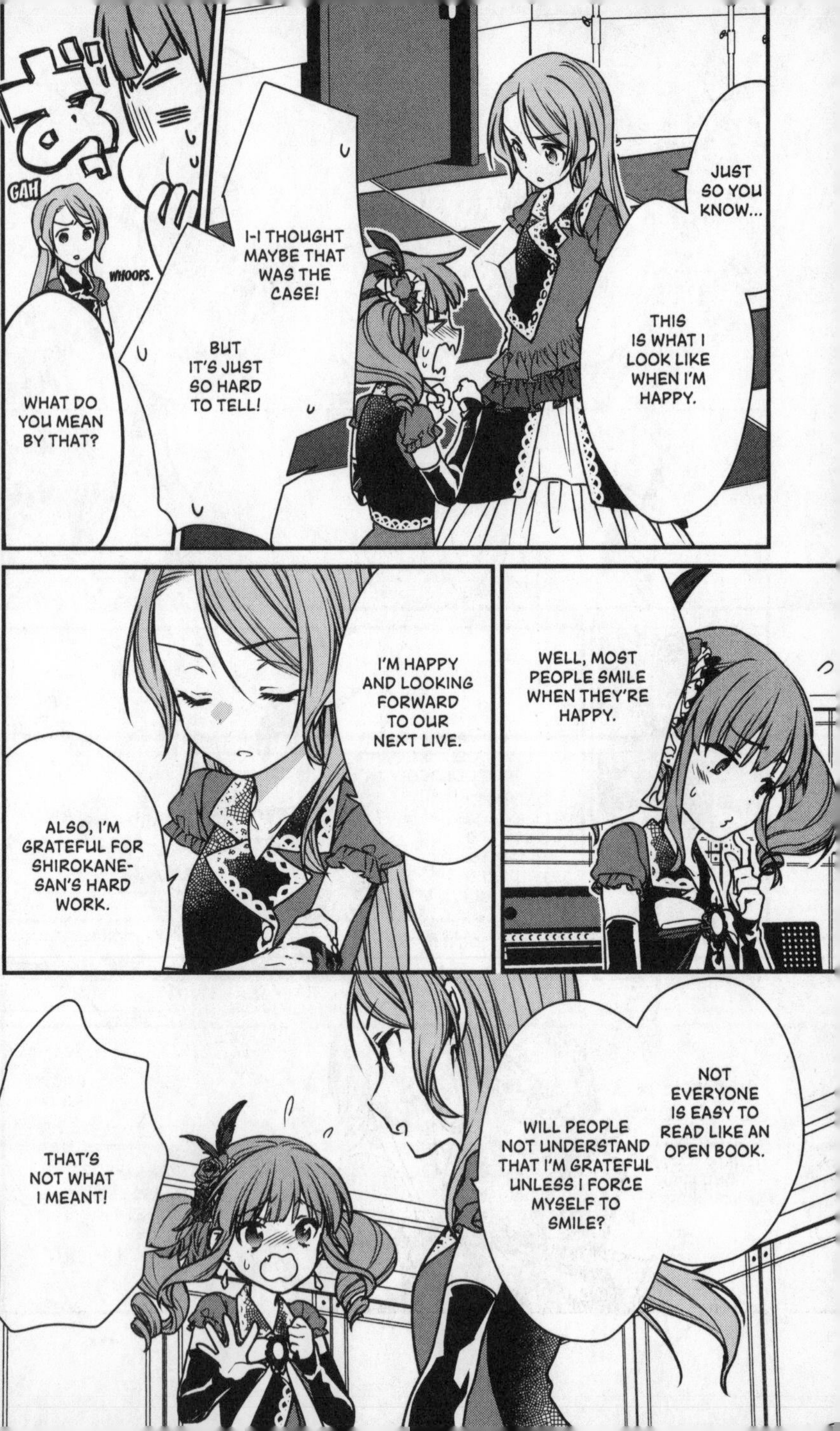
JUST SO YOU KNOW...
THIS IS WHAT I LOOK LIKE WHEN I'M HAPPY.
I-I THOUGHT MAYBE THAT WAS THE CASE!
BUT IT'S JUST SO HARD TO TELL!
GAH
WHOOPS.
WHAT DO YOU MEAN BY THAT?
WELL, MOST PEOPLE SMILE WHEN THEY'RE HAPPY.
I'M HAPPY AND LOOKING FORWARD TO OUR NEXT LIVE.
ALSO, I'M GRATEFUL FOR SHIROKANE-SAN'S HARD WORK.
NOT EVERYONE IS EASY TO READ LIKE AN OPEN BOOK.
WILL PEOPLE NOT UNDERSTAND THAT I'M GRATEFUL UNLESS I FORCE MYSELF TO SMILE?
THAT'S NOT WHAT I MEANT!

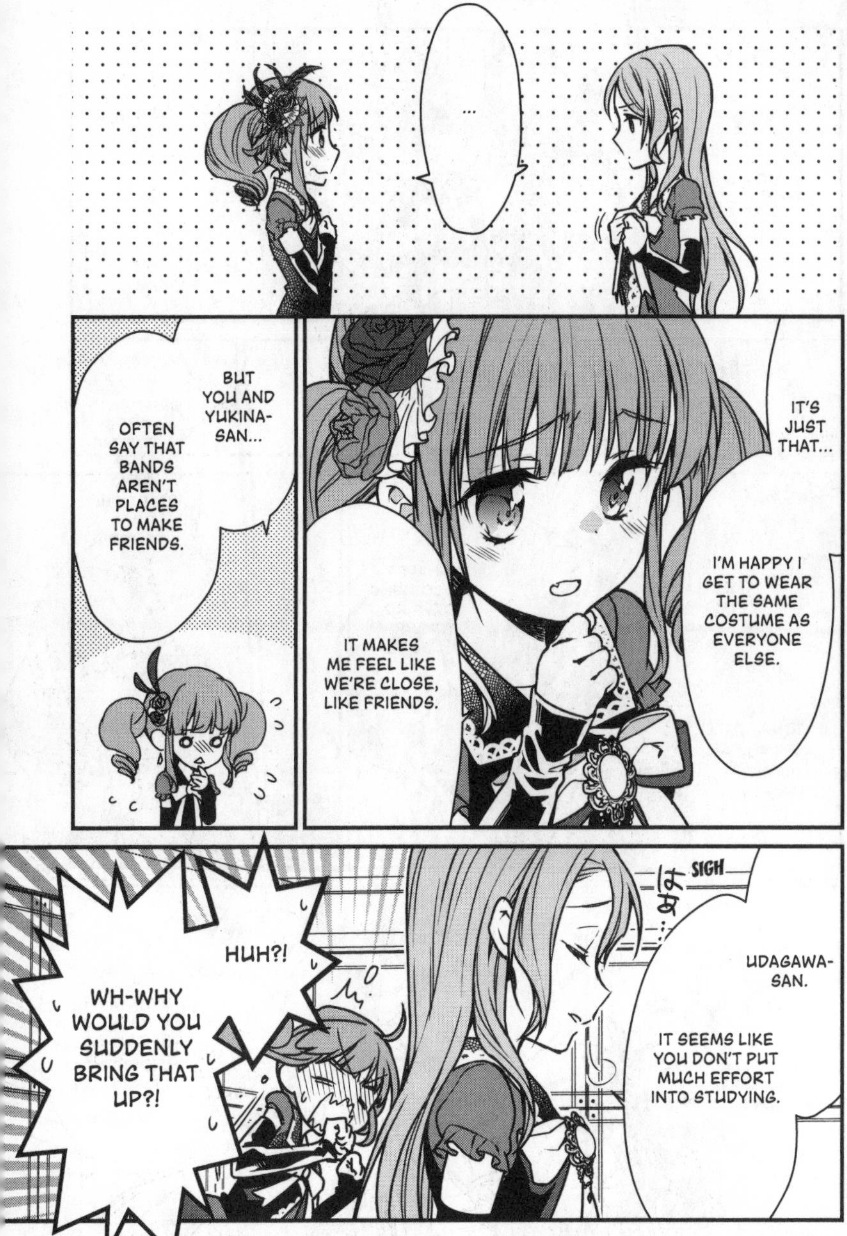
...
IT'S JUST THAT...
I'M HAPPY I GET TO WEAR THE SAME COSTUME AS EVERYONE ELSE.
IT MAKES ME FEEL LIKE WE'RE CLOSE, LIKE FRIENDS.
BUT YOU AND YUKINA-SAN...
OFTEN SAY THAT BANDS AREN'T PLACES TO MAKE FRIENDS.
SIGH
UDAGAWA-SAN.
IT SEEMS LIKE YOU DON'T PUT MUCH EFFORT INTO STUDYING.
HUH?!
WH-WHY WOULD YOU SUDDENLY BRING THAT UP?!

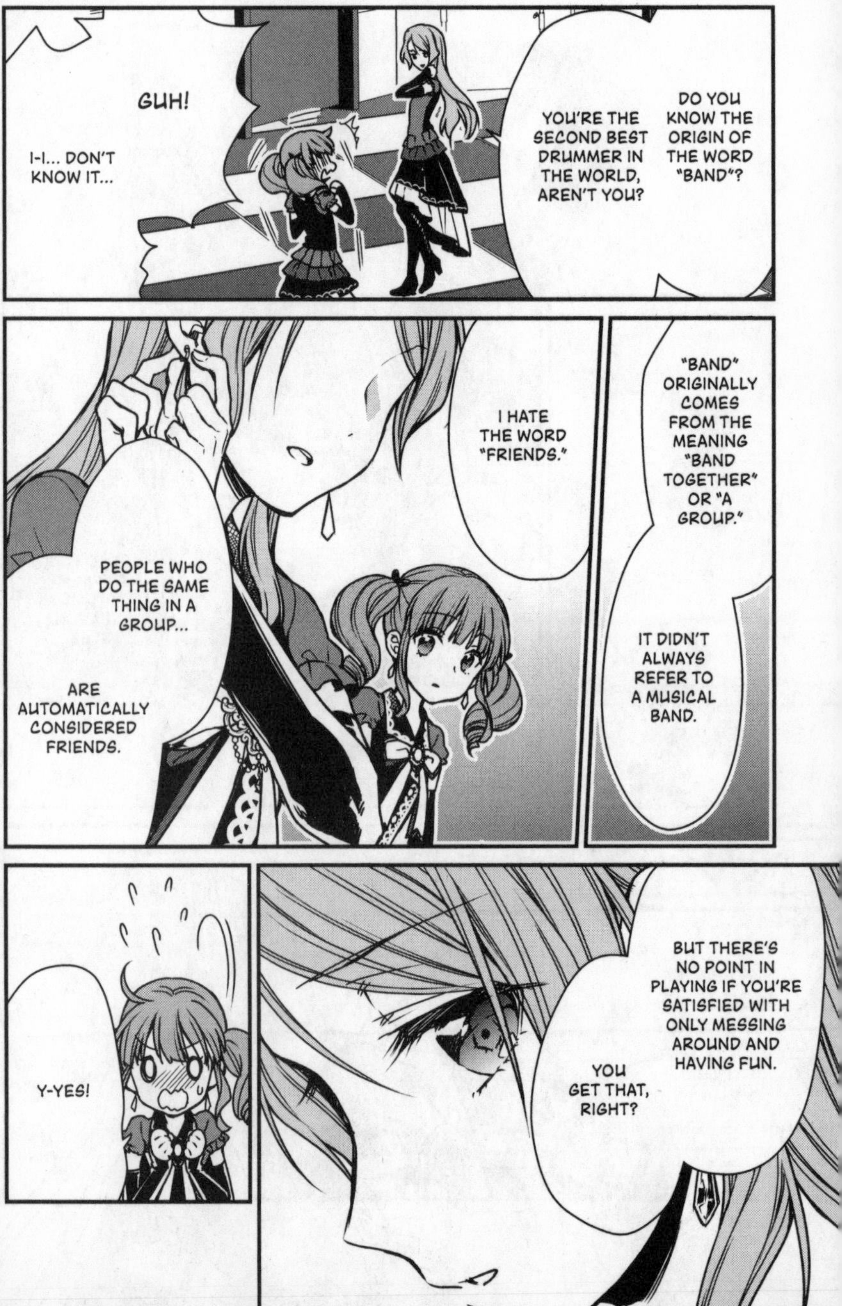
DO YOU KNOW THE ORIGIN OF THE WORD "BAND"?
YOU'RE THE SECOND BEST DRUMMER IN THE WORLD, AREN'T YOU?
GUH!
I-I... DON'T KNOW IT...
"BAND" ORIGINALLY COMES FROM THE MEANING "BAND TOGETHER" OR "A GROUP."
IT DIDN'T ALWAYS REFER TO A MUSICAL BAND.
I HATE THE WORD "FRIENDS."
PEOPLE WHO DO THE SAME THING IN A GROUP...
ARE AUTOMATICALLY CONSIDERED FRIENDS.
BUT THERE'S NO POINT IN PLAYING IF YOU'RE SATISFIED WITH ONLY MESSING AROUND AND HAVING FUN.
YOU GET THAT, RIGHT?
Y-YES!

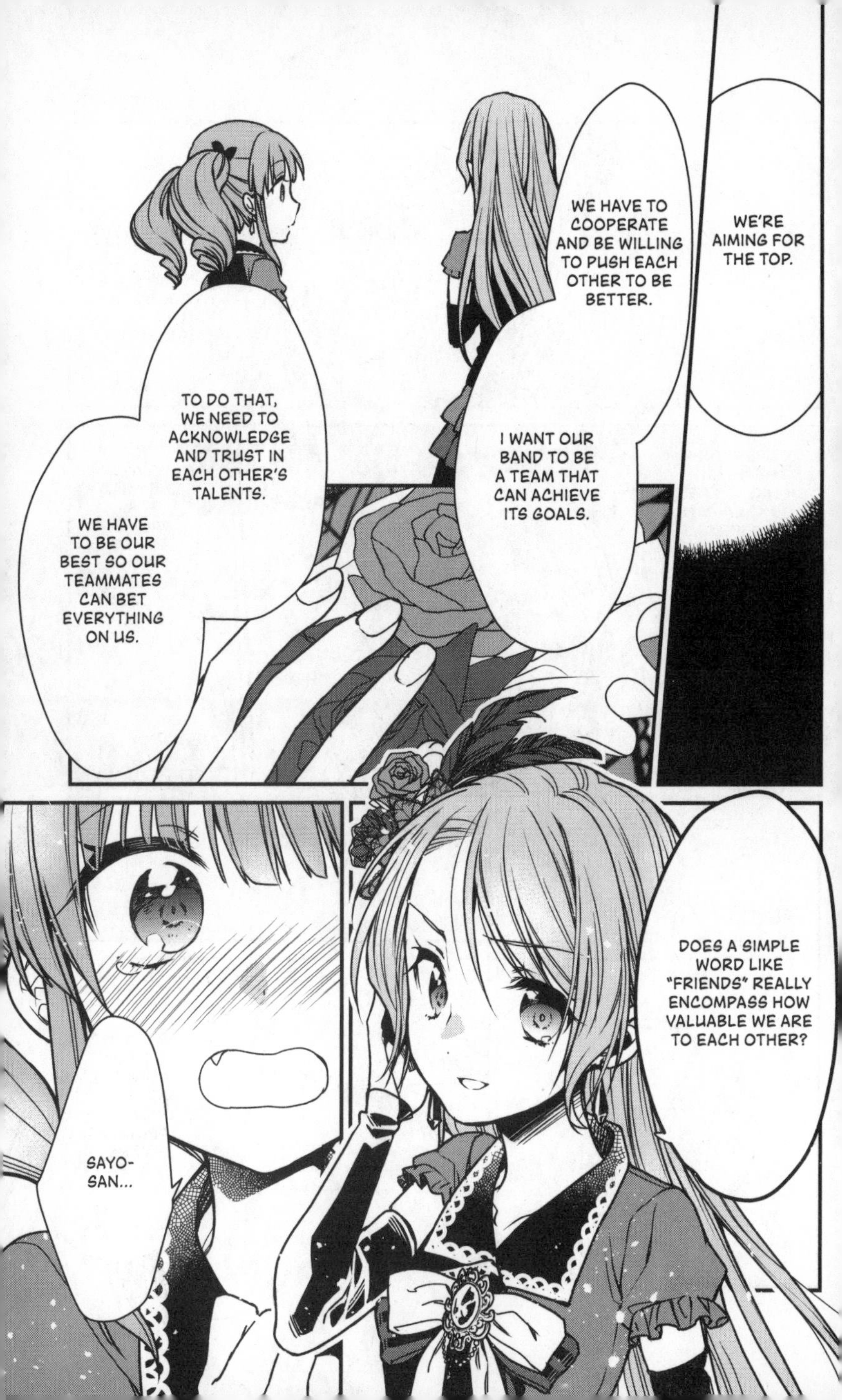
WE'RE AIMING FOR THE TOP.
WE HAVE TO COOPERATE AND BE WILLING TO PUSH EACH OTHER TO BE BETTER.
I WANT OUR BAND TO BE A TEAM THAT CAN ACHIEVE ITS GOALS.
TO DO THAT, WE NEED TO ACKNOWLEDGE AND TRUST IN EACH OTHER'S TALENTS.
WE HAVE TO BE OUR BEST SO OUR TEAMMATES CAN BET EVERYTHING ON US.
DOES A SIMPLE WORD LIKE "FRIENDS" REALLY ENCOMPASS HOW VALUABLE WE ARE TO EACH OTHER?
SAYO-SAN...

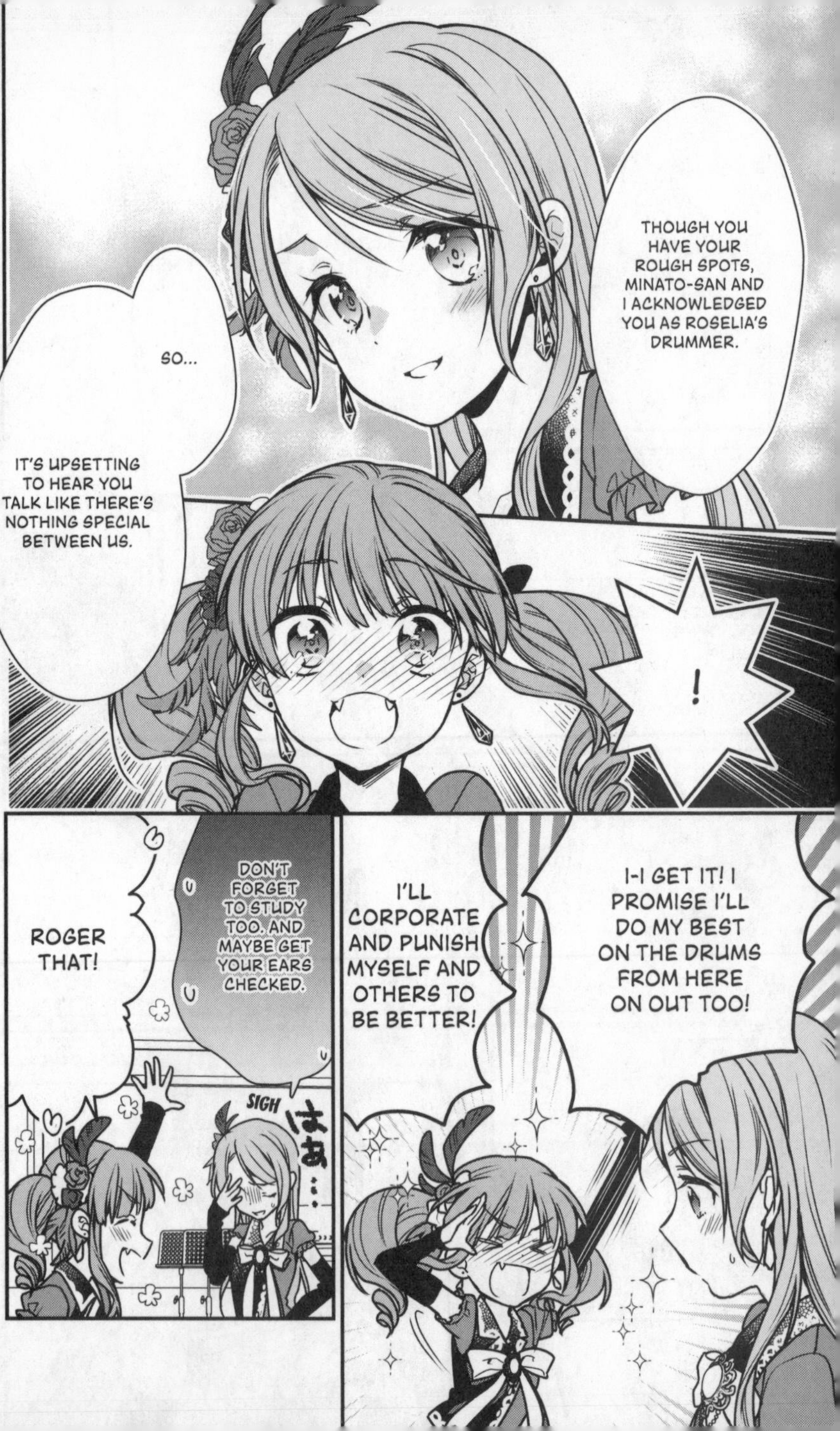
THOUGH YOU HAVE YOUR ROUGH SPOTS, MINATO-SAN AND I ACKNOWLEDGED YOU AS ROSELIA'S DRUMMER.
SO...
IT'S UPSETTING TO HEAR YOU TALK LIKE THERE'S NOTHING SPECIAL BETWEEN US.
!
I-I GET IT! I PROMISE I'LL DO MY BEST ON THE DRUMS FROM HERE ON OUT TOO!
I'LL CORPORATE AND PUNISH MYSELF AND OTHERS TO BE BETTER!
SIGH
はあ…
DON'T FORGET TO STUDY TOO. AND MAYBE GET YOUR EARS CHECKED.
ROGER THAT!

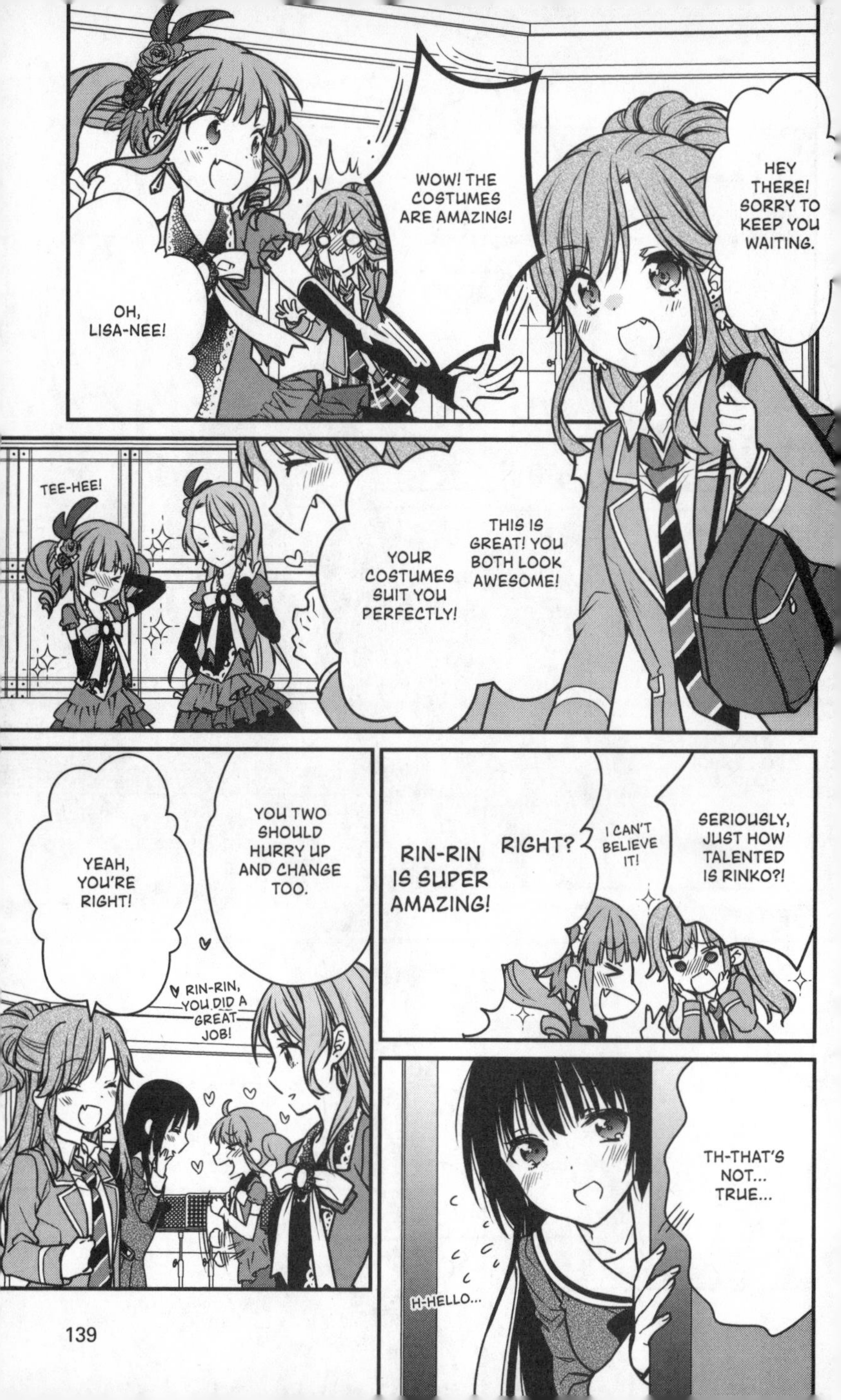
HEY THERE! SORRY TO KEEP YOU WAITING.
WOW! THE COSTUMES ARE AMAZING!
OH, LISA-NEE!
THIS IS GREAT! YOU BOTH LOOK AWESOME!
YOUR COSTUMES SUIT YOU PERFECTLY!
TEE-HEE!
SERIOUSLY, JUST HOW TALENTED IS RINKO?!
I CAN'T BELIEVE IT!
RIGHT?
RIN-RIN IS SUPER AMAZING!
TH-THAT'S NOT... TRUE...
H-HELLO...
YOU TWO SHOULD HURRY UP AND CHANGE TOO.
YEAH, YOU'RE RIGHT!
♥ RIN-RIN, YOU DID A GREAT JOB!

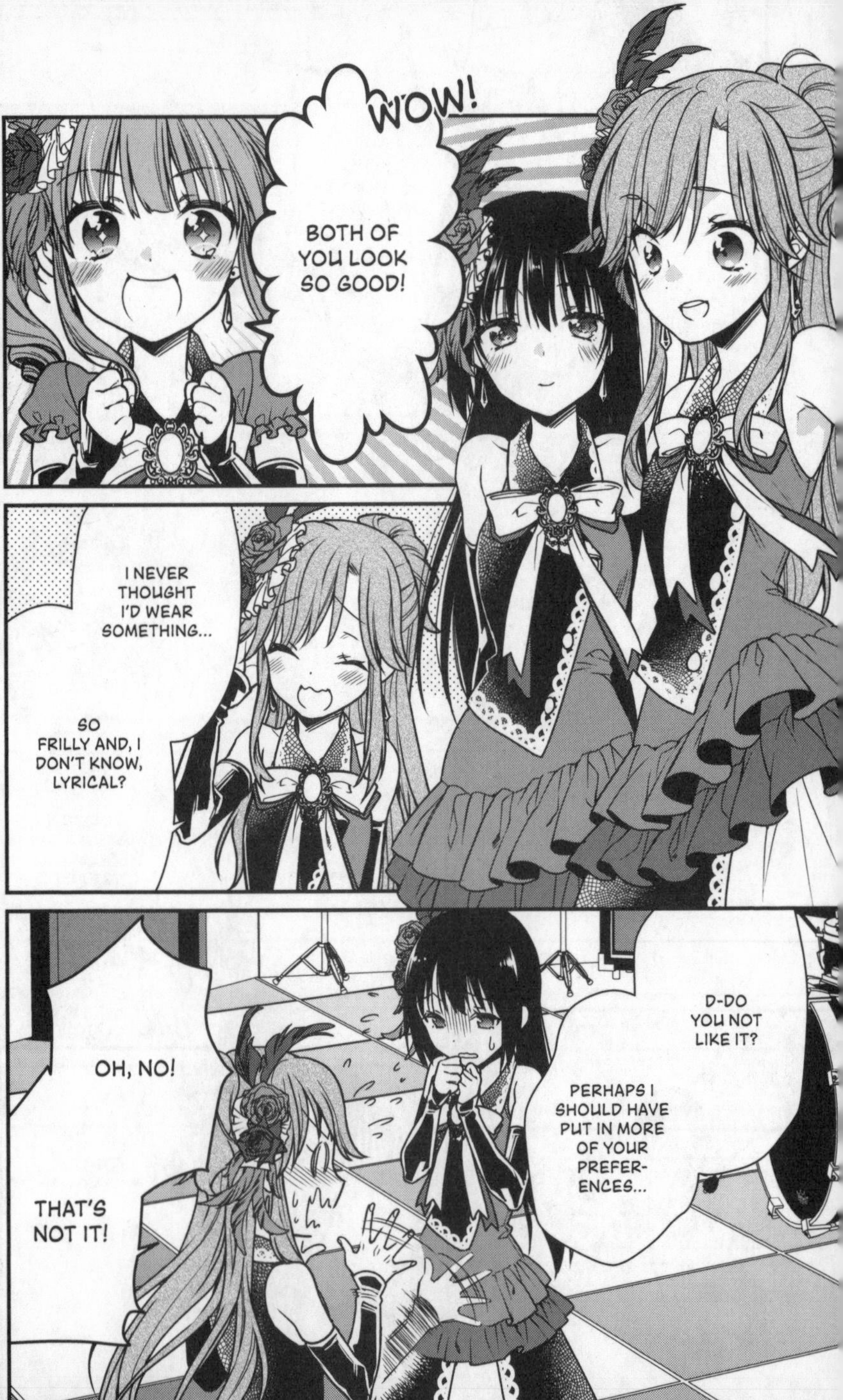
WOW!
BOTH OF YOU LOOK SO GOOD!
I NEVER THOUGHT I'D WEAR SOMETHING...
SO FRILLY AND, I DON'T KNOW, LYRICAL?
D-DO YOU NOT LIKE IT?
PERHAPS I SHOULD HAVE PUT IN MORE OF YOUR PREFER-ENCES...
OH, NO!
THAT'S NOT IT!

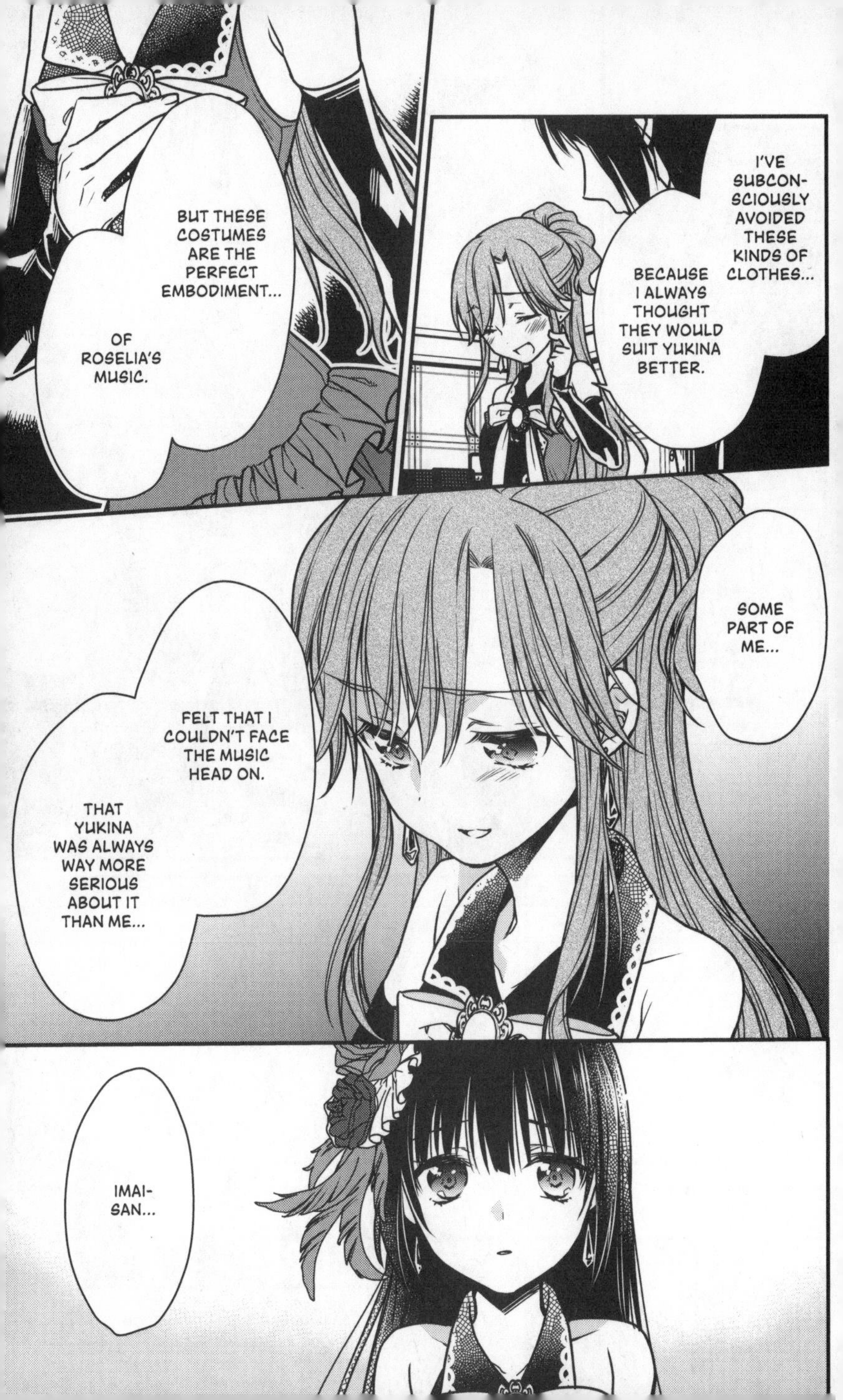
I'VE SUBCONSCIOUSLY AVOIDED THESE KINDS OF CLOTHES...
BECAUSE I ALWAYS THOUGHT THEY WOULD SUIT YUKINA BETTER.
BUT THESE COSTUMES ARE THE PERFECT EMBODIMENT...
OF ROSELIA'S MUSIC.
SOME PART OF ME...
FELT THAT I COULDN'T FACE THE MUSIC HEAD ON.
THAT YUKINA WAS ALWAYS WAY MORE SERIOUS ABOUT IT THAN ME...
IMAI-SAN...

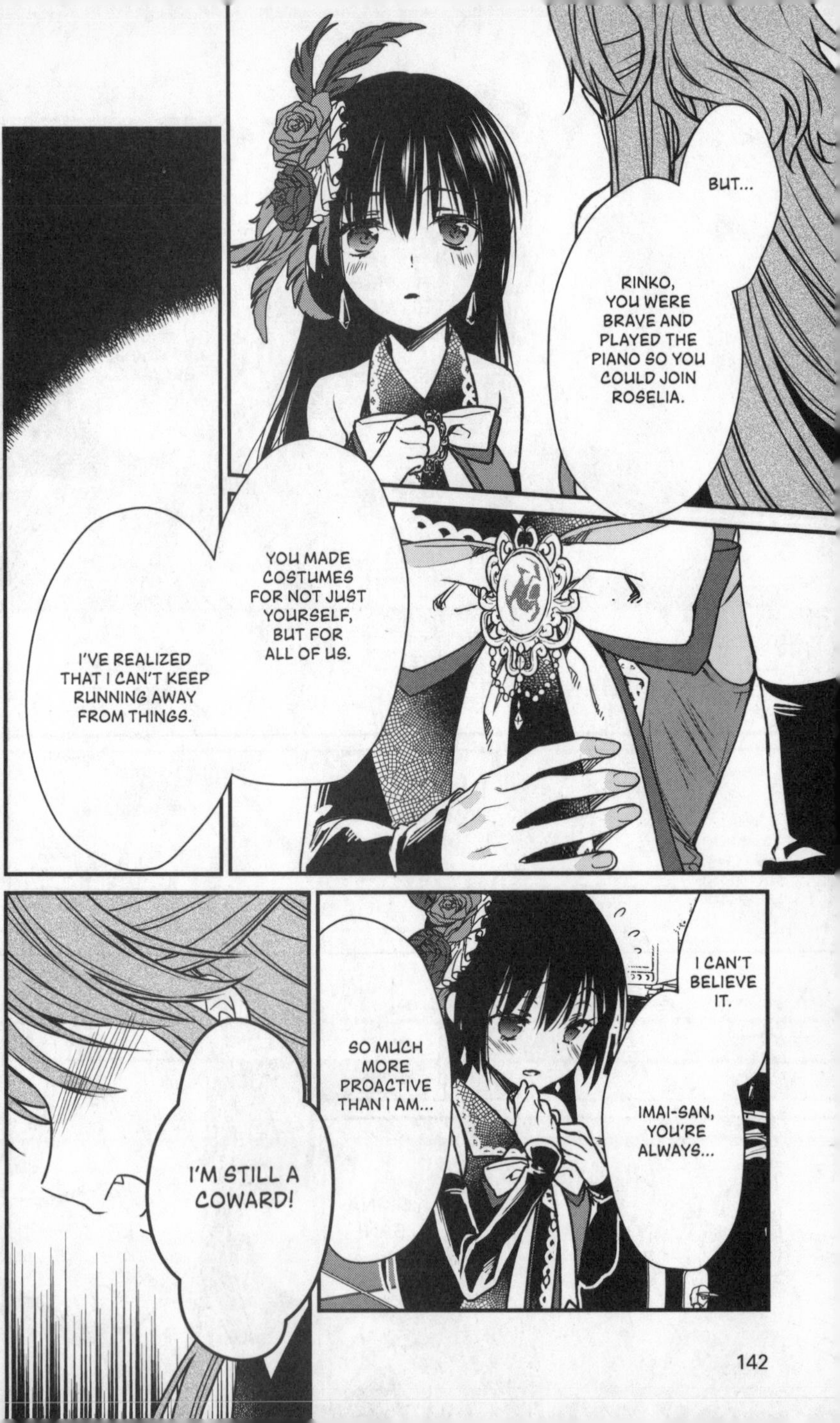
BUT...
RINKO, YOU WERE BRAVE AND PLAYED THE PIANO SO YOU COULD JOIN ROSELIA.
YOU MADE COSTUMES FOR NOT JUST YOURSELF, BUT FOR ALL OF US.
I'VE REALIZED THAT I CAN'T KEEP RUNNING AWAY FROM THINGS.
I CAN'T BELIEVE IT.
IMAI-SAN, YOU'RE ALWAYS...
SO MUCH MORE PROACTIVE THAN I AM...
I'M STILL A COWARD!

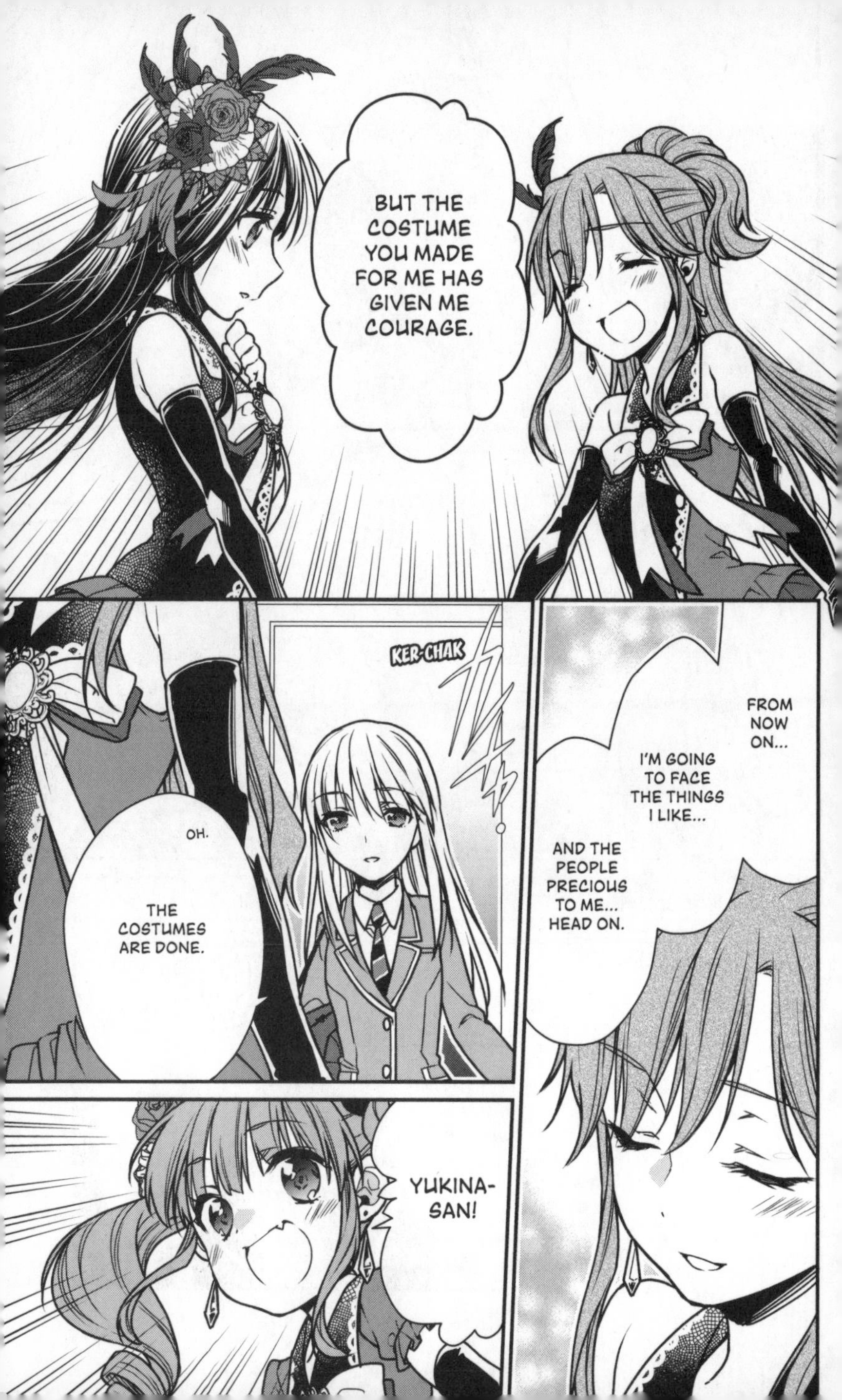
BUT THE COSTUME YOU MADE FOR ME HAS GIVEN ME COURAGE.
FROM NOW ON...
I'M GOING TO FACE THE THINGS I LIKE...
AND THE PEOPLE PRECIOUS TO ME... HEAD ON.
KER-CHAK
OH.
THE COSTUMES ARE DONE.
YUKINA-SAN!

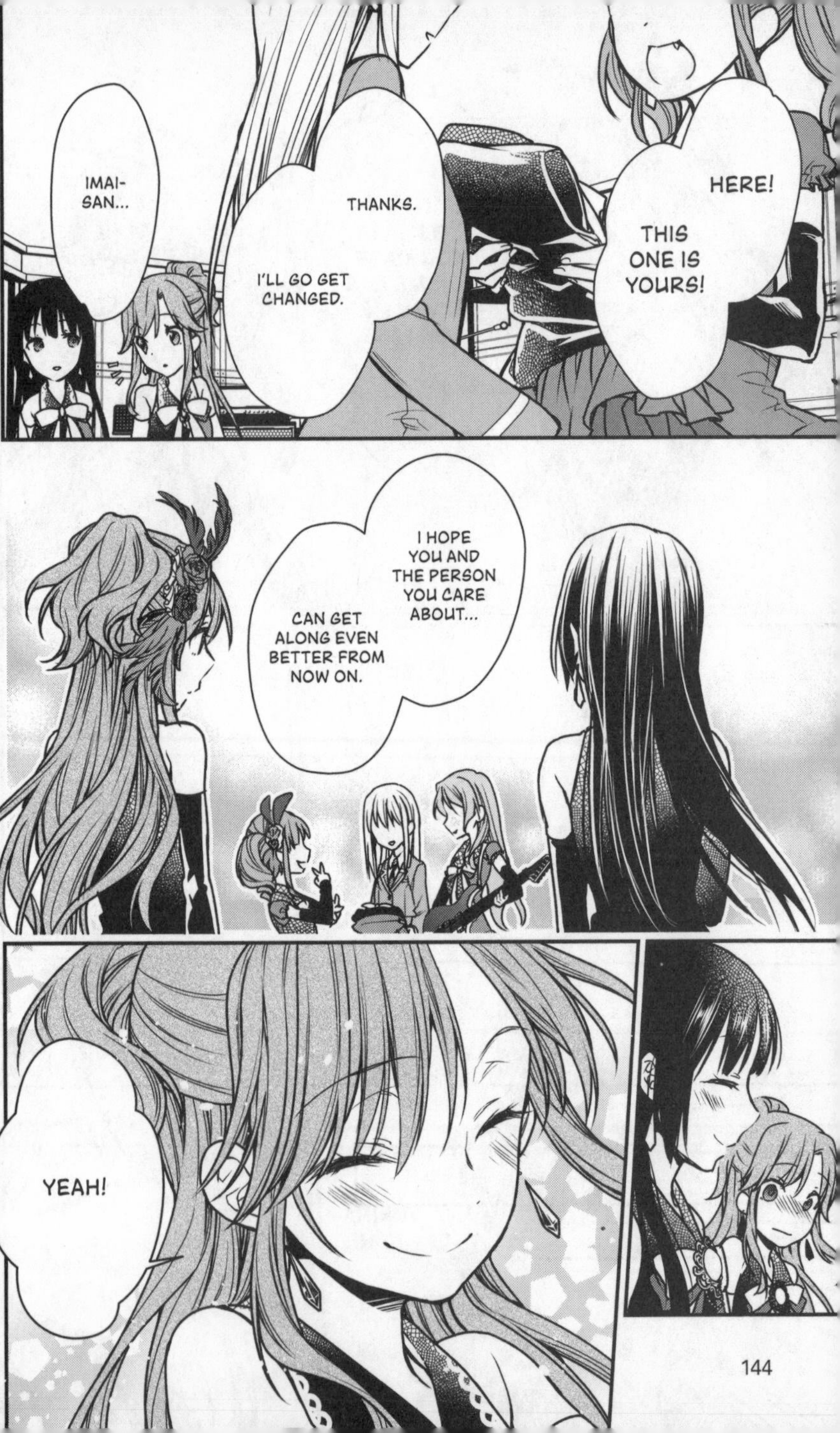
HERE!
THIS ONE IS YOURS!
THANKS.
I'LL GO GET CHANGED.
IMAI-SAN...
I HOPE YOU AND THE PERSON YOU CARE ABOUT...
CAN GET ALONG EVEN BETTER FROM NOW ON.
YEAH!

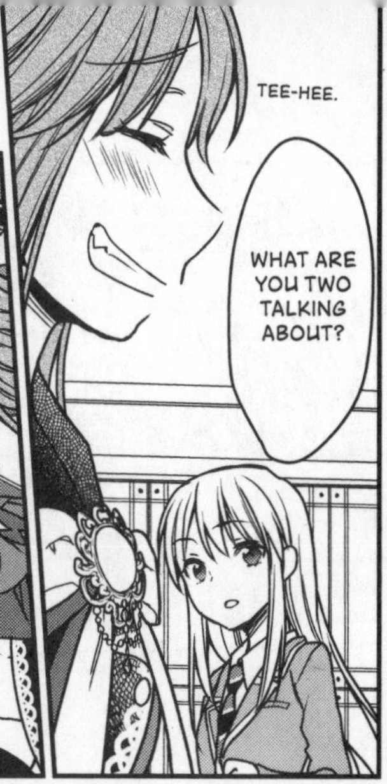
TEE-HEE.
WHAT ARE YOU TWO TALKING ABOUT?
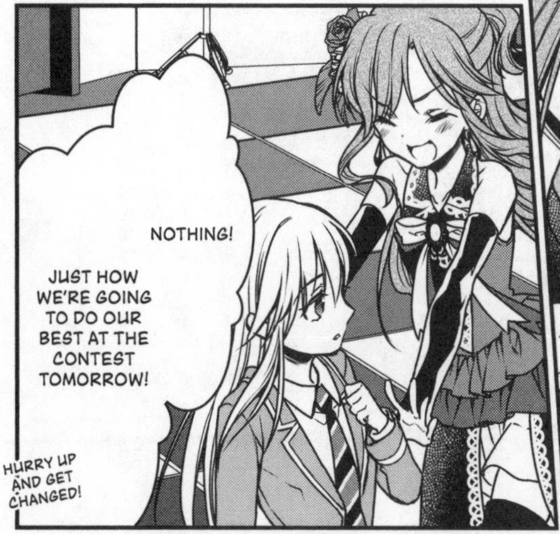
NOTHING!
JUST HOW WE'RE GOING TO DO OUR BEST AT THE CONTEST TOMORROW!
HURRY UP AND GET CHANGED!
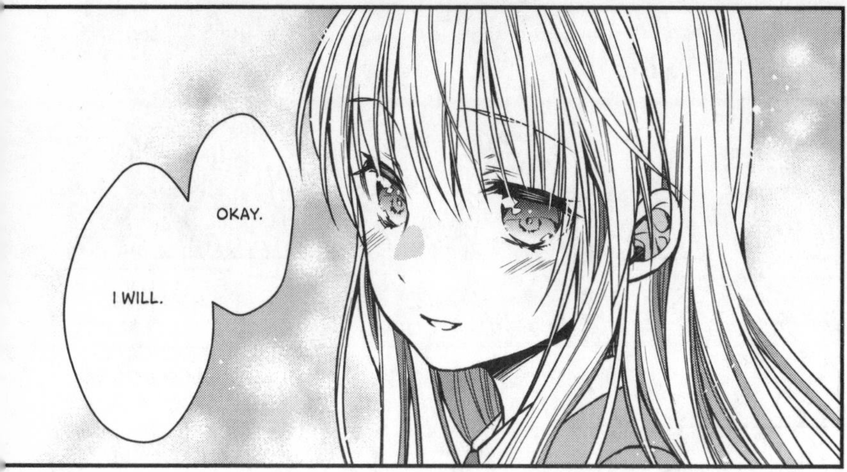
OKAY.
I WILL.

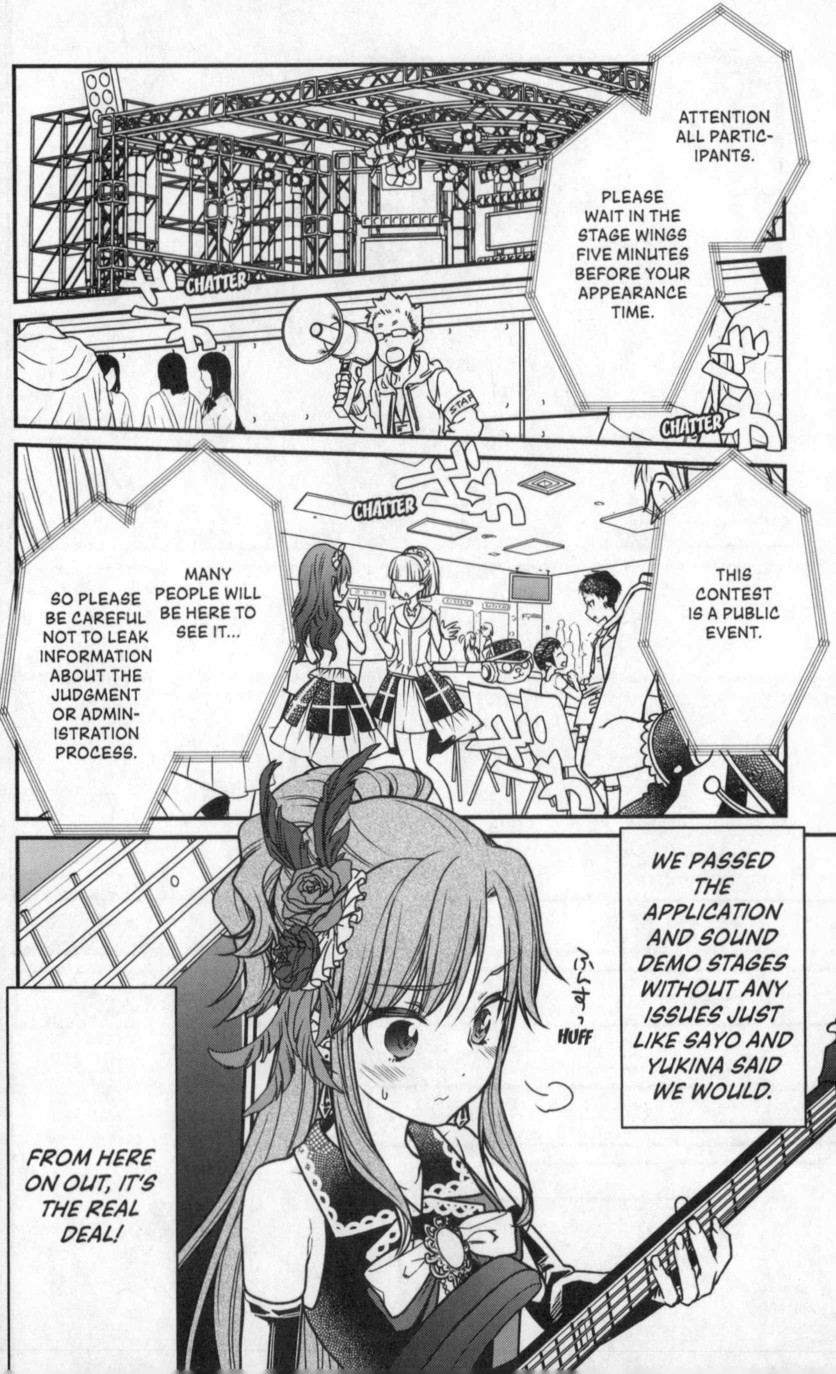
ATTENTION ALL PARTICIPANTS.
PLEASE WAIT IN THE STAGE WINGS FIVE MINUTES BEFORE YOUR APPEARANCE TIME.
CHATTER
CHATTER
CHATTER
THIS CONTEST IS A PUBLIC EVENT.
MANY PEOPLE WILL BE HERE TO SEE IT...
SO PLEASE BE CAREFUL NOT TO LEAK INFORMATION ABOUT THE JUDGMENT OR ADMINISTRATION PROCESS.
WE PASSED THE APPLICATION AND SOUND DEMO STAGES WITHOUT ANY ISSUES JUST LIKE SAYO AND YUKINA SAID WE WOULD.
ふんすっ
HUFF
FROM HERE ON OUT, IT'S THE REAL DEAL!

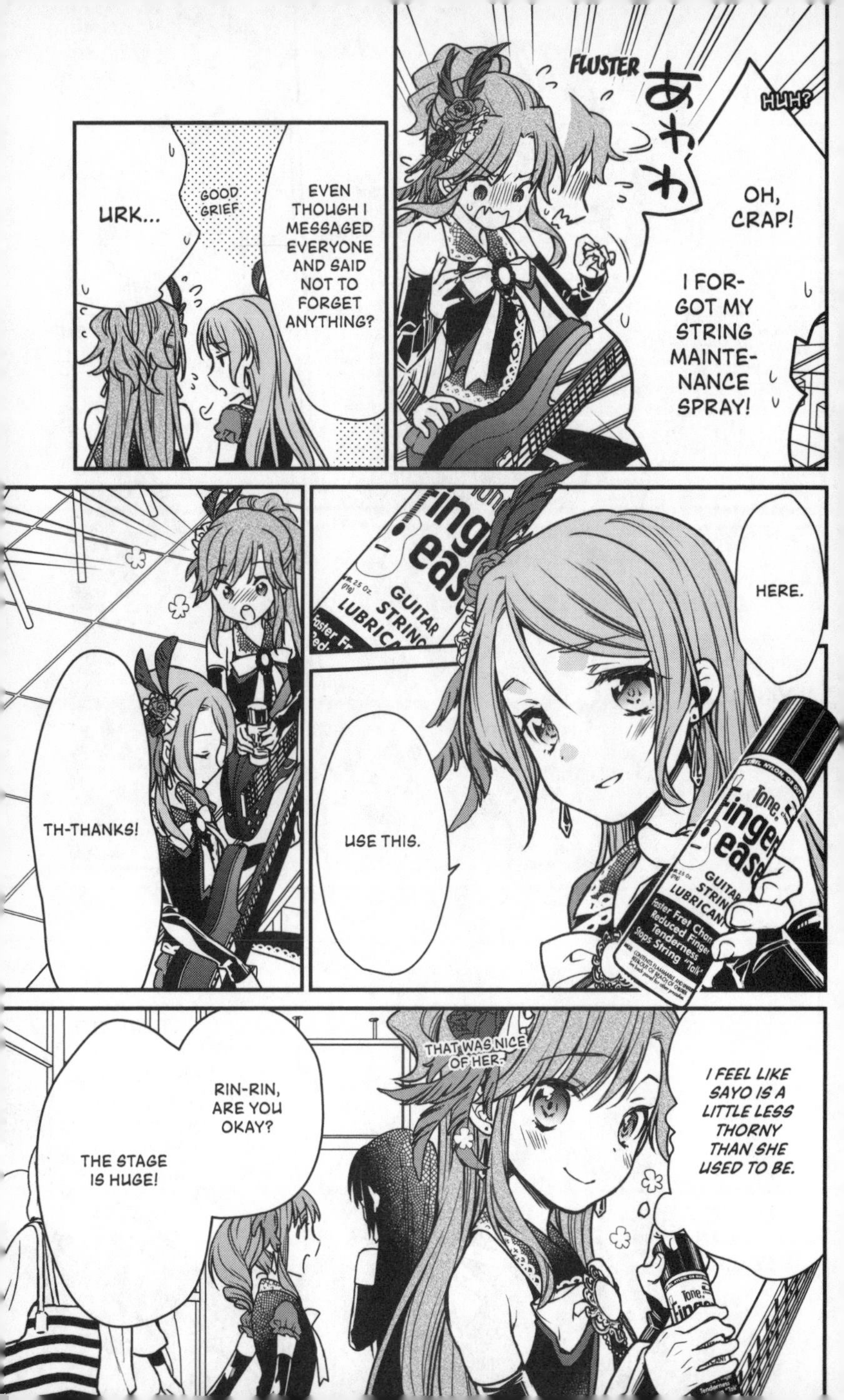
FLUSTER
あわわ
HUH?
OH, CRAP!
I FOR-GOT MY STRING MAINTE-NANCE SPRAY!
EVEN THOUGH I MESSAGED EVERYONE AND SAID NOT TO FORGET ANYTHING?
GOOD GRIEF.
URK...
HERE.
USE THIS.
TH-THANKS!
I FEEL LIKE SAYO IS A LITTLE LESS THORNY THAN SHE USED TO BE.
THAT WAS NICE OF HER.
RIN-RIN, ARE YOU OKAY?
THE STAGE IS HUGE!

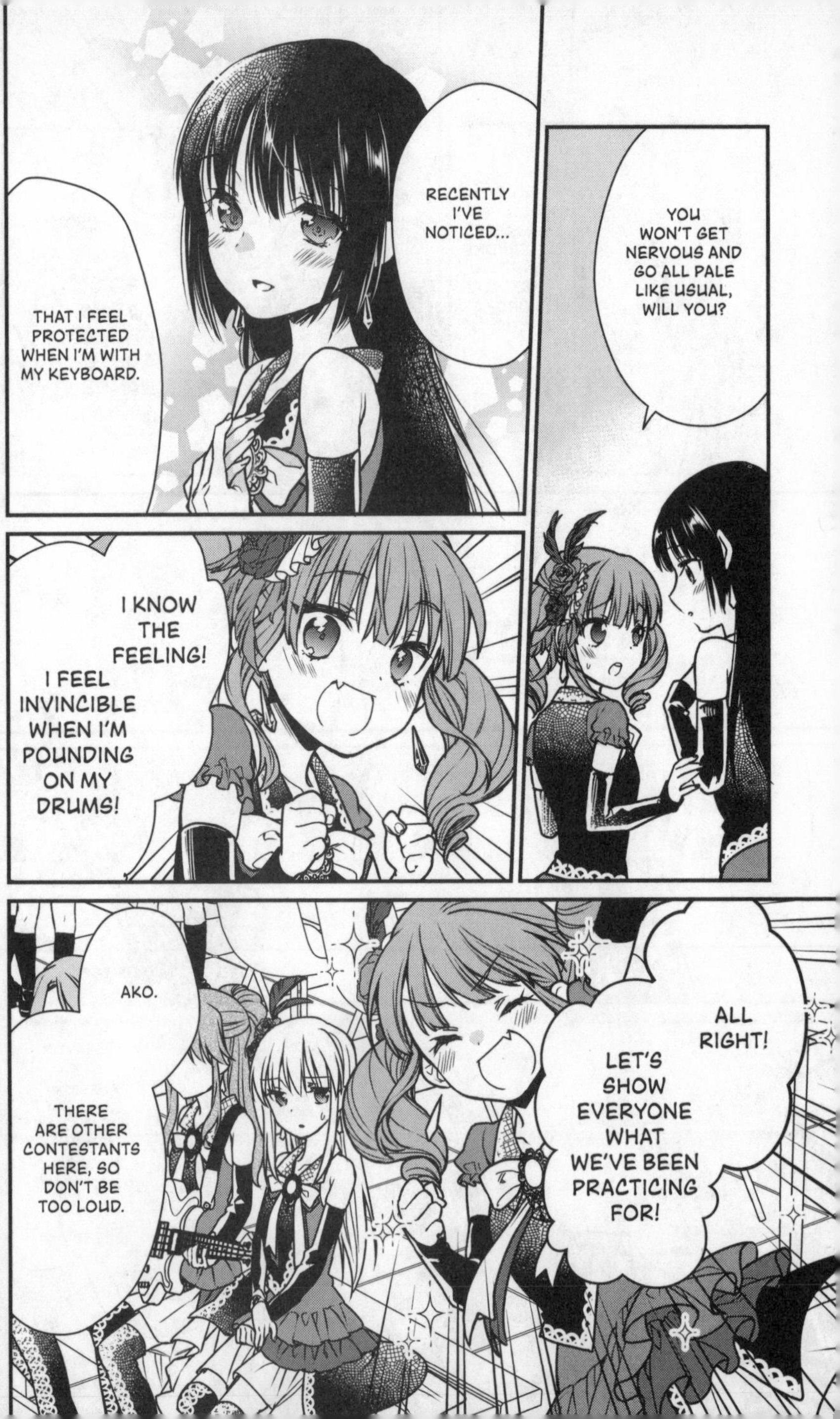
YOU WON'T GET NERVOUS AND GO ALL PALE LIKE USUAL, WILL YOU?
RECENTLY I'VE NOTICED...
THAT I FEEL PROTECTED WHEN I'M WITH MY KEYBOARD.
I KNOW THE FEELING!
I FEEL INVINCIBLE WHEN I'M POUNDING ON MY DRUMS!
ALL RIGHT!
LET'S SHOW EVERYONE WHAT WE'VE BEEN PRACTICING FOR!
AKO.
THERE ARE OTHER CONTESTANTS HERE, SO DON'T BE TOO LOUD.

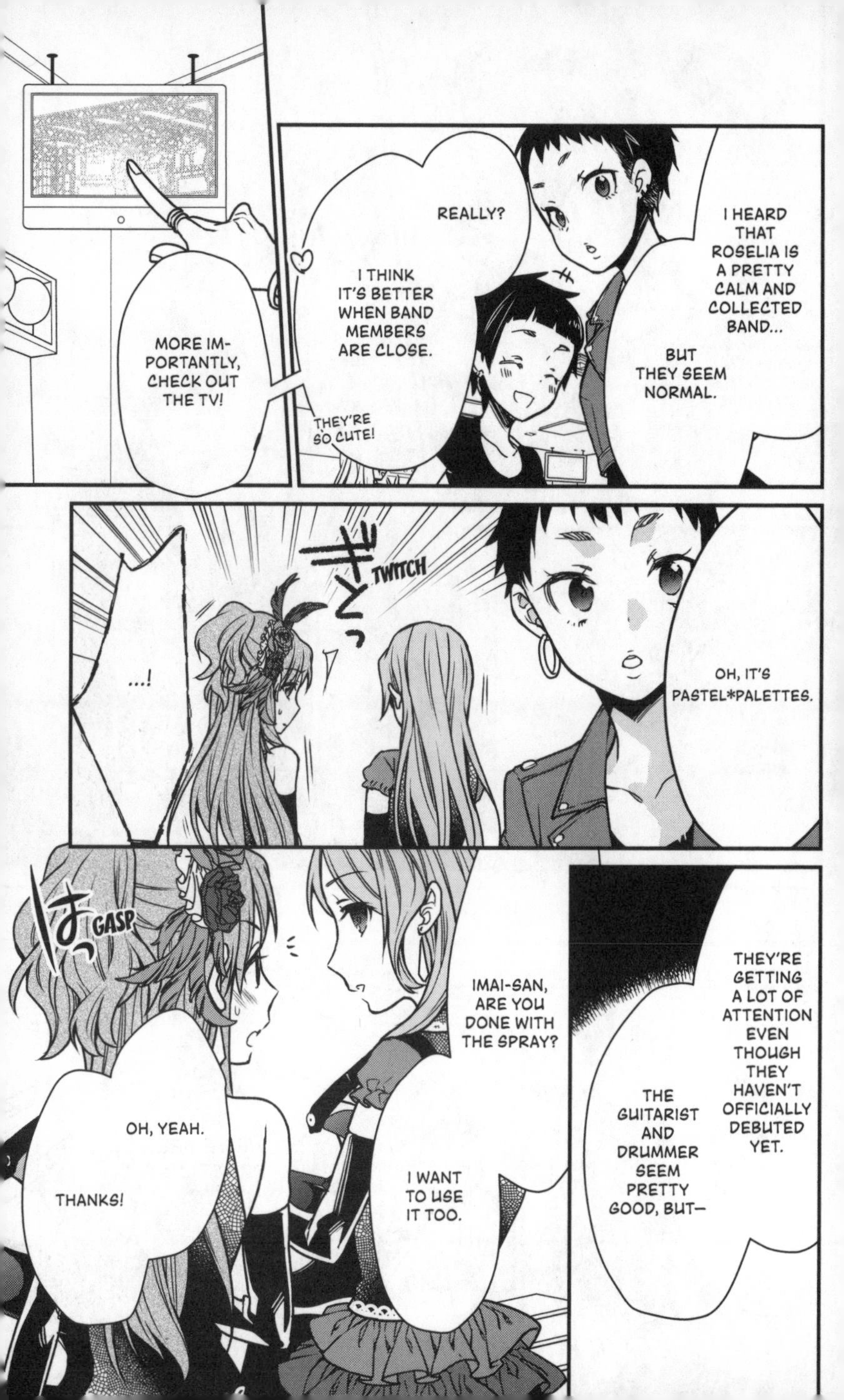
I HEARD THAT ROSELIA IS A PRETTY CALM AND COLLECTED BAND...
BUT THEY SEEM NORMAL.
REALLY?
I THINK IT'S BETTER WHEN BAND MEMBERS ARE CLOSE.
THEY'RE SO CUTE!
MORE IMPORTANTLY, CHECK OUT THE TV!
OH, IT'S PASTEL*PALETTES.
TWITCH
...!
THEY'RE GETTING A LOT OF ATTENTION EVEN THOUGH THEY HAVEN'T OFFICIALLY DEBUTED YET.
THE GUITARIST AND DRUMMER SEEM PRETTY GOOD, BUT—
IMAI-SAN, ARE YOU DONE WITH THE SPRAY?
I WANT TO USE IT TOO.
GASP
OH, YEAH.
THANKS!

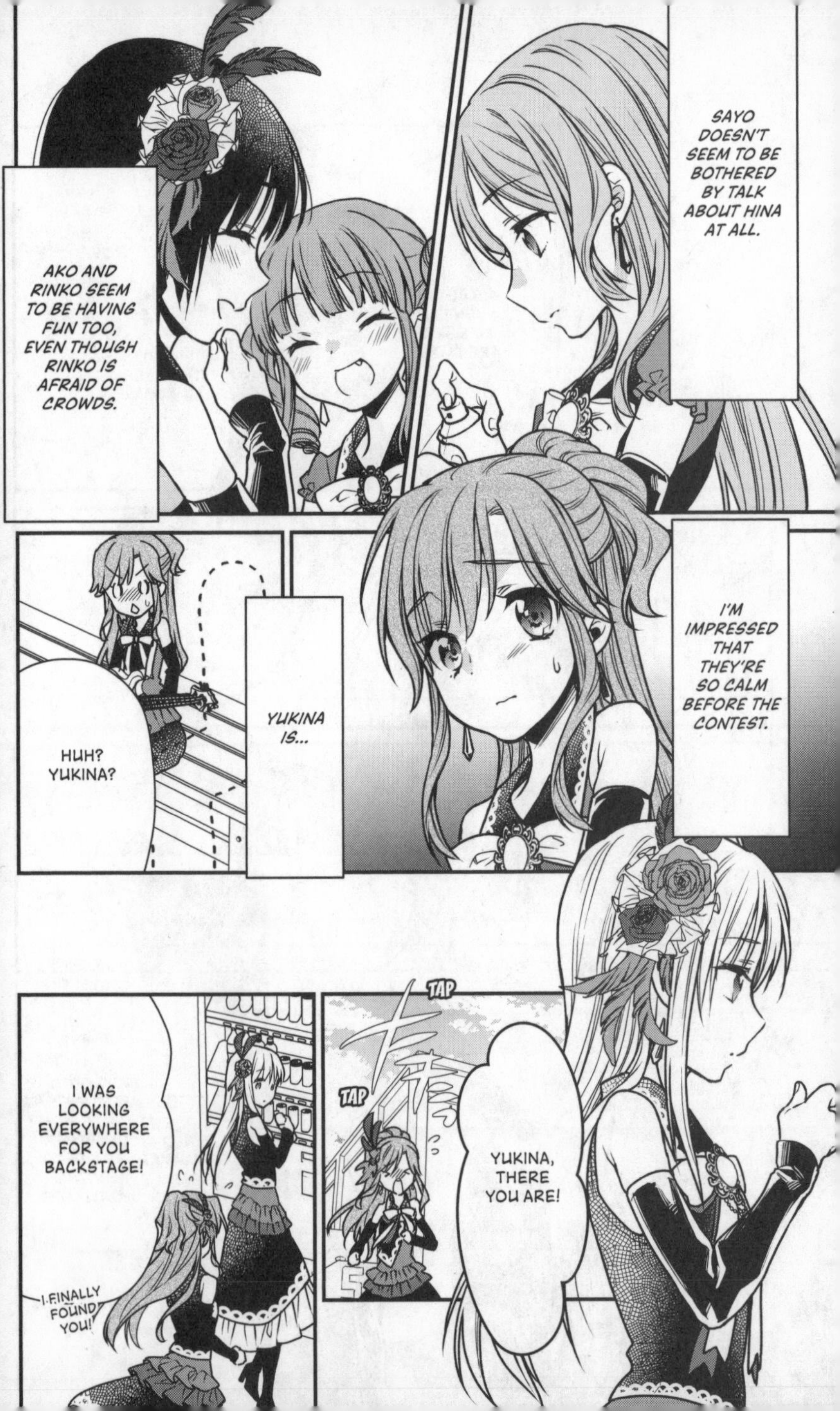
SAYO DOESN'T SEEM TO BE BOTHERED BY TALK ABOUT HINA AT ALL.
AKO AND RINKO SEEM TO BE HAVING FUN TOO, EVEN THOUGH RINKO IS AFRAID OF CROWDS.
I'M IMPRESSED THAT THEY'RE SO CALM BEFORE THE CONTEST.
YUKINA IS...
HUH? YUKINA?
TAP
TAP
YUKINA, THERE YOU ARE!
I WAS LOOKING EVERYWHERE FOR YOU BACKSTAGE!
I FINALLY FOUND YOU!

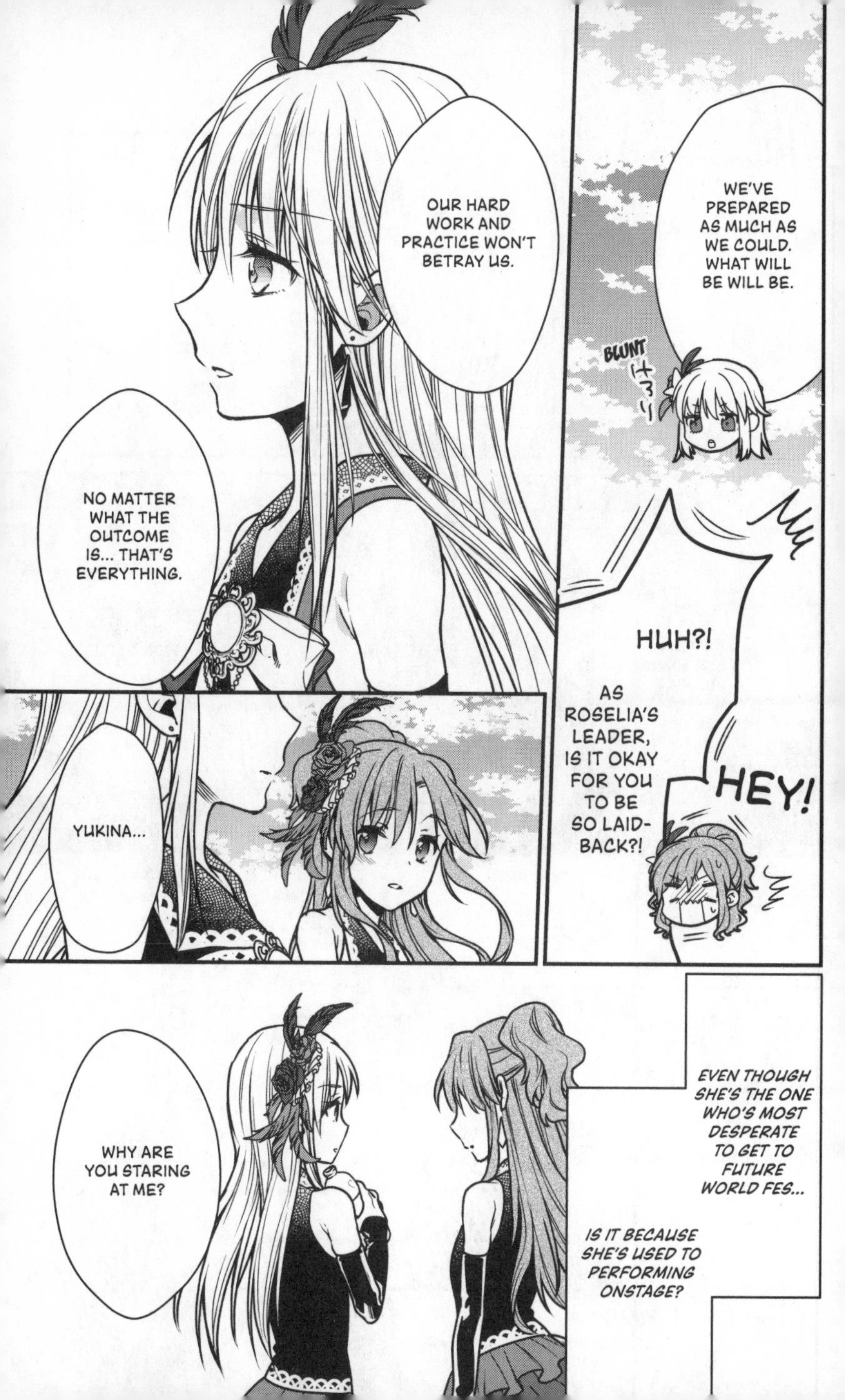
WE'VE PREPARED AS MUCH AS WE COULD. WHAT WILL BE WILL BE.
BLUNT
HUH?!
HEY!
AS ROSELIA'S LEADER, IS IT OKAY FOR YOU TO BE SO LAID-BACK?!
OUR HARD WORK AND PRACTICE WON'T BETRAY US.
NO MATTER WHAT THE OUTCOME IS... THAT'S EVERYTHING.
YUKINA...
EVEN THOUGH SHE'S THE ONE WHO'S MOST DESPERATE TO GET TO FUTURE WORLD FES...
IS IT BECAUSE SHE'S USED TO PERFORMING ONSTAGE?
WHY ARE YOU STARING AT ME?

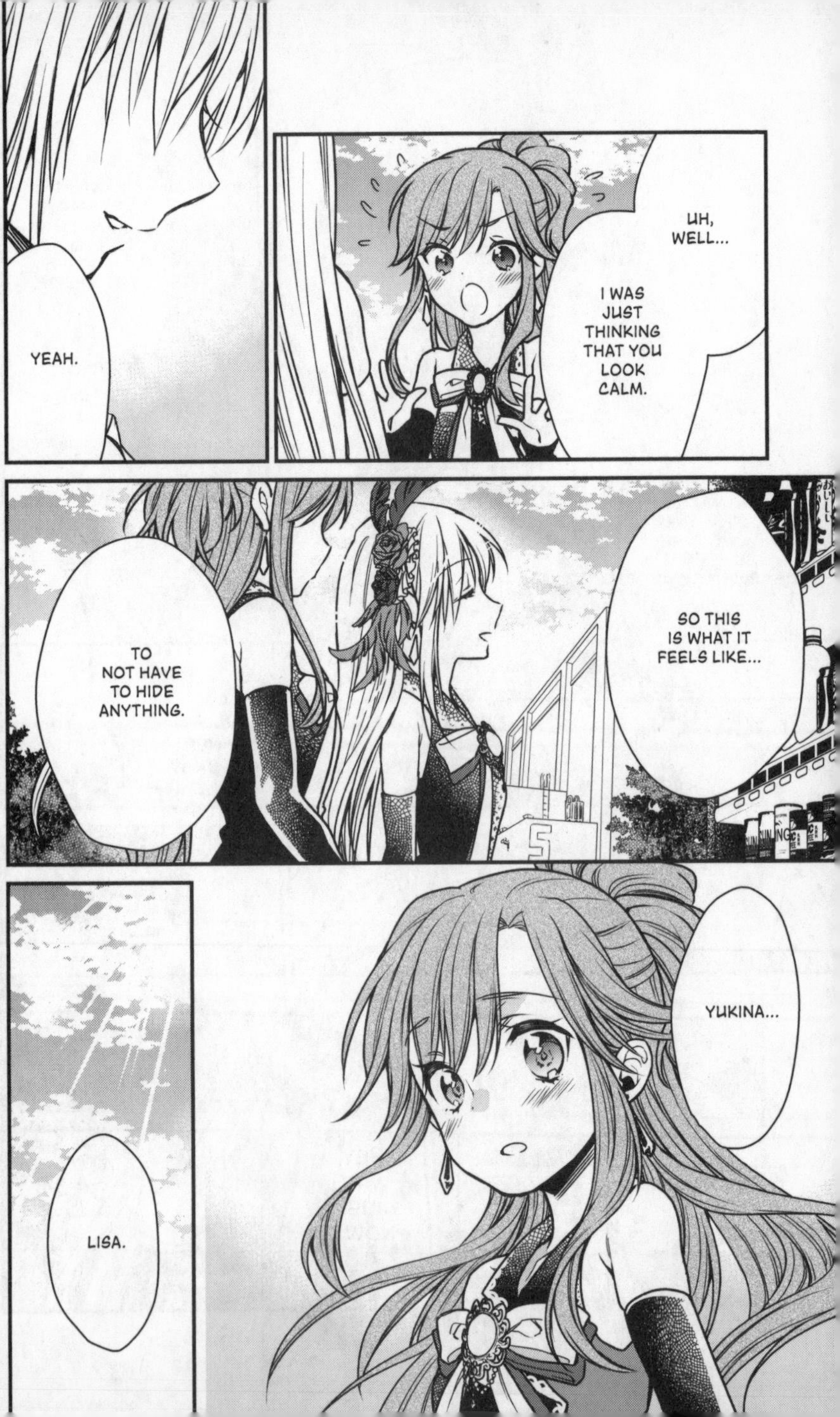
UH, WELL...
I WAS JUST THINKING THAT YOU LOOK CALM.
YEAH.
SO THIS IS WHAT IT FEELS LIKE...
TO NOT HAVE TO HIDE ANYTHING.
YUKINA...
LISA.

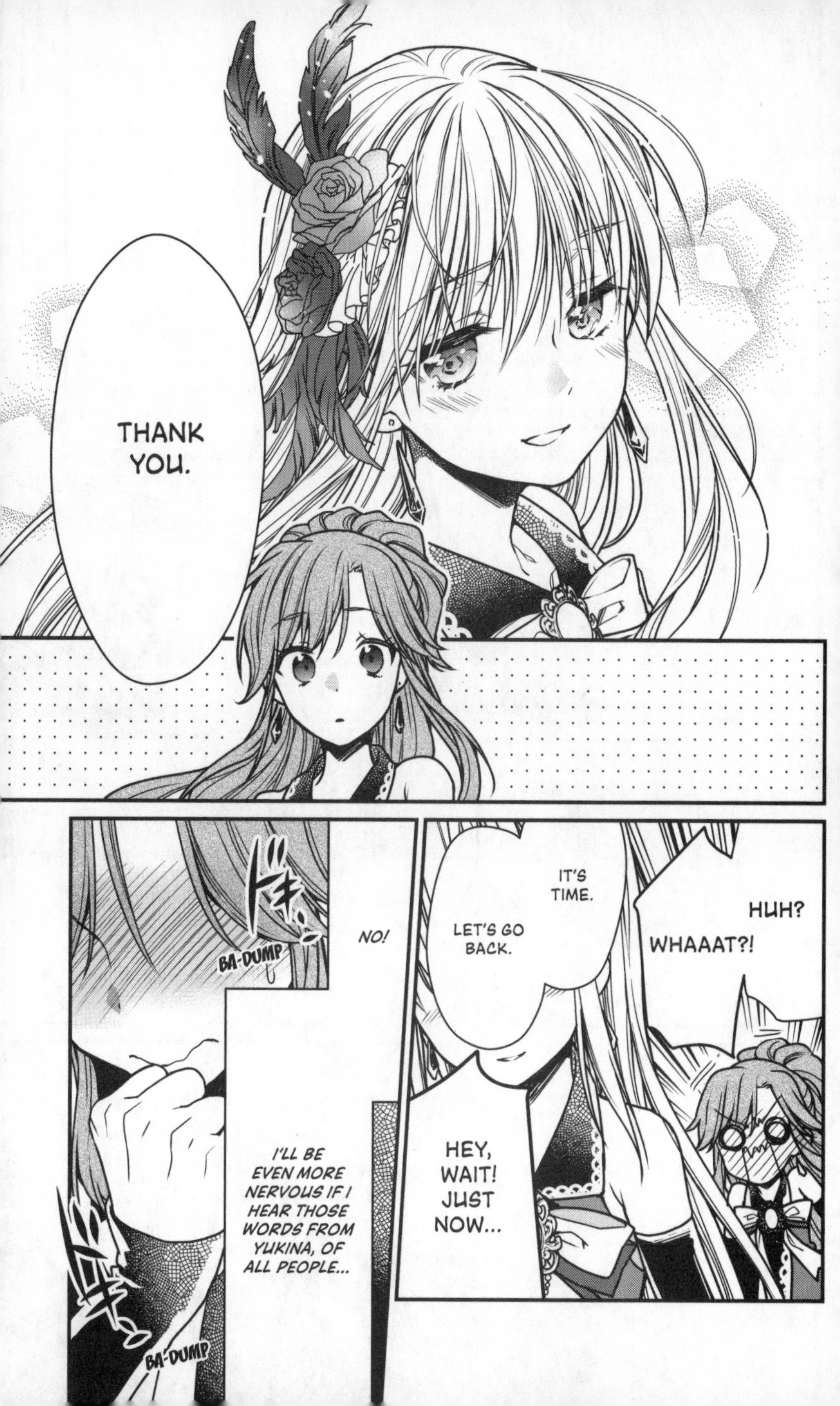
THANK YOU.
IT'S TIME.
LET'S GO BACK.
HUH?
WHAAAT?!
HEY, WAIT! JUST NOW...
ドキ
BA-DUMP
NO!
I'LL BE EVEN MORE NERVOUS IF I HEAR THOSE WORDS FROM YUKINA, OF ALL PEOPLE...
BA-DUMP

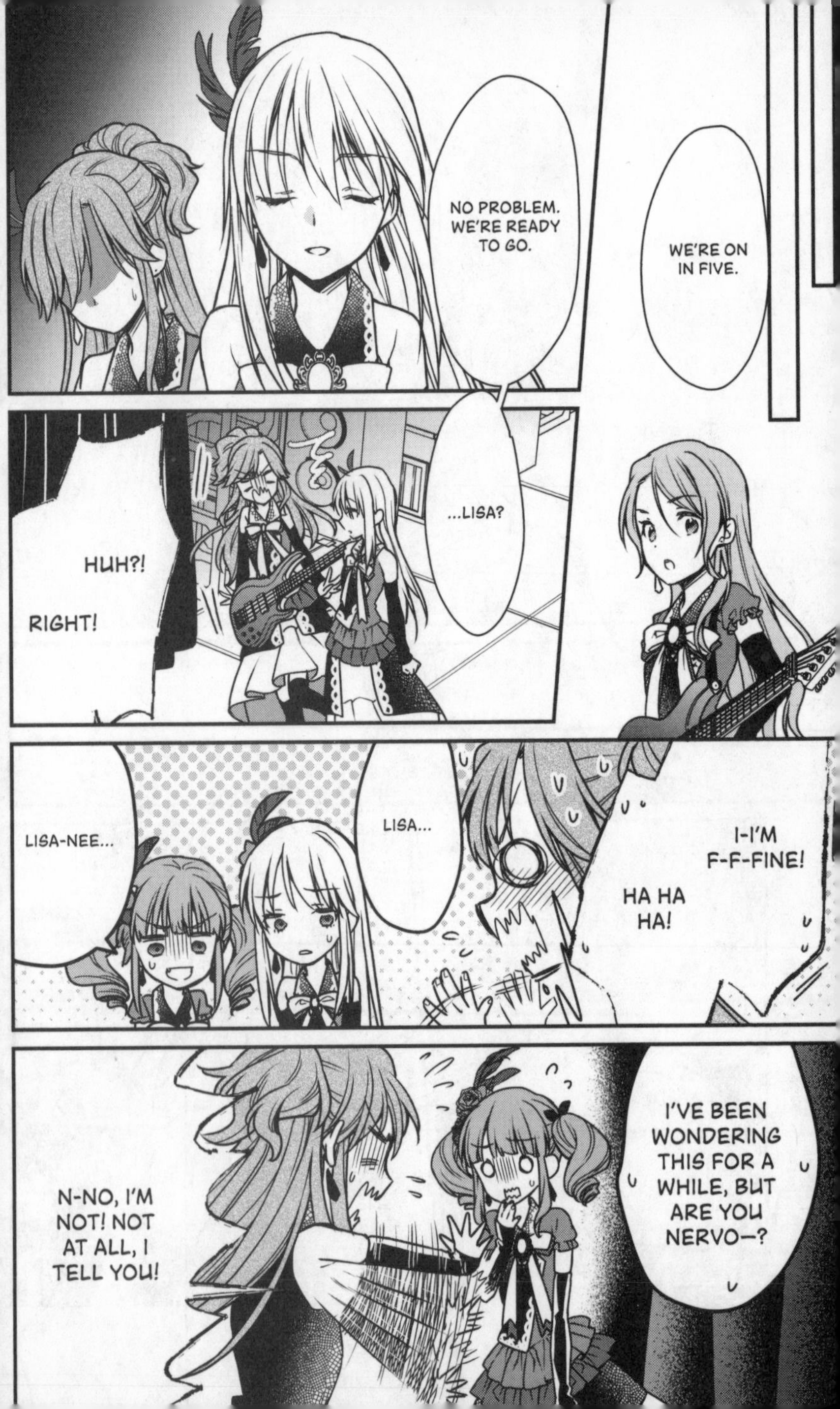
WE'RE ON IN FIVE.
NO PROBLEM. WE'RE READY TO GO.
...LISA?
HUH?!
RIGHT!
I-I'M F-F-FINE!
HA HA HA!
LISA...
LISA-NEE...
I'VE BEEN WONDERING THIS FOR A WHILE, BUT ARE YOU NERVO—?
N-NO, I'M NOT! NOT AT ALL, I TELL YOU!

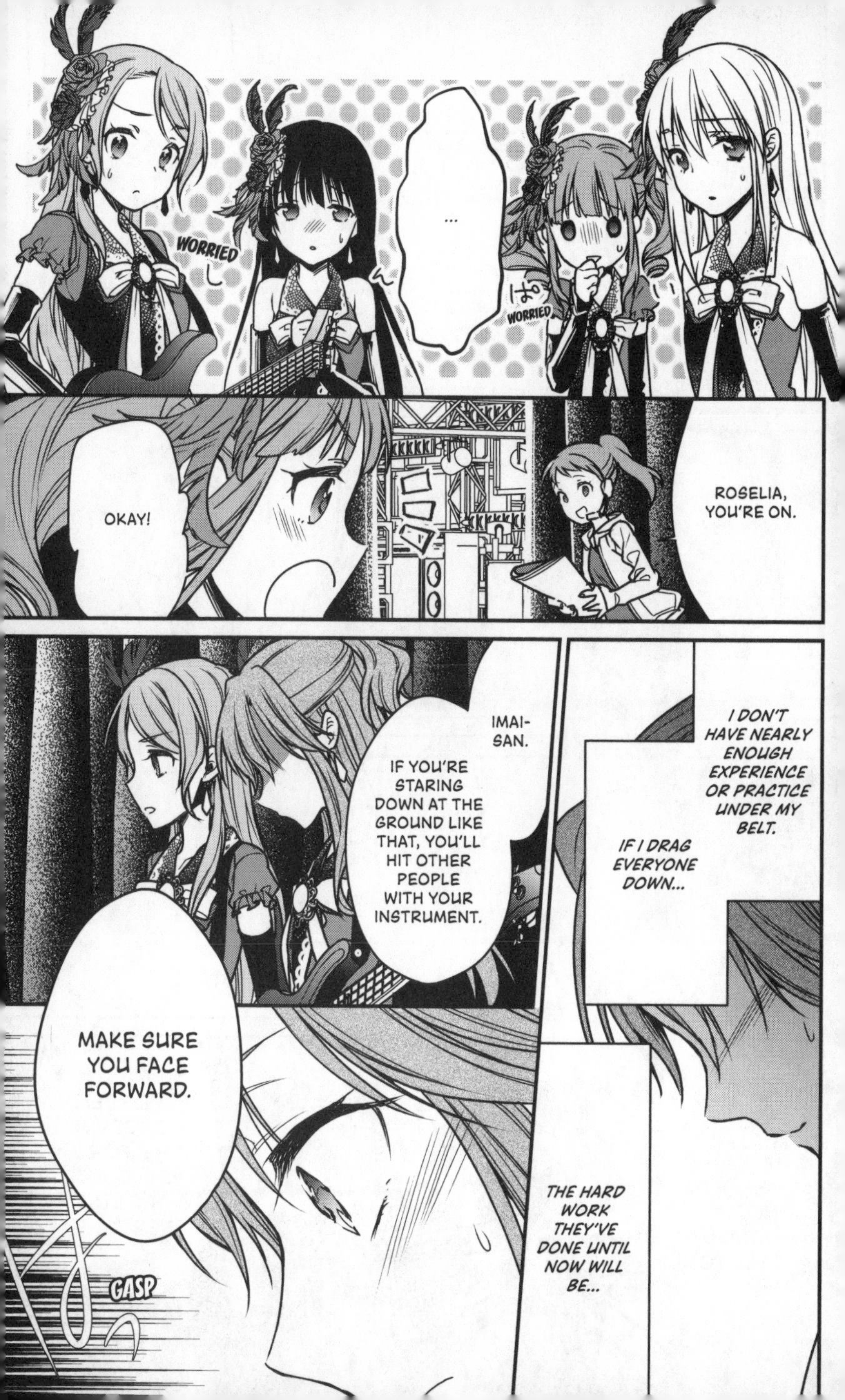
WORRIED
...
WORRIED
ROSELIA, YOU'RE ON.
OKAY!
I DON'T HAVE NEARLY ENOUGH EXPERIENCE OR PRACTICE UNDER MY BELT.
IF I DRAG EVERYONE DOWN...
THE HARD WORK THEY'VE DONE UNTIL NOW WILL BE...
IMAI-SAN.
IF YOU'RE STARING DOWN AT THE GROUND LIKE THAT, YOU'LL HIT OTHER PEOPLE WITH YOUR INSTRUMENT.
MAKE SURE YOU FACE FORWARD.
GASP

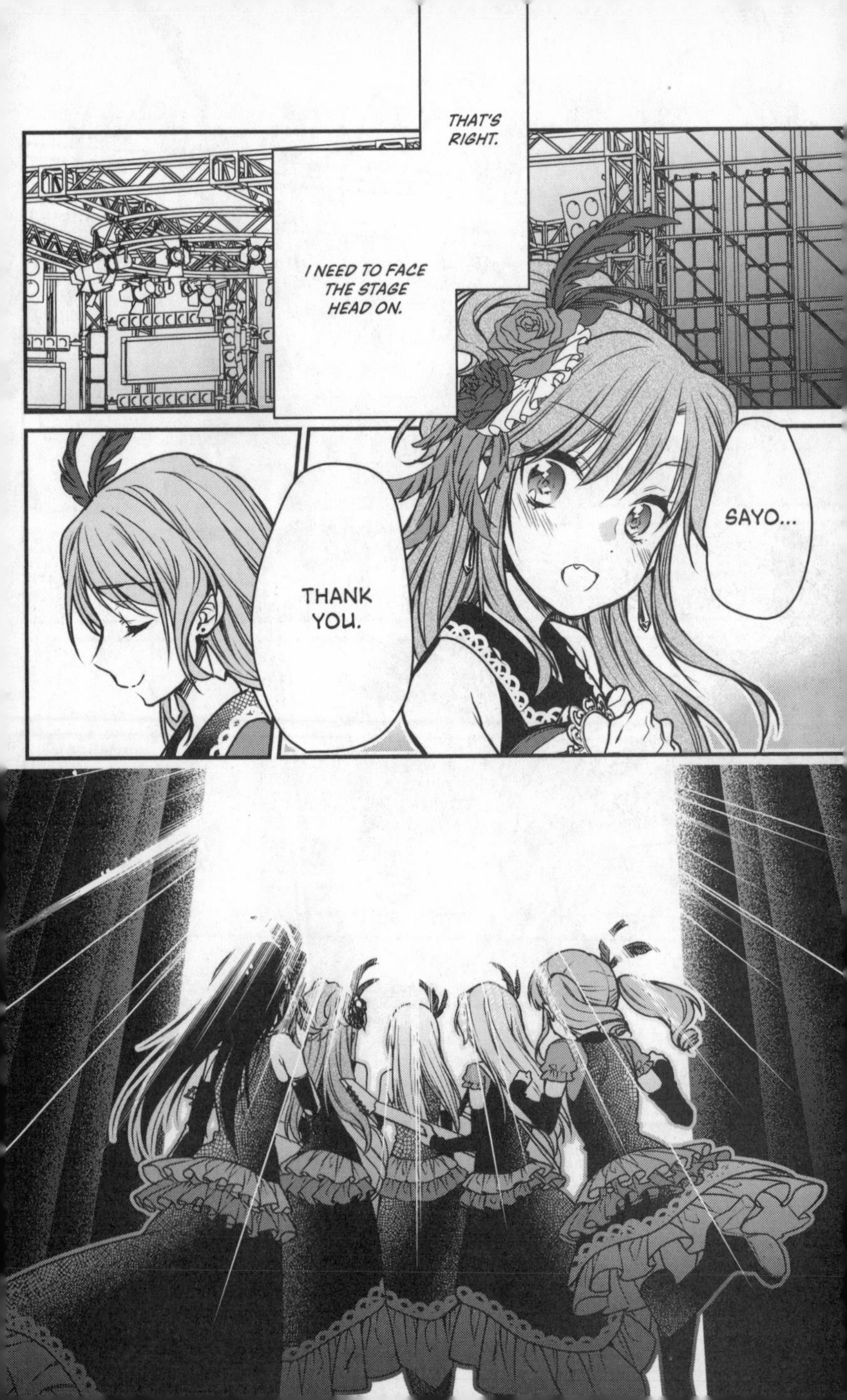
THAT'S RIGHT.
I NEED TO FACE THE STAGE HEAD ON.
SAYO...
THANK YOU.

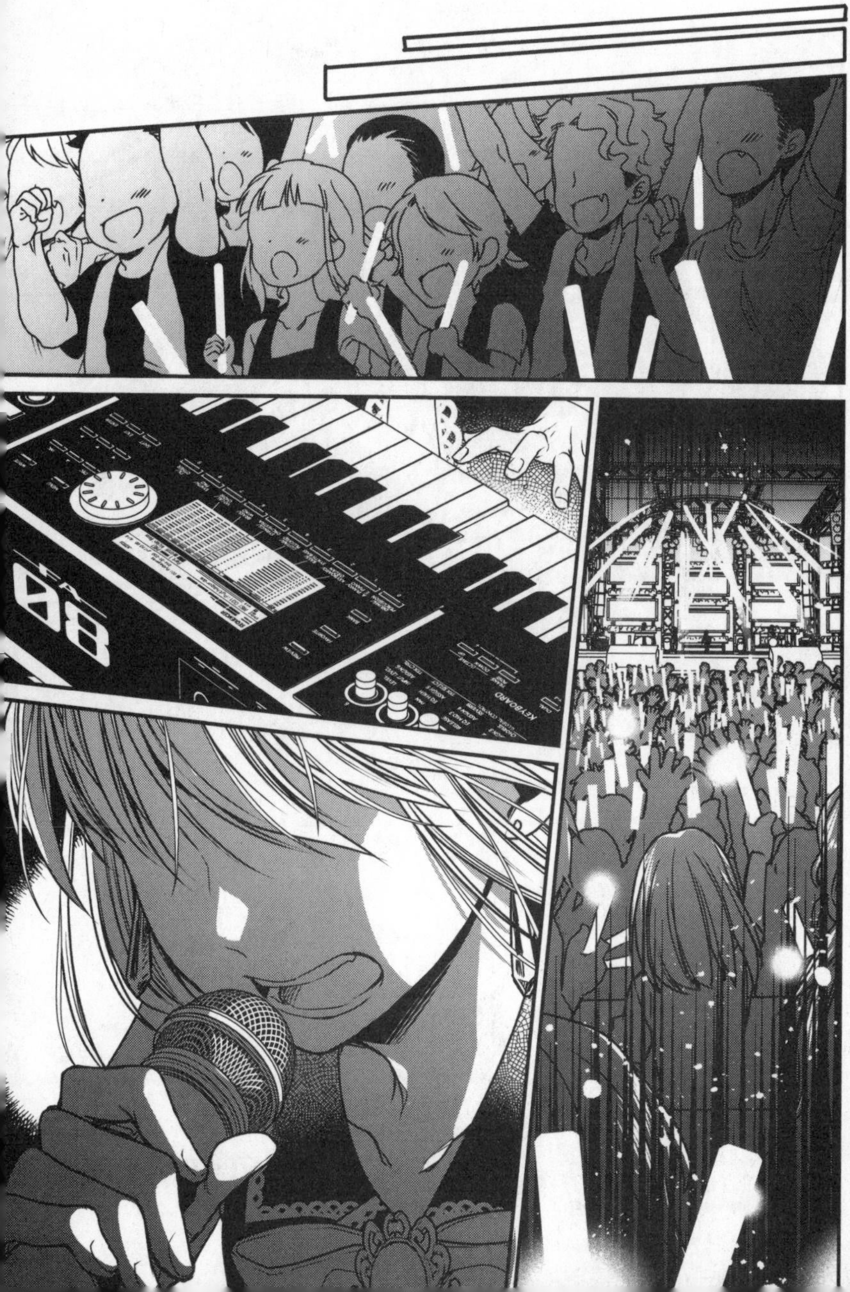

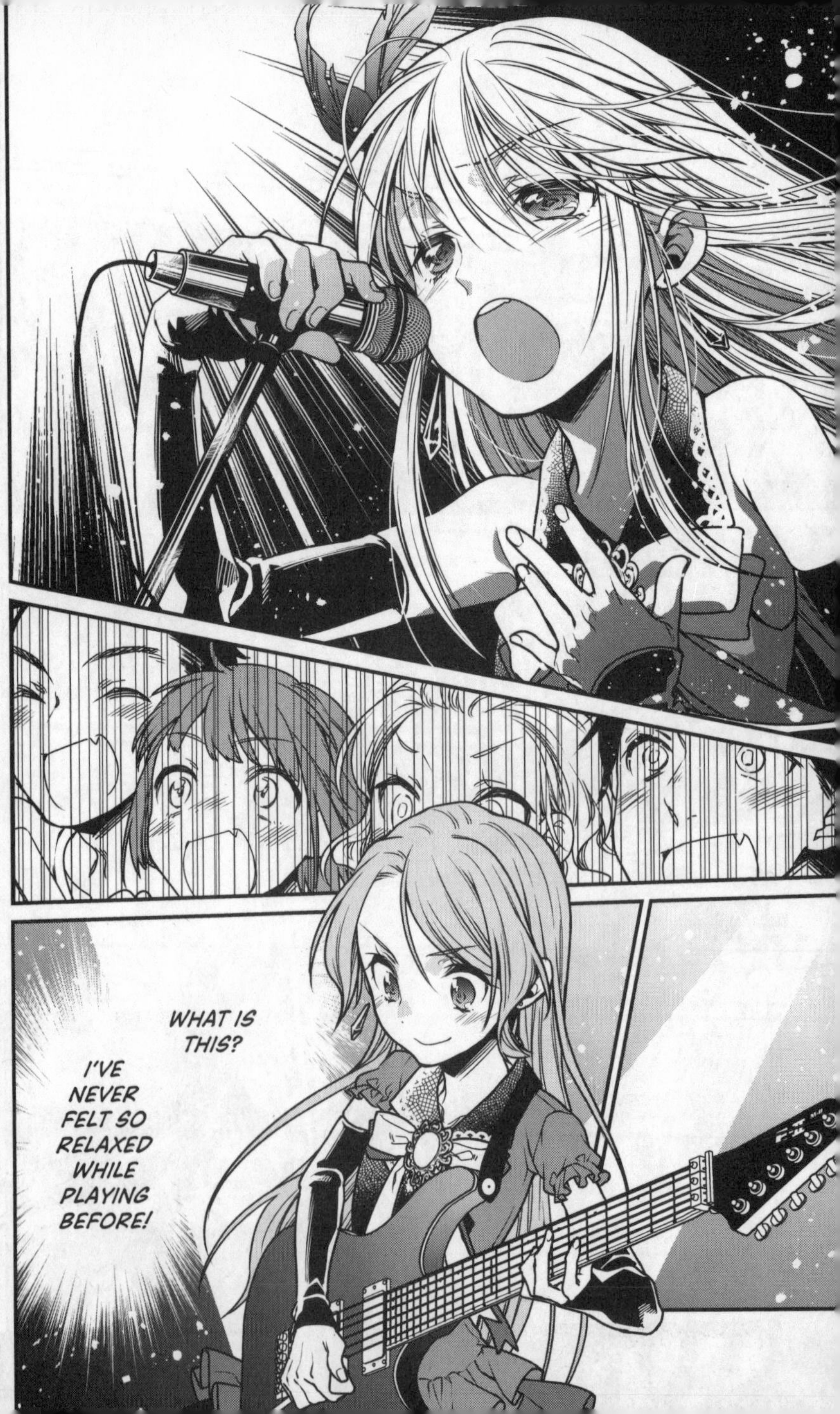
WHAT IS THIS?
I'VE NEVER FELT SO RELAXED WHILE PLAYING BEFORE!

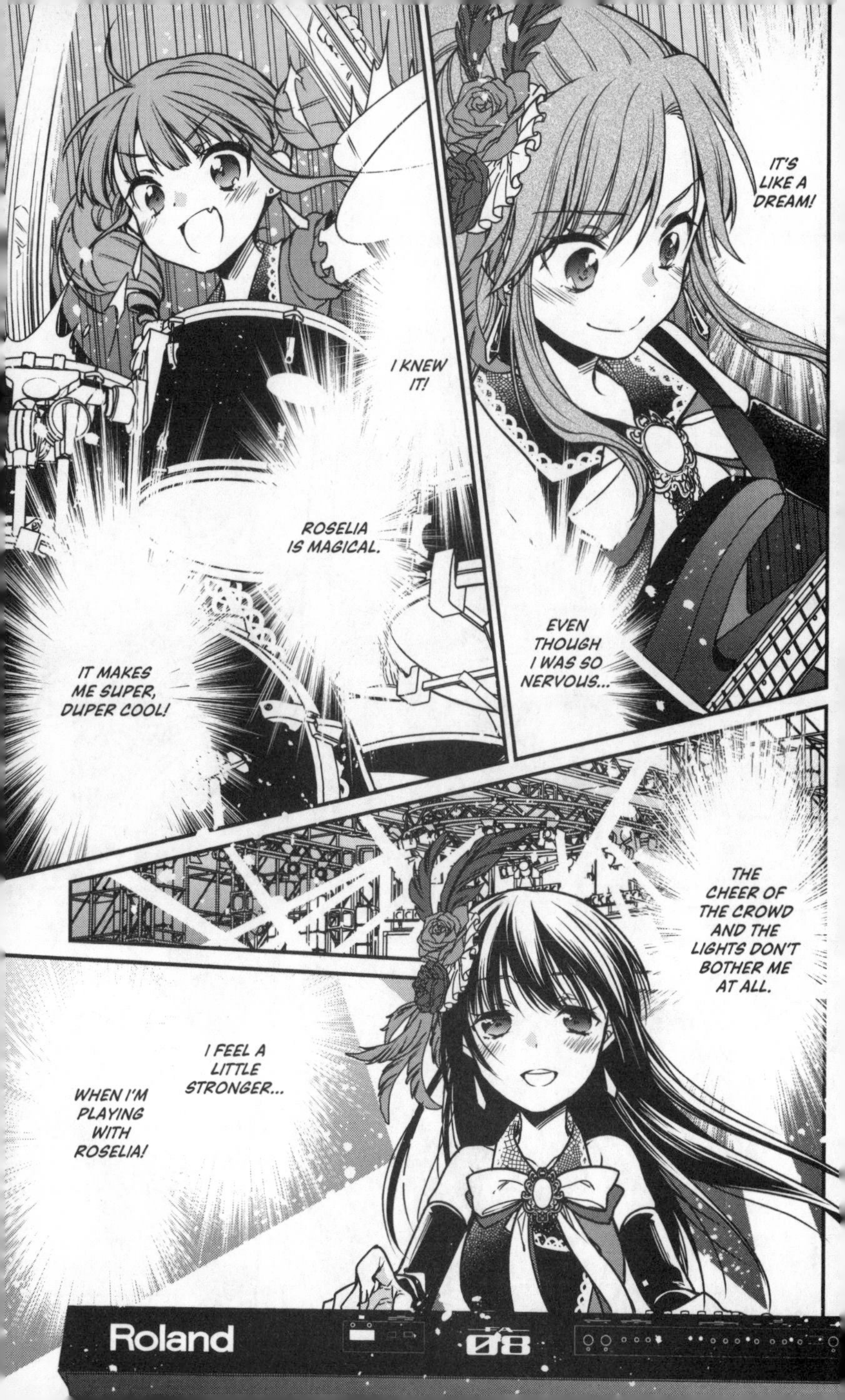
IT'S LIKE A DREAM!
EVEN THOUGH I WAS SO NERVOUS...
I KNEW IT!
ROSELIA IS MAGICAL.
IT MAKES ME SUPER, DUPER COOL!
THE CHEER OF THE CROWD AND THE LIGHTS DON'T BOTHER ME AT ALL.
I FEEL A LITTLE STRONGER...
WHEN I'M PLAYING WITH ROSELIA!
Roland

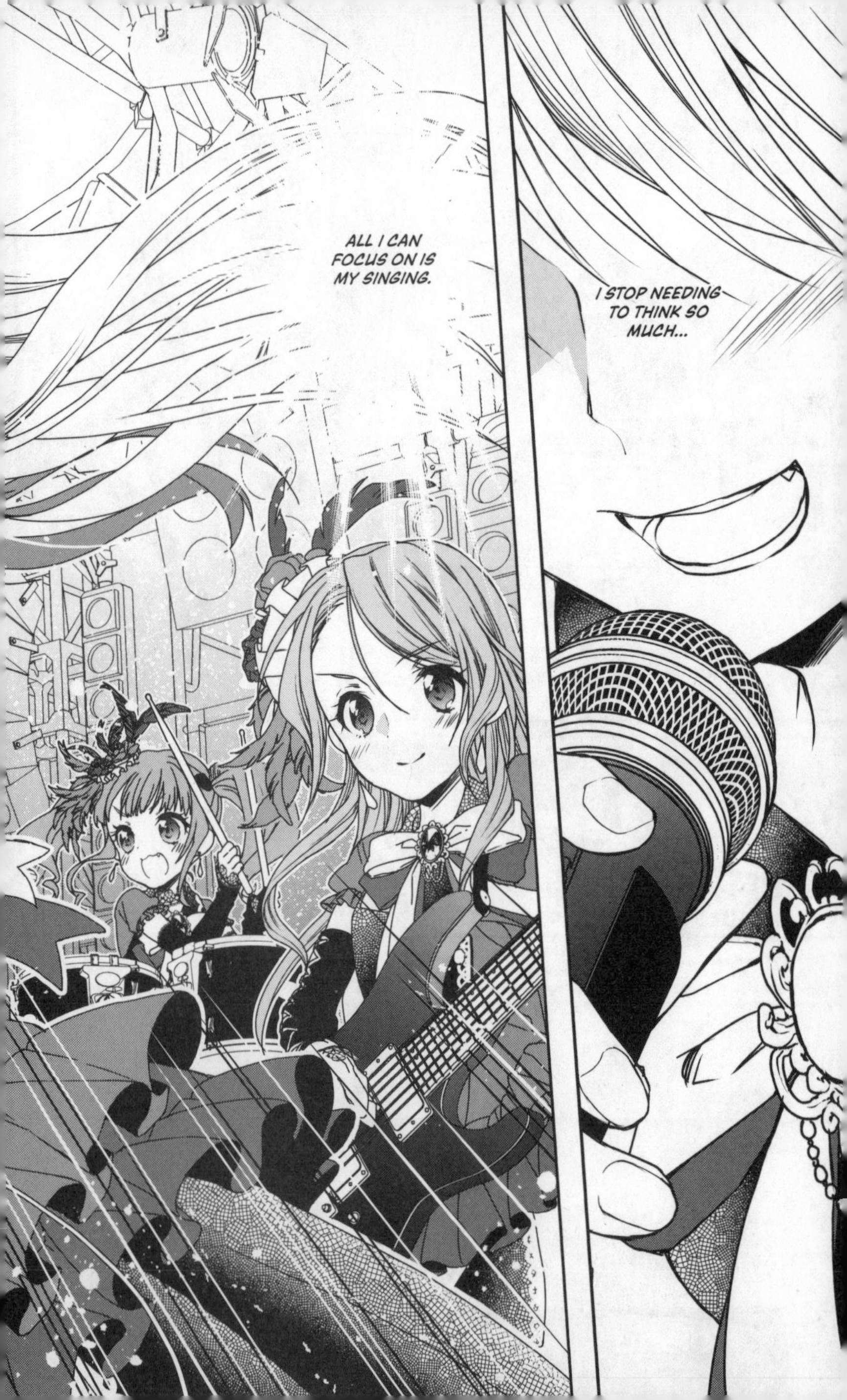
I STOP NEEDING TO THINK SO MUCH...
ALL I CAN FOCUS ON IS MY SINGING.

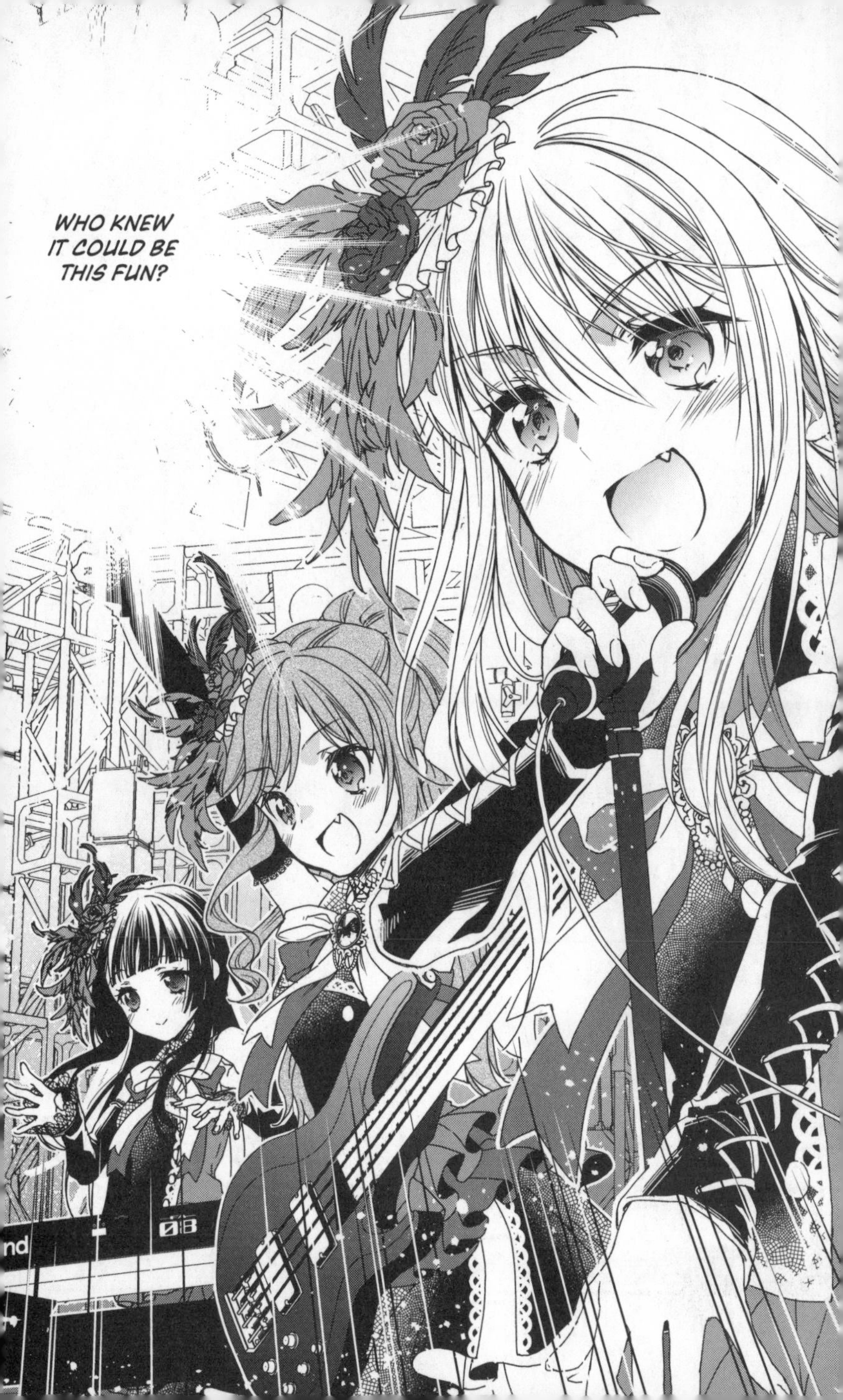
WHO KNEW IT COULD BE THIS FUN?

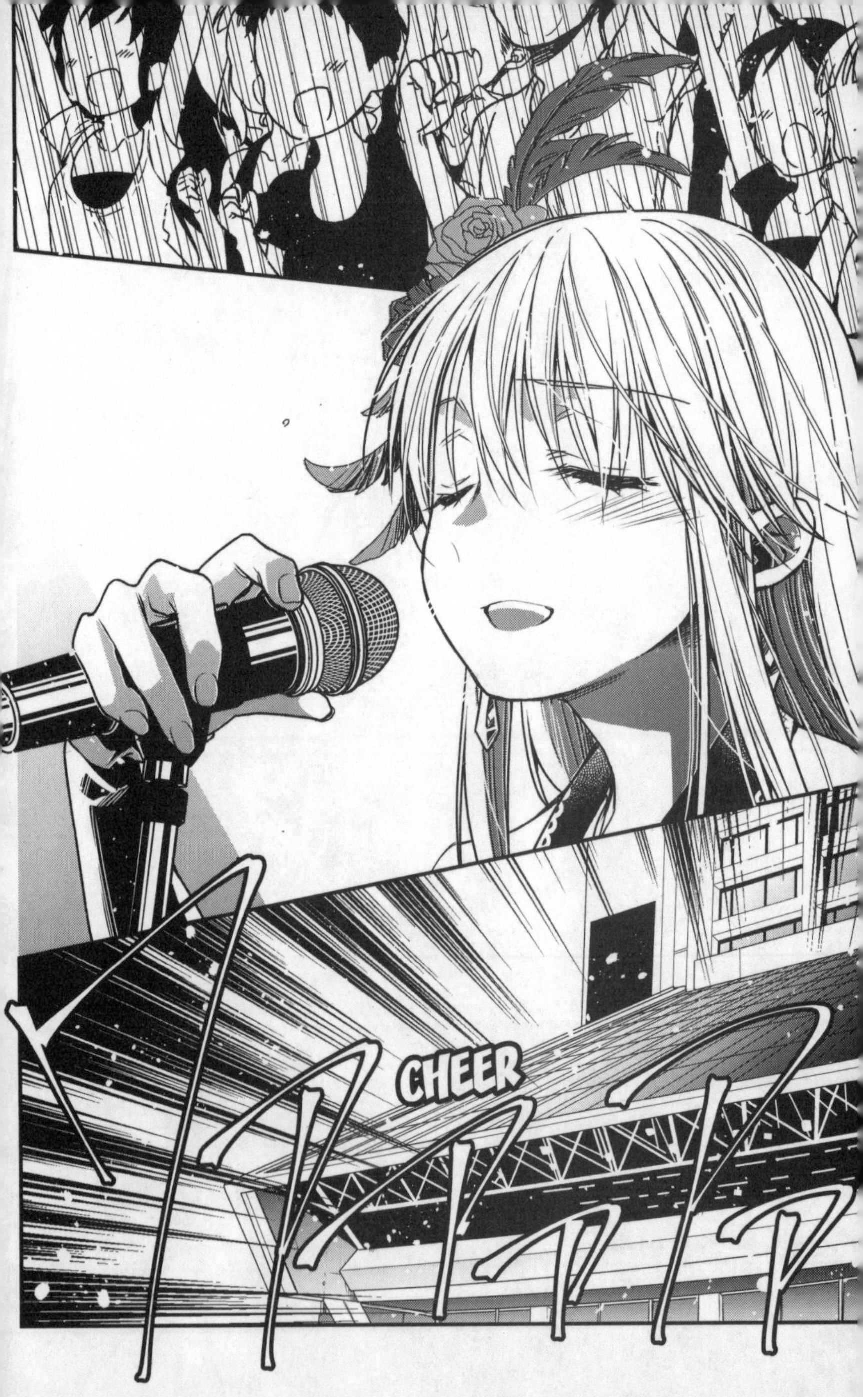
CHEER

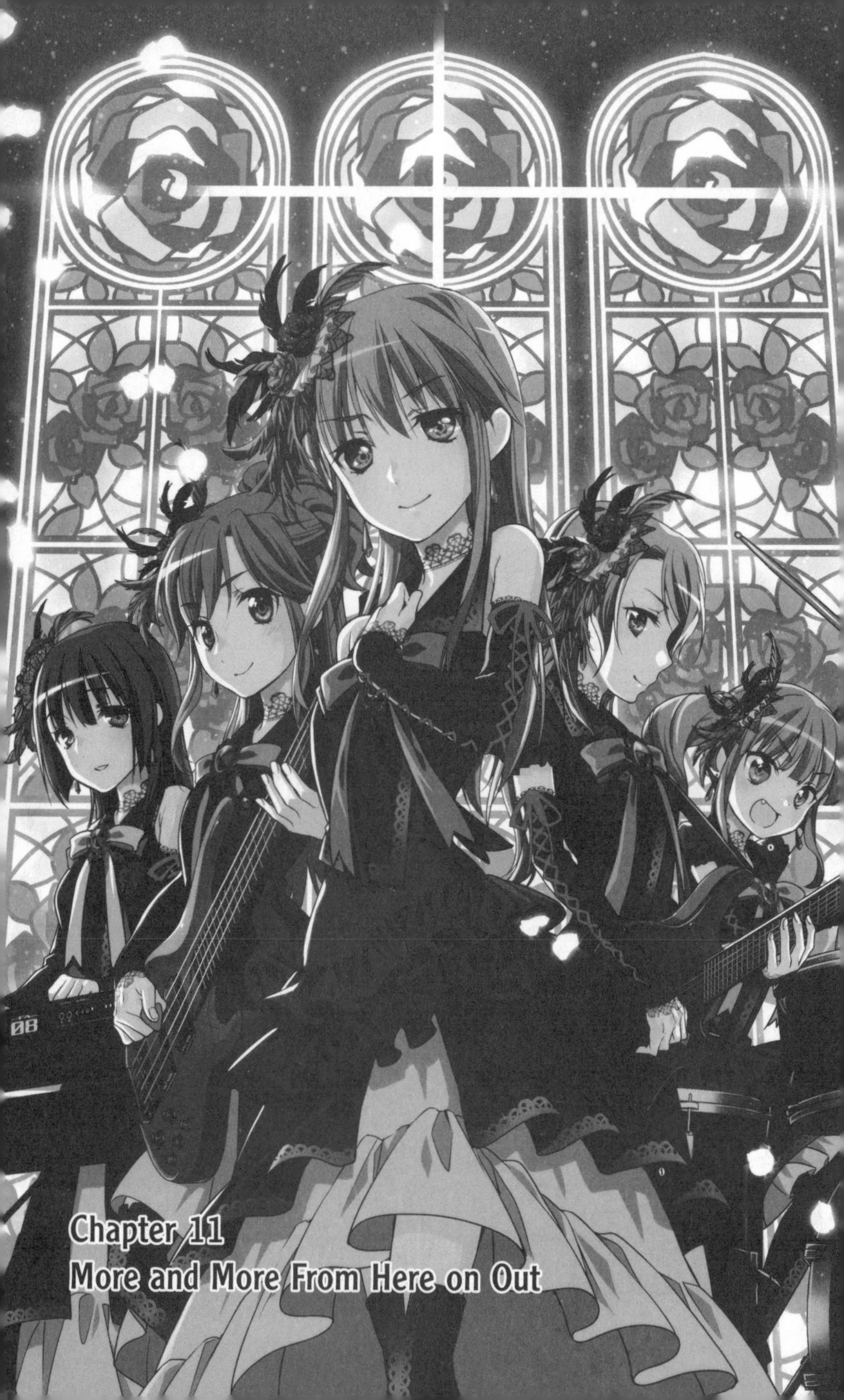

Chapter 11
More and More From Here on Out

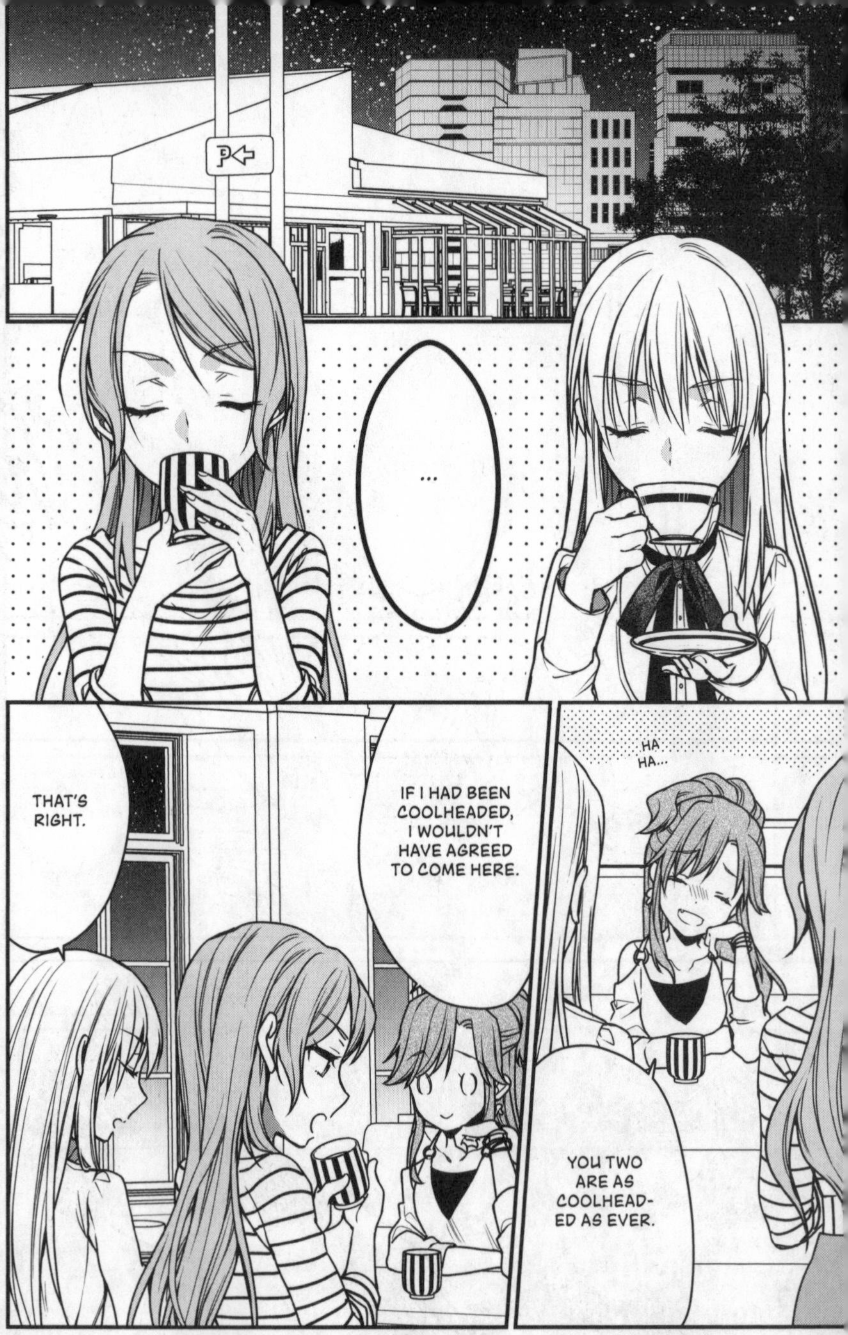
...
HA HA...
YOU TWO ARE AS COOLHEAD-ED AS EVER.
IF I HAD BEEN COOLHEADED, I WOULDN'T HAVE AGREED TO COME HERE.
THAT'S RIGHT.

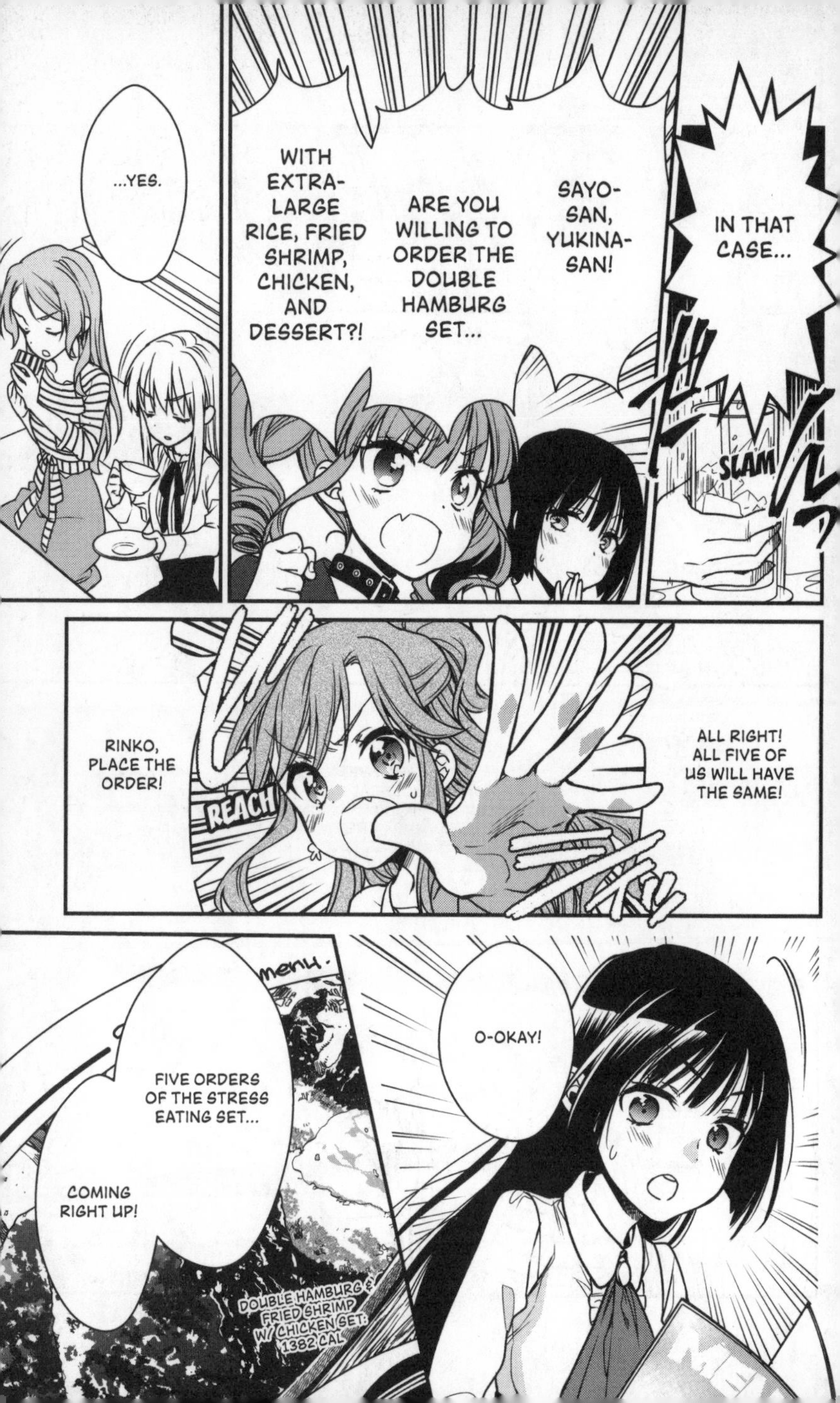
IN THAT CASE...
SLAM
SAYO-SAN, YUKINA-SAN!
ARE YOU WILLING TO ORDER THE DOUBLE HAMBURG SET...
WITH EXTRA-LARGE RICE, FRIED SHRIMP, CHICKEN, AND DESSERT?!
...YES.
ALL RIGHT! ALL FIVE OF US WILL HAVE THE SAME!
REACH
RINKO, PLACE THE ORDER!
O-OKAY!
menu
FIVE ORDERS OF THE STRESS EATING SET...
COMING RIGHT UP!
DOUBLE HAMBURG & FRIED SHRIMP W/ CHICKEN SET: 1382 CAL

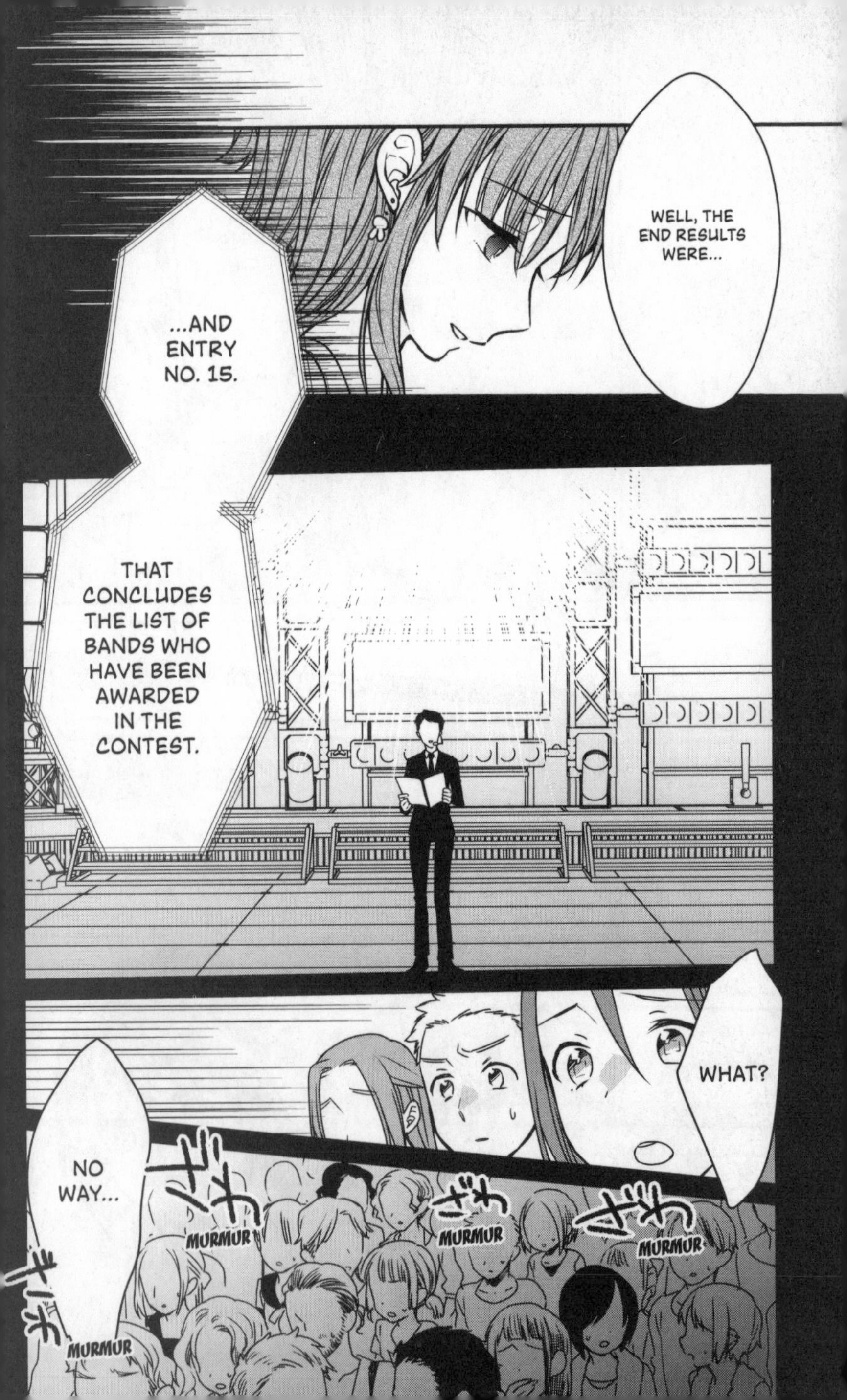
WELL, THE END RESULTS WERE...
...AND ENTRY NO. 15.
THAT CONCLUDES THE LIST OF BANDS WHO HAVE BEEN AWARDED IN THE CONTEST.
WHAT?
NO WAY...
MURMUR
MURMUR
MURMUR
MURMUR

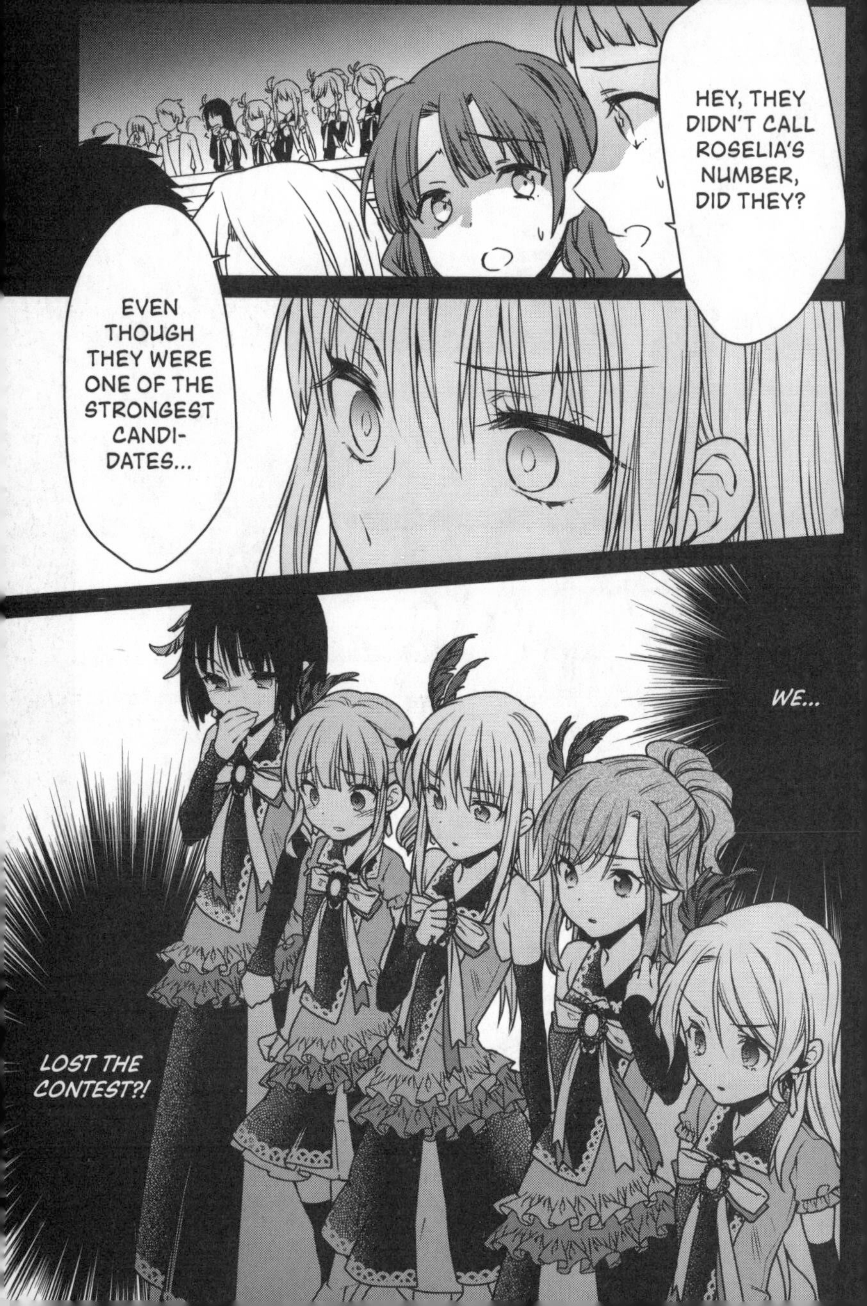
HEY, THEY DIDN'T CALL ROSELIA'S NUMBER, DID THEY?
EVEN THOUGH THEY WERE ONE OF THE STRONGEST CANDI-DATES...
WE...
LOST THE CONTEST?!

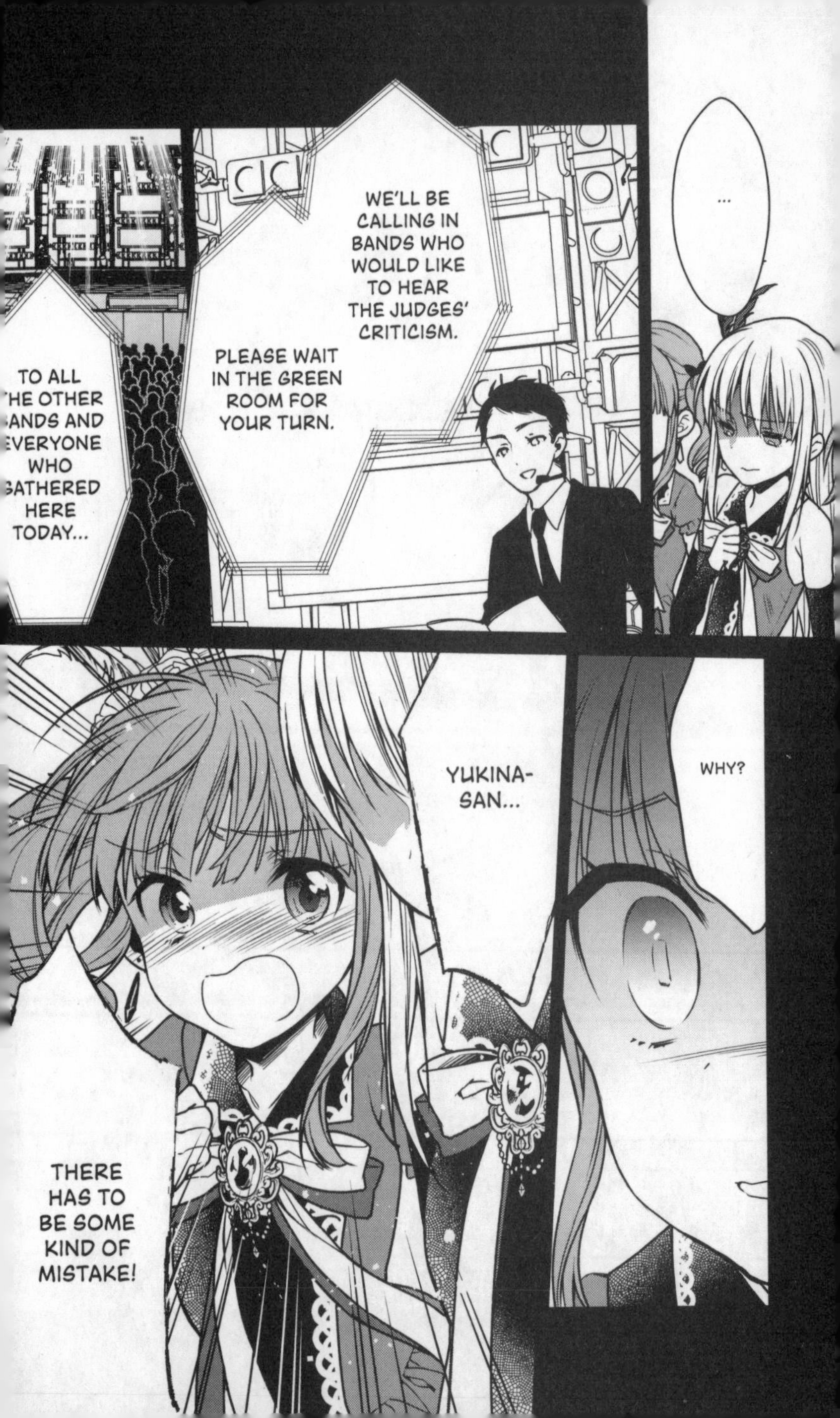
...
WE'LL BE CALLING IN BANDS WHO WOULD LIKE TO HEAR THE JUDGES' CRITICISM.
PLEASE WAIT IN THE GREEN ROOM FOR YOUR TURN.
TO ALL THE OTHER BANDS AND EVERYONE WHO GATHERED HERE TODAY...
WHY?
YUKINA-SAN...
THERE HAS TO BE SOME KIND OF MISTAKE!

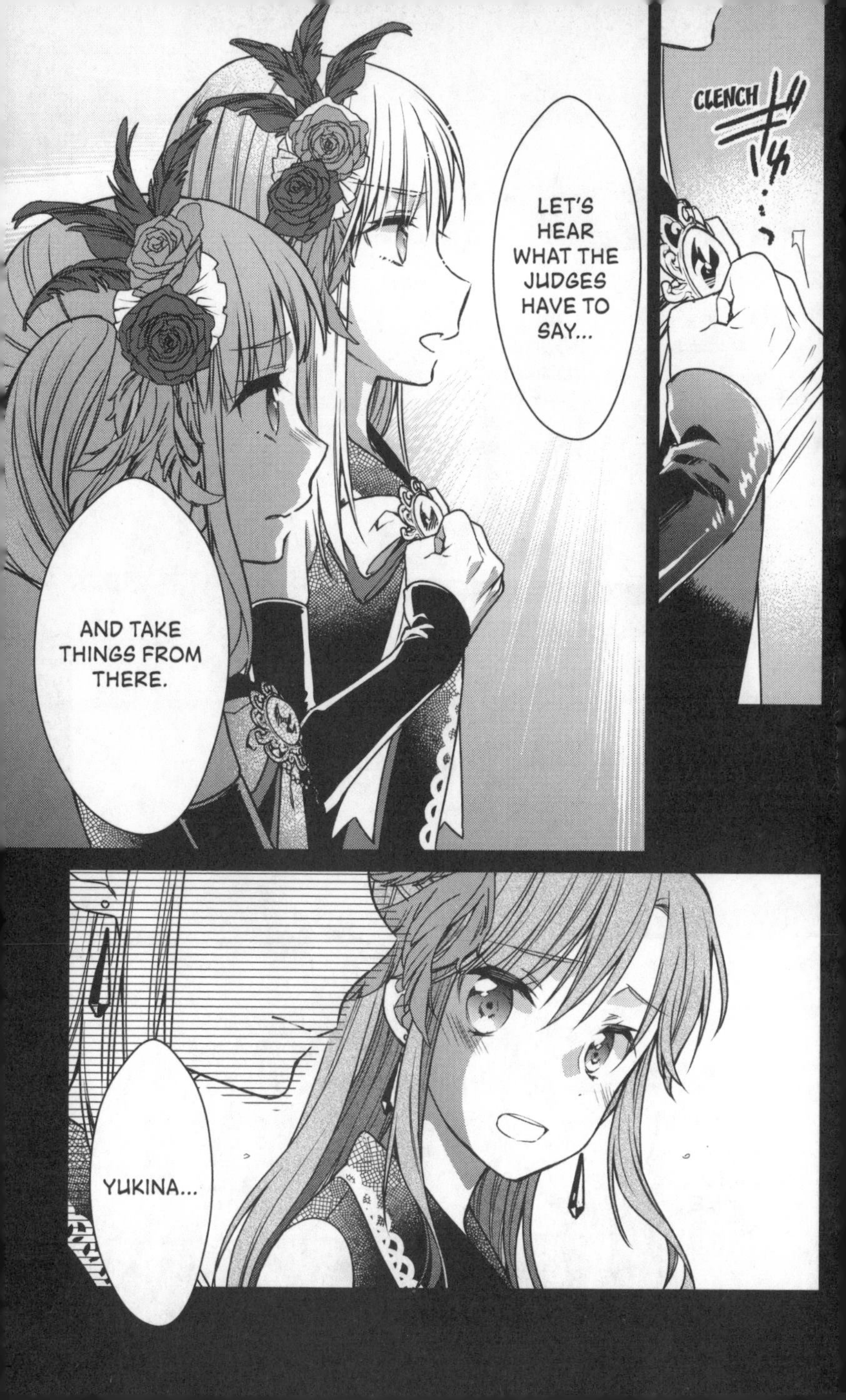
CLENCH
LET'S HEAR WHAT THE JUDGES HAVE TO SAY...
AND TAKE THINGS FROM THERE.
YUKINA...

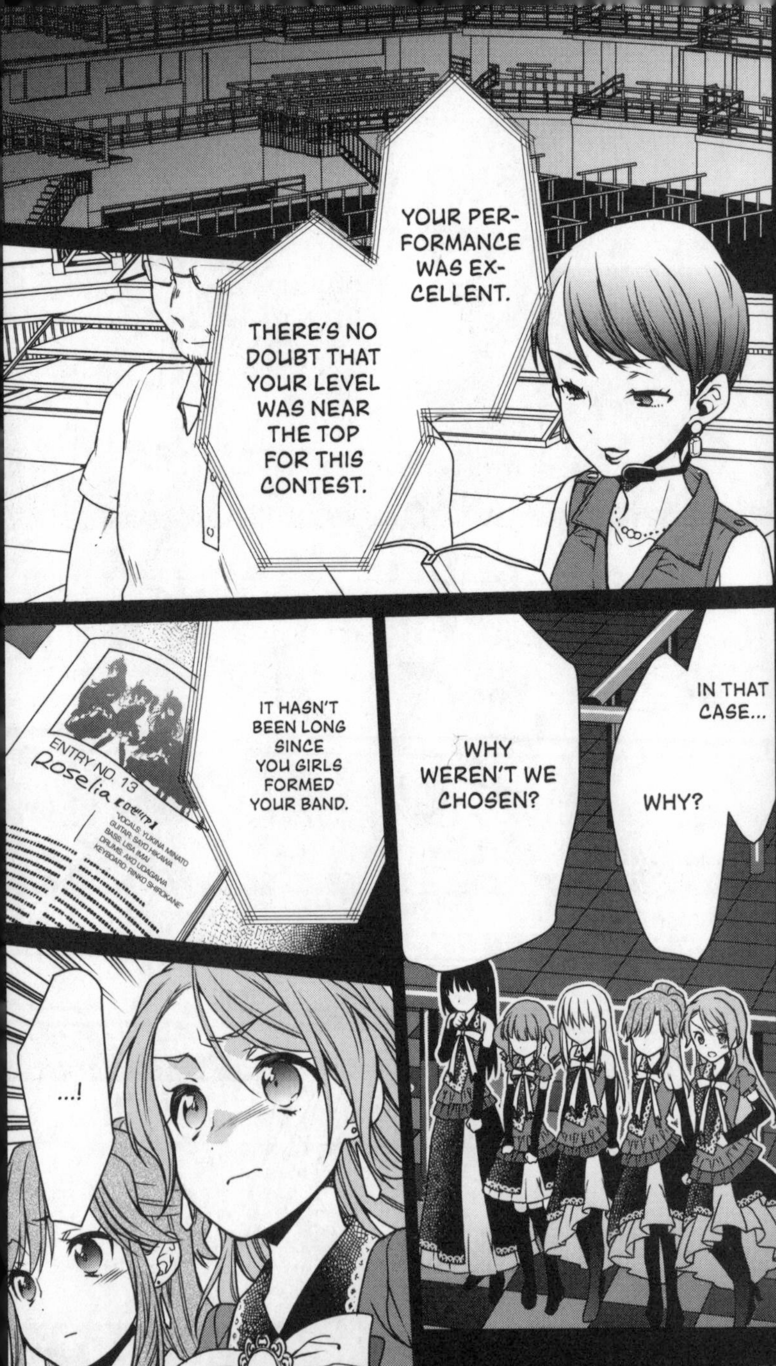
YOUR PER-
FORMANCE
WAS EX-
CELLENT.
THERE'S NO DOUBT THAT YOUR LEVEL WAS NEAR THE TOP FOR THIS CONTEST.
IN THAT CASE...
WHY?
WHY WEREN'T WE CHOSEN?
ENTRY NO. 13
Roselia
VOCALS: YUKINA MINATO
GUITAR: SAYO HIKAWA
BASS: LISA IMAI
DRUMS: AKO UDAGAWA
KEYBOARD: RINKO SHIROKANE
IT HASN'T BEEN LONG SINCE YOU GIRLS FORMED YOUR BAND.
...!

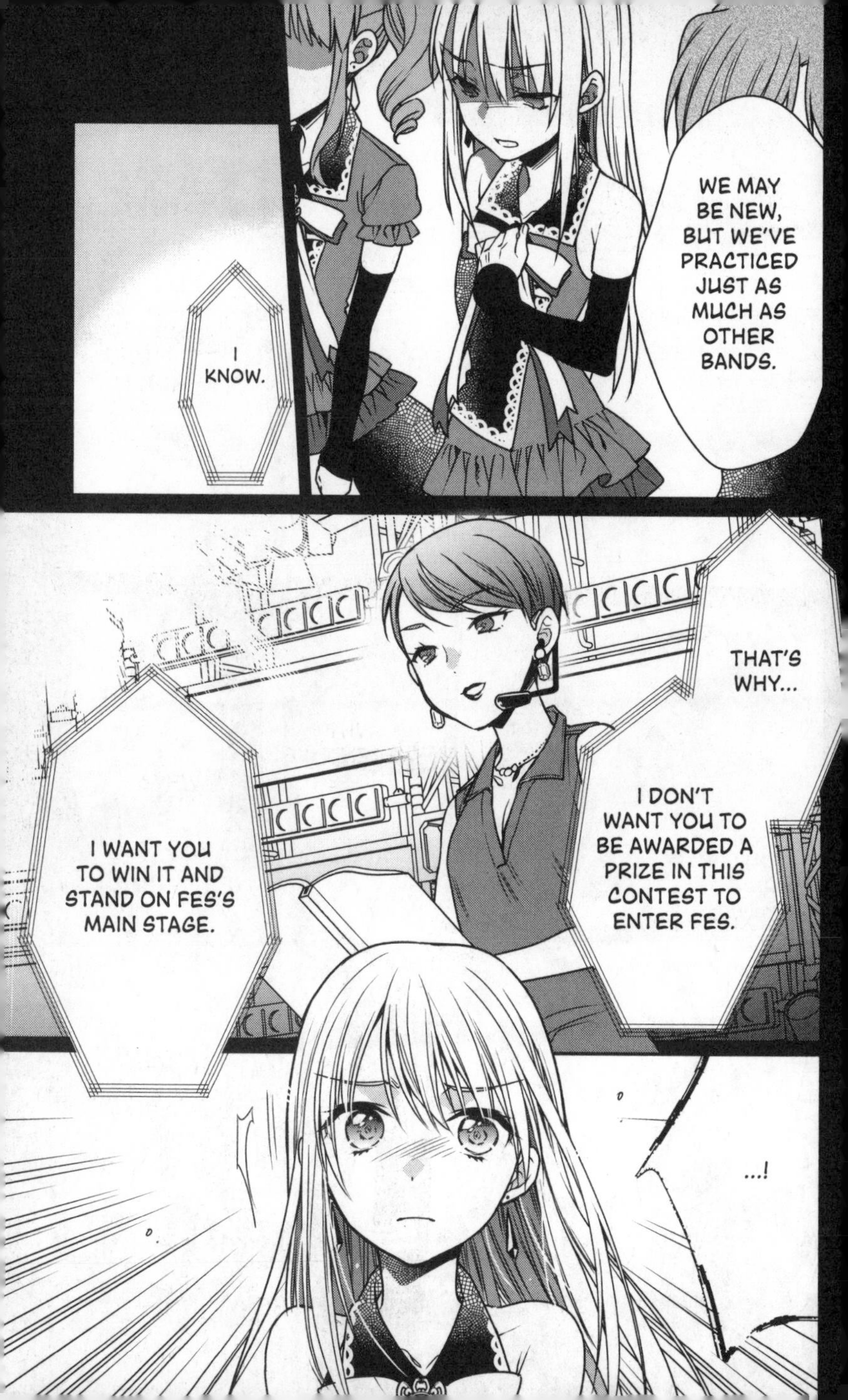
WE MAY BE NEW, BUT WE'VE PRACTICED JUST AS MUCH AS OTHER BANDS.
I KNOW.
THAT'S WHY...
I DON'T WANT YOU TO BE AWARDED A PRIZE IN THIS CONTEST TO ENTER FES.
I WANT YOU TO WIN IT AND STAND ON FES'S MAIN STAGE.
...!

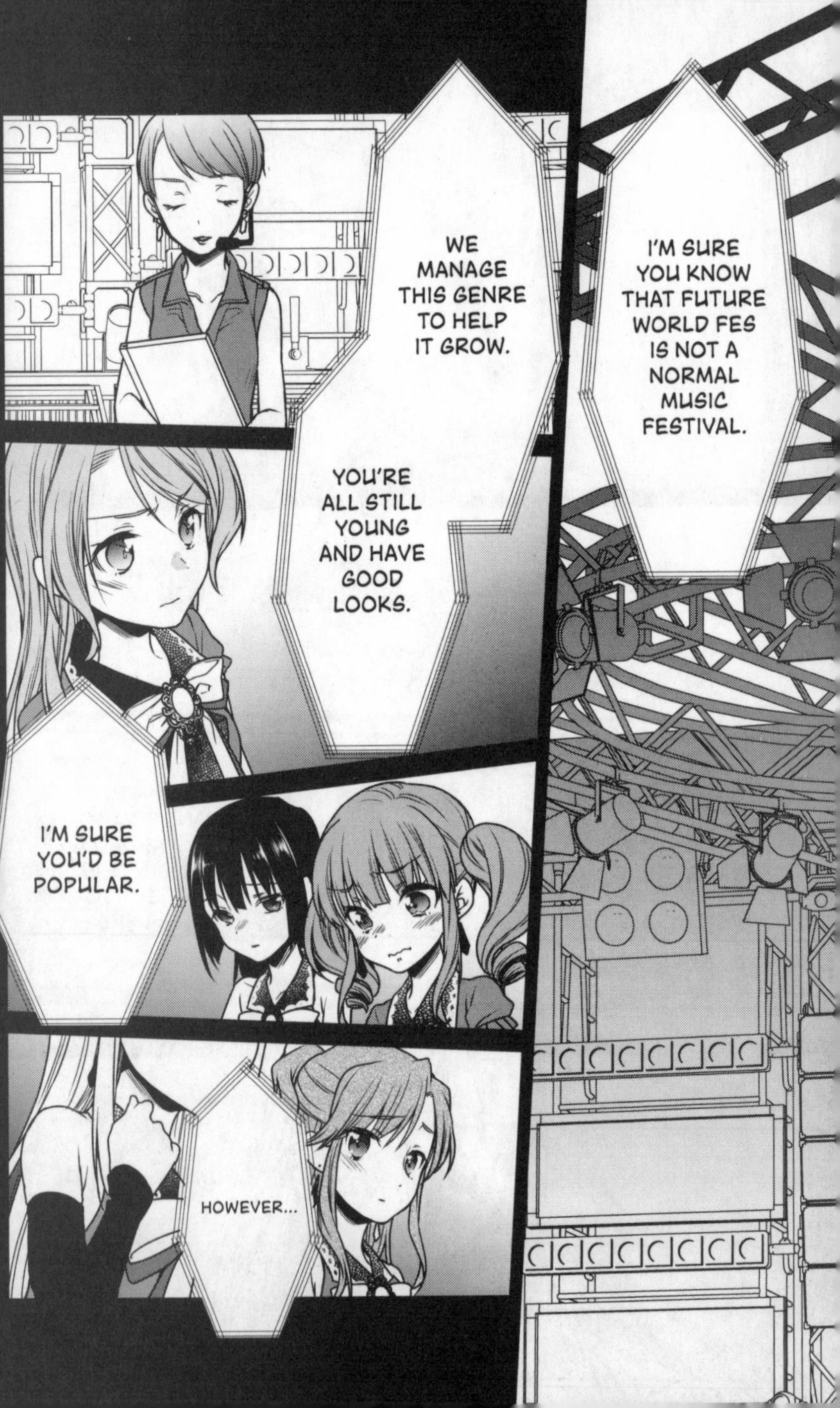
I'M SURE YOU KNOW THAT FUTURE WORLD FES IS NOT A NORMAL MUSIC FESTIVAL.
WE MANAGE THIS GENRE TO HELP IT GROW.
YOU'RE ALL STILL YOUNG AND HAVE GOOD LOOKS.
I'M SURE YOU'D BE POPULAR.
HOWEVER...

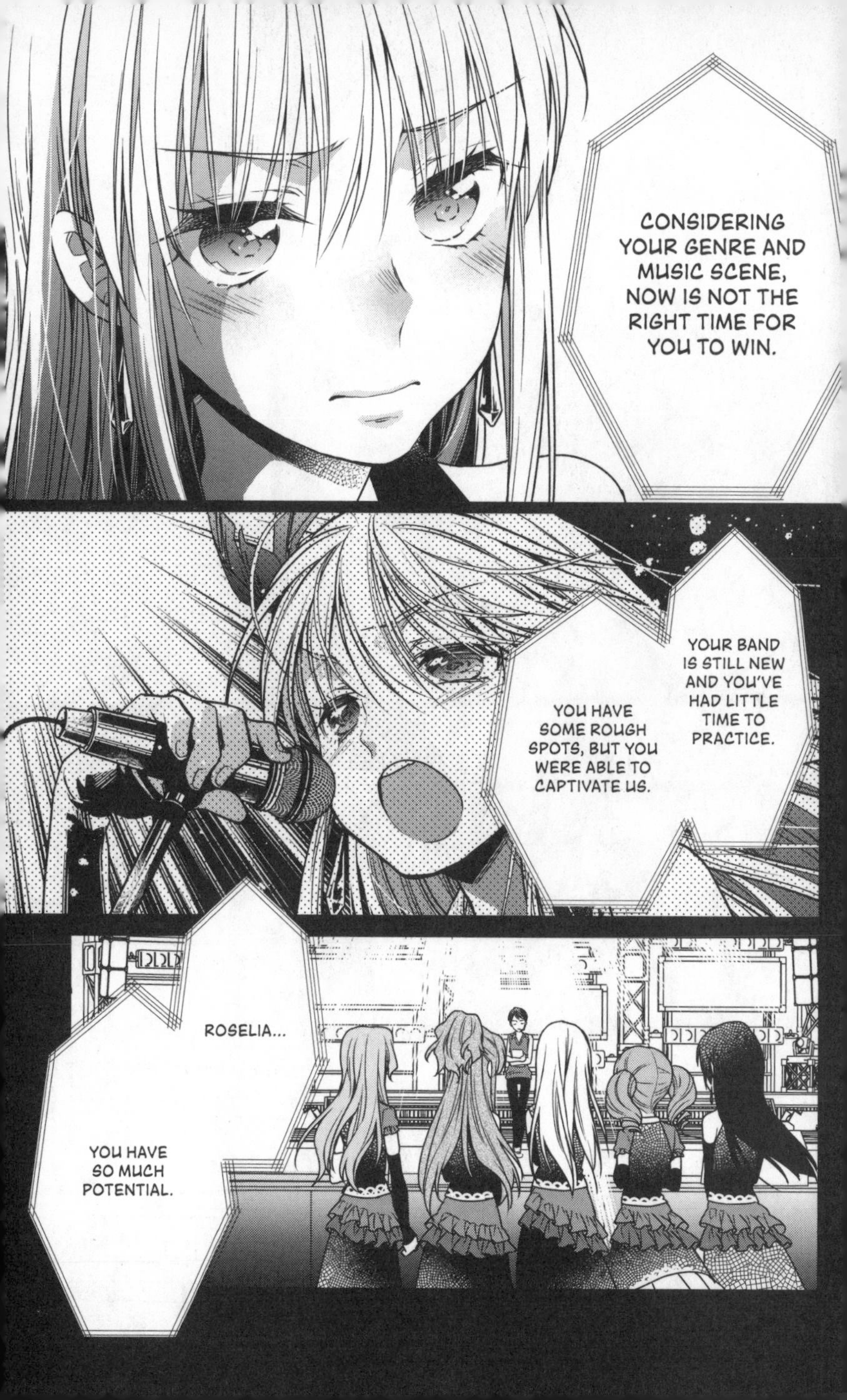
CONSIDERING YOUR GENRE AND MUSIC SCENE, NOW IS NOT THE RIGHT TIME FOR YOU TO WIN.
YOUR BAND IS STILL NEW AND YOU'VE HAD LITTLE TIME TO PRACTICE.
YOU HAVE SOME ROUGH SPOTS, BUT YOU WERE ABLE TO CAPTIVATE US.
ROSELIA...
YOU HAVE SO MUCH POTENTIAL.

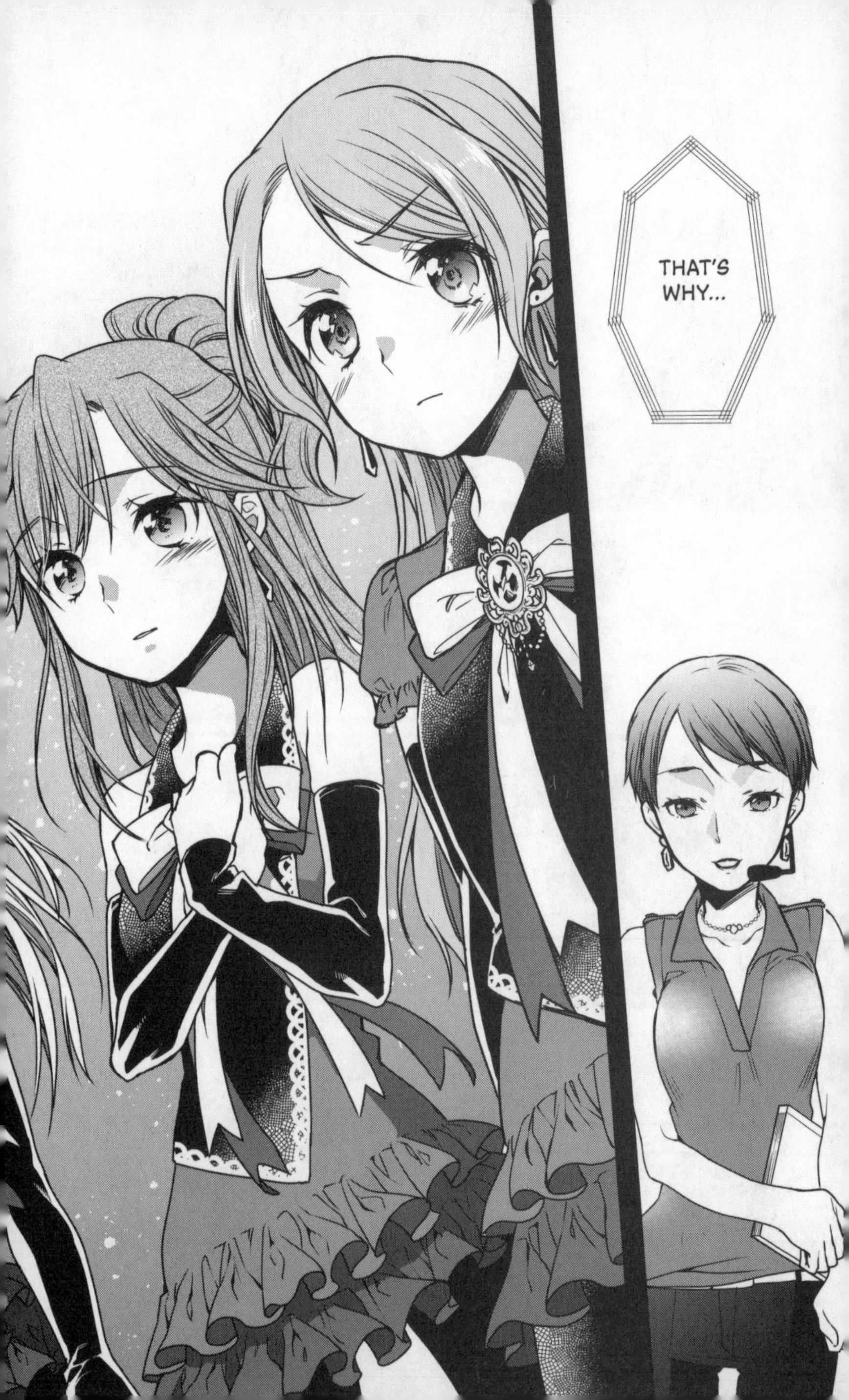
THAT'S WHY...

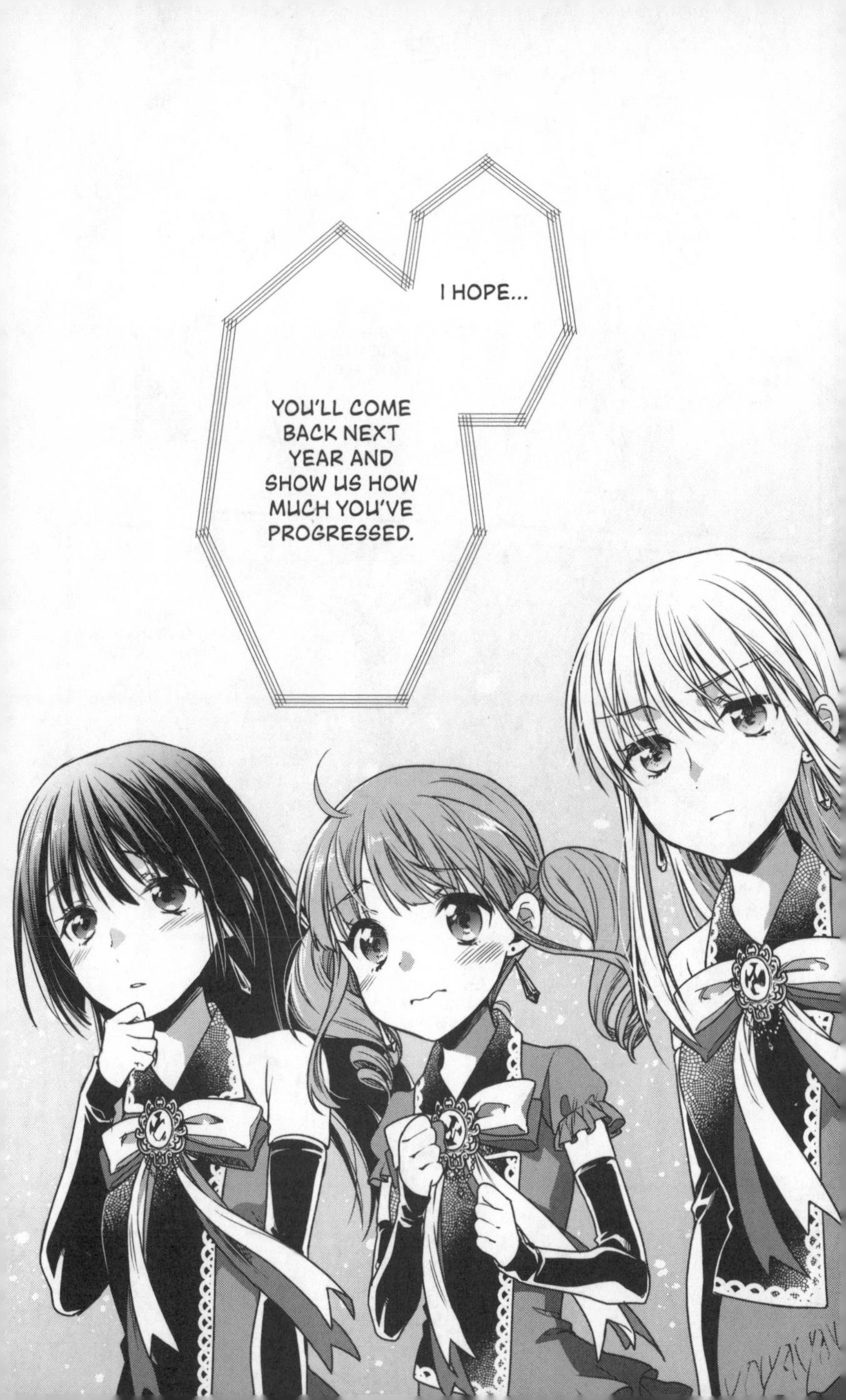
I HOPE...
YOU'LL COME BACK NEXT YEAR AND SHOW US HOW MUCH YOU'VE PROGRESSED.

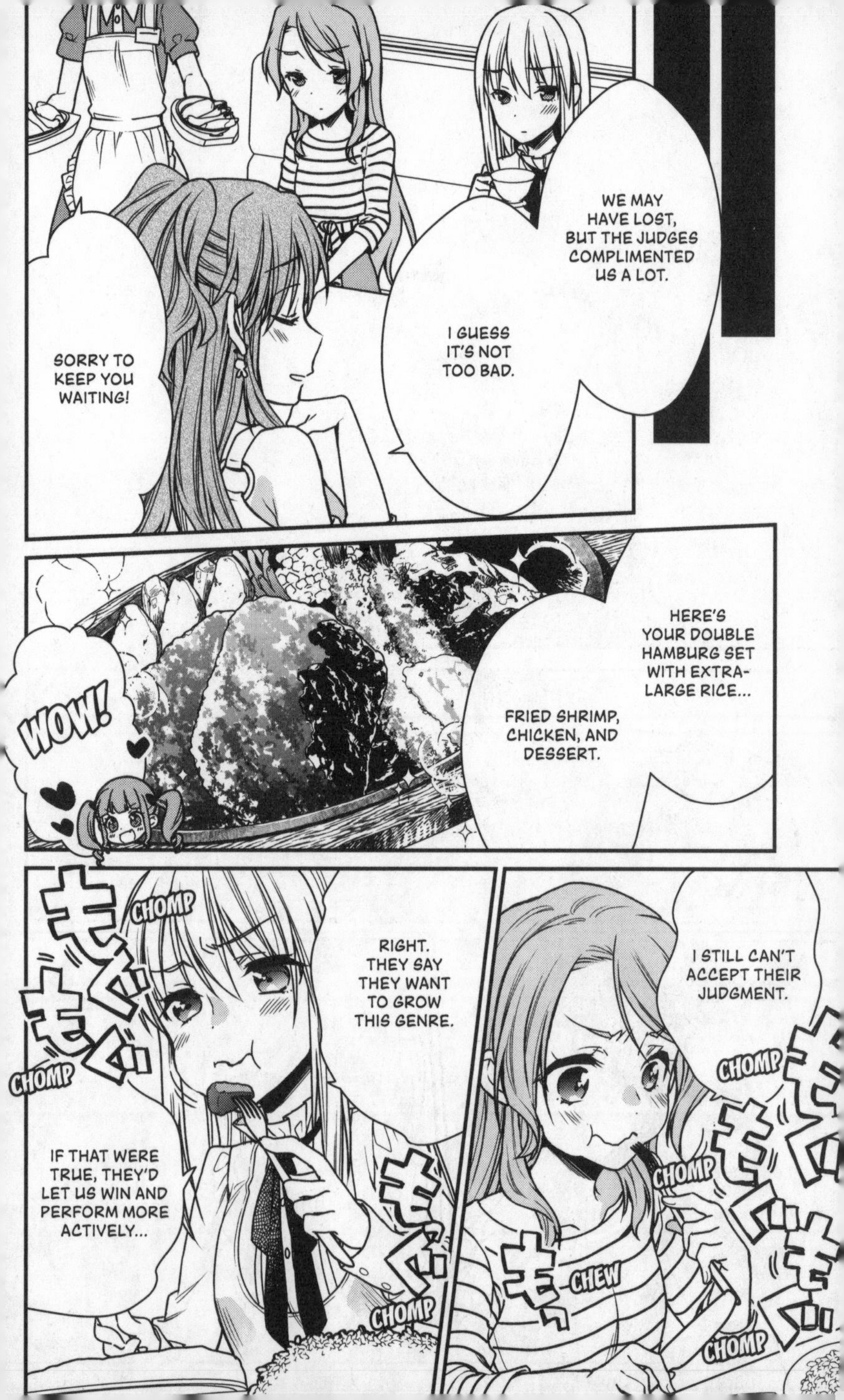
WE MAY HAVE LOST, BUT THE JUDGES COMPLIMENTED US A LOT.
I GUESS IT'S NOT TOO BAD.
SORRY TO KEEP YOU WAITING!
HERE'S YOUR DOUBLE HAMBURG SET WITH EXTRA-LARGE RICE...
FRIED SHRIMP, CHICKEN, AND DESSERT.
WOW!
I STILL CAN'T ACCEPT THEIR JUDGMENT.
CHOMP
CHOMP
CHEW
CHOMP
RIGHT. THEY SAY THEY WANT TO GROW THIS GENRE.
CHOMP
CHOMP
IF THAT WERE TRUE, THEY'D LET US WIN AND PERFORM MORE ACTIVELY...
CHOMP

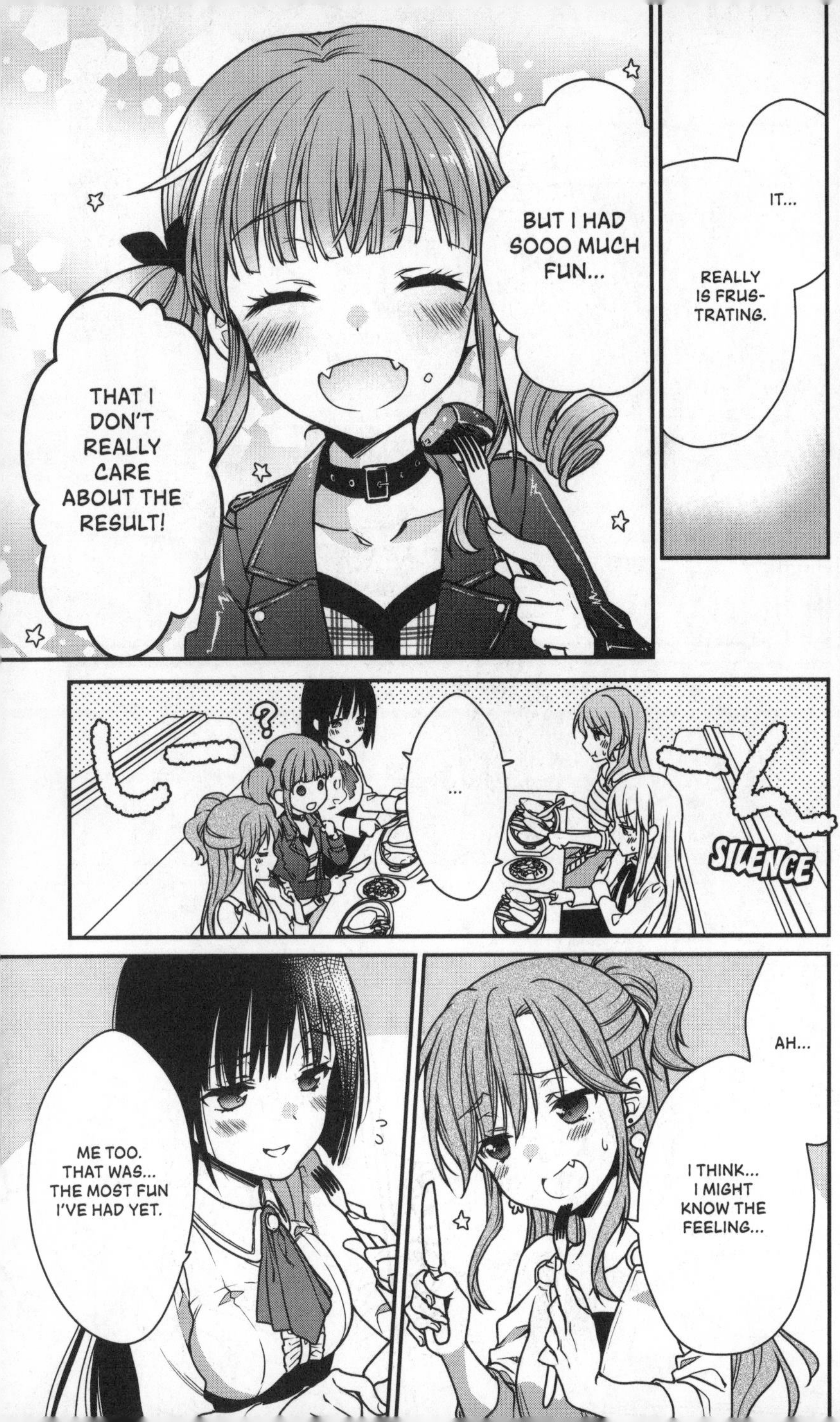
IT...
REALLY IS FRUS-TRATING.
BUT I HAD SOOO MUCH FUN...
THAT I DON'T REALLY CARE ABOUT THE RESULT!
...
SILENCE
AH...
I THINK... I MIGHT KNOW THE FEELING...
ME TOO. THAT WAS... THE MOST FUN I'VE HAD YET.

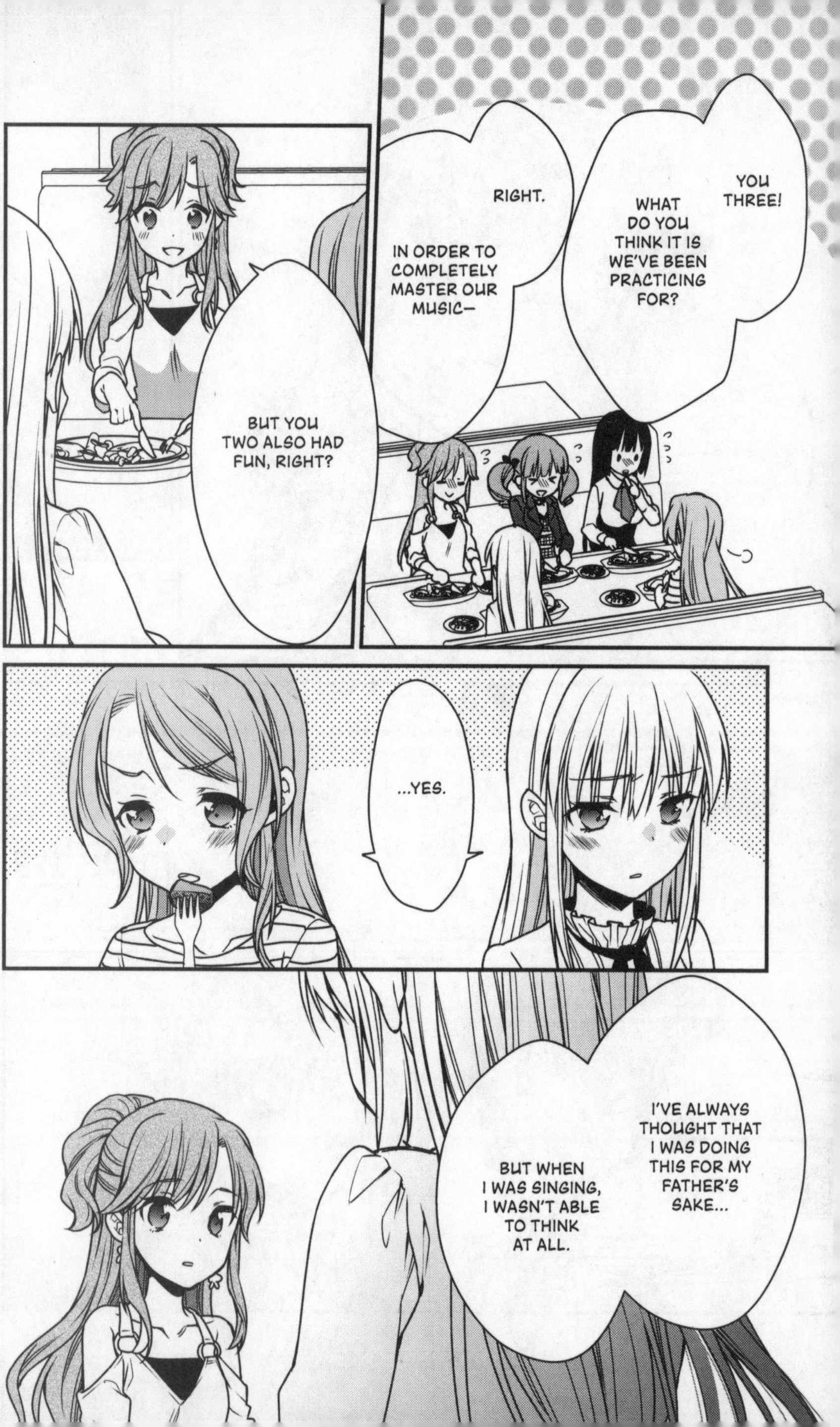
YOU THREE! WHAT DO YOU THINK IT IS WE'VE BEEN PRACTICING FOR?
RIGHT. IN ORDER TO COMPLETELY MASTER OUR MUSIC—
BUT YOU TWO ALSO HAD FUN, RIGHT?
...YES.
I'VE ALWAYS THOUGHT THAT I WAS DOING THIS FOR MY FATHER'S SAKE...
BUT WHEN I WAS SINGING, I WASN'T ABLE TO THINK AT ALL.

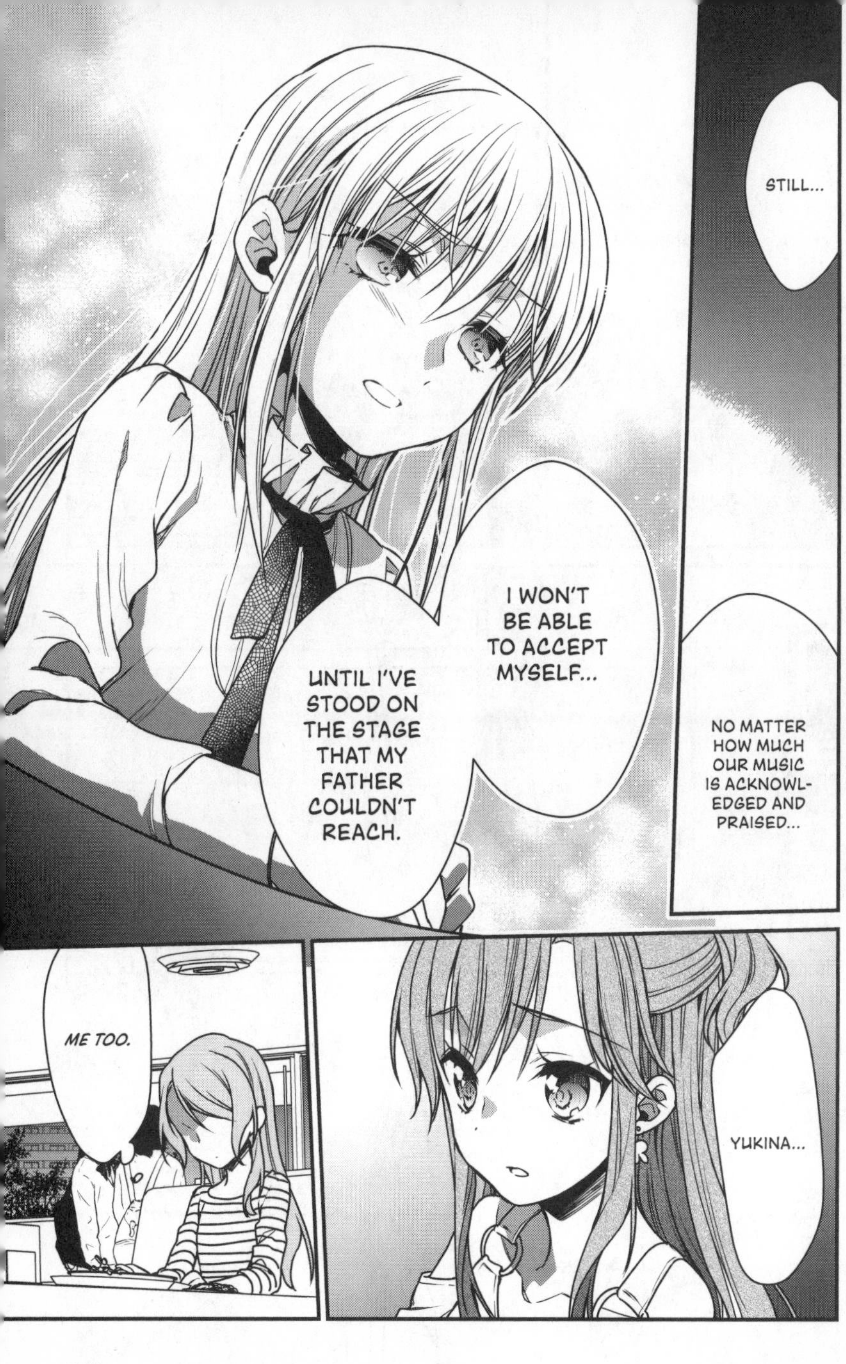
STILL...
NO MATTER HOW MUCH OUR MUSIC IS ACKNOWL-EDGED AND PRAISED...
I WON'T BE ABLE TO ACCEPT MYSELF...
UNTIL I'VE STOOD ON THE STAGE THAT MY FATHER COULDN'T REACH.
YUKINA...
ME TOO.

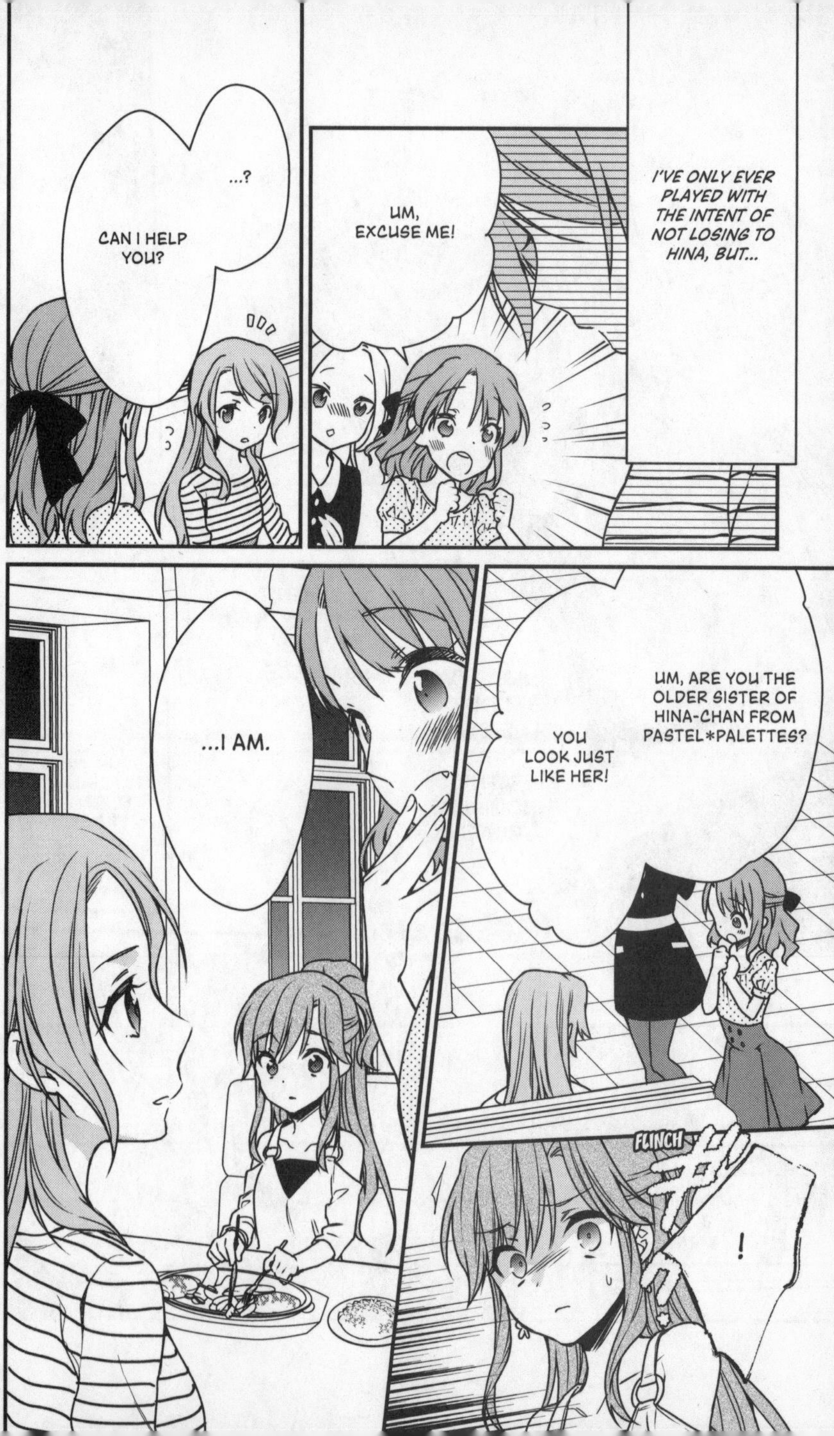
I'VE ONLY EVER PLAYED WITH THE INTENT OF NOT LOSING TO HINA, BUT...
UM, EXCUSE ME!
...?
CAN I HELP YOU?
UM, ARE YOU THE OLDER SISTER OF HINA-CHAN FROM PASTEL*PALETTES?
YOU LOOK JUST LIKE HER!
FLINCH
!
...I AM.

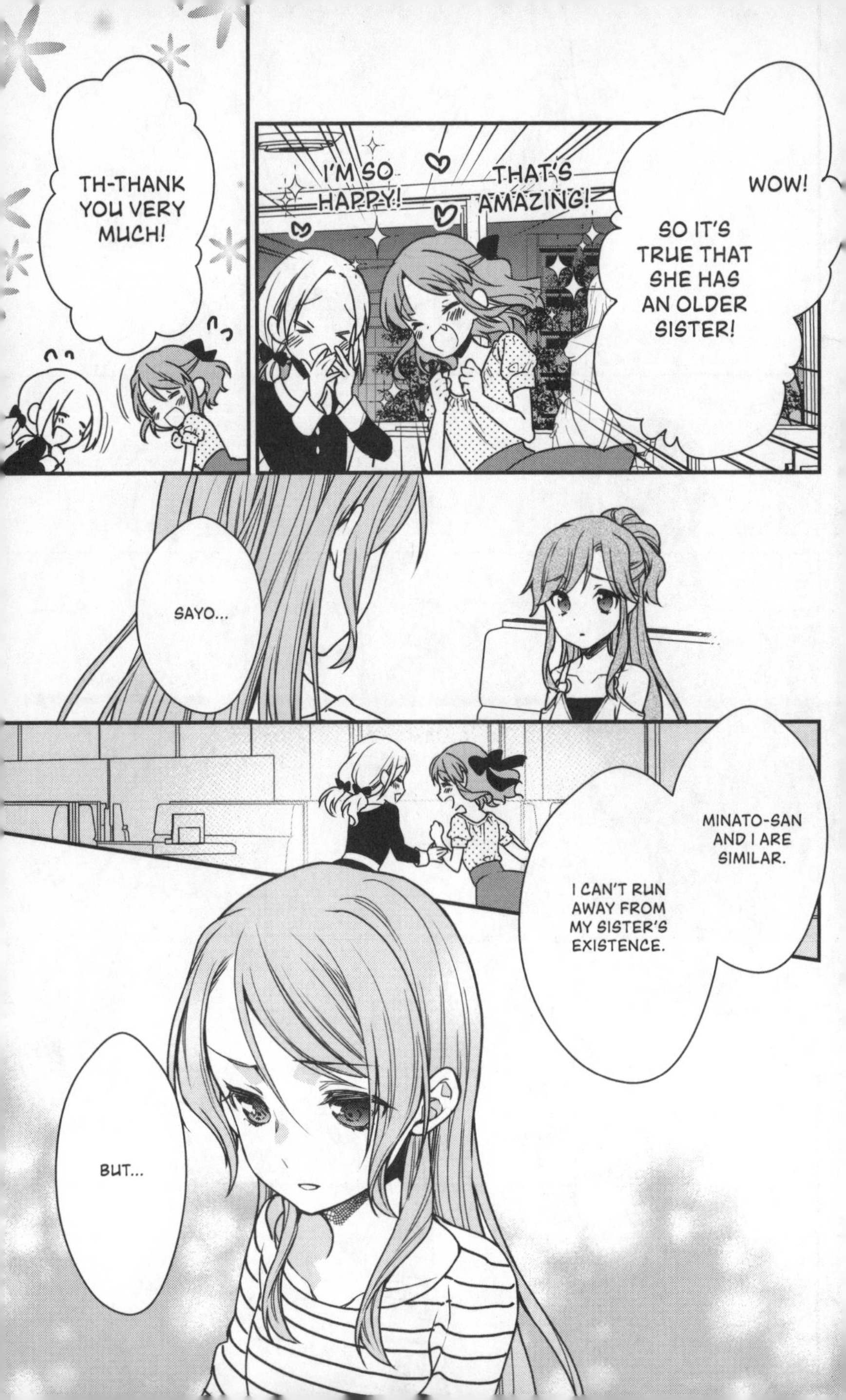
WOW!
SO IT'S TRUE THAT SHE HAS AN OLDER SISTER!
THAT'S AMAZING!
I'M SO HAPPY!
TH-THANK YOU VERY MUCH!
SAYO...
MINATO-SAN AND I ARE SIMILAR.
I CAN'T RUN AWAY FROM MY SISTER'S EXISTENCE.
BUT...

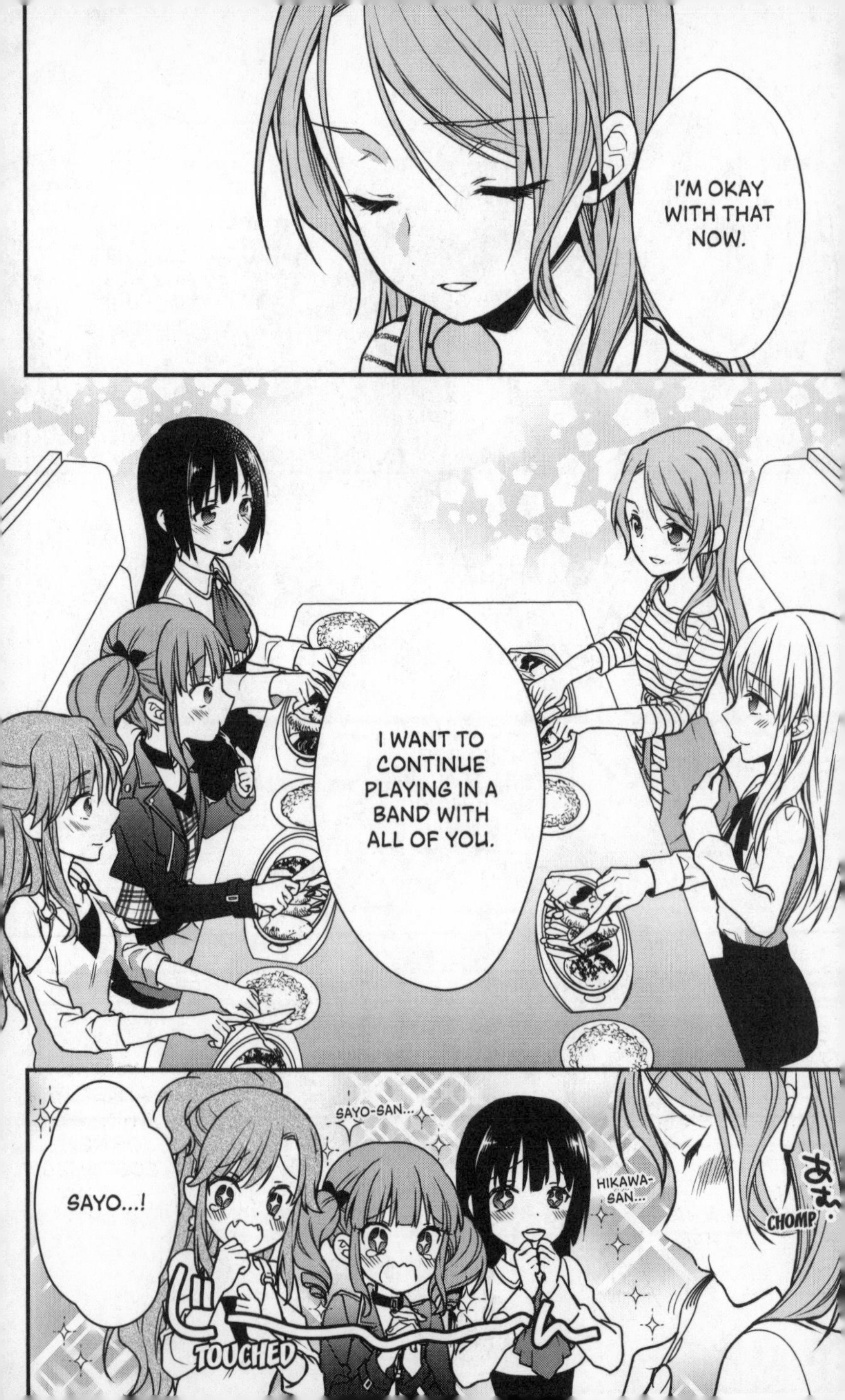
I'M OKAY WITH THAT NOW.
I WANT TO CONTINUE PLAYING IN A BAND WITH ALL OF YOU.
あむ
CHOMP
HIKAWA-SAN...
SAYO-SAN...
SAYO...!
TOUCHED

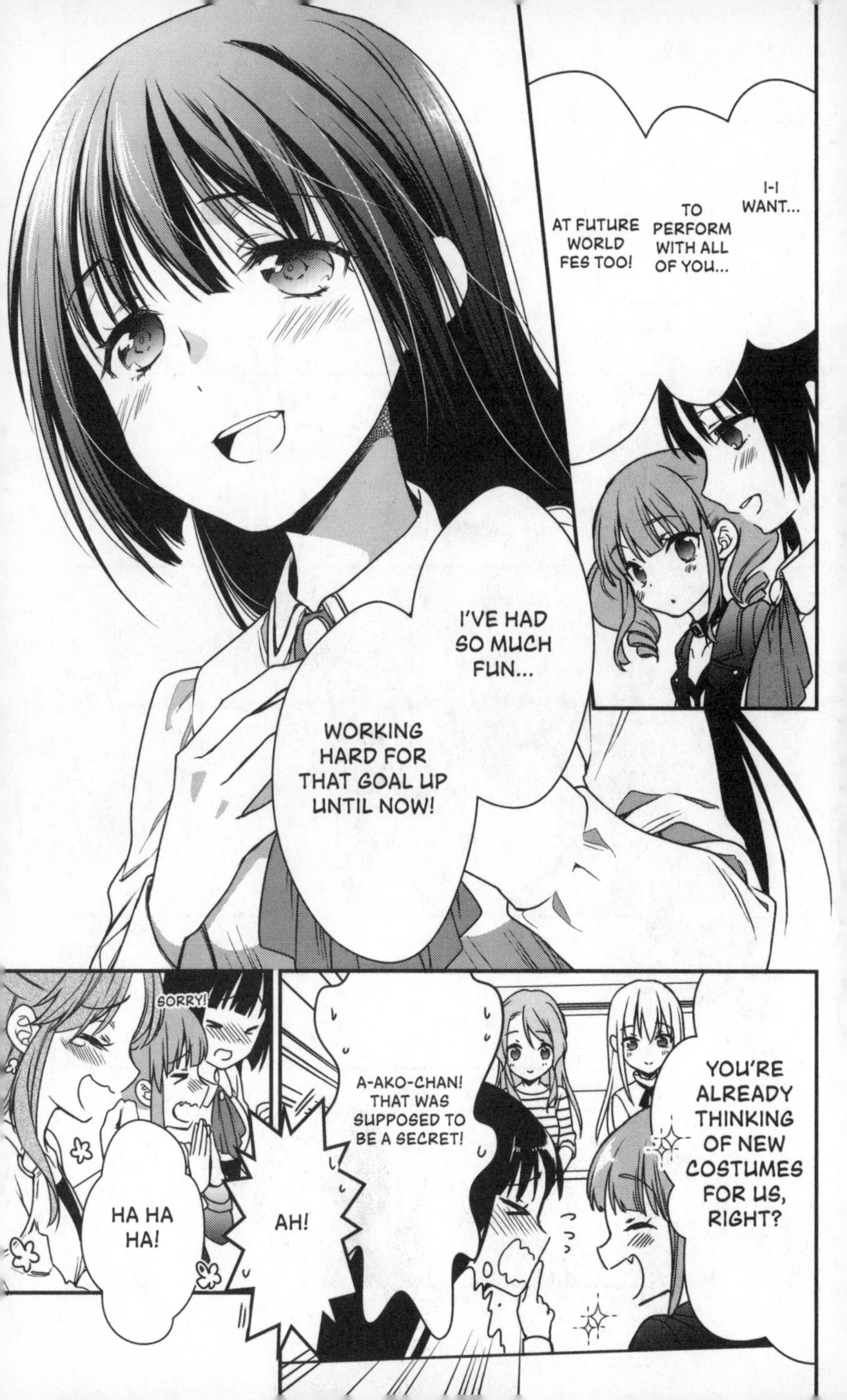
I-I WANT...
TO PERFORM WITH ALL OF YOU...
AT FUTURE WORLD FES TOO!
I'VE HAD SO MUCH FUN...
WORKING HARD FOR THAT GOAL UP UNTIL NOW!
YOU'RE ALREADY THINKING OF NEW COSTUMES FOR US, RIGHT?
A-AKO-CHAN! THAT WAS SUPPOSED TO BE A SECRET!
AH!
SORRY!
HA HA HA!

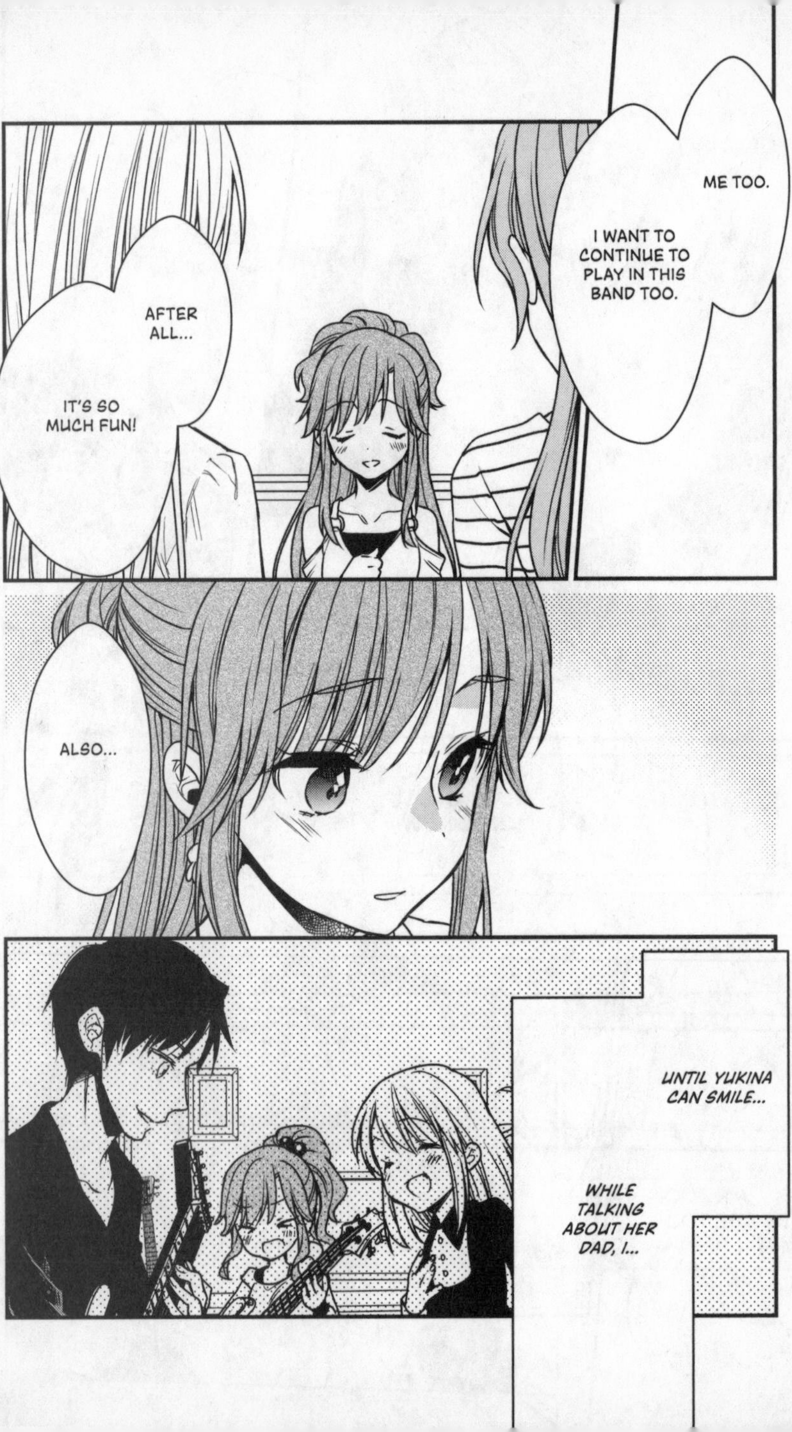
ME TOO.
I WANT TO CONTINUE TO PLAY IN THIS BAND TOO.
AFTER ALL...
IT'S SO MUCH FUN!
ALSO...
UNTIL YUKINA CAN SMILE...
WHILE TALKING ABOUT HER DAD, I...

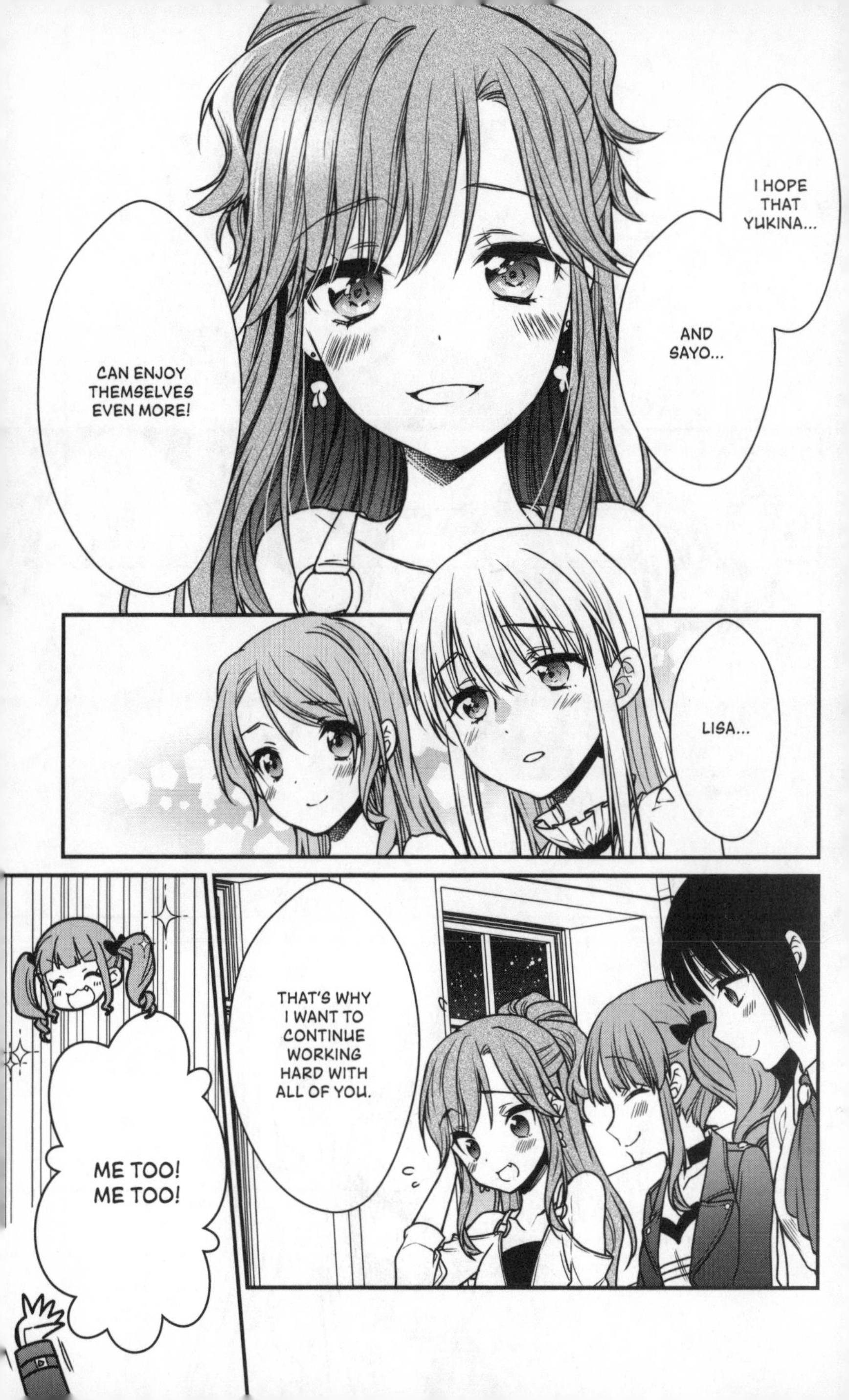
I HOPE THAT YUKINA...
AND SAYO...
CAN ENJOY THEMSELVES EVEN MORE!
LISA...
THAT'S WHY I WANT TO CONTINUE WORKING HARD WITH ALL OF YOU.
ME TOO! ME TOO!

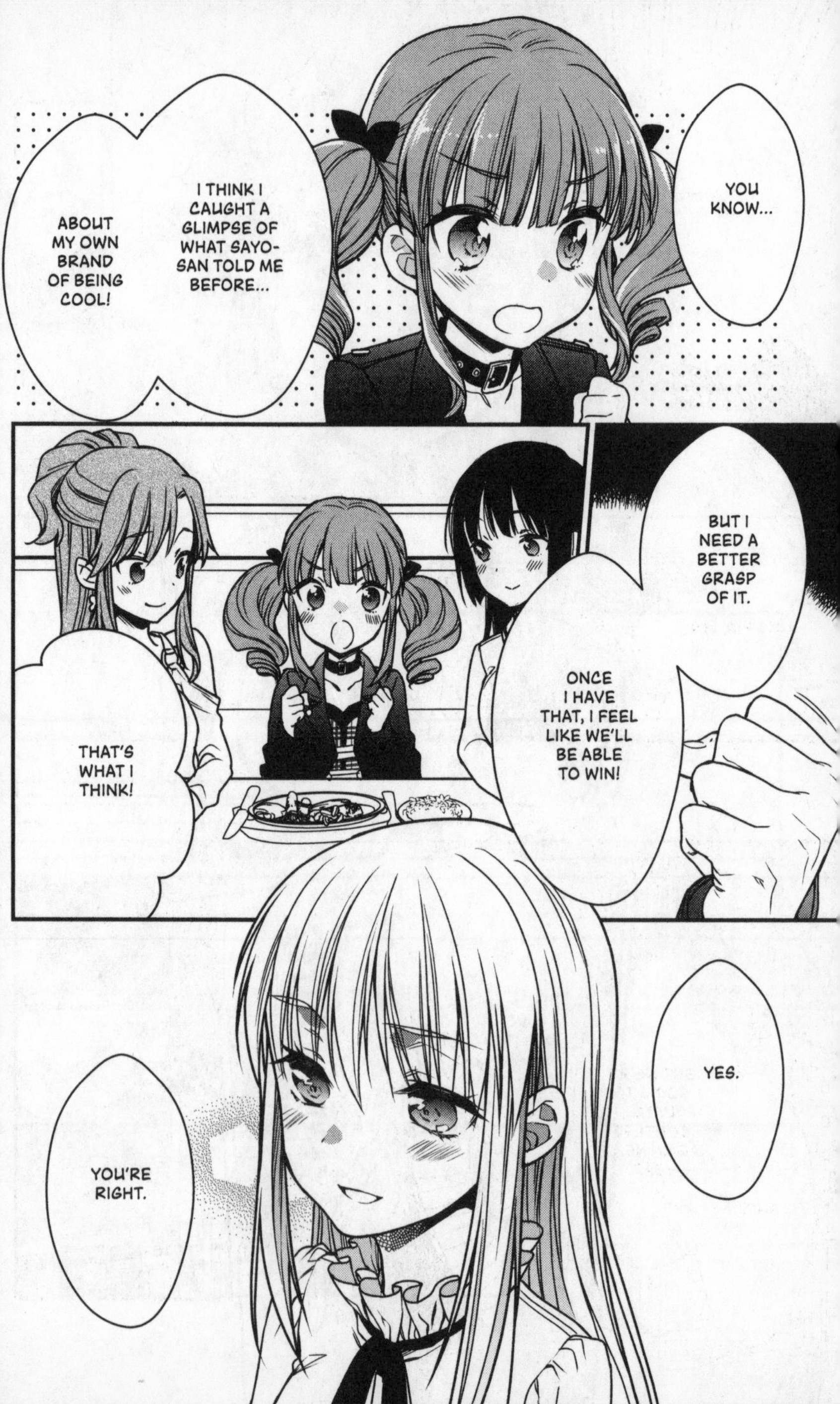
YOU KNOW...
I THINK I CAUGHT A GLIMPSE OF WHAT SAYO-SAN TOLD ME BEFORE...
ABOUT MY OWN BRAND OF BEING COOL!
BUT I NEED A BETTER GRASP OF IT.
ONCE I HAVE THAT, I FEEL LIKE WE'LL BE ABLE TO WIN!
THAT'S WHAT I THINK!
YES.
YOU'RE RIGHT.

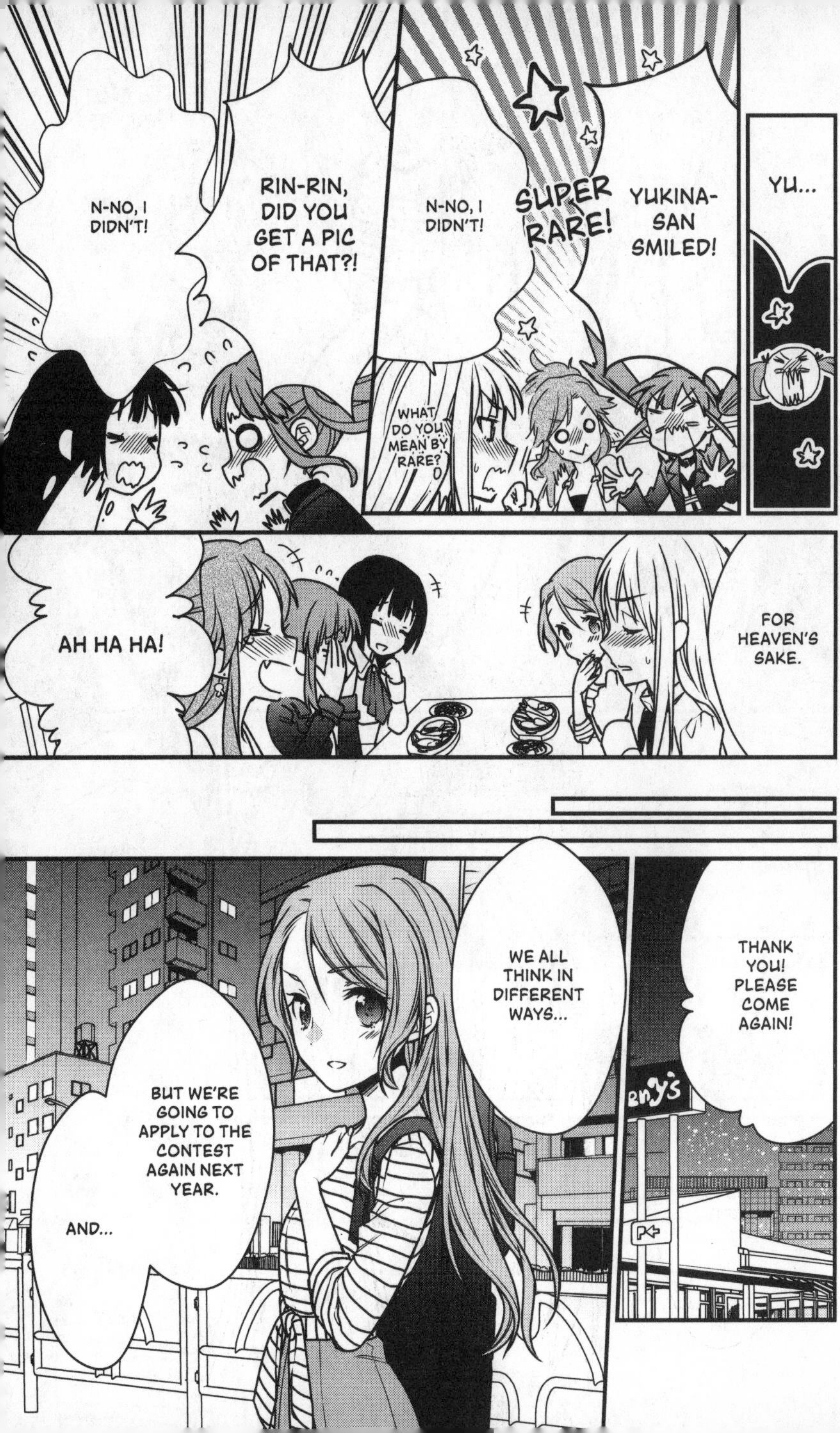
YU...
YUKINA-SAN SMILED!
SUPER RARE!
N-NO, I DIDN'T!
WHAT DO YOU MEAN BY RARE?
RIN-RIN, DID YOU GET A PIC OF THAT?!
N-NO, I DIDN'T!
FOR HEAVEN'S SAKE.
AH HA HA!
THANK YOU! PLEASE COME AGAIN!
WE ALL THINK IN DIFFERENT WAYS...
BUT WE'RE GOING TO APPLY TO THE CONTEST AGAIN NEXT YEAR.
AND...

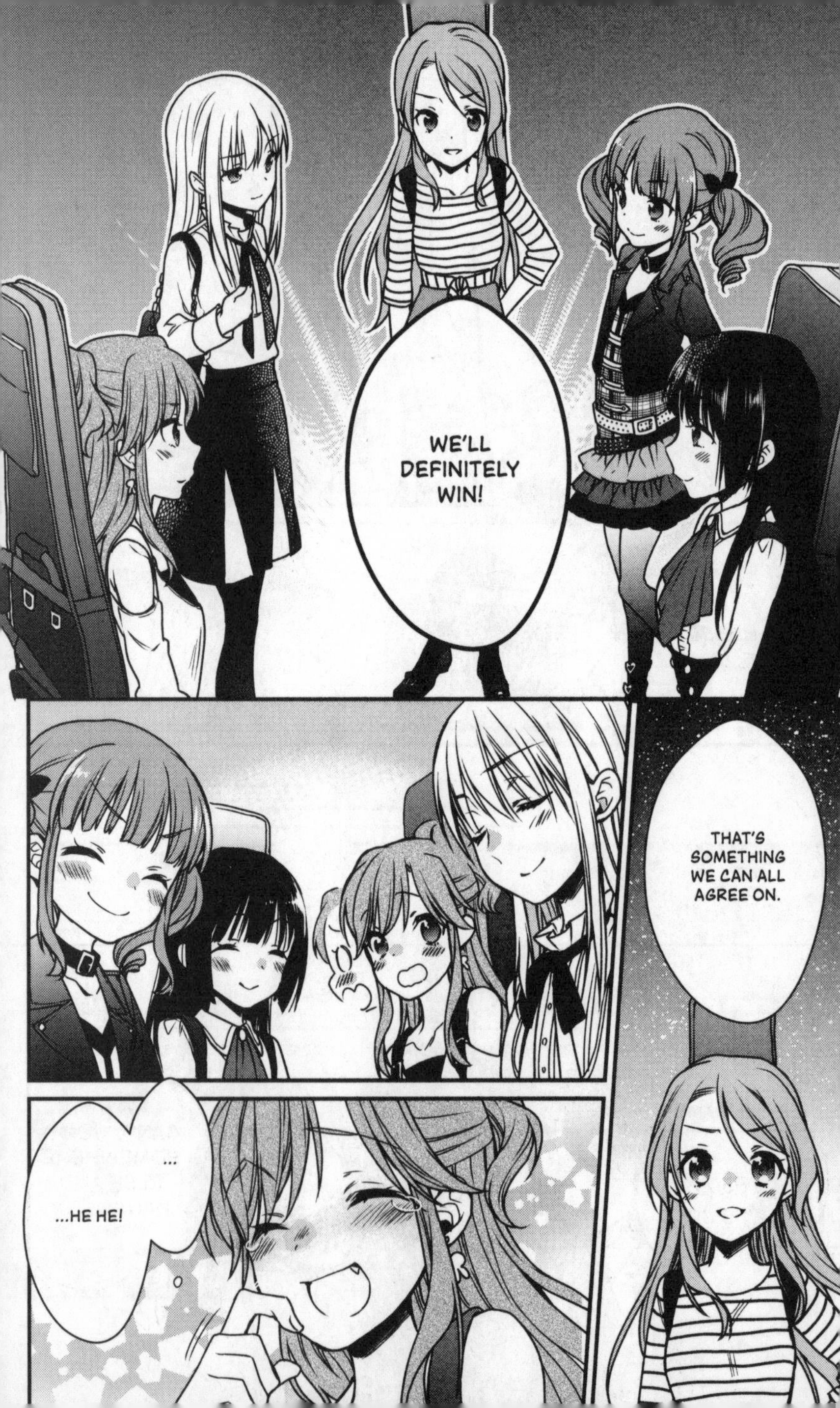
WE'LL DEFINITELY WIN!
THAT'S SOMETHING WE CAN ALL AGREE ON.
...
...HE HE!

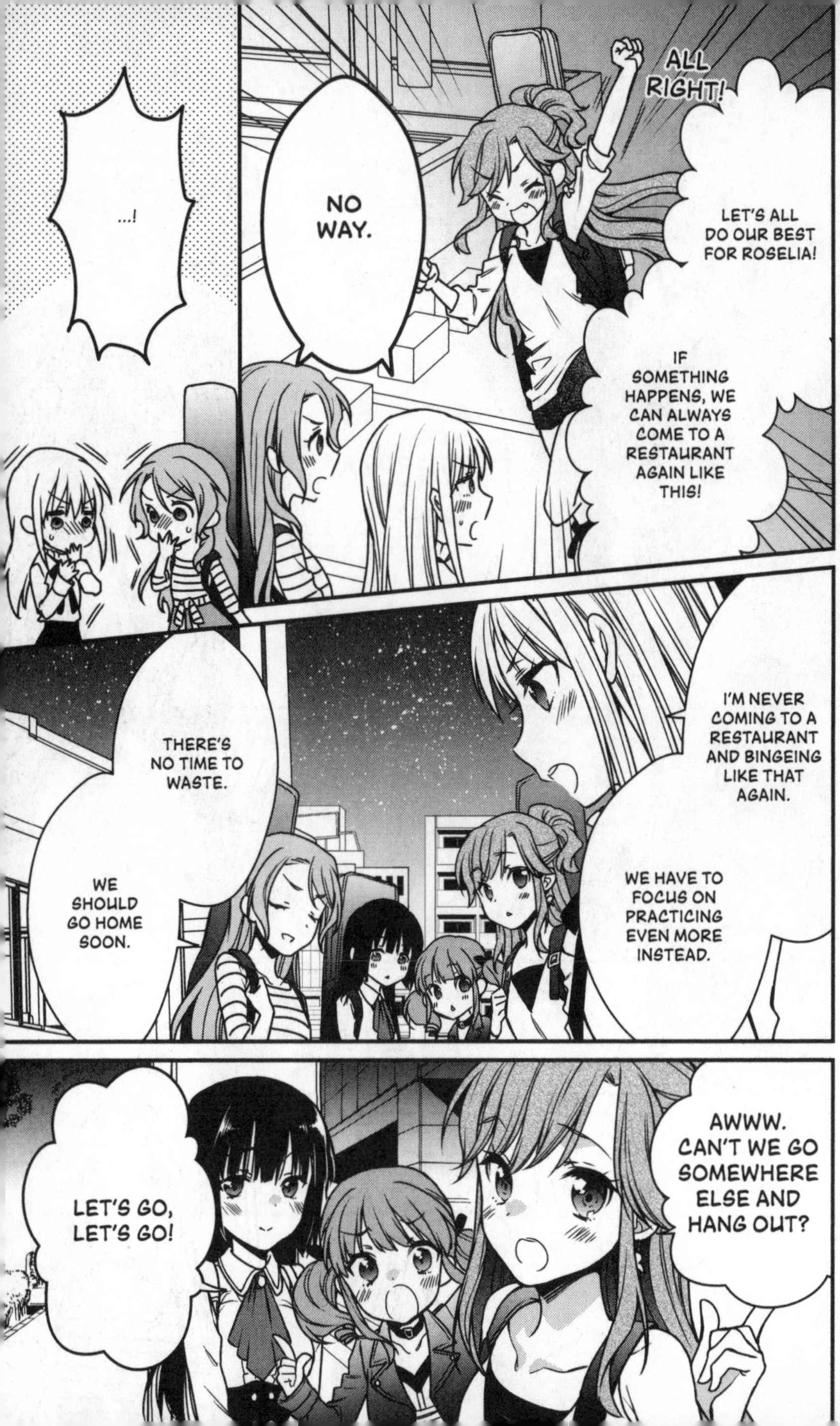
ALL RIGHT!
LET'S ALL DO OUR BEST FOR ROSELIA!
IF SOMETHING HAPPENS, WE CAN ALWAYS COME TO A RESTAURANT AGAIN LIKE THIS!
NO WAY.
...!
I'M NEVER COMING TO A RESTAURANT AND BINGEING LIKE THAT AGAIN.
WE HAVE TO FOCUS ON PRACTICING EVEN MORE INSTEAD.
THERE'S NO TIME TO WASTE.
WE SHOULD GO HOME SOON.
AWWW. CAN'T WE GO SOMEWHERE ELSE AND HANG OUT?
LET'S GO, LET'S GO!

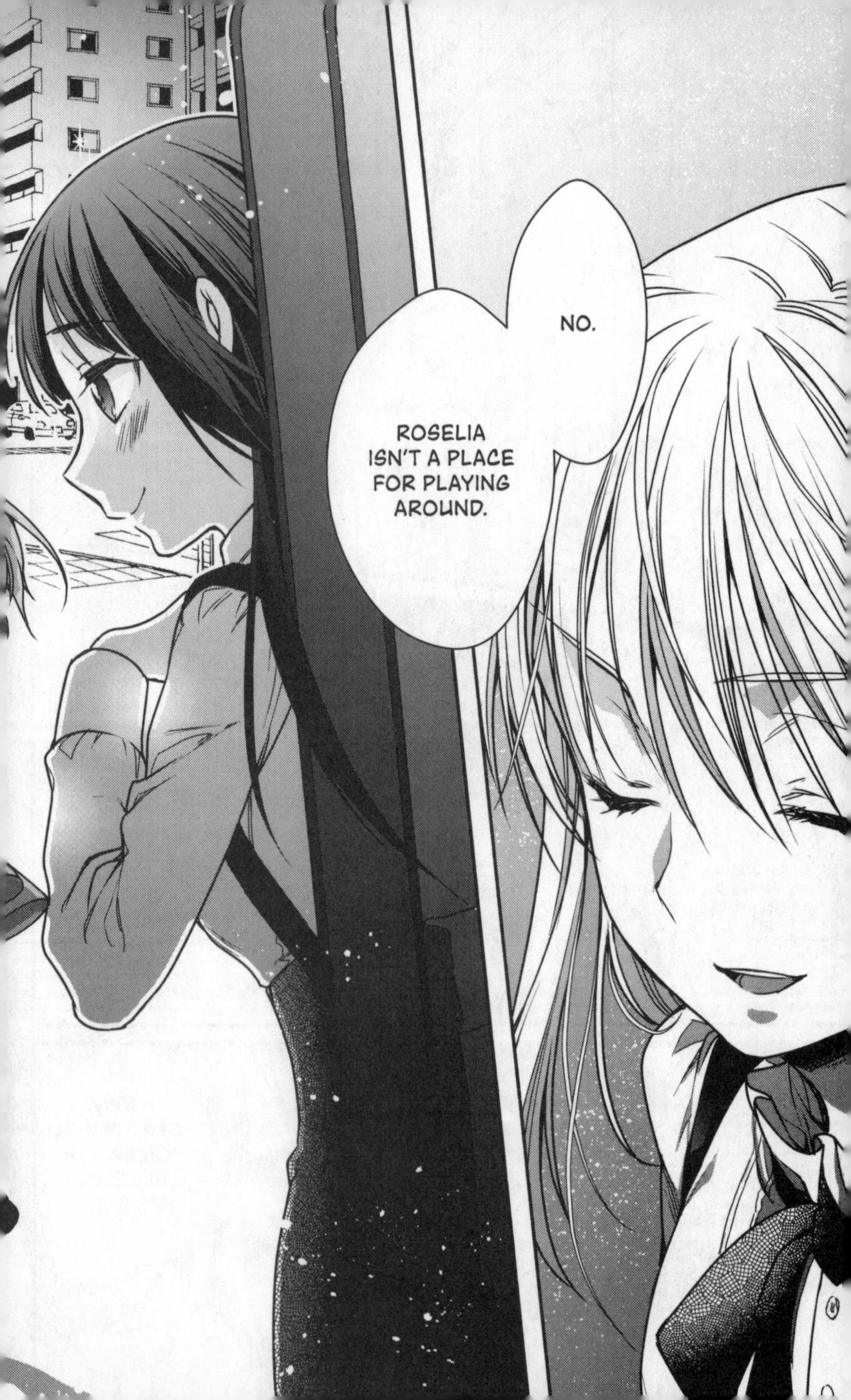
NO.
ROSELIA ISN'T A PLACE FOR PLAYING AROUND.

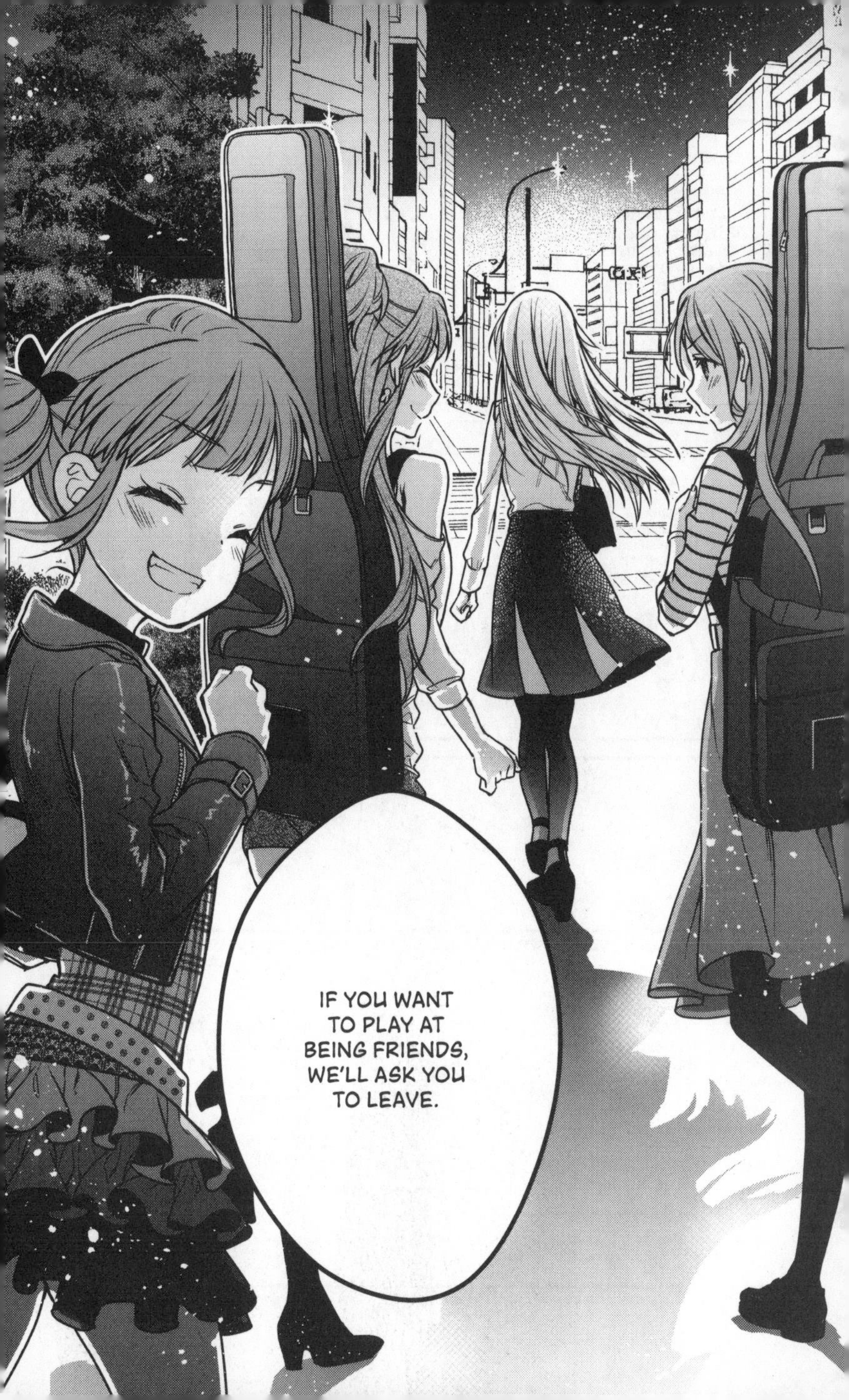
IF YOU WANT TO PLAY AT BEING FRIENDS, WE'LL ASK YOU TO LEAVE.

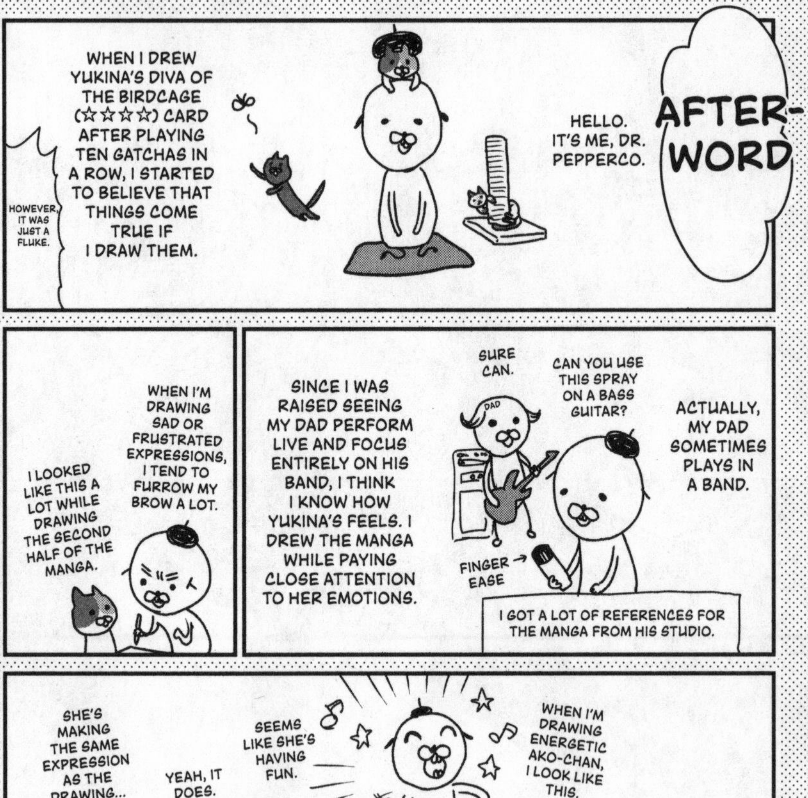
AFTER-WORD
HELLO. IT'S ME, DR. PEPPERCO.
WHEN I DREW YUKINA'S DIVA OF THE BIRDCAGE (☆☆☆☆) CARD AFTER PLAYING TEN GATCHAS IN A ROW, I STARTED TO BELIEVE THAT THINGS COME TRUE IF I DRAW THEM.
HOWEVER, IT WAS JUST A FLUKE.
ACTUALLY, MY DAD SOMETIMES PLAYS IN A BAND.
CAN YOU USE THIS SPRAY ON A BASS GUITAR?
SURE CAN.
DAD
SINCE I WAS RAISED SEEING MY DAD PERFORM LIVE AND FOCUS ENTIRELY ON HIS BAND, I THINK I KNOW HOW YUKINA'S FEELS. I DREW THE MANGA WHILE PAYING CLOSE ATTENTION TO HER EMOTIONS.
FINGER EASE
I GOT A LOT OF REFERENCES FOR THE MANGA FROM HIS STUDIO.
WHEN I'M DRAWING SAD OR FRUSTRATED EXPRESSIONS, I TEND TO FURROW MY BROW A LOT.
I LOOKED LIKE THIS A LOT WHILE DRAWING THE SECOND HALF OF THE MANGA.
WHEN I'M DRAWING ENERGETIC AKO-CHAN, I LOOK LIKE THIS.
SEEMS LIKE SHE'S HAVING FUN.
SHE'S MAKING THE SAME EXPRESSION AS THE DRAWING...
YEAH, IT DOES.
IN ANY CASE, I WAS ABLE TO ENJOY DRAWING UP TO THE LAST CHAPTER OF THE MANGA WITH THE HELP OF SO MANY PEOPLE. I HOPE THAT THIS MANGA MADE YOU FALL IN LOVE WITH ROSELIA!
THANK YOU SO MUCH FOR READING ALL THE WAY TO THE END!
I HOPE WE CAN MEET AGAIN!

2017 DR. PEPPERCO

BanG Dream! Girls Band Party!

Roselia Stage

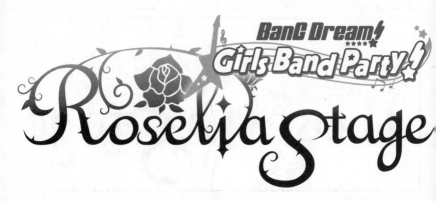

BanG Dream! Girls Band Party!

Roselia Stage

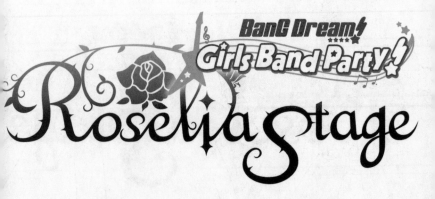

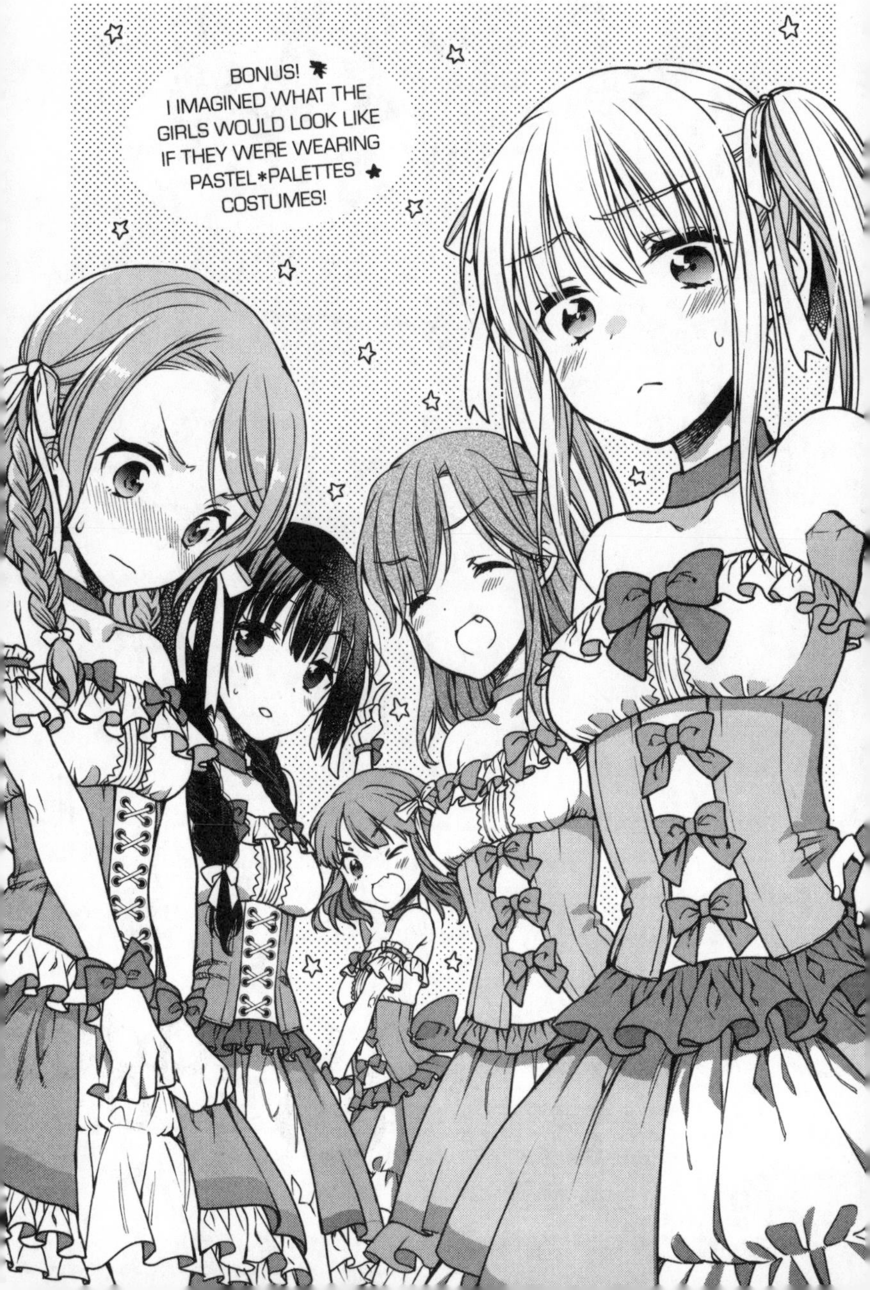
BONUS! I IMAGINED WHAT THE GIRLS WOULD LOOK LIKE IF THEY WERE WEARING PASTEL*PALETTES COSTUMES!

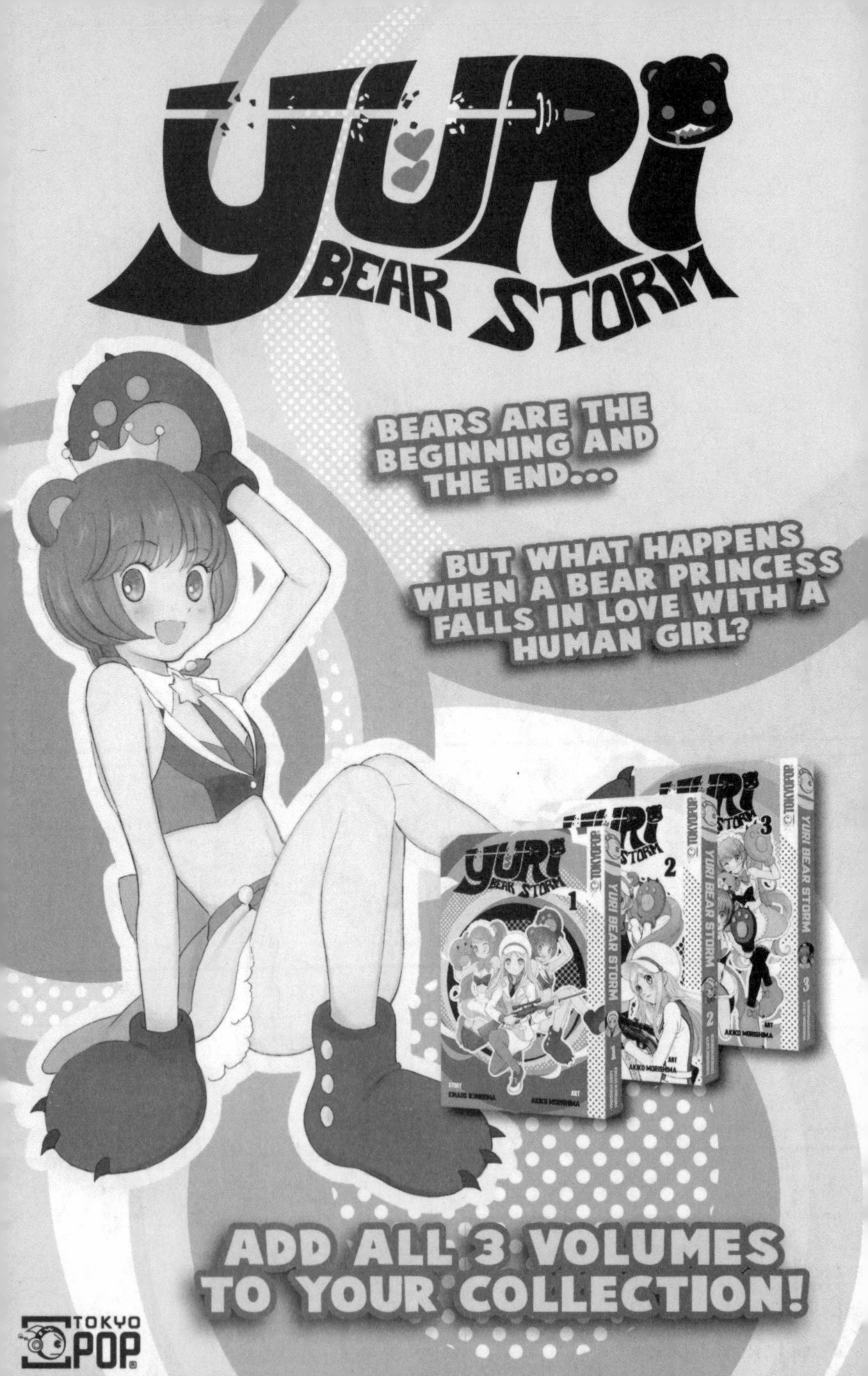
YURI BEAR STORM
BEARS ARE THE BEGINNING AND THE END...
BUT WHAT HAPPENS WHEN A BEAR PRINCESS FALLS IN LOVE WITH A HUMAN GIRL?
ADD ALL 3 VOLUMES TO YOUR COLLECTION!
TOKYO POP
LOVE x LOVE

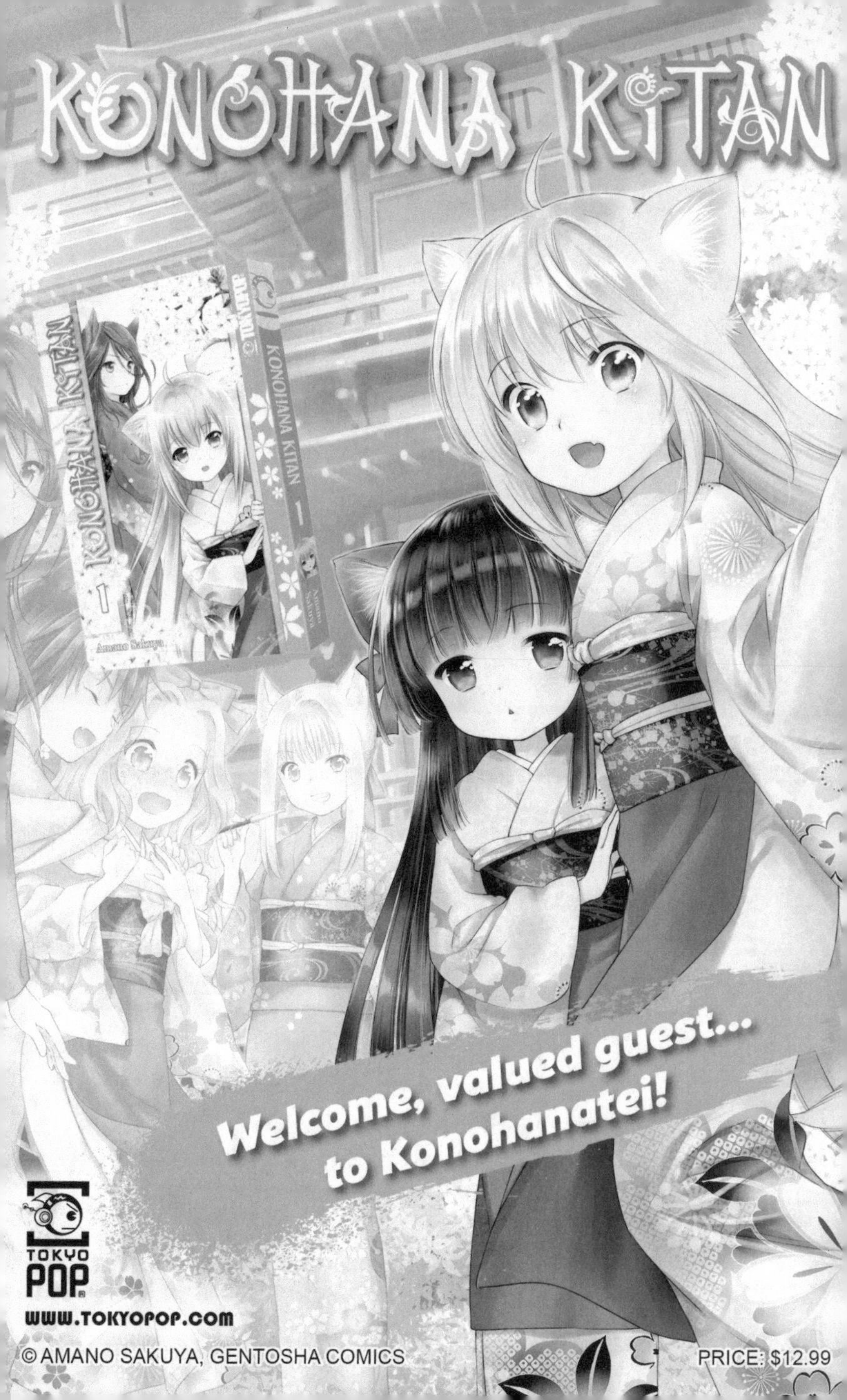
KONOHANA KITAN
KONOHANA KITAN 1
Amano Sakuya
TOKYOPOP
KONOHANA KITAN 1
Welcome, valued guest...
to Konohanatei!
TOKYO POP
WWW.TOKYOPOP.COM
© AMANO SAKUYA, GENTOSHA COMICS
PRICE: $12.99

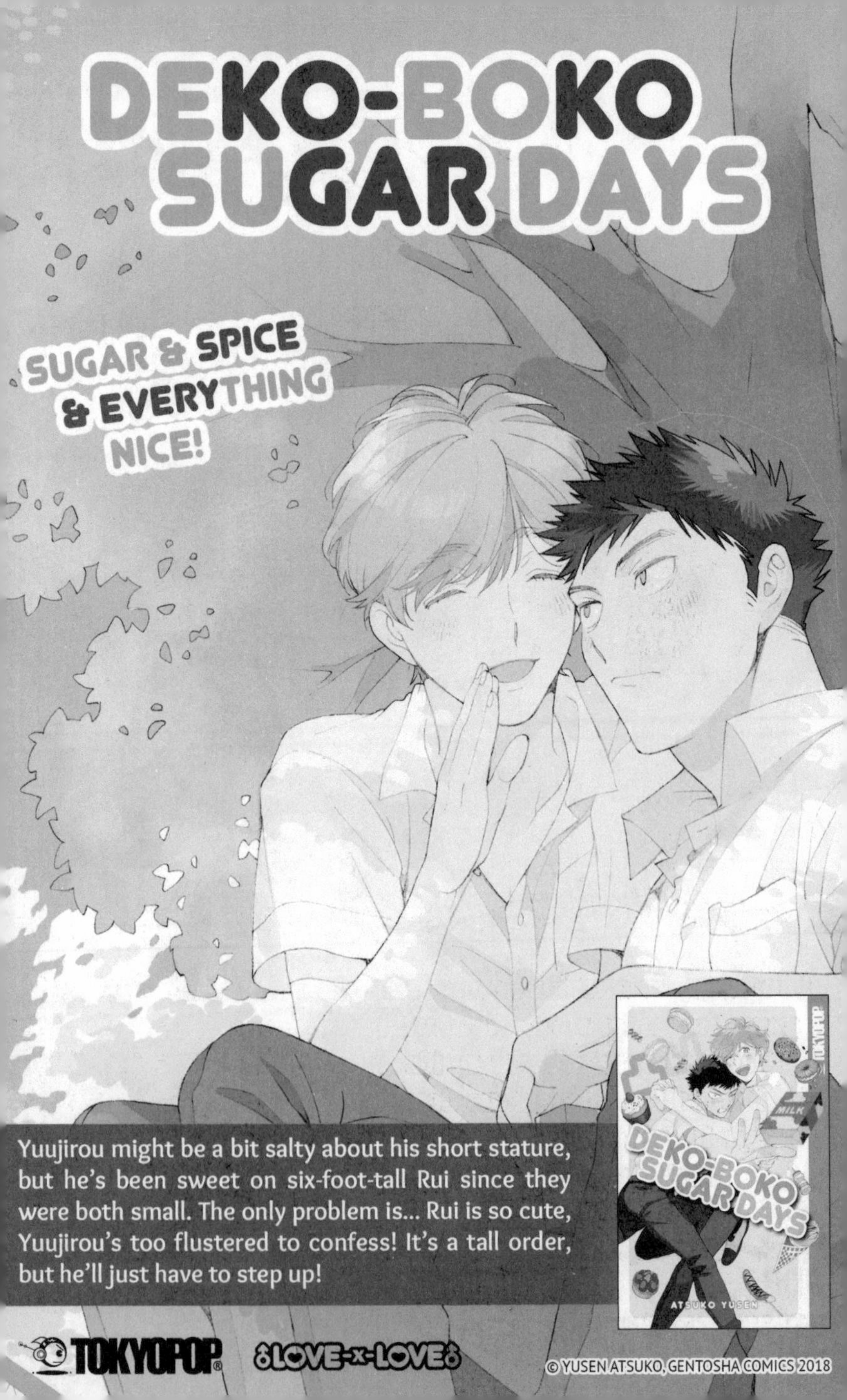
DEKO-BOKO SUGAR DAYS
SUGAR & SPICE & EVERYTHING NICE!
Yuujirou might be a bit salty about his short stature, but he's been sweet on six-foot-tall Rui since they were both small. The only problem is... Rui is so cute, Yuujirou's too flustered to confess! It's a tall order, but he'll just have to step up!
TOKYOPOP
MILK
DEKO-BOKO SUGAR DAYS
ATSUKO YUSEN
TOKYOPOP
LOVE x LOVE
© YUSEN ATSUKO, GENTOSHA COMICS 2018

SCARLET SOUL

Long ago, an ancient hero sealed away the underworld. Now, with that sacred barrier broken, it's up to Rin and the mysterious demon Aghyr to restore balance to the Kingdom of Nohmur!

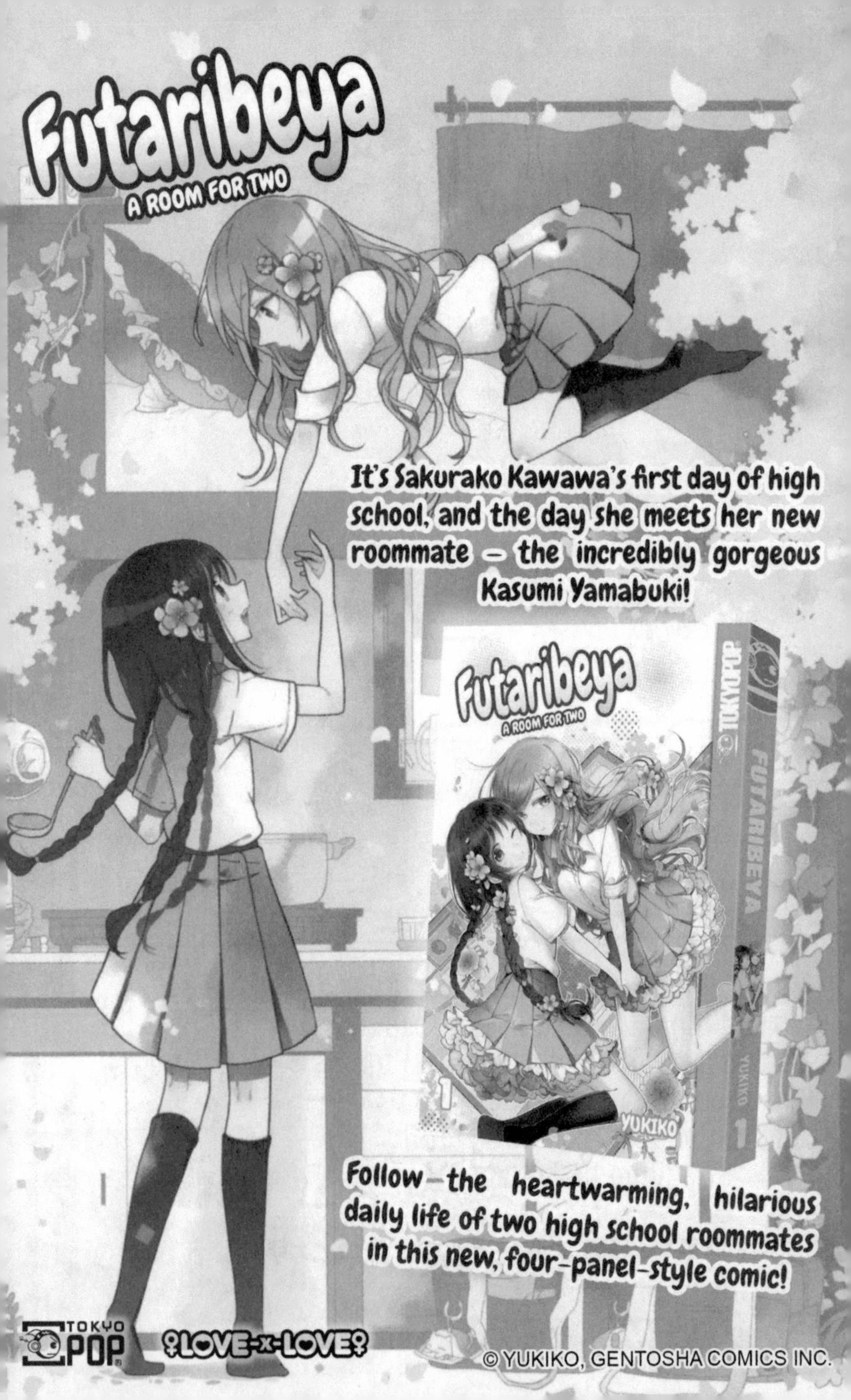
Futaribeya
A ROOM FOR TWO
It's Sakurako Kawawa's first day of high school, and the day she meets her new roommate – the incredibly gorgeous Kasumi Yamabuki!
Futaribeya
A ROOM FOR TWO
TOKYOPOP
FUTARIBEYA
YUKIKO
1
YUKIKO
1
Follow the heartwarming, hilarious daily life of two high school roommates in this new, four-panel-style comic!
TOKYO POP
LOVE-x-LOVE
© YUKIKO, GENTOSHA COMICS INC.

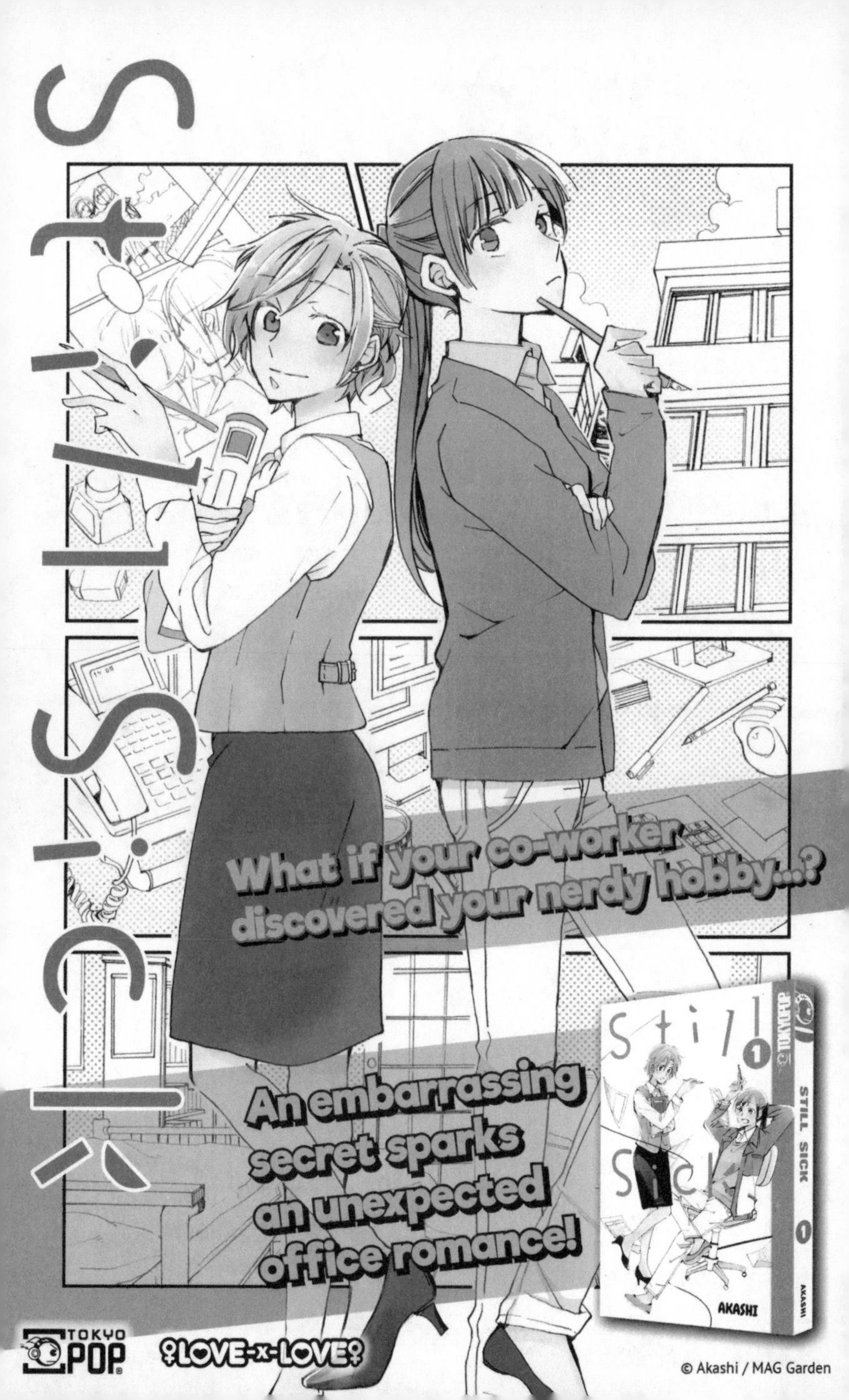
Still Sick
What if your co-worker discovered your nerdy hobby...?
An embarrassing secret sparks an unexpected office romance!
Still Sick 1
STILL SICK 1
AKASHI
TOKYOPOP
LOVE x LOVE
© Akashi / MAG Garden

The Fox & Little Tanuki

KORISENMAN

A modern-day fable for all ages inspired by Japanese folklore!

Senzou the black fox was punished by having his powers taken away. Now to get them back, he must play babysitter to an adorable baby tanuki!

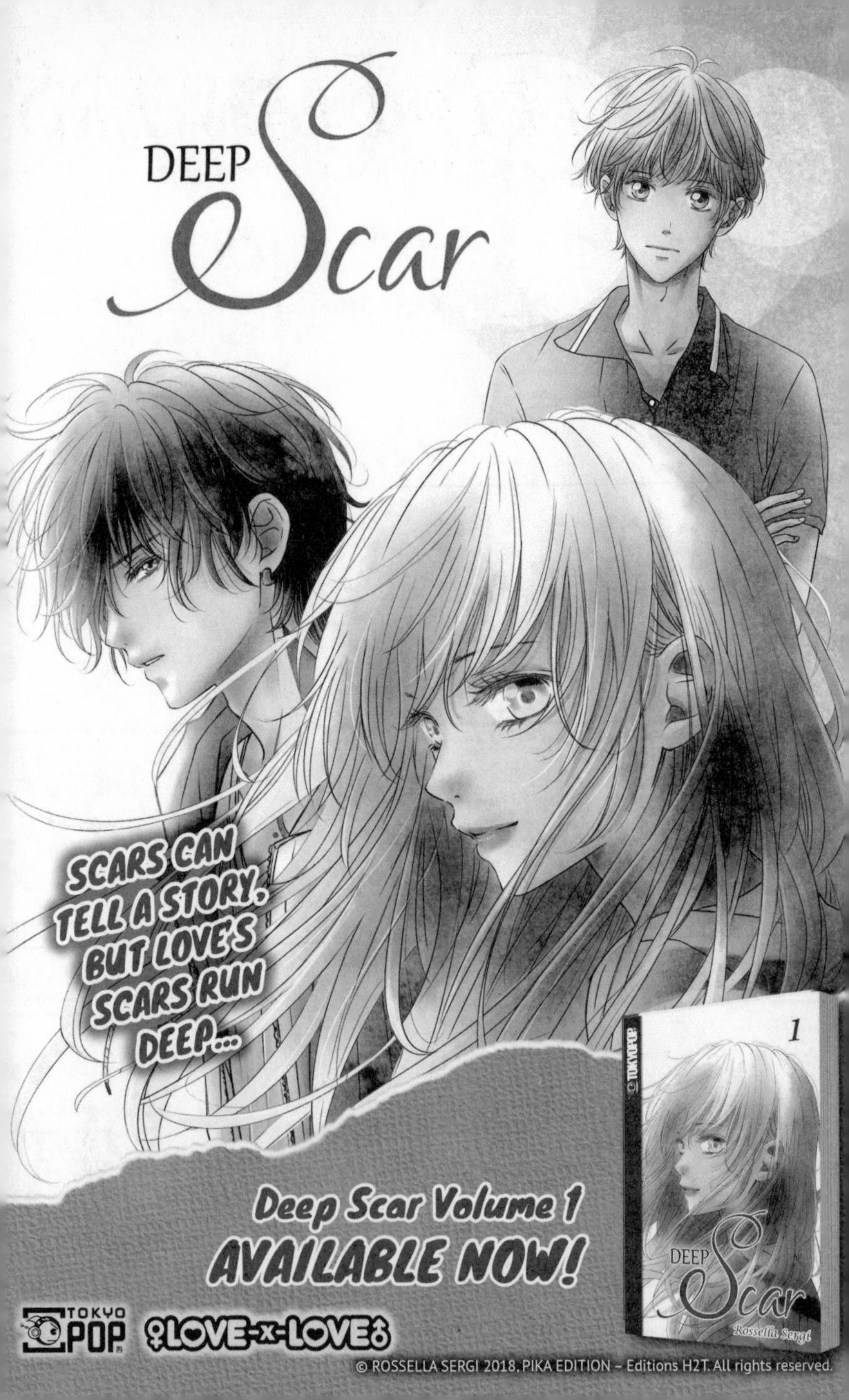
DEEP Scar
SCARS CAN TELL A STORY, BUT LOVE'S SCARS RUN DEEP...
1
TOKYOPOP
DEEP Scar
Rossella Sergi
Deep Scar Volume 1
AVAILABLE NOW!
TOKYO POP
LOVE-x-LOVE
© ROSSELLA SERGI 2018, PIKA EDITION – Editions H2T. All rights reserved.

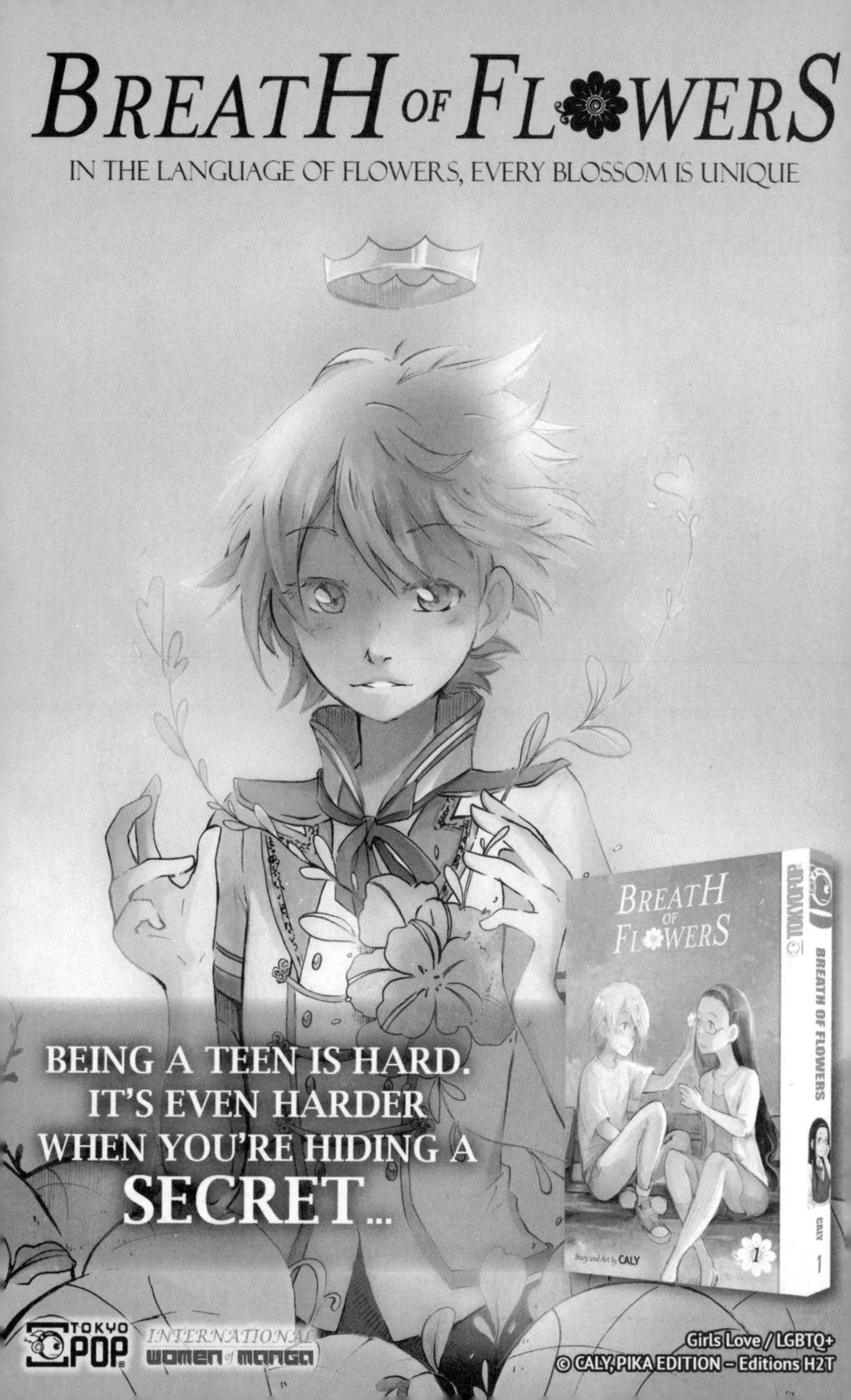
BREATH OF FLOWERS
IN THE LANGUAGE OF FLOWERS, EVERY BLOSSOM IS UNIQUE
BEING A TEEN IS HARD.
IT'S EVEN HARDER
WHEN YOU'RE HIDING A
SECRET...
BREATH OF FLOWERS
Story and Art by CALY
1
TOKYOPOP
BREATH OF FLOWERS
CALY
1
TOKYO POP
INTERNATIONAL
women of manga
Girls Love / LGBTQ+
© CALY, PIKA EDITION – Editions H2T